Jewish Family & Life

Jewish Family & Life

Traditions, Holidays, and Values for Today's Parents and Children

By Yosef I. Abramowitz
and Rabbi Susan Silverman

Produced by The Philip Lief Group

Golden Books®
New York

Golden Books®

888 Seventh Avenue
New York, NY 10106

Produced by The Philip Lief Group

Book design by Kathryn W. Plosica
Photographs by Michael Weisbrot

Manufactured in the United States of America

10 9 8 7 6 5 4 3 2 1

Library of Congress Cataloging-in-Publication Data

Abramowitz, Yosef I.
     Jewish family & life : traditions, holidays, and values for
today's parents and children / by Yosef I. Abramowitz and
Susan Silverman
        p.   cm.
     Includes bibliographical references and index.
     ISBN 0-307-44004-4 (alk. paper)
     1. Child rearing—Religious aspects—Judaism. 2. Parenting—
Religious aspects—Judaism. 3. Jewish families—United States—
Religious life. 4. Jewish religious education—Home training.
I. Silverman, Susan (Susan A.)   II. Title.
HQ769.3.A26   1997
296.7'4—dc21
                                   97-5246
                                     CIP
                                     r97

To Aliza, Hallel, Ivan, Miranda, Mikaela, and Razi; and Michal, Adin, Kyra, Benjamin, Sarah, Julia, Deena, Nili, Amit, Gilad, Ma'ayan, Nathan, Joshua, Meital, Nadav, Max, Gavri, and Liat; and *all* the grown-ups who love them—with love and appreciation for the great blessings you bring to our lives and to all the world. It really does take a village.

Acknowledgments

During the process of developing this book, we have been greatly blessed with the love, effort, brilliance, and creativity of so many incredible people. The staff of *Jewish Family & Life!* (*JFL*)—Judith Antonelli, Tovah Lazaroff, Jonathan Laden, Jeffrey Rosenbaum, and Jennifer Berkley—helped pave the way for this book; and the staff of Jewishfamily.com—Joshua Pines, Ronnie Friedland, Chad Spigel, and Nancy Schwartz—made the whole *JFL* endeavor possible. Through their dedication, creativity, and ingenuity, they make Jewish life available and alive for many families. We also thank our partners at the Jewish Communications Network as well as Rhea Basroon. And especially, the partner of partners, Susan Laden, whose vision, genius for publishing, and sense of humor, have made every step of the journey a wonderful learning experience for us.

The generosity and vision of David and JoAnn Morrison of Jerusalem, Israel, and Ronne and Donald Hess of Birmingham, Alabama, have created a revolution in the art of Jewish parenting and Jewish outreach, affecting the lives of so many families. Thank you.

We thank the Wexner Foundation for their support on so many levels, most notably the incredible community they have created and continue to build. And with love and appreciation we thank our teacher, Professor Elie Wiesel, who co-chairs the editorial advisory board of *Jewish Family & Life!* and continues to be a model of *menschlekeit* and an inspiration with his love of life and his celebration of Judaism.

Susan would like to thank all her teachers at the Hebrew Union College-Jewish Institute of Religion for sharing their love of Judaism with her; her student pulpit, Temple B'nai Israel in Laconia, New Hampshire; and her first "real" pulpit, Congregation Or Chadash in Germantown, Maryland.

We lovingly thank Rabbi Hillel Levine for modeling so much, both professionally and personally, and Dr. Susan Todd for giving us the perspective we needed to make this—and all our projects—successful. Great thanks to the staff and teachers at Gan Yeladim. We thank God every day that our children attend a school in which they are immersed in love and learning.

We deeply and lovingly thank our amazing community at "The Farm" for reasons too great and, in many ways, too intangible to enumerate; Eliza Carpenter Dennee for her constant love and support without which none of this could have happened; and Doug Wissoker for lovingly holding down the fort in times of great pressure during the writing of this book.

We thank Susan's sisters Laura, Jody, and Sarah—such incredible blessings in her life—for being absolutely essential sources of support, love, and humor; and Yosef's siblings Adam, Miriam, Sarah, and Jacob for providing a loving extended family. With love, we thank Donald "The Zaid" and Janice Silverman for their endless love and enthusiasm. We also thank, with love, Beth Ann and John O'Hara—without their doting, and the lovingkindness and faith of Martha Pleasure, we would not have had the basis from which to do our work. We also lovingly thank Martin Abramowitz and Rhoda Grill who have been such an important part of our Jewish community and have made a new city feel like home. We also lovingly thank Devora Abramowitz and Blake Voss who have been our home away from home and our sanity in a time of intense work and pressure. We also thank our grandparents, Jerry and Lea Gleich for their love and support, Goldie Halpin for her loving support, and Rose Silverman because being her favorite grandchild has always meant so much to Susan!

We are very grateful to the parents who were interviewed and who filled out questionnaires, and to the Jewish professionals who suggested families to interview. Their contributions added texture and meaning to our work.

Many wonderful and very busy people read parts of this book at various stages and we appreciate their invaluable input: Rabbi Sharon Forman, Rabbi Barbara Penzner, Sherry Grossman, Doug Wissoker, Beth Ann O'Hara, Martha Pleasure, Edna Levy-Schreiber, and Jacob Levy-Schreiber. Susan's havrusa partners, Rabbi Amy Memis and Rabbi Paula Goldberg, have also been constant sources of support and wisdom.

We also thank Carin Smilk for the interviews she conducted. Her insightfulness and kindness gently guided many people in sharing their stories which enriched this book greatly. We thank Rebecca Gutterman for her research, organizing, and beautiful writing. Thanks also to Carol Martin, whose work enabled us to do ours.

Many people generously provided information and/or materials. They include Dr. Ruth Cerano, Rabbi Herman Blumberg, Rabbi Sara Paasche-Orlow, Rabbi Ellen Nemhauser, Rabbi Judd Levingston, Rabbi Jon Spira-Savett, Judy Elkin, Marion Gribetz and the Jewish Educators of Greater Boston, Devora Abramowitz, Carol Levine, Lewis Silverman, Mimi Silverman, and Susan's teacher of history and *menschlekeit*, Rabbi Martin Cohen. Thanks to Rabbi Sandra Katz for the research assistance she provided, to Rabbi Joel Sisenwine for his "Lion King" life-cycles metaphor, and to the Jewish Feminist Center of the American Jewish Congress for their weaning ceremonies. Great thanks to Jewish educator, Lynn Golub-Rofrano, who created the annotated mediography. She has provided a great tool for readers searching to increase the power of Judaism in their lives.

Rabbi Susan Harris' comments and support guided us in forming and articulating our sense of purpose in this project. She guided, pressed, prodded, and insisted until Susan could find her own voice in this work. The loving havrusa and friendship that Susan and Susan have developed is an essential element of this book and of life in general.

Our dear friend Rabbi Susan Fendrick challenged, informed, organized, and edited. Her tireless efforts during our most stressful periods not only gave us hope, but have truly given shape and depth to this book, which would not have been possible without her. Most importantly, her abundant and unconditional love has infused this process, as it does everything else. She is a blessing.

We thank all the writers whose work is found throughout this book. They have enriched it immeasurably and their work as Jewish journalists is essential to the Jewish people. Thanks also to Gary Krebs and George Robinson, who created a vision of and foundation for this book. (Thanks Andy Polin for introducing us.) Thanks also to our editors at The Philip Lief Group. Philip Lief was a constant guiding force throughout the process. Linda Perrin at the helm guided us skillfully and clearly to this final product. Her meticulous editing is apparent throughout the book, and her vision and experience made this project successful. Thanks also to Brigitte Goldstein for her skillful editing, to Marybeth Fedele, whose administrative help smoothed a difficult process, and to Ilene McGrath, who brought order to the many Hebrew transliterations. Thanks to our editors at Golden Books, Cassie Jones and Tiffany Cale, who made important edits and asked useful and insightful questions.

Mostly, we thank our daughters, Aliza and Hallel, whom we love with all our heart, all our soul, and all our strength. To watch them grow, to teach, learn, and love with them, to sing them to sleep each night, and to greet them each morning, is to be immersed in Schechina (God's presence). And we thank God, for giving us life, sustaining us, and bringing us to each precious moment.

CONTENTS

Introduction

WHY BE JEWISH?

"I F THE STATISTICS ARE RIGHT, the Jews constitute but one per cent of the human race. It suggests a nebulous dim puff of star dust lost in the blaze of the Milky Way. Properly the Jew ought hardly to be heard of; but he is heard of, has always been heard of. He is as prominent on the planet as any other people, and his commercial importance is extravagantly out of proportion to the smallness of his bulk. His contributions to the world's list of great names in literature, science, art, music, finance, medicine, and abstruse learning are also away out of proportion to the weakness of his numbers. He has made a marvelous fight in this world, in all the ages; and has done it with his hands tied behind him. He could be vain of himself, and be excused for it. The Egyptian, the Babylonian, and the Persian rose, filled the planet with sound and splendor, then faded to dream-stuff and passed away; the Greek and the Roman followed, and made a vast noise, and they are gone; other peoples have sprung up and held their torch high for a time, but it burned out, and they sit in twilight now, or have vanished. The Jew saw them all, beat them all, and is now what he always was, exhibiting no decadence, no infirmities of age, no weakening of his parts, no slowing of his energies, no dulling of his alert and aggressive mind. All things are mortal but the Jew; all other forces pass, but he remains. What is the secret of his immortality?"

—MARK TWAIN

Harpers, 1898

Why Explore Judaism?

Since you are reading this book, you are probably Jewish or you live with Jews. You are already a part of a Jewish constellation. You seek the insight, humor, wisdom, and guidance of the generations that have led to you and your children, and you have new and different insights to lend to the great process of the generations. You may be returning to Judaism, or you may be a Jew who is coming to it for the first time, or you may be a non-Jew who practices no religion.

In any case, you want to connect yourself to something greater than the sum of the parts of your life, and to engage in a dialogue with people from the past thousand years who thought seriously about the same underlying principles of life that you think about today. You seek a life path that is intellectually and emotionally compelling. You seek to become part of something that is at once deeply personal and profoundly universal.

So, You've Picked Up This Book

Jewish Family & Life is a combination of a creative "how-to" guide, a basic Judaism course, and a gentle, humorous companion on your family's journey of religious discovery. The authors began with Jewishfamily.com, a magazine on the World Wide Web that provides articles and discussion groups for parents of Jewish children. This book is a response to the needs expressed by those readers as well as by the many seeking Jews we have met through Susan's rabbinate and Yosef's hundreds of speaking engagements across the country.

Since Jewish traditions are maintained by people's actually living them, Jewish life, like the rest of life, is a constantly evolving enterprise. If one is to integrate Judaism into his or her life in an organic, natural way, then Judaism cannot be perceived as a suit off the rack—to be put on and worn. This book is for people who are seeking a Judaism that is as open to having a relationship with them as they are open to having a relationship with it.

It is this "organic" Judaism that we hope to help you create. Your home is fertile ground for the life-affirming, relevant, spiritual, value-oriented, passionate, and richly cultural and historical power of Judaism. This book offers an overarching view to help you imagine a growing Judaism in your home, as well as practical "how-to's" and basic information on Jewish concepts and views, so that you can plant

> You will find in Judaism a powerful ally in raising moral, intellectually curious, and grounded children.

the seeds of Jewish tradition in your family garden. We have included extensive family profiles as well as brief stories and anecdotes about the many people we interviewed. These stories illustrate that there are many ways to be Jewish, and that for every Jew, being Jewish is a journey. There are many perspectives from which one may approach Jewish living and heritage. Here are a few of the people you will meet:

- Robbie took what he describes as a "brief 35-year hiatus" from Judaism, and now, with his wife (who is in the process of converting to Judaism) and their two boys, he is slowly rediscovering the joy of Shabbat—and the rest of Judaism.

- Rina and Margot are trying to combine Rina's Orthodox upbringing, Margot's tentative interest in conversion to Judaism, and their lesbian motherhood of two adopted children into a Jewish home that makes sense for their family. They are struggling—and finding a lot of joy and meaning in the process.

- Philip and Julie both came to Judaism as adults and introduced it into their home slowly over many years. Their two children, who are six years apart, have very different experiences of the role of Judaism in their lives. So Philip and Julie are thinking seriously about how to live Jewishly in a way that is as meaningful for their teenage daughter, for whom Jewish observance has become largely an intrusion, as it is for their nine-year-old son, for whom Judaism is a natural and grounding way of life.

- Jerry and his daughters did not begin to incorporate Judaism into their lives until the girls were in middle school. They had always loved the night sky, and once they discovered how much the moon guides the Jewish calendar, they became interested in incorporating some Jewish practices into their lives, beginning with those that involve looking for stars in the sky.

What all these parents have in common is their search to discover greater meaning and sense of purpose in their lives. They are experimenting with what it means to be Jewish and are striving to find concrete ways to bring Judaism into their lives as fully as possible. There are many questions that arise for a parent who is looking to bring Judaism into the home. How can I begin? What are the rituals and tradi-

NOTE TO OUR READERS

• We have included, where relevant, many traditional blessings that you can incorporate into your life. They are provided in transliteration (Hebrew words in English letters) and in English. Feel free to begin by reciting the blessings in English if doing so is more comfortable for you. You may decide to add some Hebrew later.

• If you want to learn the tunes to the songs and blessings found in this book, you can hear them on the World Wide Web by logging onto http://www.Jewishblessings.com. This will also enable you to get a feel for the Hebrew.

• The God language in this book is gender neutral, and translations from traditional Hebrew texts have been adapted to eliminate references to God as "He." Also, all language is gender inclusive, except in personal quotes, so the translations from Hebrew texts have been adapted to apply to females as well as males.

• The names of the people who have shared their stories with us have been changed. However in citations that reference a quote or statement or that use a title, the name has not been changed.

• The Resource List at the end of the book gives descriptions of books, music, periodicals, and agencies that will enrich your Jewish experience.

• In all three sections, you will find sidebars offering relevant celebrity quotes, nuggets from traditional Jewish sources, and selected ideas from readers who have contributed their insights to www.Jewishfamily.com.

tions and values? How might they fit into our lives? In what way will this be helpful to my family life?

Jewish Family & Life is divided into three sections. The first section, "Traditions," shows you step by step how to incorporate Jewish traditions, customs, and values into your home, creating Jewish space and time. It will also help you to reconceptualize your home in more Jewish terms. For example, you probably already have a bedtime ritual that you do with your children. This book will help you to add some Jewish components to that ritual and to frame that special time in Jewish terms. Also, each chapter in this section contains a family profile—a biographical account of a family's Jewish journey. Through these profiles, you will meet five families who represent a range of Jewish observance and lifestyles. These accounts show that there are many exciting and creative paths to a legitimate and organic Jewish life.

The second section is "Holidays," in which thirteen Jewish holidays are explained and a number of secular holidays are addressed in terms of how to celebrate them in a Jewish way. Following each description are suggestions for enhancing your home celebration in traditional as well as unconventional ways. This section presents a smorgasbord of options from which you can nibble or feast. It includes a profile of Steven Spielberg and his evolution as a Jew from childhood until the present. Each chapter in "Traditions" and "Holidays" concludes with a section called "Situations and Solutions," in which we address your questions and concerns in regard to managing the personal problems that sometimes occur when one introduces religious changes into family life.

The third section, "Values," is an anthology of writings about six values, each having its own chapter. There is a description of each value from our progressive Jewish perspective with an accompanying article or articles. These articles, written for Jewishfamily.com by a wide range of American Jewish thinkers and writers, provide concrete ways to think about the role these values can play in family life.

Jewish Family & Life provides information, insights, and ideas to support your journey while encouraging you to find your own way, at your own pace, in taking to heart our rich Jewish heritage. We hope that this book will help you see your own life in light of Jewish values, ideas, beliefs, and practices.

Shabbat observances, along with other rituals, holidays, and traditions, help connect us to something beyond ourselves.

A Jewish Vision for the World

Imagine a world where no child goes to bed hungry, where every child is taught how to read, where children have a positive sense of self and plenty of love. This world does not yet exist, but it can. There are enough resources, food, and love in the world to transform it dramatically for the better. And yet 40,000 children will die of hunger today, as happens every day. Not since the time of our ancestors Abraham and Sarah has there been a greater need for a system of living that can transform the world.

It is remarkable that whenever Jews are in need in any part of the world—in Ethiopia, Yemen, Syria, Russia, or New York—somehow Jews mobilize to help them, and to help others as well. Jews from all those countries were rescued by the tireless efforts of Jews around the world.

The Jewish community—less than one tenth of one percent of the world's population—provides humanitarian aid internationally far beyond what our numbers would suggest. Concern and action for the dignity and lives of human beings has been part of the legacy of Jews for 4,000 years. Whether setting up medical facilities for Rwandan refugees, taking in Vietnamese "boat people," helping Native

5

Americans improve their agribusiness, or campaigning for social justice, the Jewish community responds powerfully.

Jewish values such as *tzelem Elohim* (everyone is made in the image of God), *shalom* (peace), *tzedek* (justice), and *tikkun olam* (our obligation to repair the world) are integral to Jewish customs, holidays, rituals, and daily ways of living. Even the simplest of our rituals and observances can be rich with meaning, if they are in the context of Jewish values.

Living the Vision

The home is the Jewish nucleus. That is where Jewish living begins. But what if all the accoutrements of a Shabbat observance—candles, a Kiddush cup for wine, and challah (special bread)—were suddenly to appear out of the blue on a family's dining room table? Would the presence of those things alone help a family find closeness, a sense of purpose in their lives, and a sense of mission in the world? Probably not.

The rituals, holidays, Shabbat observances, home traditions, relationships among humans and between humanity and God all connect us to something. An understanding of that something gives context, meaning, and power to the rituals and actions of Judaism.

Some Central Jewish Concepts

What is that *something?* Several key Jewish concepts are basic to an understanding of what the essence of Judaism has been over the centuries. As we live and experience the magic moments in Jewish life on an ongoing basis, our understanding of these concepts deepens and becomes more than intellectual, pervading our hearts and souls. The place to start, however, is through an intellectual understanding of those basic concepts.

God

Shema Yisrael, Adonai Eloheinu, Adonai Echad.
"Hear O Israel! Adonai is our God and God is One!"

In a tradition that cherishes human interpretation and dissent, the unity of God is non-negotiable. God is one, alone, unique, indivisible. Regardless of differences between the different streams of Judaism, God's unity is a common denominator.

In the Bible, God is Creator, Revealer, and Redeemer—an Actor in history. God is an involved character in the biblical narratives—talking with and acting among the human characters, rewarding good behavior and punishing bad behavior. The Bible calls God many names, among them *Adonai* (my Lord), *Elohim* (literally the plural of God but understood as one), *Tzur* (Rock), and *Ro'eh* (Shepherd).

In rabbinic tradition, God is imagined in many ways. Sometimes biblical names and images for God are used with new understandings of the terms, and sometimes new images are introduced. Examples are *Makom* (Place), *Oseh Shalom* (Maker of Peace), *Shechinah* (God's presence), and *Tzayar* (Artist). More recently, God has been imagined as Mother, *Eyn Ha-Chayim* (Wellspring of Life), *M'kor Ha-Chayim* (Source of Life), and *Ma'ayan* (Wellspring).

In the Bible and in rabbinic tradition, God is not immovable and separate from us, but is actually influenced by human behavior. For example, in the Bible Abraham effectively argued with God and in rabbinic tradition it is taught that the righteous actually have the power to rule God! It is also taught that when we do *mitzvot* (religious obligations) we strengthen God, and when we disobey God's word we weaken God!

In a biblical story, our patriarch Jacob wrestles with an angel, creating a model for each generation of Jews to wrestle with God (which is how the Hebrew word *Israel* is understood). As Jews we are each responsible to wrestle with what we believe God wants from us and to create holy community based on this profound, always evolving understanding.

When Jacob awakes after a divinely inspired dream, he says, "God was in this place and I did not know it." After his "dream awareness" he achieves conscious awareness of God's presence. Part of our role in relationship to God is to see and appreciate God's magnificent presence on earth every day, manifested through the miraculous gifts of nature, life, thought, and love.

Judaism mandates actions but not emotions—with one exception. We are commanded to love God. Much more than through worship, we are expected to express our love for God by treating each other well. God is part of our daily lives, in the way we experience and treat all of God's creation.

Brit: The Covenant Between God and the People Israel

Our relationship with God holds a central place in our history. Starting with Abraham and Sarah, who separated themselves from the

> **❝** I grew up with a number of stories my rabbis told me, and when you're a kid, you get things imprinted on your hard disk that are very hard to abandon . . . repairing the world is very meaningful to me . . . we are a people who stand for a certain thing, a certain sense of justice and freedom . . . We must do right by the world. We must not treat the world as the world treats us. **❞**
>
> —RICHARD DREYFUSS,
> Actor

idolatry of their parents and the less-than-moral cultures around them, Jews have striven to affirm ethical monotheism (the idea that there is one God who is the source of what is right and wrong) and thereby to build moral community. Our miraculous Exodus from Egypt and our journey to Mount Sinai where God gave us the Torah are watershed events in defining the God-Israel partnership. Jews have continued to affirm and develop this relationship by striving to live a moral and Jewish life.

The covenantal relationship between God and the Jewish people is expressed and renewed in many diverse ways, including *mitzvot* (good deeds), the observance of holidays, rituals, life cycle events, study, worship, how we eat, what our homes look like, and activities that seek to repair the world.

Tikkun Olam: Repairing the World

Tikkun (repairing) can mean fixing something that's broken, such as the world's food and health care distribution system. It can mean finishing a task that has already begun, such as working on behalf of Judaism and democracy in Israel or furthering the civil rights agenda in the United States. We are obligated to support Jewish people and organizations, but we are also obligated to give to the poor of any community. *Tikkun olam* can also mean perfecting something that is already good, such as recycling programs.

In all of these tasks, we are in personal and communal partnership with God, and the essence of that partnership is the mission of repairing the world. The entire world is in need of healing, and Judaism obligates us to work on that task.

K'lal Yisrael: The People Israel as an Extended Family

Israel has historically perceived itself as one people. Part of what is confusing for many non-Jews, and left unarticulated by many Jews, is the concept of Israel as a nation, a religion, and a culture. It is difficult to conceptualize the essential nature of each of these three components.

This idea is powerfully illustrated by someone who converts to Judaism. That person not only takes on a religious system, but is called son or daughter of Abraham and Sarah. He or she now shares the lineage and history of the People Israel. Also, that person's soul stood at Sinai and received the Torah with all other souls of Israel, making that person an original receiver of the tradition.

K'lal Yisrael is that connection Jews feel on religious, national, and cultural levels: it is like an extended family. Therefore, *kol Yisrael arevim zeh b'zeh*, "the People Israel are responsible for one another." It is incumbent upon each one of us to ensure the well-being of every Jew.

Parenting as a Sacred Path

"How good are your tents O Jacob and your dwelling places O Israel" says the non-Jewish prophet Bil'am in the Torah as he looked over the Israelite camp. Nearly 4,000 years later, when asked by the Dalai Lama how Jews have survived so long outside their ancestral homeland, Orthodox feminist Blu Greenberg answered: "the family."

Jewish parenting is about being a creator and transmitter of tradition.

Families, in all their various configurations, give parents a mechanism and structure to raise children. The popular African saying, which was echoed by Hillary Rodham Clinton in her book, asserts that it takes a village to raise a child. This idea is mirrored in Jewish tradition's view that it takes a loving family in the context of a living community to raise a child.

Since the time of the destructions of the Temples in Jerusalem in 586 BCE (before the common era) and 70 CE (of the common era), Jewish families and communities have been rebuilding the holy space where God's presence dwells. While synagogues and schools have been the central places of study and worship, the new Holy of Holies is the home. The Temple's altar has been replaced by our decorated Shabbat and holiday tables, the Temple's menorah by the ritual candles we light with our children.

Jewish living helps us affirm the humanity, dignity, and blessing of those with whom we live, worship, and celebrate. We have regular opportunities to put aside the anxieties and criticisms of the day and focus ourselves as a family on: the story of a minor miracle (Hanukkah), miraculous redemption (Passover and Israel's Independence Day), our covenant with God (Shavuot), life's fragility and preciousness (Sukkot), creation and being made in God's image (Shabbat), the joy and meaning in Torah study (Simchat Torah), personal growth and obligations (Rosh Hashanah and Yom Kippur), our place in the world, and stories that help us in our search to discover eternal truths.

As parents, we know that the most common experiences can bring great joy. We are filled with love as we watch our children sleep. We are riveted by our children's recitals. We burst with gratitude and joy as they learn to name the world and make it their own.

Judaism recognizes this inherent holiness that parents see every day, and it offers us a language with which to name it, a context worthy of our experience, and an understanding of the greater sense of purpose for which it all exists.

Choosing a Path

Jewish parenting is not only about being a follower of tradition, but also about being a creator and transmitter of tradition by taking responsibility for helping our traditions evolve even as the values underlying them remain timeless. Your questions, complaints, and doubts as a Jewish parent are echoed every day around the world by other thinking Jews. These challenges to Judaism, and their effect on Jewish tradition, have been the lifeblood of our people.

The Jewish future belongs to parents who seek a greater sense of meaning for themselves and their children. The Jewish future belongs to you with the tough questions, the spiritual thirst, and the sincere doubts. Being an active Jewish parent is certainly difficult and requires constant learning and attention to detail. It is not for everyone—not even for everyone born Jewish. But if it is for you, its treasures are yours to seek out: its community and holidays, its challenge to affirm covenant, its ability to sanctify your home, and its invitation to follow its evolving laws. And perhaps, in the process, you will raise children who will help fill the moral vacuum of a tumultuous world searching for meaning and peace.

> **"** If you do not let your son grow up as a Jew, you deprive him of those sources of energy which cannot be replaced by anything else. He will have to struggle as a Jew and you ought to develop in him all the energy he will need for the struggle. Do not deprive him of that advantage. **"**
>
> —SIGMUND FREUD
> Founder of Psychoanalysis

Situations and Solutions

 What if I don't believe in God?
Can I still be a good Jew?

Even though belief in God is central to all religions, including Judaism, it is not necessarily an essential ingredient for good Jewish parenting. Judaism requires belief in no more than one God, but it is acceptable to doubt the existence of a single God.

Nobel laureate Elie Wiesel writes that "Some things are true that never happened, some things that happened are as if they've never been." Whether the story of God giving Moses the Ten Commandments on Mount Sinai actually happened is a matter of belief. Appreciating the "Truth" in those laws, however, takes less of a leap of faith. Similarly, the Exodus from Egypt, with its plagues and the parting of the sea, may not have happened in "real time." Yet the "Truth" of that story in terms of the values of freedom and justice—and even a belief in life's miracles—is real.

A Jewish system of living has evolved over the past 4,000 years that has withstood the test of time, geography, and crisis. Walking in the footsteps of our ancestors does not require belief in God, only a commitment to the ethics and values—symbolized by our rituals and holidays and acted upon through *tikkun olam*— that our people have passed down from one generation to the next. That means living as if there were a God.

In the Talmud, the rabbis write that God says, "Better they abandon Me, but follow My Torah." The idea is that eventually, by following Torah, by living in this life pattern, they will come closer to God.

You may want to struggle more with the idea of God. For some of us, our understanding of God has not developed and matured along with our understanding of the rest of the world. Thus as adults we may have the same understanding of God that we had as a six-year-old, one that is unsatisfying and unbelievable. If you wish to make Judaism, and the Divine presence, meaningful to you at your level, seek out books, people to talk with, or adult education programs and continue to learn. These activities will enrich your search. They will model for your children that when one grows up, the questioning, growing, and searching increase.

11

PART I

TRADITIONS

Chapter One

MAKING YOUR HOME JEWISH

And you shall write [My words] on the
doorposts of your house and upon your gates.

(DEUTERONOMY 6:9)

I T IS KYRA'S THIRD BIRTHDAY. She comes home from the playground with her dad to find the house decorated with signs and crepe paper ribbons. She may be only three, but she knows what it all means. She is elated: "My birthday!" Her surroundings send her a very clear, exciting message. She starts singing "Happy Birthday" to herself and greets her friends.

Such is the power of environment. We make our homes child-safe. We put locks on cabinet doors and fence off the top of the stairs. We make our homes warm and attractive by putting art on the walls and family photos on the shelves. We reinforce our children's sense of self and bolster their confidence. We display their artwork on the refrigerator door and good report cards on the bulletin board. We root for them at their plays, concerts, and games. We send them off to sleep with love and assurance and greet them in the morning with the joy of a reunion. We wish them good days from the bottom of our hearts and send them off to school. In short, by our words and actions, by the way we decorate our homes and treat our children, we create a place that is warm, safe, and loving.

In the same way we create a Jewish home. Through our surroundings, our actions, and our words, we convey certain messages. What does having a Jewish home mean? It means to do in a Jewish way what you either are already doing or want to do. It means sanctifying the space in which you live, making holy the relationships between parents and children.

The Jewish home contains certain items, not for conspicuousness, but for their symbolic meaning for the family. The various Hebrew words for holiness share the root letters *kuf* ("k"), *daled* ("d"), and *shin*

15

("sh"). You may recognize the word *Kiddush,* which is the blessing made over the wine on Shabbat and on many holidays. Literally it means "sanctifying" the day. *Kedushah* is the Hebrew word for holiness. If the Hebrew letter *mem* ("m") is placed before the other three letters to create the noun *mikdash,* this root for sanctity then indicates "a sacred place." The Jewish home is a sacred place. It is no accident that in Jewish tradition, two places are called *mikdash me'at* or little sanctuary; one is the synagogue, the other is the home.

Creating a Jewish Milieu

The Mezuzah

Perhaps the best place to begin to create a Jewish home is at the front door. When Susan's parents were first married, they received a mezuzah as a wedding gift. They knew that it was something one affixed to the doorpost, but on which side and at what angle they were not sure. While the groom was unpacking, the bride examined the mezuzah. She was happy to discover the scroll inside until she got a close look at it. "Oh no!" she exclaimed, "the instructions are in Hebrew!"

A mezuzah is a casing that contains a small parchment (called a *klaf*) with handwritten biblical verses from the Shema prayer, including those referring to the mezuzah itself. The *klaf* is rolled up and placed in the casing which is mounted on the doorposts. (*Mezuzah* literally means "doorpost.") The letter *shin,* from one of the Hebrew names for God (Shaddai), or the entire name, can be seen through a small hole in the vessel, or it may be written on the outside of the vessel itself. The mezuzah is placed at a slight tilt, top pointing inward, on the top third portion of the right doorpost as you face the room for which it is intended. A mezuzah can be placed on every door of the house except that to a bathroom or closet.

The origin of this custom goes back to the eve of the Israelites' exodus from Egypt. When God brought down the tenth and final plague, the death of firstborn Egyptian males, the Israelites were instructed to dab lamb's blood on their doorposts as a sign for the Angel of Death to "pass over" their homes. The biblical requirement to have a mezuzah on the doorposts has evolved since then, so to observe this practice, don't go to the local butcher! Go to a Judaica store, or find a Judaica mail-order catalog. The handwritten scroll and its case are sold separately, but most Judaica stores will sell both. Mezuzah casings come in a great variety of beautiful designs; we were given a bride-and-groom mezuzah for our wedding.

Older children will know that the mezuzah contains the words of the Shema and that this tradition has been a part of our people since the time they left Egypt. Younger children see that these objects mark our doorways and perhaps they see people kiss them as they pass through. Becky, a social worker, and Paula, a college professor, put the mezuzah on the doorway to their seven-year-old daughter's bedroom at a height she can reach. "I haven't ever seen Eliana kiss it," said Becky, "but she helped us figure out the right height for her."

The presence of the mezuzah is one way in which even a small child internalizes Jewish values, traditions, and rituals. Later, when the child studies the Shema and learns it is written on parchment placed within the mezuzah, the visceral knowledge of the mezuzah as a symbol in their home will fall into place with an intellectual understanding of its theological and cultural significance.

"The mezuzah recontextualizes the whole house," says Rabbi Susan Harris. It states that ours is a Jewish home. That statement casts a light over the entire home. It is in this light that we think about what a home is, what qualities make up our home: What is safety? What is refuge? How does our home guide us and inform our family relation-

---

THE SHEMA

Shema Yisrael Adonai Eloheinu Adonai Echad.

Barukh shem kevod malchutoh l'olam vaed.

Hear, O Israel, Adonai is our God, Adonai is One.

Blessed be the name of God's glorious majesty forever and ever.

You shall love Adonai your God with all your heart, and with all your soul, and with all your might. And these words which I command you today shall be in your heart. You shall teach them diligently to your children, and you shall speak of them when you are sitting at home and when you go on a journey, when you lie down and when you rise up. You shall bind them for a sign on your hand, and they shall be for fontlets between your eyes. You shall inscribe them on the doorposts of your house and on your gates.

—DEUTERONOMY 6:4-9

ships and give us strength? The beginning verses of the Shema read, *V'ahavta et Adonai Elohecha, b'chol l'vavcha u'v'chol nafshecha u'v'chol me'odecha,* "You shall love Adonai your God with all your heart, with all your soul, and with all your strength" (Deuteronomy 6:5). What meaning does this command have in the context of the home? We weave Jewish practices and principles into daily life. The mezuzah serves as a constant reminder of what we already have but often need to remember—God's omnipresence and the potential for our home to be a holy place. The mezuzah is not merely a decoration. The custom of touching and kissing it as we enter the doorway brings us into constant interaction with it and reminds us of the sanctity of our home. Some people have a special house dedication, a *chanukat bayit,* at which they hang the mezuzah formally. This is usually done when one is moving into a new house, but it can also be done to give ritual expression to a new level of religious observance.

Jewish Art and Decorations

There is no reason to wait for a special occasion to fill the house with Jewish art. Every room, including the children's bedrooms, can be adorned with beautiful artwork with Jewish themes. For example, many Judaica stores carry decorative lithographs with biblical phrases such as *Tzedek, tzedek tirdof*—"Justice, justice you shall pursue"; or *Kol ha'neshamah t'hallel yah,* "Every soul praises God." A *mizrach* is a work of art on which the word *mizrach,* meaning "East," is inscribed; it is placed in Western Jewish homes on the eastern wall of a room, indicating in which direction to face when praying toward Jerusalem. For the children's rooms, put up a Hebrew *aleph-bet* poster along with the English alphabet poster. Make a family trip to a local Judaica shop, or browse through a Jewish products catalog to find art pieces Choosing them can be a family activity. So can figuring out their meaning.

Kathy, a single mother of two, says she and her children look at a Jewish painting they have on the wall, and the children make up stories about it. Her children love to hear the stories of gifts and purchases—who gave them and on what occasion. The stories do not have to be dramatic. Something as simple as "Your grandma gave us this menorah when you were just two" places a ritual or art object in the family history.

Attractive ritual objects are in keeping with *hiddur mitzvah* (beautifying a commandment). Not only should we engage in ritual activities, but we should do so in ways that beautify the surroundings and the entire experience, such as having beautiful Shabbat candlesticks or finding a mezuzah of striking design. Many holiday ritual objects can also be displayed all year round. A beautiful *hanukkiyah* (Hanukkah candleholder), a Rosh Hashanah apple and honey bowl, a seder plate, and a shofar all are part of *hiddur mitzvah.*

Some objects are used at once-in-a-lifetime events but continue to have great meaning throughout life. If a special *chuppah* (wedding canopy) was made for your wedding or commitment ceremony, it can serve as a wall covering, a bedspread, or canopy. If a *tallith* (prayer shawl) was used as a *chuppah*, it can be worn at Shabbat morning services. A framed *ketubah* (marriage contract) is a daily reminder of the commitment of your relationship. The Kiddush cup from your wedding, or special pillow or blanket used at your child's *brit milah* (circumcision ceremony) or naming can be kept in a prominent place. If you do not have any of these items from a past life-cycle event, you can begin to acquire some of them. A decorative *ketubah* marking an anniversary becomes a comparable symbol if you have no such artwork from your wedding day. Photographs from any of these life-cycle events depict your family's love, history, and connection to the Jewish people through ritual.

One mother reports, "Our daughter likes to hear the story about when I was eight months pregnant with her and we went on a pilgrimage to the Lower East Side [of Manhattan] to buy a mezuzah for the baby's room. At several shops the owners said, 'That's bad luck.' They told us not to buy one until the baby arrived. After trying several shops, we found a Noah's ark mezuzah. The merchant said, 'For a baby! This will bring you very good luck!' So we bought it."

With a story behind it, an object gains a special place in your family history. In turn, your family history has a very concrete place in our people's history. The personal level interacts with the traditional purpose or understanding of the object and a new meaning is born.

What other kinds of things are normally around your house? Do your children play with stickers? There are Jewish symbol and holiday stickers. Do they like to collect things? There are "Torah cards" with drawings of various biblical characters on one side and information about the person and the story context on the other. There are games and activities that have Jewish themes and teach values and traditions along the way.

> **"**Jewishness ain't chicken soup or Israeli politics or affection for guilt. Jewish identity is rooted in a distinctive old religion that builds individual character and group loyalty through close family life. That is how the Jewish people have survived through five millennia and is the light the Jews. . .must continue to offer the world.**"**
>
> —WILLIAM SAFIRE
> Newspaper Columnist

The Tzedakah Box:
Decorative and Meaningful

An excellent way to teach Jewish values and traditions in your home is through your attitude toward money (See Chapter 12: "The Value of Money"). Many children have piggy banks because their parents want them to learn the value of money. But "value" in this context means the dollars-and-cents value. In Jewish tradition, money has ethical value, the power to improve (or damage) the world. Money is associated with tzedakah, a word that means "righteousness." Although it is often loosely translated as "charity," there is an important difference. Charity is something given out of the goodness of one's heart. And although it is better to give with a generous heart than to do it begrudgingly, tzedakah is an obligation. It is incumbent upon every one of us whether we have warm, "charitable" feelings or not.

The Hebrew word *tzedakah* has the same root as the word *tzedek,* "justice." We teach this value to our children by making the practice of putting money in the tzedakah box a part of our life—something as basic as doing homework or saying please and thank you. A good beginning is to place a tzedakah box next to the child's piggy bank. Mark and Susan's three children put money in the tzedakah box at allowance time. Each child puts one-third in the bank, puts one-third in the tzedakah box, and keeps one-third for spending money. Janice and Kevin and their three children have three tzedakah boxes: one for a Jewish organization, one for a secular organization, and one for the orphanage in India from which their son was adopted. These boxes, always displayed, remind them "of the connection between our obligation to the world around us and our own very great blessings."

Many families sit down together when the boxes are full to look over pamphlets from various nonprofit organizations and decide how to distribute their money. Older children may have a discussion about the various organizations. Younger children may talk about giving in more general terms—feeding hungry children or finding homes for people who have nowhere to live. (For younger children, it may be more effective to sort clothing or toys for giving away, since these things have more concrete, understandable purposes than

Yose ben Yochanan of Jerusalem said, **"**Let your house be open wide; let the poor be members of your household...**"**

—PIRKEI AVOT 1:5

Note to readers: *Pirkei Avot* is a portion of the Talmud consisting of a compilation of rabbinic sayings, probably dating from 300 BCE to 200 CE, that teach Jewish ethical principles. Citations from *Pirkei Avot* appear throughout this book.

money.) This is an important opportunity to have a discussion about the many problems people face, about the Jewish obligation to repair the world, and about your child's ability to make a difference. Asked to decide where to give her money, Eliana says, "To the people who sleep on the steps by the church down the street." She is learning from an early age how much individual action matters.

There is a wide variety of tzedakah boxes, and they can be very beautiful, cute, or amusing. We have two ceramic tzedakah bears (one wears a pair of glasses like our older daughter), a blue one in the shape of a house, and a big tie-dyed one.

Words and Music

Many contemporary Jews have to do a lot of searching and reaching out to find a community and rhythm with which they are comfortable. Jewish directories and Jewish websites can aid in the search. There is also a wide spectrum of national and local Jewish magazines, newspapers, and newsletters that may be consulted.

Regular mailings from Jewish organizations keep a family informed of local activities and issues of interest to Jews. As our friend Rabbi Ellen Nemhauser says, "I go to the door and, passing my mezuzah, I lean down to pick up the Jewish periodicals that have arrived in the mail. For that brief moment I am standing quite literally with the Jewish past at my back and the Jewish present and future in my hands."

There is a plethora of Jewish media products: videos, audiotapes, and CD-ROMs. In addition to watching *Cinderella*, small children can travel through time with Mitzvah Mouse (and their folks can learn something, too!). In addition to listening to Phish, your children can sing along with Debbie Friedman's songs about our culture. Keep a few tapes or CDs of Jewish songs in the car. Our four-year-old walks around singing Hebrew and Jewish songs to herself. When traditions found in video presentations are reflected in your own lives, or when the songs you have learned from the CD are sung on Friday night or at a holiday celebration, a connection is made. As Becky says, "We bring musical joy into our home in a Jewish way. In many ways it shapes our family.

Robbie and Lynn play Jewish music in the morning as they get ready to start their day. "When our children come down in the morning, they hear lively Jewish children's music. It's a happier start to the day as we make lunches and put on coats. It's especially nice when the morning is rushed—which is almost always—and in addi-

> **"The best kind of love I know is Jewish love. I was brought up by it. I was enveloped by it, and taught and nurtured by a loving, giving, closely knit, supportive Jewish family."**
>
> —MELISSA GILBERT
> Actress

Rabbi Yishmael
would say,
**"Be speedy to obey
God; be dignified
before the young;
and greet every per-
son with joy."**

—PIRKEI AVOT 3:12

tion to making lunch we're preparing bagels for breakfast in the car. It just takes two seconds to press 'play' and it changes the atmosphere so we feel more in control of our environment. These days we play Debbie Friedman's *Live at the Del* tape on the way to school. Our boys love it.

"Our 12-year-old plays clarinet and saxophone in a jazz band. He got a hold of *Gates of Song* (the Reform movement's anthology) and has taken to playing Jewish songs. We're so happy that he's added these songs to his repertoire. We live in a community with almost no Jews, so when he plays one of the 'Gates' songs at band practice, his friends ask about it. He loves the opportunity to tell people about being Jewish."

We often play Jewish music for our daughters Aliza and Halleli when they come home from school in the afternoon, especially in the winter when they cannot spend as much time outside. It creates a festive atmosphere on a dreary day, and the festivity is Jewish in nature.

Music can have a very powerful influence on us. Songs from our childhood and teenage years, which remain in our heads, define who we are and how we locate ourselves in the world. For many people, a particular experience will call to mind a certain song from the past, or vice-versa. Susan would love it if, in times of anxiety, her mind played the Hebrew song *"Ani V'Ata"* (You and I can change the world), rather than the Beach Boys' "Help Me Rhonda!"

There are Jewish songs in English, and Hebrew translations and transliterations are available. There is also beautiful adult Jewish music to enjoy and expose children to. Sharing music with our children is a wonderful way to express our love for them. Singing songs with Hebrew words is a time of family connection in the Jewish language.

Many Paths to Family Kedushah

The word *kadosh* (holy) has a place not just in our prayers but in our everyday language. "We use *kadosh* to relate how we treat people and certain objects," one mother explains. "Eliana understands not to put a book on the floor, because it is *kadosh*. And she knows she is expected to be kind to people because they are *kadosh*. It's really not so different from teaching children manners and appreciation for the world. We just use words that are meaningful in a Jewish context."

Many Jewish practices allow us to slow down and appreciate moments we might otherwise gloss over. Making a blessing is a major part of this. The blessings over bread and other foods are very short and take just a few seconds to recite, but they add an element of holiness to the moment and the act of eating. The mundane act of eating a sandwich is transformed into a moment of connection and gratitude to the Source of Life—as well as a recognition of the raw materials and of the human beings at each stage who produce the food, including the family member who prepared the meal. A bless-

A blessing before eating creates a contemplative atmosphere for the meal.

ing before eating unites the people around the table and creates a contemplative beginning to the meal. Concluding with *Birkat Ha-Mazon* (the grace after meals) or other prayers of gratitude plays a similar role. In an age of fast food and faster meals, these moments of connection allow us to take a breath and remember the miracle of food and all the different forms of *kedushah* (holiness)—divine, natural, and human—that brought it to our plates.

Robbie describes himself as a "born-again Jew." "I was raised Jewish and took a brief 35-year hiatus," he says, "from the time I was bar mitzvah until three or four years ago, when I realized my children would have no Jewish identity if I didn't become involved in this. As soon as I started to read, I was captured." Robbie's wife, Lynn, is a Chinese Catholic in the process of converting to Judaism. "All of our rituals have started out very small. That's the way we've introduced them. Now we say the Motzi (blessing over bread) before we eat, have Shabbat dinner every week as a family, and are very focused as a family on tzedakah. The children reinforce Judaism in our home. They remind us of things we're supposed to do. There's a constant interchange and communication. I think it's made our family stronger and brought us closer together. It has strengthened our sense of identity as a family, and the boys really know who they are, which is important because we live in such a small town, two hours from any substantial Jewish community. I'm sure they're the only Yiddish-speaking Chinese Jews here!"

As Art, father of two teenage boys, beautifully phrases it, "Jeanette and I try to weave all the different aspects of our Judaism

Profile

MEETING CHALLENGES; MAKING HOLY TIME

AS ONE WALKS THROUGH THE HALLS OF THE LOCAL CHILDREN'S HOSPITAL, conversations among the mostly non-Jewish hospital personnel can be overheard. "Mmmmm. What is that wonderful smell?" "Oh, that's Adam's stew, his special Sabbath stew."

Adam has cystic fibrosis and, at age 17, has spent half of his life in the hospital, so it has become important for him to make a life there. Sometimes on Shabbat, Adam gets permission to plug in a crock pot for his cholent, a Sabbath stew. His friends who have become bar mitzvah (reached adulthood in the Jewish community at age thirteen) make trips to the hospital with a Torah scroll to conduct a Shabbat morning service. Every Friday evening Adam dresses in a suit and tie and lights Shabbat candles.

Explains his mother, "One side effect of hospitalization is that time has no meaning and every day feels like the day before, so he needs to put on that suit. It helps him to get in the right frame of mind. And he does. Whenever he's in the hospital he touches somebody."

Four years ago Adam held a Passover seder for people who could not be home with their families. The group that gathered in his small, semi-private room consisted of a mother and her daughter who belonged to the Conservative branch of American Judaism; an Israeli cab driver and his son who did not speak English and had no religious Jewish identity; and an Israeli Chasidic woman, who did not speak English, with her infant. She was terrified because she was unaccustomed to speaking with members of the opposite sex. Adam pulled them all into his room for the seder. He led it as best he could, and everyone contributed what they knew.

Adam is the oldest of five children. His father, Jonny, is a lawyer, and Amy, his mother, is working toward a Ph.D. in Special Education. His brother Naftali, 15, is a gifted student. His brother Ze'ev, 13, has been diagnosed with autism. Then there is his sister Aliza, 11, and the youngest, David, 10, who shows some symptoms of autism. So making the everyday, even great, challenges into holy time is a way of life for Adam's family.

"Every single moment with Adam has been perceived by me, and I'm sure by Jonny as well, as a gift. Having a child like this really heightens all your senses to appreciating the moment, and it's very hard to live that way. Appreciating the moment means that you're not so overcome with worry about tomorrow and next week and next month and what you have planned and what you've got to get done. You can stop, run around the house, kiss all your kids, and thank God they're under one roof. You know, when you stub a toe, your whole body becomes a toe, that's all that exists. But you don't appreciate it when you're feeling pretty decent. It takes a long time and a lot of training just to appreciate everyday things. So the lesson of Adam is appreciating every day, squeezing as much joy out of every single day as you possibly can."

A few years after Adam was born, they had Naftali, who is gifted. Says Amy, "The very child we were discouraged from having for medical reasons is the one who may discover a cure for cystic fibrosis."

> "Appreciating the moment means that...You can stop, run around the house, kiss all your kids, and thank God they're under one roof."

A couple of years after Naftali, they had Ze'ev, who is autistic. "Ze'ev is one of the happiest people you'll ever meet. We were just at a wedding of a very close friend this weekend and you cannot understand what it means to be *m'sameach chasan v'kallah* (joyful with the groom and bride) until you see a Ze'ev. One hundred percent joy. He was just so totally thrilled. Ze'ev really does love life intensely. Now, autism is as if your inside and your outside aren't really connected, and sometimes you can get to the inside of a child and sometimes you can't. But he's really happy in that world of his. And sometimes we can have a window into who Ze'ev is. If the lesson of Adam is to appreciate each moment, the lesson of Ze'ev is to recognize each child's potential and celebrate it. With Ze'ev, a single word is precious."

Aliza is the only girl, a blond, blue-eyed preteen ball of fire. She is what her mother calls "typical," since she was not born with special needs. Amy describes Aliza's loving way of connecting with others. "When she was ten, I saw her out on the playground being the first to approach the Russian children who had just arrived. She saw them standing alone and kind of lost, and so she befriended them. I'm sure that had a lot to do with growing up in a home with three brothers who wouldn't quite fit into the crowd. Judaism infiltrates everything we say and do and feel. It's how I look at the special needs population and how I teach my children to see the world. This has ramifications for my daughter."

So, from what kind of home emerged these children with their abilities to reach out and bring meaning to people's lives, to make people feel welcome and comfortable, to celebrate so wholeheartedly at someone else's *simcha,* joyous occasion?

"Jonny was brought up in a home like that—that's what his parents' home was about," says Amy. "My father really worked hard to make sure each holiday was beautiful and exceptional as I was growing up. The Sunday school kids came over one class at a time to see our sukkah and shake the *lulav* and *etrog.* I think you become better at welcoming guests when you've seen it modeled by other people. Our home is a pretty wild place. We have expandable walls! That's how the Temple was in Jerusalem. The walls miraculously expanded to hold as many people as was needed. And that's kind of what our house does."

> **"We have expandable walls! That's how the Temple was in Jerusalem...And that's kind of what our house does."**

One Shabbat Amy and Jonny invited two couples for lunch. By the time the meal was over they had 50 people there. "The college kids in the area know that this is the place they can come without calling first. They can bring a friend and pick up a little bit of *shabbes* atmosphere. A pile of people came to visit Adam. There were people here of all ages. It was a lot of fun and pretty out of control. That's pretty typical for our house. I mean, no one will walk away saying that it's elegant or spotless but they'll tell you it was a nice warm place with a lot of good conversation. They'll tell you it felt like home."

Amy and Jonny and their children take the obligation to welcome people into their home very seriously. "Everyone chooses the mitzvah that they really thrive on, and our mitzvah is *ha- khnasat orchim* (welcoming guests). It's just the thing that we do, and we really study it like a science. If we have someone who's never had a *shabbes* experience or has never sat in a sukkah before, we talk to our children about it and try to explain how the guests might feel and what the children can do and say to make them comfortable. And we try to invite people in groups—again, to add to their comfort level. Once Jonny was out of town and I was under the weather— Adam was about 11 at that time—he happened to see someone in synagogue he didn't recognize. He walked right up and invited the stranger for lunch."

into a tapestry blanket that helps keep the family warm." The reminders are on the doorposts of our house and upon our gates.

Bathing, Resting, Rising

Parents often bathe their young children before putting them to bed and reading to them. In Nancy Fuchs's wonderful book on parenting as a spiritual journey, *Our Share of Night, Our Share of Morning*, she writes about bath time:

> Most adults don't think much about baths. We usually take showers to get clean, and that is the end of the matter. Children challenge that utilitarian perspective. For the parents of small children, baths have only a little bit to do with getting children clean and a lot to do with the actual process of giving a bath. It is an integral part of the cycle of the day. Parents speak not about a "bath" but about "bath time." It is a time for soaking away the stains of the day (or sometimes the week), watching our children becoming clean, fresh, and pure once again. As we wash away our children's grime, we can let ourselves believe that our hearts, too, may become clean again.

There is an unspoken *kavanah* (spiritual intention) at bath time. Acknowledging this *kavanah*, Rachel and Jonathan apply a mealtime ritual to bath time. Before sitting down at the table to eat, it is customary to ritually wash one's hands. Symbolically, the table is an altar, and we purify ourselves before approaching the altar of God. After washing, we say a blessing. It is customary to remain silent between saying this blessing and taking a bite of the bread, so as to make it all a single action. It is not a washing of the hands as much as a symbolic purification of the spirit.

After getting out of the bath, Rachel and Jonathan's children dry off and put on their pajamas. Then they say a blessing: "Thank You, God, for a clean, fresh body and this time to rest." Jonathan explains, "There is a heightened sense of focus on preparing for rest and shared quiet time. I would even call it spiritual. We attempt to transition from activity-filled day to peaceful night by expressing our appreciation for a cleansed body and the blessing of rest."

You may already be using certain bedtime "rituals." As you review the day together quietly, why not phrase some of your observances of the day in Jewish terms? For example, the words *tzedakah*

> **❝**[I am] just a nice Jewish girl from New York. Going back through my life now, the Jewish family feeling stands proud and strong, and at least I can say I am glad I sprang from that. I would not trade those roots—that identity.**❞**
>
> —LAUREN BACALL
> Actress

(righteous giving) and *g'milut chasadim* (acts of lovingkindness) can be used. If your child shared her sandwich with a classmate who forgot her lunch, or if a classmate took the time to explain the instructions for tomorrow's math assignment to your child, one comment could be, "What an act of *g'milut chesed* [singular]!" If your child gave money to a person in need or to an organization, one way to express parental pride is to acknowledge the act of tzedakah. Our days are full of these small acts of kindness, and they are so easily forgotten. Jewish tradition teaches that blessings—even miracles—are everywhere. What did your child notice today for the first time? You do not have to be familiar with all the traditional blessings to say one for having a lovely new experience, encountering a special new person, or seeing a beautiful sight.

Singing to or with your children at bedtime will make them feel Jewish in a special way. First of all, teach them the Shema, which is traditionally recited at bedtime every night.

You may want to add some popular children's songs as well. We sing "Twinkle, Twinkle Little Star" interspersed with some Hebrew words and an added verse written for each child. In this way we move from the universal to the Jewish to the personal.

> Twinkle, twinkle, little star, how I wonder what you are.
> Up above the world so high, like a diamond in the sky,
> Twinkle, twinkle, little star, how I wonder what you are.
> When I go to sleep at night, thanks for keeping me in sight.
> Please keep watch upon the earth, keep it safe 'til morning
> light.

> Twinkle, twinkle, *kokhavim* [stars], shining in the *sha-ma-yim*
> [heaven].
> If you'll say a Shema tonight, everything will be all right.
> Twinkle, twinkle, *kokhavim*, shining in the *sha-ma-yim*.
> (Adapted by Renee Boni)

> Twinkle, twinkle, Aliza Rose, I love you from your head to
> your toes.
> You're my bright, shining light, in our house everything's all
> right.
> Twinkle, twinkle, Aliza Rose, I love you from your head to
> your toes.

Here is an interpretation of the prayer Ahavat Olam from the evening worship service, which speaks of God's love for us.

We are loved by an unending love. We are embraced by arms that find us even when we are hidden from ourselves. We are touched by fingers that soothe us even when we are too proud for soothing. We are counseled by voices that guide us even when we are too embittered to hear. We are loved by an unending love. We are supported by hands that uplift us even in the midst of a fall. We are urged on by eyes that meet us even when we are too weak for meeting. We are loved by an unending love.

Embraced, touched, soothed and counseled...ours are the arms, the fingers, the voices; ours are the hands, the eyes, the smiles. We are loved by an unending love. Blessed are You, Who loves Your people Israel.
(Adapted from Kol Ha'neshama by Rabbi Rami M. Shapiro)

Just as we treat "goodnights" as departures, saying "goodnight" and separating from our children, we treat "good mornings" with the joy of a reunion. However, fewer people are likely to have a formal morning ritual for awakening. There is a traditional Jewish prayer, *Modeh Ani*, which is said upon waking in the morning. Judaism views sleep as a little taste of death, and so we express our appreciation to God for granting another day.

Modeh ani lifanecha melekh chai v'kayam.
Shehekhezarta bi nishmati b'chemlah raba emunatecha.

I am thankful before You, Living and Sustaining Ruler, Who returned my soul to me with mercy. Your faithfulness is great.

For little children, you may want to try this interpretive translation. We sing it.

Thank you *Ha-Shem* for another day.
For another chance to learn and dance and play.
Thank you *Ha-Shem* for loving me so I'll try to be good.
This I want you to know!

Reading

Through reading and studying books and texts we delve into the Jewish past, connect with the Jewish present, and inform our ability to shape the Jewish future. You probably already read to your young chil-

Not living our Judaism while expecting our children to develop an attachment to it is like being an art lover who expects her children also to love art even though she doesn't bring them to museums or teach them art history or create artwork with them. Like dedication to art or anything else, Judaism is not genetically coded for replication. We might be born with Jewish parents, but being Jewish involves education, experience, and commitment. In this voluntary, open society, every Jew is ultimately a Jew by choice.

dren or encourage your older children to read on their own. Reading time is extremely precious in many families. It provides loving interaction between family members as well as a joint educational venture into worlds beyond our own. If we incorporate Jewish books into our normal reading schedule, our children's Jewish knowledge and connection increase exponentially! And perhaps you have not read many of these books yourself. Here is an opportunity to begin an endeavor together with your child. Whether you

have read the books before or not, remember there are seventy faces of Torah (the breadth of Jewish texts) and with your child you can discover a new one every time.

Next time you are searching for a good read, browse through the Jewish bookstore or the Judaica section of your local store or library, or get a Jewish book mail-order catalog, and see what interests you and the children. For little ones, there are many beautifully drawn picture books, dramatizing folk tales and holiday stories. Then there are the Chelm stories, a series of tales about life in a fictional Jewish community whose inhabitants take the long road to logical thinking. Their often ridiculous and always hilarious mishaps will appeal to everyone in the family. There is also a wealth of Jewish books for older children which delve more deeply into important issues, such as coming of age, assimilation, and the Holocaust.

You may want to look for actual Jewish texts such as a *Chumash* (Five Books of Moses), *Siddur* (prayerbook), or *Midrash* (Jewish legends based on the Torah); there are bilingual versions in Hebrew and English, and others with pictures and commentary. Books for every Jewish holiday and area of interest abound, from rabbinic stories to Jewish history, fiction about life in Jewish communities around the world and through the centuries, to books on death and dying. In terms of making decisions on age-appropriateness and topical appeal, use the same standards you would use for the rest of your children's book collection.

As you explore, you will find much to reflect on. You will find that your Jewish family life is illuminated by the words and worlds that live in books.

Creative Bedtime Rituals

by Debra Nussbaum Cohen

WHEN I WAS PREGNANT WITH MY SON, Aryeh, who is now 17 months old, I promised myself that I would do something Jewish with him before tucking him into bed at night. The problem was, I didn't know where to begin. I didn't have a Jewish bedtime ritual growing up and so I lacked any personal experience on which to draw. I looked into a few prayerbooks but did not feel strongly connected to the traditional bedtime reading of the Shema, which seemed too intricate, too heavy, to recite with my baby. My religious experience since Ari's birth has been richer than at any time before. The most wonderful moments of connection with the divine energy that fuels the universe have been as Ari lies relaxed in my arms, gazing up into my eyes while sucking lazily on his first bottle of the morning or his last one at night. It's the quiet times, the lulls between the structure and activity of your days, that are the most precious and full of prayer. I wanted to find a bedtime ritual that would match these moments.

One evening I was chatting with a neighbor, an evangelical Christian, when she said she had to go say prayers with her son and daughter. This neighbor had been born a Jew. At the time she began wondering about God and faith, she was approached by evangelical Christians, who invited her into a life of connection with God. When she challenged a rabbi for Jewish answers to her questions, he was unable to provide her with meaning. So she turned to those who promised her spirituality. This was a powerful reminder to me that if I did not give Aryeh a sense of spiritual intimacy with God, someone else might. Following is a sampling of creative Jewish bedtime (and some other) rituals developed by friends.

Cara Saposnik of Brooklyn, who lived most of her youth in Israel, and her husband, Rich Kirshen, rock their fifteen-month-old daughter, Gili, to sleep singing two Israeli songs—one by Natan Alterman about the Jezreel Valley going to sleep, and the other, the pop song *"Ye'hiyeh Tov,"* meaning "It Will Be Good."

During the second six months of Gili's life, Kirshen, a Reform rabbi, would get up with her at dawn and take her to the dining room window, where they would watch night turn into day. "She watched it with such intensity, so amazed as she looked at everything," Kirshen says. "This impromptu ritual stopped my jadedness and opened me up to each new day. We were very present and didn't have to fill up the space with words."

Daniel Lehmann, an Orthodox rabbi and the principal of a Boston area day school, says the traditional Shema with his son Hillel, who is three. Several months ago, after they read the Shema out loud in Hillel's Jewish nursery school class, he began his own new supplement. As Hillel says, "Adonai is One," he extends his pointer finger, which Lehmann touches with his own extended finger, like Adam and God in Michelangelo's fresco.

Shai Gluskin, a Reconstructionist rabbi in Philadelphia, sings two Israeli songs, which he learned as a boy in Habonim camp, to his daughter Sophia Pearl—a folk song called *"Lilah, Lilah,"* and a song sung to the tune of "Taps." The English translation of the lyrics is, "It's

the end of the day/The sun is silent/Stars are glimmering in the sky/Night has come for us to rest/Peace, wholeness, peace."

In the early morning, just after Sophia has had her first drink of the day and she is lying in bed with her parents, "all smiling and perky," says Gluskin, he says the first line of the *Modeh Ani* over her. This is the morning prayer of gratitude to God for returning one's soul, which is traditionally said upon waking.

Larry Magarick, a New York City lawyer, began making bedtime music and prayer tapes for his sons when Benjamin, the oldest, was three. The first one he compiled was about welcoming Shabbat with Kiddush, some *zemirot* (Sabbath songs), and *niggunim* (tunes without words). Then Magarik compiled a Goodnight-to-Ben tape, on which he recites the Shema. At age eleven, Ben does not usually listen to his father's tapes any more, but his younger brothers, who are five and three, often listen to them as they go to sleep.

Melanie Schneider, the director of a Reconstructionist organization in New York, puts her 16-month-old daughter Sasha to sleep with the *"Cha"* Shema. She recites the *Ve-ahavta* paragraph, which contains many words ending in the sound "cha." At the appropriate moments at the ends of the words, Schneider pauses and points to Sasha, who understands her cue and says, with great enthusiasm and many giggles, "Cha!"

When her six-year-old son Yonaton was younger and afraid of the dark, Susan Grossman developed a prayer about the protecting angels surrounding him. When Yonaton is comfortably settled in his bed, she sings the prayer about the angel Michael on his right, Gabriel on his left, Uriel at his feet, Raphael at the head of the bed, and above him like a canopy, watching over him and all Israel, is *Shekhinat-El*, or God's Presence. Then they say the central line of the Shema.

In traditional "angelology," explains Grossman, a Conservative rabbi in Tuckahoe, New York, the angel Michael's flaming sword scares away frightening monsters; Gabriel's horn calls the celestial beings to his aid; Uriel lights a path with a flaming torch; Raphael is a healer; and Shekhinat-El protects children from harm.

Debra Nussbaum Cohen is a staff writer at the Jewish Telegraphic Agency and focuses on religious and spiritual issues.

WHEN MYSTERY ROCKED ME TO SLEEP

Mute, invisible, God lived in my house when I was little, along with my parents and my brother. God was in my room when I woke up in the morning, had a place at our table during meal times, and watched over me while I slept.

I loved this mysterious force that felt close enough to touch yet could hold the whole world in the palm of the hand. So it was logical that God's language was, to my English ear, a stream of foreign sounds. I had memorized many of these words by the time I was four. At night my parents turned out the lights and together we would recite the Shema. I never asked them what the words meant, nor did I need to know. I saw it almost as a secret code letting God know it was time for guard duty. Then, while I drifted into sleep, my parents read me a bedtime story.

I have known Hebrew fluently for many years. But every night before I go to sleep, I recite this ancient prayer, slipping for a moment from comprehension and returning to that moment on the edge of knowing, when mystery rocked me to sleep.

—TOVAH LAZAROFF
Journalist

Chanukat Bayit: Dedication of the Home

The author/playwright David Mamet and the actress/singer Rebecca Pidgeon tell the story of their family's *chanukat bayit* (house dedication). When they moved into a new home, they invited friends to celebrate with them as they affixed the mezuzah to their front doorpost. The guests were asked to step onto the front porch and, after the mezuzah was affixed, to file back in, giving the family a blessing as they came through the door. In the front of the line was a very reserved couple who, after exchanging awkward glances, moved quickly to the back of the line.

Not everyone feels comfortable participating spontaneously in a new ritual in front of a group of people. Others will pour their hearts out. A *chanukat bayit* ceremony need not be anything more than friends and family joining you as you symbolically consecrate your home and make the public statement that yours is a Jewish home.

After the words are spoken, the mezuzah is affixed to the doorpost as follows:

Stand outside the door facing in. Reach to the top third of the right doorpost. Place the mezuzah at a slant, with the top leaning in and the bottom leaning out. Hammer the nails part way through the holes at the top and the bottom of the mezuzah. Then say the blessing for affixing the mezuzah followed by the blessing for a new event.

*Barukh ata Adonai Eloheinu Melekh ha-olam, asher
kidshanu b'mitzvotav v'tzivanu likbo-a mezuzah.*

Blessed are You, Adonai our God, Ruler of the universe, who sanctifies us with holy commandments and commands us to fix a mezuzah.

*Barukh ata Adonai Eloheinu melekh ha-olam,
shehekhiyanu v'kiymanu v'higiyanu lazman hazeh.*

Blessed are You, Adonai our God, Ruler of the universe, Who has given us life, sustained us, and brought us to this moment.

Then finish hammering in the nails. The ceremony focuses on the main entrance to the home. Afterwards, the remaining mezuzot are affixed privately. You can follow the ceremony with food to celebrate and socialize. Here are some additional ideas to precede the affixing of the mezuzah.

- Ask your child to write about what "home" means, and especially a Jewish home. This can be read as part of the ceremony.

- A younger child may draw pictures of the home that may serve as decorations.

- Have a reading or readings that highlight ideas and values you wish to incorporate into your home. Read a passage from the Bible or rabbinic literature. For example: "Through wisdom a house is built and through understanding it will continue to grow, and through knowledge the rooms are filled with all precious and pleasant treasure" (Proverbs 24:3-4). You can also talk a little about what the passage means to you.

- Have a guest book (or a large poster board) on which your visitors can write their wishes for you.

- Give tzedakah to organizations that represent the values you want to embrace in your home.

Hands-On Judaism

1. Make a Jewish object. Look up background information in an encyclopedia about a particular item you want to make with your child. Learn a little of the history and traditional meaning of the item as you work. This may also be an opportunity to learn more about the history and meaning of the Jewish art and objects that are already in your home.

2. Add a Jewish theme. Even the kinds of projects children normally do can be infused with Jewish themes. For example, paper cuts or potato stamps can use Jewish religious and holiday symbols. Decorate a coffee can and cut a slit in the lid to make a tzedakah box. Write *Tzedakah* in Hebrew or English. You might also write a phrase such as *Tzedek, tzedek tirdof*, "Justice, justice you shall pursue." Or decorate a necklace box to make a mezuzah holder. You can roll up a

> **"**You have to be a storyteller, a banker, a chef, a psychologist, Darth Vader, a friend, a director—it's a job that really keeps you on your toes and helps you keep your sense of humor. But, in this day and age we focus more on our gratification than on our long-term needs and our children translate that into violent behavior. . . . As the old Chinese adage goes: All the seeds of today are the flowers of tomorrow. That is the legacy of being a Jew. We must take the task seriously.**"**
>
> **—HENRY WINKLER**
> Actor, Director

prayer your child creates and put it in the holder. (This will not be a kosher mezuzah for your home, but it is wonderful for a dollhouse!) With a little creative thinking, you can inject many of your normal arts and crafts activities with Jewish themes.

3. Write or read a prayer. Suggest that your child write a prayer or choose one from the liturgy. A small child can also draw a picture of the meaning of the prayer or of something related to your home. Read the traditional prayer together and write a related prayer for your family.

4. Help build an understanding of God. Your children are the first generation to grow up without hearing God being described exclusively in masculine terms. There are many new as well as ancient images of God that broaden and enrich our understanding of our relationship to the Divine Being. Talk with your children about God as: Rock, Wellspring of Life, Shekhinah (Presence), Place, King, Source of Life, Creator, Artist, Mother, Father, Judge, Merciful One, Comforter, Maker of Peace, Man of War, Maker of Good and Evil, Maker of All, Holy One, Friend, Ancient One, Shepherd. Write stories, draw pictures, or make art that answers a question about God.

5. Make a family mitzvah tree. On a large piece of heavy paper draw a tree with a branch for each member of the family. At the end of each branch glue a piece of Velcro. Using heavy cardboard or construction paper, cut out leaves. On each leaf write the name of a mitzvah (commandment or good deed) and glue a piece of Velcro to the back.

Every time a member of the family does a mitzvah, attach the leaf with Velcro to that person's branch. Mitzvot may range from taking care of a sibling to visiting the sick, from giving tzedakah to doing volunteer work, from writing to a politician on an issue of concern to making blessings and lighting Shabbat candles. You can remove the leaves and start fresh at the end of each Shabbat.

6. Trace your roots and history. Go to a local Judaica store to find books, videos, games, music and/or art for your home. Ask older Jewish relatives, especially grandparents, what Jewish symbols and decorations were in their home as they grew up. Take out family photos while you are having this discussion and encourage your children to be part of it. Find out about forgotten traditions that you may want to revive in your home. Tape the interview.

7. Enjoy the symbols in your home. Organize a treasure hunt using the Jewish symbols in your home. The first clue can read, "We want every year to be sweet for you." Then the clue in the Rosh Hashanah honey bowl can read, "Moses and Miriam put this on their door so we are able to put one on our door." Then, taped next to the mezuzah they find a note that reads, "Who gives to the poor shall not lack" (Proverbs 28:27). Then when they find the next clue, hidden under a pile of coins next to the tzedakah box, they put the coins in the box and read the next clue, or find a gift. This can be a birthday game with a gift at the end. For small children, we recommend *The Jewish Home Detective*, published by the Union of American Hebrew Congregations (UAHC).

8. Set up a Jewish calendar. This is a regular calendar with Jewish dates and holidays and Torah portions added. Linda Golub-Rofrano, a Jewish educator from Washington, D.C., wrote a calendar with a suggested Jewish children's activity for each day of the year. You may want to incorporate some of the following ideas into the calendar you create for your children: Make a point of taking the fifth—commandment, that is—honor your father and mother; ask your parents how they chose your Hebrew name; say the Motzi over bread; visit a Jewish museum and write about your favorite exhibit; practice reading Hebrew out loud to your parents; write a poem about something Jewish or write a Jewish short story; learn about a Jewish value and make it part of your life and write about it; talk about what you like best about Shabbat and why.

Linda Golub-Rofrano has many more suggestions for specific Jewish holidays as well. For Rosh Chodesh, the beginning of the Jewish month, she suggests the following: Find out the name of the Hebrew month that begins on a particular day and the date of the Hebrew month when there is a full moon. Why is Rosh Chodesh a "women's holiday"? For the High Holidays she suggests discussion of the symbolism of blowing the shofar, for example, and of other rituals. (For many family activities related to the holidays see Chapters 6 and 7 of this book.)

Situations and Solutions

Q | The Jewish music I grew up with was "schlocky" and much of it was in Yiddish. I want my children to have a strong Jewish identity, but they are into Metallica and Jewel. They won't tolerate the Jewish music of yesteryear. What should I do?

A For a humorous approach, note that there is some Jewish music that uses the music of popular songs, with just the words changed. Your children may not think this is cool, but they may find it amusing. There is so much modern Jewish music that is beautiful and meaningful in its own right, and the car is a good place to introduce it. First, you have control of the tape player. Second, there is a wealth of music out there for children of all ages: children's and adult holiday songs; feminist music; Jewish songs from across continents and generations; Israeli folk and popular music; a capella groups singing everything from parody to liturgy. You may find that your kids like it and actually request it the next time you take a trip. Another good time to introduce Jewish music is at holiday times. Have it playing in the background during your Hanukkah party or while you braid challah or make salad with the children for Shabbat.

Also, for your preteens and teens: some great rock musicians are Israeli and you can find their music in the United States. Just as kosher wine is now every bit as sophisticated as other wines, Jewish music includes quality revivals of older forms as well as innovative contemporary new sounds, reflecting the whole range of music in general culture.

Q My husband is afraid that if we put up a mezuzah, we might become victims of antisemitic vandalism. Is he over-reacting or am I missing something here? I think he is uncomfortable with being Jewish, but I don't know how to broach this with him.

A Antisemitic attitudes and incidents are at an all-time low and are steadily decreasing. But that does not mean that your husband's fear will also naturally decrease! Often fears cannot be dealt with on a rational level. One way to respect your husband's fear and achieve your desire to have a mezuzah on your door is to place it behind the door. That may be a comfortable compromise while you discuss the underlying issues. Also, mezuzot belong on interior doorways as well, so you might put them up inside your house.

Chapter Two

OBSERVING SHABBAT

ARELY DO WE EXPERIENCE AN OBLIGATION THAT IS ALSO A GIFT. Your boss does not say, "I have a present for you. Finish six reports by five o'clock today." As parents we don't hand our teenager a gift box with a note inside: "You have to baby-sit for your brother Saturday night." Nor does the government send you a card, "Thinking of you this season. Send your tax forms with a check by April 15!" But Shabbat (the Sabbath) is truly both an obligation and a gift. We are commanded to cease the activities that at other times define us and shape our world. We are commanded to leave life's projects and constructions behind for a day.

Shabbat begins just before sundown on Friday and ends when three stars appear in the Saturday night sky. Within this span of time, there are certain restrictions and certain obligations, which create what 20th century rabbi, philosopher, and activist Abraham Joshua Heschel called "a palace in time."

On the Seventh Day . . .

Shabbat was first introduced in the biblical account of the creation. "The heaven and the earth were finished and all their array. On the seventh day God finished the work that God had been doing, and God ceased on the seventh day from all the work that God had done. And God blessed the seventh day and declared it holy, because on it God ceased from all the work of creation that God had done. Such is the story of heaven and earth when they were created" (Genesis 2:1–4). Humanity was created on the sixth day—only one day before the creation of Shabbat. "God created humanity in God's image. In the image of God, God created humanity. Male and female, God created them" (Genesis 1:27). On the

> **"**In the Biblical traditions of the People Israel, there seem to be two strands of thought about Shabbat. One strand sees Shabbat as a reflection and expression of cosmic rhythms of time that are rooted in the process of creation. The other views Shabbat as an expression of human freedom, justice, equality and dignity.**"**
>
> —ARTHUR WASKOW
> *Down-to-Earth Judaism*

sixth day, humanity was created in God's image, and on the seventh day God rested.

The commandment to observe Shabbat in the Book of Exodus combines these two ideas (Shabbat as a divinely ordained holy day and humanity as made in God's image), and from them a third concept emerges: the covenant. Humanity is created in the Divine image. And the Israelites are commanded to symbolize—in fact, to act out—being made in God's image by keeping Shabbat. Their doing this, in turn, is a sign of the covenant between God and the Jewish people. The biblical passage containing this covenant is known in the Shabbat morning liturgy as *V'shamru*. "The Israelite people shall keep the Shabbat, making the Shabbat throughout the generations as a covenant for all time. Between Me and the Israelite people it will be an eternal sign. For in six days God made the heaven and the earth and on the seventh day God rested and was refreshed" (Exodus 31:16–17).

We seek to bring peace and justice to the world through the message that every human being is created in the image of God. This is made more explicit within the version of the Ten Commandments found in Deuteronomy (Deuteronomy 5:12-15). God tells us that we, our children, our workers, and our slaves shall rest on Shabbat. And then God says something that is a constant refrain throughout the Hebrew Scriptures and subsequently in other traditional texts: "Remember that you were slaves in the land of Egypt and Adonai your God freed you from there with a mighty hand and an outstretched arm. Therefore Adonai your God has commanded you to observe the Sabbath day." Shabbat is directly related to treating others justly.

The biblical passages about Shabbat have been interpreted through the centuries to mean avoidance of acts that are considered *m'lakhah* (work), as well as of objects that might lead to doing *m'lakhah* or that otherwise violate the spirit of Shabbat. M'lakhah consists of 39 kinds of work grouped into seven categories: growing and preparing food, producing and preparing garments, doing leather work and writing, providing shelter, providing fire, doing an action that completes an activity, and transporting/carrying. Why these particular categories? The Rabbis based the 39 *m'lakhot* (plural of *m'lakhah*) on the types of labor the Israelites used to build the Tabernacle, the desert sanctuary, according to God's specific instructions.

The rabbis describe God as *Tzayar*: Artist, Creator, Former. We imitate God during the week by being molders of the world and of relationships around us. For six days we try to transform and repair the world through *action*; on the seventh day we anticipate and model a transformed world through *being*.

Shabbat is a taste of the messianic era—of a perfect, harmonious world. We create *ruach Shabbat*, the spirit of Shabbat, which the biblical prophet Isaiah calls a "delight." This spiritual "delight" is created through various Shabbat activities. We eat favorite foods, sing and dance together, study, make love, pray, join together with friends, play with our children, meditate, talk, take walks. On this special day we pause, unwind, and get in touch with ourselves, our spirits, our loved ones, and we experience a soulful taste of what perfect living could be.

This is what enables us to work during the week. All week we strive to align our work with God's will, to imbue it with the Jewish values of peace, justice, acts of lovingkindness, and *tzelem Elohim* (the belief that everyone is made in the image of God). If we did not have a taste of the world to come, how could we maintain a vision toward which to work? How could we keep our efforts in the world from becoming a blur? It would be like planting trees with no sense of the forest. On Shabbat we experience the vision, so that we can maintain that vision in everyday life and imbue our work with the values of that vision.

Shabbat is like a wedding: we are merged with God. In fact, one rabbinic interpretation describes God on the seventh day as a king who had made a bridal chamber that he plastered, painted, and adorned. With the room and its accoutrements in place, what was missing? A bride to enter it. Similarly, after six days of creation, what did the world lack? Shabbat.

There are many other metaphors for Shabbat in rabbinic literature. It has been compared to a queen, a jewel, and even a choice fruit or flower. It is the weekly oasis in which our people have experienced God as Creator, a symbol of our covenant with the Creator, the remembrance of our having been redeemed from slavery in Egypt, and a foretaste of the messianic time for which we yearn.

> Shabbat is like half-time in a football game. While the game is on hold, we try to enjoy ourselves differently—the music, the dancing, the food. We aren't tense, and we are not watching the clock so closely. It's a good time to talk and catch up, about the week, about the plays we just saw.

The Oldest Continual Revolution

Historically, Shabbat has always served an important purpose in the life of the Jewish people. When we faced cruelty and oppression, Shabbat helped us remember our one true Ruler. Many oppressors derided the Jews for this observance because they did not see (or, more likely, because they did see!) the revolutionary nature of this day when we remember that God is the only true ruler.

Shabbat is a day when we stop working, regardless of the material gain that work may bring. It is a day when we insist that there is something higher, greater, more compelling than ceaseless

Most days we walk because we have to be someplace. On Shabbat we can walk and appreciate the things around us.

The rabbis teach that there are three incomplete phenomena: the incomplete experience of death is sleep; an incomplete form of prophesy is the dream; the incomplete form of the next world is the Sabbath. It is also taught that there are two more. The incomplete form of heavenly light is the sun; and the incomplete form of heavenly wisdom is the Torah.

production. How could we have continued the ancient practice of slavery once we learned that we must all rest as God rested because each one of us is made in God's image?

The Jews in Ethiopia realized this. When they were being harassed by Christian missionaries to name the savior of the Jews, they replied, "The savior of the Jews is Shabbat." This day of rest was the anchor that helped the Jewish people maintain their identity and sense of purpose throughout history. For the Israelites freed from slavery, for the Jews under Roman rule at the beginning of the common era, for the secret Jews in medieval Spain, for the Jews living under Nazi terror, for the contemporary Jews of Ethiopia and Russia and Yemen and Iran, and for us who sometimes lose ourselves in mundane pursuits, Shabbat is a reminder of our partnership with the Redeemer and of our hope for freedom. What greater gift could God give us than our very selves? We are not allowed to become our tasks or burdens. We may not enslave our souls to the work of our hands. We may not extinguish the divine flame that burns within us, or even ignore it. Shabbat is the gift of holiness in time.

In the Torah God tells us, "You are holy, because I the Eternal your God am holy." On Shabbat we imitate the Creator by becoming the created, not as formers of the world around us but as shapers of our souls and our family relationships. The observance of Shabbat is the oldest continual revolution, still overthrowing the forces of dehumanization and bolstering the power of human compassion and holiness.

A Time to Stop and Smell the Roses

The belief that every human being is created in God's image extends far beyond one single day. Contemporary society does not often affirm the Divinity in all of us. We often see others in terms of their role in our lives, the jobs they do, the money they have or do not have, the power they wield, the support they give us, or the demands they make on us. What if we first saw each other as images of God? Would we take each other more seriously? Would we listen more carefully? Would we tend to judge less and appreciate more? How would our social interactions and obligations be affected? What would be the effect on how we treat a poor person in the street, a co-worker who is being discriminated against, a child who cannot read, or a spouse who is unhappy? How would this new view play out in our priorities and decisions as a society?

Too many of us grew up thinking that Shabbat was primarily a day of "don't do this and don't do that." It was often associated with missing the big football game, with going to unbearably long services, or with facing an anachronistic set of complicated rules that were never adapted or explained in a modern context.

Shabbat is about joyful connection to our true selves, to our family, to our community, and to God. It is the cornerstone of Judaism's recognition that both our bodies and our souls need nourishment. We are not merely creatures engaged in constant search for food or sexual gratification, but humans in whom glows a Divine spark that must be rekindled.

A Day to Look at the Sky

A STORY IS TOLD OF THE CHASIDIC TEACHER, Rabbi Nachman of Bratslav, who noticed his disciple, Chaim, rushing along the street. Reb Nachman opened the window and invited Chaim to come inside. Chaim entered the home and Nachman said to him, "Chaim, have you seen the sky this morning?"

"No, Rebbe," answered Chaim.

"Have you seen the street this morning?"

"Yes, Rebbe."

"Tell me, please, Chaim, what did you see in the street?"

"I saw people, carts, and merchandise. I saw merchants and peasants all coming and going, selling and buying."

"Chaim," said Reb Nachman, "in fifty years, in one hundred years, on that very street there will be a market. Other vehicles will then bring merchants and merchandise to the street. But I won't be here then and neither will you. So, I ask you, Chaim, what's the good of you rushing if you don't even have time to look at the sky?" (as found in *Gates of Shabbat*, Marc Dov Shapiro, Central Conference of American Rabbis, New York, 1991.)

> **"**To really observe the Sabbath in our day and age! To cease for a whole day from all business, from all work, amidst the frenzied hurry-scurry of our age! To close the stock exchanges, the stores, the factories—how would it be possible? The pulse of life would stop beating and the world perish! The world perish? To the contrary; it would be saved....**"**
>
> —SAMSON RAPHAEL HIRSCH
> "The Sabbath" in *Judaism Eternal*

The rabbis teach:

- the Sabbath garments shall not be like the weekly garments

- walking on the Sabbath shall not be like walking on the weekdays

- affairs of the week are prohibited, heavenly affairs are permitted

- speech on the Sabbath should not be like speech on the weekdays

- mundane speech is forbidden but mundane thoughts are allowed

We take walks and look at the sky too rarely. We walk because we have someplace to be or something to accomplish. On Shabbat, however, we look at the sky.

Rabbi Abraham Joshua Heschel teaches us that Shabbat is an opportunity "to collect rather than to dissipate time." We as American Jews, like many Americans, have endless demands placed on our time—work obligations, social pursuits, activities for ourselves and our children. We give a little of our time here, a little of our time there, until our days disappear bit by bit. Shabbat is when we stop and say to ourselves, "I am not going to rush." As the sun sets on Friday evening, a family "making Shabbat" will slow down, switch gears, and begin to transform itself into a unit of modern holiness.

Kindling a Divine Spark

Somewhere between long work days, school activities, social obligations, household demands, and the lure of slumping in front of the television, parents are searching for ways to have meaningful family time. For many parents, Shabbat is an opportunity to shape an entire day that is unhampered by rigorous demands.

Traditional Shabbat observance entails the following:

1. Refraining from activities that are considered *m'lakhah* (work) or are otherwise not in the Shabbat spirit.

2. Lighting candles at the beginning of Shabbat, eating three festive meals, and ending Shabbat with the Havdalah ceremony.

3. Going to synagogue or staying at home to daven (pray) one or more (sometimes all) of the following: Kabbalat Shabbat (the Friday night service for welcoming Shabbat) and Ma'ariv (evening prayers), as well as Shabbat Shacharit (morning prayers) and Minchah (afternoon prayers). Both of the latter include a public Torah reading.

It is a mitzvah to take delight in celebrating Shabbat. Jewish learning, spirited singing, and restful family time are important aspects of the day. Special foods, clothing, ritual objects—even children's treats—are often part of the day's observance.

If we approach Shabbat as a new endeavor by asking ourselves whether we should observe Shabbat or not, we are limiting ourselves. That question suggests that there is one kind of Shabbat day and we can decide only whether to observe it or not. That is not the case. A better question is, "How can Shabbat become a meaningful part of my family life?"

To find an answer to this question, many parents turn to a blueprint of Shabbat basics and then work with it to create something that is their own. This process may extend over a period of time, growing and changing as the family grows and changes. Many American Jewish families observe Shabbat by examining traditional prohibitions and requirements and factoring in the less concrete goals of Shabbat, such as achieving a true sense of rest, having a more peaceful home, and experiencing a sense of God's presence. The requirements of a traditional Shabbat are theoretically in line with the latter goals, and for many people they serve those ends. Others feel the need to do some creative reconfiguring, taking into account their community's norms and values, to fashion a meaningful Shabbat for their family.

Personal Approaches

One mother remembers that her first attempts at Shabbat rituals felt overwhelming. "But it's worth taking the risk," she adds. "It's like wearing a new pair of jeans. It takes about four times to feel comfortable."

Amy, a photographer and mother of two, says that her approach to Shabbat "is like photography. I only use one standard-sized lens despite the myriad equipment available. Why? Because my eye, my perspective, my self can be lost in the layers of technology. The photograph is not about what a lens can do, or what a fancy piece of equipment can record. It's about finding the unique perspective of one of God's creatures. When I am limited technologically and in terms of available activities, I am forced to apply myself fully. And this is the case for my family on Shabbat. We cease moving automatically and instead actively invest ourselves in developing a deeper awareness of the meaning in our own lives."

When Sandra's daughter was two, they would sometimes take early morning walks in the park. They would walk once around the perimeter of the park and then leave so that Sandra could get to work. One harried morning, when Julia squatted down by a flower to smell it, Sandra took her hand and said, "Come on, Sweetie. Let's keep moving." There was literally no time to smell the flowers.

Shabbat is when we say to ourselves, "I am not going to rush. In fact, my child can smell the same flower all day, and I can relax and watch her observe, smell, and touch God's world."

Profile

RINA AND MARGOT'S SHABBAT: ALWAYS SINGING!

t is a quiet Sunday morning. Even though it is a largely Jewish neighborhood, with many Hanukkah menorahs in the brownstone windows, Rina and Margot's home stands out with its colorful and plentiful handmade Hanukkah decorations. The inside of their home is just as colorful, with handmade Hanukkah "stained glass" in the kitchen windows and music in the air.

Rina and Margot are preparing brunch when the children run in. Razi and Toby are both seven. But they are not twins. Razi's birth parents were Puerto Rican and African American, and Toby was born to Caribbean American parents. Both were adopted as babies. Razi is dressed in jeans and sweater, quite conservatively, which is in keeping with his personality. He starts to tell a story about his Bubbi (Yiddish for "grandmother") when his *ima* (Hebrew for "mom") was a little girl. Toby joins in, almost taking over. She is as effusive and "out there" as Razi is reticent and cautious.

The children sit down to their bagels and each says a quiet Motzi before they eat. Margot points out that the children are the ones who remind her and Rina to bless their food. The blessings fit very naturally into the somewhat chaotic atmosphere. To look around that kitchen is to believe in God. How many paths had to cross in just the right places for this group of people to become a family?

Rina, who directs an organization that assists elderly Holocaust survivors, is the child of survivors and was raised in a Modern Orthodox family. After college her connection to Judaism began to lapse. "It really started to fall apart and I drifted for a long time."

Margot is an architect who was raised in a nominally Christian military family. "My family had an overblown sense of patriotism and extreme racial and religious prejudice. I didn't really take any values from them." Margot begins to talk about how she and Rina met.

"We each had decided to adopt a child and joined our area's Singles Adopting Children organization. That's where we met." Rina adds, "Razi came home to me on February 7, and Toby came home to Margot on February 8. We both went to the next meeting to show off our babies and that's when we really noticed each other. Within a few months it was a done deal."

"Rina was very brave," Margot continues. "Razi was a bundle of health and legal risks, but Rina knew that he was her son. Period. She took him to the doctor the day after he came into her home. Originally Razi's doctor thought he had AIDS, but for complicated legal reasons no one would test him. So Rina tested his blood under her name. In the end, he was not infected with HIV, and he's very healthy now. His birth mother was a crack addict who left him in the hospital. Now he plays chess and classical guitar and studies Hebrew and the Torah portion every night with his mother and sister before going to bed."

At the time Razi came into Rina's home, she was not consciously connected to Judaism. But even so, as soon as he was healthy enough, he was converted to Judaism and had a *bris* (a ritual circumcision). When Rina and Margot and the children moved in together, Razi was one year old and Toby was nine months. Rina and Margot thought about the role of religion in their home. Rina expressed an ambivalent interest in having a Jewish home, and Margot did not care enough about Christianity to justify the confusion two religions would cause for the children.

Rina had not yet begun any Jewish practice in their home, but she was still going to her parents' house every *Shabbes* and *yontif* (holiday). "I couldn't bring Margot and the kids because my father didn't want anything to do with my lifestyle." That situation was very stressful, and she knew something would have to change. Change came after Rina's father died.

"He died when the children were just about three. It was at that point, with Margot's encouragement, that I shifted into another gear. There was a lot of negative in my Jewish experience, but there was also a tremendous amount of positive, and I didn't want it to be lost: the music, *Shabbes*, my father. In many ways it was emotional and irrational. I kept saying to Margot, 'If I don't believe [in God], being Jewish doesn't make any sense.' But I wanted to come back even though I couldn't figure out how to do it. Margot told me not to get all worked up about it and just do it. We both wanted the kids to have something."

So after Rina's father died, she and Margot decided to have Toby converted. She was four years old when she went into the mikvah (ritual bath) and became a Jew. She was given the Hebrew name Rivka, after Rina's aunt who was killed in the Holocaust.

It was right after Toby's conversion, at the unveiling ceremony of the gravestone for Rina's father, that Margot first began to think about converting herself. At the unveiling, Rina spoke with some of her relatives, who were Chasidim, and she found out that one of them was named Rivka, named after the same woman for whom Toby had been named. Margot recalls looking over at this woman with a wig and at her husband with sidecurls, black hat, and long black coat and marveling that she was named after the same woman as her little black baby with the dreadlocks. "It was very powerful," she says, "that they are both carrying on Rivka's name."

> "His birth mother was a crack addict who left him in the hospital. Now he plays chess and classical guitar and studies Hebrew and the Torah portion every night."

Carrying on the tradition of generations can be a daunting task. Rina describes her approach to bringing Judaism into her home as very slow, without self-judgment, and without trying to have it make complete sense.

"For example, we keep kosher in a way that most people would not consider kosher. For health reasons, Razi has to eat meat, but only organic meat. So we had to choose between kosher meat and organic meat, and, of course, his health came first. We keep meat and milk separate and have separate dishes and utensils. The meat is from a kosher animal but not slaughtered kosher."

Rina believes that Jewish life in general does not always make sense and demands flexibility. "If you try to say, look, you can only have *Shabbes* in this way because the rabbis say so, then you're lost—because what if it doesn't feel right, what if you can't do it? I think we started out with Margot and the kids coming to my mother's house for *yontif*. So it was about trying it out. Seeing what it feels like to take off every *yontif*. Seeing what it feels like to set *Shabbes* aside each week."

Friday night dinners are spent together at Rina's mother's house: Jewish rituals, Razi-and-Toby style. When they arrive at the house, Razi immediately complains that he's hungry. Rina and Margot ask him to be patient, but it's only Bubbi who can calm him down. The family gathers around the Shabbat candles, and the children stand hugging their Bubbi while Rina lights. The children run and hide under the table while the adults cover their eyes and say the candlelighting blessing. With her eyes still closed, Rina asks God to keep her children, Margot, and her mother healthy. When the women open their eyes, the children are gone.

"Where are Razi and Toby?" Bubbi asks with feigned worry.

"Don't worry, Momma," Rina replies, "you'll see, by the time we're done singing Kiddush, they'll be back." They start making Kiddush, and at the appropriate moment they hear two little "amens" from under the table. By the time Kiddush is over, the children have emerged.

After Kiddush, they do the ritual hand washing before sitting down to a meal, and the children say the Motzi blessing over the challah. Then they eat. And then they sing. And this is where it has been a struggle for Rina.

"Part of relating to *Shabbes* for us as a family is seeing what it feels like to sing together," Rina explains. "Growing up, we sang a lot. But we hadn't sung in my mother's house for a long time. I was always there for *Shabbes*, even without Margot and the kids, but my parents were so angry and hurt [about my lifestyle] that we stopped singing. So now I was going to start singing and my father wasn't there? It felt awful. So I was singing for the kids, and every time I'd start singing my mother would tell me, `Stop singing. You're making me cry.'

"I began to teach the kids songs at home. And they learned them on tapes in the car, and from their videos. Toby has a beautiful voice and both children are very musical. So they have come to know and love the *Shabbes* songs.

"Finally, we began singing a little bit after *Shabbes* dinner. And the children sang their hearts out. My mother loves it when they sing! Now we sing the same songs we did when I was a child, but it's in a whole new light. Razi and Toby have really brought singing back to *Shabbes*."

Margot leads the Tot Shabbat art projects at synagogue, and many of Toby and Razi's creations can be seen around their house. Rina leads the Tot Shabbat service and has a question and answer time at the end, which Margot loves to watch.

"When Rina asks questions, Razi always knows the answers. I once overheard the other parents whispering, `Does she prep him ahead of time?' And actually, she does. Every night before bed the children sit with Rina and practice writing Hebrew letters in their *makhberet* (notebook), read one line of the week's Torah portion, and at least once a week read and talk about a child's version of the Torah portion. They roll their Torah scrolls (they each have a complete printed scroll) to the correct place for the week. Sometimes they sleep with the Torah at the foot of their beds. Razi and Toby are ready for any questions."

At home on Shabbat afternoon there is one rule: No obligations! No one has to make his or her bed, do homework, practice anything. They don't have to do anything, but they always end up singing.

At the end of Shabbat, each child holds the candle, the spice box, or the Kiddush cup as Rina sings the Havdalah blessings. They hold the candle as high as they can so their future spouses will be tall (following an old tradition).

"Shabbes is so fundamental to being Jewish," Rina muses. "The whole idea of a day off, of not getting into a car, not doing anything that you normally must do—the whole Jewish idea of thinking about more than yourself, whether about what you eat, how you celebrate, or how you live your life, even about discrimination, which, God knows, these black, Hispanic, Jewish children of lesbian parents will experience. *Shabbes* is the time when we imagine a better world.

"I want them to have the positive side of Judaism—*Shabbes*, music, holidays, the obligation of tzedakah, belonging, knowing how to learn. And if nothing else, if I succeed in giving my children the opportunity to believe in God, then I'll be pleased. Because I think people who believe in God are blessed. They feel safe. So right now they do believe in God—and we'll see where that takes them."

> At home on Shabbat afternoon there is one rule: No obligations! No one has to make his or her bed, do homework, practice anything. They don't have to do anything, but they always end up singing.

❝One of my fondest boyhood memories is getting up early on Saturday mornings to walk to shul with my dad. It was a special time. My father would take my hand in his and begin to sing a Shabbes song. His baritone voice would echo through the empty streets, and I would join in with my youthful soprano.

"More than school, more than the synagogue, more than any teacher, it was on those walks that I learned to be a Jew. I think it was also then that my father planted the seeds that enable me to be a nurturing Jewish father to my own boy.❞

—ARI GOLDMAN
from his essay "Jewish Fathering" in the *Hadassah Magazine* (Source: *Jewish Parenting Book*, ed. Roslyn Bell. New York: Free Press, 1989.)

Becky and Paula developed their own Shabbat practice by having a conversation about what they were each looking for in that day. Becky says, "I feel bound to Jewish life, and then from that sense of obligation I look for ways to be Jewish that feel enriching. Paula and I brainstorm together on things we can do at the *Shabbes* table. We have collected and created rituals that feel meaningful. We started with different vantage points, but through trial and error, we have ended up close together in establishing our Shabbat goals for our family."

Robbie, a father of two, recounts, "When we first started introducing active Judaism into our home, we began with Shabbat. Just Shabbat. At first I thought, 'Oh my God, this is going to seem so contrived, the kids are going to complain, they're not going to like this. But they really took to it. In fact, I took them on a weekend fishing trip to a lake in Canada. We arrived on Friday afternoon. We went out and got some grape juice and a piece of bread, and made a little portable Shabbat kit. So we lit candles and were going down to dinner and my twelve-year-old said, 'Hey, Dad. I have an idea for a new family tradition. When Shabbat comes, after we light candles we should keep our kippot (yarmulkes) on for the rest of the night.' I told him that was a great idea and we'd start doing it as soon as we got back home. He said, 'Well, why don't we start doing it now?' I explained that we were in a place where there weren't any Jews, and it would seem a bit unusual. He looked up at me, 'I thought part of being Jewish was being different, Dad. You're not ashamed of being Jewish, are you?' So we went down to the restaurant, all three of us with our kippot on."

Mike and Shirley both work, and making time to cook a meal for Shabbat dinner is burdensome. So they thought about what would make it special but not time-consuming. "So we order pizza. The kids love it and we have it only Friday night, so it's special. Also, only on Friday nights they are allowed to have soda. Shirley and I love our Friday night dinners—they are less work than even the simple meals we cook all week, it's less mess, and we love the food!" Adds Shirley, "Because there is little mess, I am able to be a guest at my own table and not flinch at the pots and pans piled in the sink."

For Karen, Shabbat is a day for celebration. "I'm a party girl," she explains. "For some people Shabbat is *menuchah* (rest); for others it's *kedushah* (holiness); for me it's *oneg* (delight). It's a time for getting together with family, eating and socializing. I sit with my husband and cousins and talk, while all our children run around and play together. It's social. Every week it's a party."

Lynn and Joe drive wherever they need to go if it is in the spirit of Shabbat. "For us, going to a museum is in the spirit of Shabbat if it means having quality family time, being relaxed, focusing on each other, and learning. We will also travel to go hiking or boating. While in the car, we play Jewish music. That way, even traveling in the car feels *Shabbesdik.*"

Taking Leave of Shabbat

At the end of the day, when three stars appear, it is time for the brief ceremony of Havdalah (literally, separation or distinction), at which time we take leave of Shabbat. Our rabbis teach that on Shabbat we are given an extra soul. At Havdalah we relinquish that extra soul but hope that the sweetness and holiness of the day will remain within us during the week. We take a cup of wine, a box of spices, and a beautiful braided Havdalah candle, and we sing or recite the blessings. These blessings talk about distinctions between the holy and the everyday, between light and darkness, between our people and each of the peoples of the earth, and between the seventh day of rest and the six days of work. We then make a blessing over the wine, a symbol of joy, to sanctify the moment, and we sniff the spices to carry the sweet spice of Shabbat into the week and to wake us gently to our earthly responsibilities. Then we make shadows on our hands with our fingers in the candlelight in order to display the distinction between light and darkness.

This light is the first fire of the new week. It is a sign that the time to begin creating again has arrived. No more dreamlike days until next week. It is now time to invest ourselves in our work again. As we make the transition back to our week, we also make the connection between creation and the messianic era (a time of justice and peace) by invoking the prophet Elijah. Tradition teaches that he will herald the coming of the Messiah. Some add that Miriam the prophetess will lead the Jewish people in

66"When the sun sank at the termination of the Sabbath, darkness began to set in. Adam was terrified. . . . [So] what did Adonai do for him? God made Adam find two flints which he struck against each other; light came forth and he uttered a blessing over it. . . . Samuel asks, 'Why do we recite a blessing over fire at the termination of the Sabbath? Because it was then created for the first time.'99

—GENESIS RABBAH
11:2

joyful song and dance to a time of a perfection. We then drink the wine, douse the candle, and wish each other a good week. Shabbat is a taste of that perfection, but our work in the world is needed to bring it about.

Some Basic Steps for Making Shabbat

1. Preparing ahead: Some people have Friday night dinner and Saturday lunch ready before candlelighting on Friday. Traditionally, cooking is forbidden on Shabbat—remember the 39 *m'lakhot?* Some people also prepare *seudah shlishit,* the third meal, which is a pre-sundown, late Saturday afternoon meal.

We enhance the mitzvah of observing Shabbat by arranging a beautiful table setting and by wearing our *Shabbes* best. Both activities are part of *hiddur mitzvah,* beautifying a commandment. We use our most beautiful white tablecloth and finest dishes and silverware (unless putting out your best dishes for the children makes you a nervous wreck). There is a mystical tradition of dressing all in white on Shabbat to symbolize the purity of the day.

It is also important to prepare mentally. Some ways to do that are to shut out thoughts and conversation about work; to take a long hot shower; to put on music; or even to spend some meditative time arranging the flower bouquet.

2. Setting out the tzedakah box: Put a few coins into the tzedakah box just before lighting the candles, which signals the start of Shabbat. (Handling money is not traditionally permitted during Shabbat.) Jewish tradition teaches that each time a person gives tzedakah, it is as if he or she has personally received the Divine Spirit.

3. Lighting the candles: Check a Jewish calendar or newspaper to determine candle-lighting time, the beginning of Shabbat, which occurs just before sundown. It is customary to light two candles, made especially for Shabbat, which remain burning until they go out. One explanation for the two candles is that they represent the two Torah commandments concerning Shabbat: "keep" and "remember." Keeping Shabbat is understood as the obligation to observe Shabbat, and remembering Shabbat is associated with preparing for it.

Lighting two candles is not a hard and fast rule. Many people light a candle for each member of the family so that each person gets

FOR US, SHABBAT IS MARKED BY TWO SPECIAL SALADS:
YOSEF'S SHABBAT SUPER-SALAD

Boil: Sweet potatoes, white potatoes. Let cool in fridge. Cut into chunks.

Combine in a big bowl: cut lettuce; chopped tomatoes; cut string beans; sprouts; chopped cucumber chunks; green, red, yellow, and orange peppers cut into chunks. Add cooled chunks of potatoes.

On top, place sliced rings of red, orange, and yellow peppers; crumble your favorite kind of cracker, and sprinkle pine nuts, dried cranberries, chopped dates, walnuts, and pecans. Let people add their own dressing.

DAVID ROSENN'S SALAD

Combine chopped fresh spinach, chopped avocado, whole chick peas (from a can), fresh lemon juice, and a little Italian dressing.

to light one. Instead of candles, some people use little oil lamps that resemble the source of light used in ancient times. These are available in Judaica stores. (Not recommended for young children!)

Between saying the blessing and lighting the candles, some people symbolically draw in the light from the candles with gentle circular hand motions over the flame. Traditionally the candles are lit by the woman of the house or a daughter, who will cover her eyes while reciting the candlelighting blessing. (But there is no reason why other members of the family could not perform the mitzvah.) The reason for covering the eyes is that the usual order is to say the blessing before doing the action, but in this case, if we said the blessing first, thereby beginning Shabbat, we technically could not light a fire! So we light first just before the beginning of Shabbat, then we bless with our eyes covered—and afterwards we take our

hands away to see the candles magically lit. Many people take an extra moment before saying the blessing to take a deep breath and feel the peacefulness of Shabbat.

Barukh ata Adonai, Eloheinu Melekh ha-olam,
asher kidshanu b'mitzvotav, v'tzivanu l'hadlik ner shel Shabbat.

Blessed are You, Adonai our God, Ruler of the universe,
Who has sanctified us with commandments and
commanded us to light the Shabbat candles.

4. Blessing each other on Friday night: It is customary for parents to bless their children and each other, concluding with the priestly blessing. The sources of the tradition for blessing children are biblical. Isaac blessed his sons, Jacob and Esau. And Jacob blessed his grandsons Ephraim and Menasseh, a blessing that is recalled in the Shabbat table blessing for boys. The blessing for girls recalls the matriarchs of our people.

The priestly blessing is taken from the biblical book of Numbers (6:24-26). As the parents say the blessing, they place their hands on the children's heads.

Traditional blessing for a girl:

Yesimakh Elohim k'Sarah, Rivkah, Rachel, v'Leah.
May God make you like Sarah, Rebecca, Rachel, and Leah.

And for a boy:

Yesimkha Elohim k'Efraim v'chi'Menasheh.
May God make you like Ephraim and Menasseh.

This is followed by the Priestly Blessing (modified):

Yivarekh'kha Adonai v'yishm'rekha.
Ya'er Adonai panav alekha viychuneka.
Yisa Adonai panav alekha v'yaseim l'kha shalom.
May God bless you and keep you.
May God turn toward you and be gracious to you.
May God turn to you and grant you peace.

Many couples also bless each other, or say a few loving words. Traditionally, a man sings to his wife a passage from Proverbs (31:10-31), which is known as *eyshet chayil* (a woman of valor). There are mutual options also. If you have your *ketubah* (marriage contract), you may want to choose a few lines from it to recite together, or one of you to the other, alternating each week.

Another possibility is for each person to say briefly what the others have done for him or her. This is a good time to acknowledge the good that goes on each week within your family. It also is an opportunity to make the focus of Shabbat the blessings in your family and put aside quarrels and misunderstandings.

5. Singing Shalom Aleichem on Friday night: As we sit down at the table on Friday night, it is traditional to begin with singing *"Shalom Aleichem."* This popular song welcomes the Shabbat angels into the home. Some parents point out to their children the angels dancing in the candlelight. The same tune fits the English as well as the Hebrew version.

Shalom aleikhem mal'khei ha-shareit malakhei elyon
Mimelekh mal'khei ha-m'lakhim ha-kadosh barukh hoo.
Bo-akhem l'shalom, mal'khei ha-shalom malakhei elyon
Mimelekh mal'khei ha-m'lakhim ha-kadosh barukh bu.
Barkhuni l'shalom, malakhei ha-shalom malakhei elyon
Mimelekh mal'khei ha-m'lakhim ha-kadosh barukh bu.
Tsetkhem l'shalom, malakhei ha-shalom malakhei elyon
Mimelekh mal'khei ha-m'lakhim ha-kadosh barukh bu.

Peace unto you, ministering angels, messengers of the
Most High, Ruler of Rulers, the blessed Holy One.
Come in peace, messengers of peace, messengers of the
    Most High,
Ruler of Rulers, the blessed Holy One.
Bless me with Peace, messengers of peace, messengers of
    the Most High,
Ruler of Rulers, the blessed Holy One.
Go in peace, messengers of peace, messengers of the Most
    High,
Ruler of Rulers, the blessed Holy One.

6. Saying Kiddush (the prayer of sanctification of Shabbat that is said over wine): Many of the positive commandments emphasize the joyousness of Shabbat. In that spirit it is no wonder that Shabbat begins with the blessing over the wine which is a symbol of joy.

On Friday night the Kiddush has four parts. The first part recalls the biblical account of the creation of Shabbat. The second part is the blessing over wine. The third describes the gift of Shabbat, its meanings and symbolism. And the fourth describes Shabbat as a sign of the covenant between God and Israel.

And there was evening and there was morning, the sixth
day. The heaven and the earth were finished and all their
array. And on the seventh day God finished God's work

The Friday night Kiddush and the Grace after Meals (Birkat Ha-Mazon) appear here in English and in abridged form. The entire Hebrew and English texts are available, along with the rest of the songs and blessings in this book, at http://www.Jewishblessings.com.

which God had done. And God blessed the seventh day and sanctified it, because on it God ceased from all God's work of creation which had been done.

Barukh ata Adonai, Eloheinu Melekh ha-olam, borei peri ha-gafen.
Blessed are You, Adonai our God, Ruler of the universe, Creator of the fruit of the vine.

Blessed are You, Adonai our God, Ruler of the universe, Who sanctifies us with commandments and favors us with the holy Shabbat, with love and graciousness bestowed upon us, a remembrance of the works of creation. For it is the first of the holy assemblies, a remembrance of the going forth from Egypt.

For You have chosen us and sanctified us from among all the peoples. In love and graciousness You have bestowed upon us Your holy Shabbat.

Barukh ata Adonai, m'kadeish ha-Shabbat.
Blessed are You, Adonai, Who sanctifies Shabbat.

On Saturday morning the Kiddush begins with *V'shamru*, a biblical passage describing Shabbat as a sign of the covenant between God and Israel, for Israel must rest as God did on the seventh day. It

---

Seven-year-old Aviva wrote a blessing that her family recites every Friday evening. There is a part in it for every member of the family. It is an acrostic, spelling out the words **ABA** ("father"—he reads this part); **EMA** ("mother"—she reads this part); and **HAPPY**—which they all read together. At the end, Aviva added the line about Yonah ("dove" and her brother's name), and Yonah adds the last line!

As the week closes up/**B**ad things will disappear from your heart/**A**ll will be happy

Everything rests/**M**ay you do the same/**A**nd we will say Amen

Have a good Shabbat/**A** Shabbat of Peace/**P**rayer will rise/**P**eace will come some day/
   Yes, peace will come some day

Aviva: And with the peace will be a Yonah ("dove")
Yonah: And there will be Aviva ("spring")

consists next of a biblical passage outlining the revolutionary idea
that Shabbat rest from work applies to everyone in the community—
including the slaves and the animals (Exodus 20:8-12). It concludes
with a statement that God blessed and sanctified the seventh day and
a blessing over the wine.

*V'shamru b'nei Yisrael et ha-Shabbat, la'asot et ha-shabbat l'dorotam
brit olam. Beini u'vein b'nei Yisrael, ot hee lei'olam. Kee sheshet yamim,
asa Adonai, et ha-shamayim v'et ha-aretz. Uvayom hashviyee, shavat
vayinafash.*

Remember to make the day of Shabbat holy. Six days you
shall labor and do all your work. But the seventh day is a
Shabbat for Adonai your God. On it you will not do any
work—you, your son or daughter, your male or female servant, your cattle, or the stranger who is within your gates—
for in six days Adonai made the heaven and the earth, the
sea, and all that is within them, and on the seventh day God
rested.

Therefore Adonai blessed the day of Shabbat and made it
holy.

Barukh ata Adonai, Eloheinu Melech ha-olam, borei peri ha-gafen.

Blessed are You, Adonai our God, Ruler of the universe,
Creator of the fruit of the vine.

After you say the blessing over wine or grape juice, drink from
the cup. You may pass it around or give everyone individual cups to
drink from. Silver Kiddush cups come in a variety of sizes and beautiful designs.

7. Washing the hands: Between the blessing over the wine and the
blessing of the bread, some people do a ritual hand washing followed
by a blessing. Judaica shops have beautifully ornate special *netilat
yadayim* (washing of the hands) cups, which have no spout—the
water is poured over the side. They often have two handles to make
it easier to pour water onto each hand.

*Barukh ata Adonai, Eloheinu Melekh ha-olam, asher kidshanu
b'mitzvotav v'tzivanu al netilat yadayim.*

Blessed are You, Adonai our God, Ruler of the universe,
Who sanctifies us with commandments and commands us to
wash our hands.

It is customary to be silent after the hand washing, or to sing softly, but not to speak until the blessing over the challah has been said and everyone has taken a bite. This practice makes washing, blessing, and eating one continuous action. The washing is a reminder of the priestly purification rites in the ancient Temple, and the Shabbat table with its foods becomes like the Temple altar.

8. Reciting the blessing over the challah: In Jewish tradition the challah (braided Shabbat bread) remains covered while the Shabbat is being sanctified with the blessing over the wine so as not to embarrass the challah. The reasoning goes that if we are so concerned with the feelings of an inanimate object, how much more concerned should we be about the feelings of another human being?

The person saying the blessing traditionally holds two loaves of challah together. These correspond to the two portions of manna that fell from heaven on Fridays so that the Israelites, wandering in the desert, would have enough food to last through Shabbat, when no manna would fall.

> *Barukh ata Adonai, Eloheinu melekh ha-olam ha-motzi lechem min ha-aretz.*
> Blessed are You, Adonai our God, Ruler of the universe, Who brings forth bread from the earth.

9. Reciting the grace after meals: After each meal we recite a long spirited prayer, the Birkat Ha-Mazon—the Grace after the Meal—to thank God for the generous gift of the bountiful food. Here is the first passage.

> Blessed are You, Adonai our God, Ruler of the universe, Who sustains the whole world in goodness with grace, kindness, and compassion. God gives food to all creatures because God's mercy is eternal. In God's abundant goodness, we have never and never will lack food, for the sake of God's great Name. God sustains and provides for all, and does good to all, and provides food for all the creatures that God created.

> *Barukh ata Adonai, Hazan et ha-kol.*
> Blessed are You, Adonai, Sustainer of all.

10. Celebrating in song: So that everybody can participate, hand out a small song and prayer book, called a *benscher,* which contains the various Shabbat blessings and also *zemirot* (table songs). After the meal it is customary in many households to engage in spirited singing before reciting the Birkat Ha-Mazon, the song of thanks to God the provider of plenty.

11. Making Havdalah: Havdalah, the concluding ceremony of Shabbat, takes place on Saturday evening. To make Havdalah you will need a braided candle, a spice box filled with spices, and a Kiddush cup for wine or grape juice.

Form a circle in a fairly dark room and have different people hold the candle, the spice box, and the Kiddush cup. The Havdalah blessings are recited in Hebrew or English either by one person or by all together. As each blessing is said, the relevant item is made accessible to the group: The Kiddush cup is held up for all to see, but the wine is not sipped yet. The spices are passed around and each person takes a moment to smell their sweetness. The candle is held high, and every person puts a hand up into the candle's light, turning the hands over, palms in, and bending the fingers. Some people look into the eyes of those near them to see the light reflected there.

When the blessings are concluded, each person takes a sip from the wine. The remainder is poured into a nonflammable basin in which the candle is then extinguished. An alternative, which is more fun but also more dangerous, is to pour whiskey into the basin and extinguish the candle in it. It will burst into a big, quick burning flame, sure to enchant the children.

Havdalah blessings:

Behold, God is my unfailing help; I will trust in God and will not be afraid. God is my strength and song; my Deliverer. With joy shall you draw water out of the wells of salvation. God alone is our help; may God bless His people. God of the universe is with us; the God of Jacob is our protection. There was light and joy; gladness and honor for the Jewish people. So may we be blessed. I will lift the cup of salvation and call upon God's Name.

Each person takes a moment to smell the sweet spices in the spice box during Havdalah.

Blessing over the wine:

Barukh ata Adonai, Eloheinu Melekh ha-olam, borei peri ha-gafen.
Blessed are You, Adonai our God, Ruler of the universe,
Creator of the fruit of the vine.

Blessing over the spices:

Barukh ata Adonai, Eloheinu Melekh ha-olam, borei minei v'samim.
Blessed are You, Adonai our God, Ruler of the universe,
Creator of many kinds of spices.

Blessing over the flames of the Havdalah candle:

Barukh ata Adonai, Eloheinu Melekh ha-olam, borei m'orei ha-eish.
Blessed are You, Adonai our God, Ruler of the universe,
Creator of the fire's light.

Blessed are You, Eternal our God, Ruler of the universe, Who distinguishes between the sacred and the profane, between light and darkness, between Israel and other people of the world, between the seventh day and the six days of the week.

In the dim twilight, the people in the circle join hands and sing *"Shavua Tov"* (a good week), which is sung in Hebrew and English. This is followed by *"Eliahu Ha-navi,"* sung in Hebrew only. Some people add *"Miriam Ha-neviya."*

Shavua tov, Shavua tov, Shavua tov, Shavua tov, Shavua tov, Shavua tov, Shavua tov, Shavua tov, Shavua tov
A good week, a week of peace, may gladness reign and joy increase. (repeat twice)

Eliahu ha-navi, Eliahu ha-Tishbi, Eliahu ha-Giladi. Bimheira v'yameinu, yavo ayleinu, im mashiach ben David.
Miriam ha'Neviya, oz v'zimra v'yada. Miriam tirkod itanu l'hagdil zimrat olam. Miriam tirkod itanu l'taken et ha-olam. Bimheira v'yameinu, hee t'vi'einu el mei ha-yishua.

May Elijah the Prophet come to us, heralding the Messiah, soon and in our days!
Miriam the Prophetess, strength and song in her hand, will dance with us to increase the world's song. Miriam will dance with us to repair the world. Soon, and in our days, may she bring us to the waters of redemption!
(The Miriam verse was written by Rabbi Leila Gal Berner.)

Finally we wish each other a happy, healthy week—"*Shavua tov!*"— and the lights are turned on. Shabbat has ended.

> It is said that after Shabbat lunch tiny little Shabbat angels swing from our eye-lashes, making it almost impossible to stay awake.

Hands-On Judaism

Here are some family activities for Shabbat:

1. **Attend services.** Go to Friday night and/or Saturday morning services at a local synagogue.

2. **Study and learn together.** See Chapter 4, "Learning as a Family."

3. **Go for a walk.** Take a long walk before or after lunch.

4. **Sing.** Learn a few Shabbat songs. (See Resource List at the end of the book.)

5. **Take a nap.** This is a time-honored Shabbat tradition.

6. **Play Shabbat tapes or CDs and dance!** (Note: Traditional Jews do not use electricity on Shabbat because turning the light switch is like kindling fire, which is prohibited on Shabbat.)

7. Have a family discussion. Discuss the past week and compare the week's activities with the goals and priorities of individual family members and the family as a whole.

8. Play games. Play Scrabble and allow all "Jewish" words such as *Kiddush, Shabbat, schlep,* and so on.

9. Invite or visit. Invite friends to your home or go to another's home for a meal, some singing, a discussion.

10. Read. Read a book to the children (maybe that book that you have been meaning to read which requires a little time for discussion), or encourage them to read to you.

11. Tell stories. Tell stories from Jewish tradition. There are wonderful books of children's *midrashim* (rabbinic stories) and other wonderful stories.

12. Act. Act out a scene from the week's *sidrah,* the Torah portion.

13. Teach. Take small children who are learning to identify things outside and find things that God made.

14. Focus on values. Choose a *m'lakhah,* a form of work that is forbidden on Shabbat, to add to the list of family Shabbat prohibitions. This can be a wonderful exercise of clarifying values as well as an exercise in interpretation. Why is a particular act considered work and outside the spirit of Shabbat? If it is an act that is not generally practiced by most families today, what are its modern equivalents?

15. Discuss the Torah. Choose one story—or even one line—from the Torah and make up a story about it, or discuss or act out answers to questions about the text, such as: What's missing? What do you think each character was thinking, or really wanted to do? If you were one of these characters, what would you have done? If this situation came up today, what would be different? What would be the same? Does this situation happen in some form today? Characters can be animals or inanimate objects as well as people!

16. Make love. It's a mitzvah for a couple to make love on Shabbat. While the children are napping, the parents should share some private time together.

17. Tell family stories. Share your family's history with your children. Tell them stories about their grandparents, their great-grandparents, where they came from, what they went through, their accomplishments, their most memorable qualities, and the like.

18. Go to a museum. While driving and paying an entrance fee might eliminate this as a Shabbat activity for some Jews, the leisurely enjoyment of beautiful art in the company of loved ones may be in the spirit of Shabbat for others.

19. Go to the beach. Pay special attention to the beauty and vastness of God's creation. An Israeli friend once said, "I love Shabbat in Israel. As my wife and kids and I are piling into our car in our bathing suits, my next door neighbors are dressed up and going out their door to walk to synagogue. Even though we experience Shabbat in very different ways, it is still an important time for both families. We wave to each other and call out a happy 'Shabbat Shalom!'"

20. Go on a hike. Rarely do we feel at one with God's creation. Shabbat is the time to do that, and a hike among the trees might be a way to do it.

Situations and Solutions

Q How can we introduce Shabbat into our family life? With very few exceptions we have not observed Shabbat before. We are afraid that our children will resent such drastic changes in our weekend activities and expectations. (They attend public school, where they participate in Friday night dances and Saturday afternoon sporting events.) But we are both committed to bringing a greater degree of Jewish observance into our home.

A You clearly have an understanding of the importance of *shalom bayit* (peace in the house). It seems unlikely that a teenager would willingly sacrifice weekend activities for the sake of family religious time. And it would be counterproductive to make Shabbat into a struggle for control and power. Instead, let your wishes be known. Explain your reasons for making these life changes and invite your children to be a part of it. You may choose to explain to them that you would love them to participate in the different aspects of Shabbat (Friday night dinner, Saturday lunch, synagogue attendance, family activities) but that it is not required and that you will make every effort to continue facilitating their normal activities through transportation and money (to the extent that this is true and comfortable for you).

Having made that clear, start to build your family Shabbat. During the week, give your children age-appropriate opportunities to participate in creative ways—baking dessert, arranging the flower bouquet, writing a Shabbat poem to be read at the Friday night dinner or Saturday lunch. Invite friends, and encourage your children to invite a friend.(Your guests do not need to be Jewish!) Feel free to be unconventional. Play Trivial Pursuit or Scrabble. Put the stress of the week aside. Forbid yourself to bring up subjects of tension, such as a poor grade or irritating teenage behavior. Eventually your children may opt for family Shabbat over the football game. Be clear on what they must do and what they may do.

Q We would love to explore the possibility of observing Shabbat more religiously, but we are close to our secular Jewish and Christian extended families who live an hour away and we see them every week on Saturday or Sunday. Should we limit those visits to Sundays? How can we balance family obligations with religious ones?

A Many Jewish families who have non-Jewish extended family are struggling to reconcile their own religious observance with conflicting family customs and expectations. The decision to increase Jewish observance can be hard to understand for those who do not share that Jewish connection (whether they are Jewish or not). Therefore, tensions may arise.

As always, keep lines of communication open. Describe your Shabbat observance, and be up front about your desire to observe Shabbat in a more meaningful way. Talk with your family about their religious experiences and what becoming more observant means to you. If you are not yet sure what Shabbat will mean for you but have a desire to try, tell them that. It is all right to experiment and be unsure. Make it clear that your expectations of them and their personal religious behavior has not changed. When we have our nonobservant family over on Shabbat, we make sure they know that they can use electricity, watch television, use the telephone, and generally do as they wish. One of our sisters tells us that she used to come to visit in spite of Shabbat, and just "live around it." But then she slowly came to appreciate the peacefulness, and she began to want to come especially for Shabbat.

Perhaps you could make Sunday the day to visit your extended family and reserve Friday night and Saturday as a home-centered Shabbat. Let your family know that they are welcome to join you. A Saturday afternoon/evening get-together is nice because it does not mean an extended stay on Shabbat itself and it ends with Havdalah. Havdalah is good for a mixed group because it is so beautiful with wine, spices, and a beautiful candle. And children love it because it is mysterious—a burning candle in a darkened room or outside under the stars.

 My wife converted to Judaism when we got married. Now she wants to go to synagogue on Friday nights and observe Shabbat. I don't want to give up our old ritual: getting the children to bed and watching a video.

Consider moving your old ritual to Saturday nights. We all need time just to put our feet up and be entertained. While Shabbat is restful, it does not have that wonderful mindless quality we all need sometimes.

You two are not alone. There are many couples of which one partner is a convert to Judaism and has a greater desire to observe traditions than the partner who is Jewish by birth. Those of us who grew up as Jews often don't feel the need to behave in certain ways or observe religious laws to be Jewish. We simply are Jewish. One thing a partner who is a Jew by choice can teach us is that it means something to be a Jew. It is good to remember that our partner has taken on something that is not merely a new label but rather a new way of life.

Your wife has made a commitment and she is trying to fulfill that commitment through her words and actions. And it certainly poses a challenge to the status quo, with which you are probably comfortable. Yet leaving the religious dimension of your home and family to her will likely make you feel more alienated and put upon down the road. Your wife's religious desire is an opportunity in your relationship to grow and explore together. This does not mean that her approach always dominates. In fact, if you take part in this process, the end result will reflect your combined aspirations and values. The enjoyment and the power will come from both of you as a team, as you interpret the meaning of Judaism and live according to that evolving interpretation. Some couples who explore Jewish tradition together, either in a classroom setting or informally at home, have found that the process injects a new perspective and energy into their relationship.

 We decided to give Friday night services a try but they start late for the children and they are not very family-friendly. Is this typical and what should we do?

 The time and the general atmosphere of the services vary from synagogue to synagogue. Shop around. Talk to other parents to see what they like or what they have heard about the best places to go with children. Go to different services and see how they feel.

First and foremost look for a place that is welcoming, stimulating, and child-friendly. More and more synagogues are becoming family oriented. They have weekly children's services, monthly family Shabbat services and lunches, and special, earlier services to accommodate families with young children.

Some questions to ask a member of a congregation you are considering joining: Would I find a nice community within the community with which to celebrate Shabbat and holidays? Is it involved in social action? Is it a community of comfort in hard times and a community of joy in happy times? Is it a place where your children feel happily connected to Judaism? Are you happy with the Jewish education provided for your children? Are people interested in and knowledgeable about Judaism? Can I feel comfortable and safe learning and growing here? Is the rabbi accessible to the congregants? At the *oneg* (literally "joy," it refers to the festive food and socializing that follows services) ask people the questions that are important to you.

Some families, however, find even the most accommodating synagogues still too "institutional." If you can't get comfortable in a synagogue, you can still find a way to celebrate Shabbat more fully. There are thousands of *havurot* (small, informal groups unconnected with a synagogue) that meet once or twice a month for Shabbat meals, services, learning, and fellowship. Some havurot are small groups of three or more families that rotate hosting responsibilities; others are larger, established groups of people who pray together in a Jewish community center or in a room in a synagogue where they may then share a meal.

Chapter Three

TRADITIONS THROUGH THE LIFE CYCLE

I F YOU LOOK BETWEEN THE LINES OF THE DISNEY FILM *The Lion King*, you may notice a very Jewish story. Thanks to his encounter with Rafiki, the baboon and ritual master of the jungle, Simba seeks out his dead father by looking into a pond. He is disappointed to find only his own reflection. "Look deeper," says Rafiki. After a good, hard look, Simba finally connects with something greater than himself. He hears the voice of his father, his conscience, his teacher. "Remember who you are. Remember your destiny," it comes booming back. "Remember . . . ."

Connecting with his past empowers Simba to move forward and reclaim his proper place in the circle of life. His past includes not only Rafiki, but Nala, a childhood friend.

Powerful memories are created most often by relationships with people and by events. *The Lion King* is not only about relationships but also about the importance of life-cycle rituals. As we watch this film with our two daughters, we point out that the movie starts with a ceremony that is like a *bris* (rite of circumcision), with Rafiki acting as rabbi. After the private ceremony in the lion's home, the newborn is presented to all the animal kingdom with much fanfare. Simba grows into a young cub, asserting himself, testing rules, making friends, and trying out his roar. His adolescence is spent with his buddies, Timon and Pumbaa, without a care and without any higher values. Only after he returns to claim his place in the circle of life does he take responsibility for the fate of his community, and also marries Nala. And in classic fashion, the movie ends with the *bris* of his son, officiated by Rafiki. (Thank you "Rabbis" Katzenberg and Eisner!)

Susan's father often reminds us that children remember three things: regular dinners together, family vacations, and life-cycle events. In our family we have interpreted these highlights to mean: Shabbat, visits to grandparents, and every opportunity—from haircuts to birthdays to weddings—to instill the magic and beauty of Jewish life through life-cycle rituals.

The traditional milestones in Jewish life-cycle events are birth, bar/bat mitzvah, marriage, and death. These are certainly significant events in the life of any person. Yet the yearning for ritual to mark other life passages is so great, and our tradition so rich with sources, that any modern family will find numerous other events that merit commemoration, including a child's starting Hebrew school, a teen's first date, and a young person's obtaining a driver's license. Grasping the hands of time in a deliberate and Jewish way gives us the potential for transforming many moments into memories of transcendence —into empowering occasions to reclaim our heritage and make it relevant to our modern lives.

There are many ways in which we can affirm our special bond with family and friends, with a living Judaism, and with God. And let us not forget Susan's mother's rule: Never miss an opportunity to take pictures or videotape a joyous event.

> **"**The greatest Jewish tradition is to laugh. The cornerstone of Jewish survival has always been to find humor in life and in ourselves.**"**
>
> —JERRY SEINFELD
> Comedian

Birth and Bris

In a memorable scene from the television show *thirtysomething*, Hope and Michael are arguing whether their newborn son should be circumcised at a *bris*, a Jewish circumcision ceremony. Hope is not against the ritual but wants to know why it is important to Michael, who has married a non-Jew and is openly ambivalent about his Jewish identity. The answer, supplied by Michael's uncle, is that the chain of tradition cannot be broken. With a touch of nostalgia, their little one enters into the covenant between the Jewish people and God, on prime time and now on reruns.

What is it about a *brit milah*, the covenant of circumcision often called a *bris*, that is so enduring and powerful? Our Patriarch Abraham, already at an advanced age, circumcised himself to set himself apart from all the nations, and then circumcized his son Isaac on the eighth day as God commanded. Since that time 4,000 years ago, Jewish males have undergone this rite on the eighth day of their lives.

> And God took note of Sarah as God had said and God did for Sarah as God had spoken. Sarah conceived and bore a son to Abraham in his old age, at the set time of which God had spoken. Abraham gave his newborn son who Sarah had borne him the name of Isaac. And when his son Isaac was eight days old, Abraham circumcised him as God had commanded him. Now Abraham was a hundred years old when

his son Isaac was born to him. Sarah said, "God has brought me laughter; everyone who hears will laugh with me." And she added, "Who would have said to Abraham that Sarah would suckle children! Yet I have borne a son in his old age."

(Genesis 21:1-7)

Just as the bat mitzvah ceremony emerged in the early twentieth century to mark the entrance of Jewish girls into Jewish adulthood, *bris* (covenant) ceremonies (without circumcision) have developed for baby girls as well. This development is a response to the need for ritual to affirm the place of women as a part of the Jewish people and of our covenant with God.

Aliza's birth was one of the most spiritual moments of our lives, a time when God's presence could be seen and felt dramatically—for with the birth or adoption of a child we put ourselves in God's hands. It has been said that there are no atheists in a foxhole. It is equally difficult to imagine atheists in a delivery room or holding their child for the first time. For relatives and friends, the *bris* is the landmark occasion of welcoming the newborn into the world and into the family. It is a time to affirm the ancient covenant between God and the Jewish people that has been sustained for another generation, and to give voice to the hope that this child will bring the world closer to a time of peace and wholeness.

The bris gives family members an opportunity to celebrate with the parents and to welcome the child into the Jewish community.

With ritual, song, and food, the community of family and friends celebrate the new gift to the world and acknowledge the community in which the child will grow and develop. Missing the opportunity to welcome your child publicly into the community and the covenant deprives your family of the opportunity to celebrate with you and to articulate a pledge to bring this child to a life of Torah and good deeds. The significance of this ritual goes far beyond a surgical procedure. It gives you, the parent, a ritual place to acknowledge the transformation of your growing family and to strengthen your place in the generational chain of the Jewish people.

The traditional ceremony for boys usually takes place in the home of the parents or grandparents. It is performed by a *mohel*, who is specially trained and certified to perform the circumcision. Until recent-

THE POWER
OF A NAME

The rabbis teach:
"The names of the
wicked are like
weaving implements,
as long as you use
them they remain
taut, if you lay them
aside, they slacken.
Thus, have you ever
heard a man call his
son Pharoah, Sisera,
or Sennacherub?
No: He calls him
Abraham, Isaac,
Jacob, Reuben or
Simeon."

GENESIS
RABBAH.49:1

ly only men received this training, but the Reform and Conservative movements now certify both male and female physicians to serve as *mohels*. (The more traditionally trained *mohels* need not be doctors.) You can find a *mohel* by looking in the ad section of your Jewish newspaper or by asking at your synagogue. The best reference is other Jewish parents.

A good *mohel* will walk anxious and sleep-deprived parents through the ceremony. It is extremely important to select a Hebrew name in advance of the *bris*—usually a name in memory or honor of a family member. (Sephardic Jews name children for living relatives while Ashkenazic Jews name children for relatives who have passed away.)

The key to having a good *bris* is to delegate: the food, the invitations, the ritual objects, and the program. Program? Yup. Not only does it make a nice souvenir, but a simple program put together on a computer can give a little family history, explain the significance of the baby's Hebrew and English names, list a charity for donations in honor of the birth or adoption, and explain the ceremony and its significance. Maybe you have non-Jewish co-workers, friends, and relatives, and this is a way to affirm that they are part of your community too. It is also a helpful guide to those Jews who are not familiar with the tradition.

Grandparents and other relatives can be invited to hold the baby and say a few personal words. We have videos from the ceremonies for both of our girls. As Aliza watches her video, we tell her about all the people she sees there and about how she was welcomed into the Jewish people. Traditionally, baby girls are given their Hebrew name in the synagogue about a month after they are born. We chose to give our girls their names on the eighth day in a home ceremony in which we used some of the language of the *brit milah*, the covenantal circumcision ceremony for boys. We wanted our daughters to know—and our community to affirm—that they too are in a covenant with God.

When our first child was born, word went out that we were having a *bris* on the eighth day. Some neighbors made the assumption that it was a boy and brought some adorable boys' clothing as gifts! Now we hear that more and more parents of daughters are opting for a ceremony on the eighth day. Whether on the eighth day, the thirtieth, or the first convenient Shabbat, Jewish families have almost routinely begun to welcome their daughters with the giving of a Hebrew name, a public declaration and ritual symbolizing her place in the covenant, and the giving of tzedakah.

Another ritual to consider is planting a tree in honor of the baby, either in Israel or in your backyard. In ancient days a tree was planted for a newborn, with the hope that its branches would years later be used as poles to hold up the *chuppah*, the wedding canopy.

Brit Ceremony

HERE'S MOST OF THE CEREMONY WE USED FOR BOTH Aliza and Hallel. It was compiled by Susan and was based on the work of Rabbi Shohama Wiener and on other, unattributed ceremonies. Feel free to be creative and tailor it to particulars of your family.

Welcome

> *Brukhot ha-ba'ot tachat kanfey Ha-Shekhinah,*
> *brukhim ha-ba'im tachat kanfey Ha-Shekhinah*
> May you be blessed beneath the wings of Shekhinah,
> be blessed with love, be blessed with peace.
> (By Debbie Friedman, 1988)

Covenants

Leader: When Israel stood at Mount Sinai to receive the Torah, the Holy One said, "Present to Me good guarantors that you will guard My Torah, and then I shall give it to you."

Everyone: They said, "Our ancestors are our guarantors."

Leader: The Holy One said, "Your ancestors are not sufficient guarantors. Bring Me better guarantors and I shall give you the Torah."

Everyone: They said, "Ruler of the universe, our prophets are our guarantors."

Leader: God said to them, "The prophets are not sufficient guarantors. Bring Me better guarantors and I shall give you the Torah."

Everyone: They said, "Our children will be our guarantors."
(Midrash Shir Ha-Shirim)

Elijah

We invite Elijah, whom our tradition calls the messenger of the covenant, to sit among us as he has done at every *brit milah* of our people for thousands of years.

Eliahu ha-navi, Eliahu ha-Tishbi, Eliahu ha-Giladi. Bimheira v'yameinu yavo ayleinu, im mashiach ben David, im mashiach bat David
May Elijah the Prophet come to us,
heralding the Messiah, soon and in our days.

Blessings

The baby is placed on a pillow and handed to each *sandak,* grandparent, to receive a blessing.

Parents: *N'varekh et m'kor ha-chayim asher kidshanu b'mitzvat ha- brit v'tzivanu l'hakhnisa b'vrit Sarah v'Avraham.*
We bless the Source of Life Who sanctifies us with the Mitzvah of Covenant and commands us to enter our baby into the covenant of Sarah and Abraham.

Everyone: Amen. Just as she has entered into the covenant, so may she enter into the Torah, the marriage canopy, and good deeds! Amen.

Prayers

We are prepared to fulfill the mitzvah of entering our child into the covenant. Just as God chose a name for Sarah our matriarch at the same time the *brit* of circumcision was commanded, so do we give our daughter her name on the eighth day.

Our God and God of our mothers and fathers, sustain this child through her parents' loving care. Let her be known among our people Israel by the name [child's name] *bat* [parent's name] *v'* [other parent's name]. Let her father rejoice in his offspring, and her mother be glad with the fruit of her womb. Thank you O God, Source of goodness. The love You show the children of Your covenant reaches into every time and place. May her name be a source of joy to her and inspire her to serve our people and all humankind. May her parents rejoice in her growth of body and soul. May we, her family and friends, witness her entrance into the covenant, assist her entrance into a life of Jewish learning and Torah, the blessing of marriage, and a life of good deeds. Amen.

May God Who blessed our ancestors Abraham, Isaac, and Jacob; Sarah, Rebecca, Leah, and Rachel, bless this infant. May her father and mother have the privilege of raising her, educating her, and encouraging her to attain wisdom. May her hands and her heart be faithful in serving God. And let us say, Amen.

May God bless you and keep you, May God turn to you and be gracious to you, May God be with you and bring you peace.

(Parents speak here.)

Reader: After God made a covenant with Abraham and Sarah, they were blessed with a baby. But between these two events, we learn that they were visited by three angels. Abraham and Sarah welcomed these Divine messengers by washing their feet. Then Abraham and Sarah were told that their covenant with God would be continued through a child. We do the same today with our little angel who is the newest recipient of the *brit*.

Reader: The waters of creation, the waters of passage. Waters that can sustain and nourish. Waters that can drown. So it was with the birth of the Jewish people. In their birth canal the waters parted and they crossed in safety. For the Jews, the sea was *mayim chayi*m, waters of life. The waters closed after them, and evil ones were submerged. For evil, the waters were waters of death.

And Miriam, the prophetess, took all the women and sang unto them: "*Mi chamokha…*"(Who is like You?) Miriam recognized the safe passage across the sea as a sign of God's covenant, for the Holy One had promised, "I will deliver you, and I will take you for my people, and I will be your God."

Legend says that because of Miriam's great leadership, God created a well of water that followed the Israelites in all their journeying in the wilderness. It was named Miriam's Well. From this well flowed *mayim chayim*, living waters, that quenched their thirst and nourished their spirits. In the waters that poured forth from this well, fruit trees flourished and fragrant herbs and grasses sprouted.

Miriam's Well is one of the symbols for Torah, for the Jewish tradition and the wandering years in the wilderness are a metaphor for the physical and spiritual journey all of us must take. Today, [child's name], we mark the beginning of your journey as a member of the Jewish people. We will welcome you with the ancient ceremony passed down to us from Abraham and Sarah. May your journey through life be sustained and refreshed by the waters of Miriam's Well, by God's care, by the words of Torah, and by the traditions of the Jewish people.

(Adapted by Rabbi Shohama Wiener from *Menorah*, IV, 3-4)

N'varekh et m'kor ha-chayim zokher ha-brit b'rechitzat raglayim.
Let us bless the Source of Life who remembers
the covenant through washing of the feet.

N'varekh et eyn ha-chayim borah peri ha-gafen.
We bless the Source of Life, Creator of the fruit of the vine.

N'varekh et m'kor ha-chayim yotzreinu,
shehecheyanu v'kiymanu v'higiyanu lazman hazeh. Amen.
We bless the Source of Life, our Creator,
Who has kept us alive, sustained us, and brought us to this time.

Future

In ancient Israel, a tree was planted at the birth of a child, and branches from the tree were later used for the *chuppah* at the child's wedding. This tradition is taking root once again. Today we plant a dogwood in our yard for [child's name], who will care for the tree. We hope one day to use its flowering branches for her *chuppah*.

The Torah is described as a tree of life in our prayers. As this tree grows, we hope, [child's name], that your knowledge and love of Torah grows. We invite each member of this community to add a shovel of earth and to participate in the planting of this tree.

Song to conclude ceremony:

Shavtem mayim b'sason memaanei ha-yeshua (repeat)
Mayim, mayim, mayim, mayim, hey, mayim b'sason (repeat)
Hey, hey, hey, hey,
Mayim, mayim, mayim, mayim, mayim, mayim b'sason (repeat)

You will draw water with joy from the wells of salvation!
Water, water, water, water, hey! water with joy!

Hey, hey, hey, hey
Water, water, water, water, water, water with joy!

Situations and Solutions

Q My wife's parents, who are not Jewish, are very unhappy that our child will not be baptized. They say it is all right if he is raised as a Jew, but he still should be baptized. Should we do it?

A How you initiate the entrance of your child into a faith community will set an important pattern in your family's ritual life. Letting your in-laws make those decisions sets a bad precedent, both in terms of your religious identity and in terms of your family dynamics. The question ultimately is not what your in-laws want, but how you and your wife feel about this issue.

If your wife has converted to Judaism, she probably understands the significance of ceremony in marking a milestone in a religious life and will likely object to her parents' request. If this is the case, you have an easier time respectfully saying no to them. If, however, she is not Jewish and also wants the baptism, then you have a problem faced by many interfaith couples. You need to decide as a family where you see yourself on the religious spectrum.

Children of interfaith couples who live a dual religious life are robbed of any firm identity as they grow up. By not deciding the religion of your home, you are shifting the problem onto your child, who then has to choose between the mother's faith and the father's. This is an unfair burden to place on any child. Teach your children that beliefs are deep and valuable. If you baptize the child, then take the steps to establish a Christian home and resolve to give up any Jewish claim on your child. Or choose the beauty and joy of establishing a Jewish home and raising Jewish children while finding other ways of validating the love you have for your in-laws. If you intend to create a Jewish home for your children, even without your wife's conversion to Judaism, baptism contradicts that goal.

Your in-laws probably understand the role of religious faith when instilling values. The grandparents can become your allies in your efforts to raise moral and ethical children. You are beginning a long journey—equal measures of loving patience and sincere commitment will matter a great deal.

Pideon ha-Ben (Redemption of the Firstborn)

In the biblical book of Exodus we read that every first-born male is to be dedicated to the service of God in appreciation of God's having protected them on the night of the Exodus when the first-born Egyptian males were slain. Pideon ha-Ben is done on the thirtieth day for first-born boys, and now for girls too. It involves paying money to "redeem" the child from this obligation. Parents often use this opportunity to make contributions to organizations that work for the values they want their child to grow up to embrace.

Breast Milk Weaning

Not so very long ago, most newborns were fed from a bottle. It was considered the modern thing to do. Now breastfeeding is modern again. As more and more Jewish mothers choose to nurse their children, weaning ceremonies, which have their roots in the Torah, are also experiencing a revival.

We learn that Hannah brought offerings of thanks to God for granting her Samuel, who would later become a prophet to Eli the priest. And she brought Samuel to dedicate him to service of God. She did this at the time of his weaning and not at the time of his birth (I Samuel 1:22–28).

The rejoicing and thanksgiving around the time of weaning may have been grounded in a high infant mortality rate in ancient times. A child who can start eating food has passed a milestone of development and is more likely to grow into a healthy adult. So Hannah gives thanks only after it has become clear that her child is strong.

Just as there is no uniform way to welcome baby girls into the covenant, there is no set ritual for weaning ceremonies. Most, however, contain some of the following basic elements, which can be adapted for your family:

> **"**The child grew up and was weaned, and Abraham held a great feast on the day that Isaac was weaned.**"**
>
> GENESIS 21:8

1. **Reading biblical passages.** Recite Genesis 21:8 and I Samuel 1:21–24.

2. **Saying Motzi, the blessing over bread.**

> *Barukh ata Adonai Eloheinu, melekh ha-olam, ha-motzi lechem min ha-aretz.*
> Blessed are You, Source of life, Who brings forth bread from
> the earth.

The father feeds the baby some soft challah to symbolize the child's
independence from the mother's milk and his now equal ability to
nourish the child.

3. **Saying prayers and blessings.**

> Mother:
> *Barukh ata Adonai, Eloheinu Melekh ha-olam, asher patach et didai
> vehenakti et pere bitni.*
> Blessed be the Source of life, Creator of the universe, Who
> opened my breasts to nurse the fruit of my womb.

> Father:
> *Barukh ata Adonai, Eloheinu Melekh ha-olam, mesameyakh horim
> b'yeladeyhem.*
> Blessed be the Source of life, Creator of the universe, Who
> has enabled parents to rejoice in their children.

4. **Presenting the baby with a tiny Kiddush cup.** Recite the blessing
over the white grape juice.

> *Barukh ata Adonai, Eloheinu Melekh ha-olam, borei pere ha-gafen.*
> Blessed are You, Adonai, Ruler of the universe, Creator of
> the fruit of the vine.

5. **Breaking the baby bottle.** Under the *chuppah* (the marriage
canopy) it is traditional to break a glass. One of the interpretations of
breaking a glass is that it symbolizes the end of the children's dependence on parents. Similarly, breaking a baby bottle can symbolize
entering a new phase of independence for the child.

6. **Giving to a children's fund.** Make donation to UNICEF, AIDS
babies, or the like in the amount or multiples of the baby's weight—
for a baby who weighs 25 pounds at the time of weaning, for example, donations of $25, $50, $75, and so on.

Situations and Solutions

Q My husband is pushing me to wean our one-year-old child, since nursing her interferes with our private time as a couple. I am not ready to part with nursing yet, but I also don't want to alienate my husband.

A A couple should expect to have less private time when their children are young, especially when a child is still nursing. Making enough time with your partner without eliminating the satisfaction that nursing brings to you and your baby is the real challenge.

Explain the importance of the special bonding that breastfeeding provides. Work to find ways of "stealing time" from your hectic lives for more intimacy—a weekly date, an occasional overnight at a nearby hotel while friends or family members take the baby, an early bedtime on Friday night. Or have private time while the baby naps on Shabbat.

Birthdays, Jewishly

by Lisa Farber Miller and Sandra Widener

The *Encyclopedia Judaica* could not be more blunt: "The celebration of birthdays is unknown in traditional Jewish ritual." In fact, it says, the only birthday party mentioned in the Bible is for Pharaoh! (Genesis 40:20).

As a result, parents searching for ways to make birthdays Jewish will find few traditions to guide them. There are, of course, certain birthdays that do receive special recognition in Jewish tradition—the bar and bat mitzvah and, among Chasidic Jews, a boy's third birthday. Superstition may have played a part in spoiling the party. Jews have long believed that to call attention to a good thing—like overpraising a child—is to tempt the evil eye, a faux pas that demands the immediate recitation of *keyn eyn harah*, or *kinahora*, meaning "no evil eye" in Yiddish.

The tradition also holds that your birth alone is not as significant as the way you live your life. After all, King Solomon is thought to have said, "The day of death is better than the day of one's birth" (Ecclesiastes 7:1). As a midrash explains, "When a person is born, it is not known what he will be like when grown and what his deeds will be—whether righteous or wicked, good, or evil. When he dies, however, if he departs with a good name and leaves the world in peace, people should rejoice." With that in mind, traditional communities are more likely to mark the anniversary of a revered leader's death than his birth. Nevertheless, under the influence of secular culture, birthday celebrations have become a fact of family life. Why not create your own Jewish traditions and customs to celebrate your child's birthday?

A birthday can be an opportunity to bring a spiritual element into your child's life and yours. You can celebrate in a reflective way that helps you think about the blessings and changes the past year has brought. You can celebrate the qualities you most like about your child or reminisce about funny or heartwarming things your child did. And you can reflect out loud about what your child means to you. As your child grows older, this custom is likely to become a highlight of the birthday celebration. The following ideas adapt old rituals for modern celebrations.

Plan a birthday Shabbat dinner. Many families, especially those with older children, celebrate twice—once at a party for friends and a second time with just family. You can make the family celebration on Shabbat. On the Friday night closest to your child's birthday, dedicate the Shabbat dinner to him or her.

In some families the birthday child uses a special plate reserved for this special event. And don't forget the Hebrew version of the happy birthday song: *"Yom huledet samayakh, yom huledet samayakh!"*

You can also have a tzedakah party. Give birthday children change to put in their own tzedakah box. Don't worry if a very young child does not yet understand the significance—the idea is to create a tradition that grows in meaning as your child grows older. You can also give a charitable gift in honor of the birthday.

You can involve the birthday child in selecting the charity or project. The bulletins of the Ziv Tzedakah Fund (see Resource List) list dozens of child-friendly tzedakah ideas, like buying a cow for a kibbutz or a horse for an Israeli organization that provides disabled people with therapeutic riding lessons.

Do a mitzvah together. Birthdays are a good time to convey the importance of mitzvot. Here are some mitzvot ideas that can easily be incorporated into a young child's special day.

- Bring a piece of birthday cake to an ailing relative or friend.
- Donate food to a local food bank.
- Make an art project together and bring it to a nursing home.
- Start a Saturday slumber party with a havdalah ceremony.

For Aliza's fourth birthday, we began a family tradition. On her invitation we wrote, "No gifts, please. Instead, we will be collecting nonperishable food. Please bring a couple of cans and yourselves!" Then after the party we took Aliza to the local food pantry. She was so proud to hand over her birthday tzedakah. And frankly, we were relieved not to have to explain away materialism to a four-year-old. Birthdays are a time to be thankful for the blessings we have in our lives. What better way to teach this idea to a child than having a celebration of her life be a celebration of sharing?

Plant a tree. An ancient and lovely tradition is to plant a tree when a new baby is born. According to the Talmud, in biblical times a cedar was planted for a son, a cypress for a daughter (*Talmud Gitten* 57a). The cedar symbolized strength and stature; the cypress gentleness and sweetness. The children cared for their own trees, and when the child was ready to be married, branches were cut from the tree to make the *chuppah*.

You can build on this custom by planting a tree at every birthday. Children can watch their "family" of trees grow. You can use the occasion to tell the story of Honi, the Circle Maker, the miracle worker of Second Temple times (first century BCE), who planted carob trees throughout Israel. Once when a passerby asked why Honi bothered to plant a tree that would take 70 years to bear fruit, Honi replied, "As my ancestors planted for me, so do I plant for my children." If you cannot plant a tree in a yard, arrange to plant one in the Children's Forest in Israel.

It is an ancient and lovely tradition to plant a tree when a baby is born. You can plant a tree in your yard— or you can arrange to have a tree planted in Israel.

Stage a Jewish puppet show. Puppeteers and other entertainers who cater to Jewish audiences often advertise in the local Jewish weekly. Or parents or older siblings can adapt a Jewish children's book or Bible story using bought, borrowed, or handmade puppets.

Give a Noah's Ark costume party. Guests can come as their favorite real or imagined animal, and a deck or a balcony can serve as an ark. Lead a "parade of the animals," serve animal crackers, and, in commemoration of the symbol of God's covenant with humankind, play up the rainbow theme by making homemade pizzas decorated with rows of tomatoes, mushrooms, and green and yellow peppers, and serve tutti-frutti sherbet with the cake.

Have a holiday party. Build Jewish festivals into the birthday celebration. Make a Purim mask party for February or March birthdays, or an outdoor tent party at Passover to remember the Jews' wandering in the desert.

Give gifts with a Jewish content. If you want to show your children that you value Jewish heritage, show it with a Jewish birthday gift. Here are some suggestions: a tzedakah box, a Noah's ark and animal set, a kiddie Kiddush cup, a personalized kippah (skullcap), a mezuzah decorated for children, video or audio tapes with Jewish stories and themes.

Recite special prayers: Special times call for special blessings. The following prayers appropriate for birthdays are suggested in *On the Doorposts of Your House: Prayers and Ceremonies for the Jewish Home,* edited by Chaim Stern (Central Conference of American Rabbis).

> God of days and years, Author of life, our times are in Your hand. We thank You for the blessing of life and for all that enriches our lives. We gather today in special thankfulness to share in the happiness of [your child's name]. Be with him (her) always as the joy of his (her) life.
>
> May he (she) be blessed with health and happiness, and with the strength to overcome sickness and sorrow. May we have the joy of coming together for many more years, united by mutual reverence and love. Then will our lives be filled with abundance and blessing.

As on all other occasions, say the appropriate blessings over a glass of grape juice or wine. Before cutting the birthday cake, say this blessing.

> *Barukh ata Adonai, Eloheinu Melekh ha-olam,*
> *shehecheyanu, v'kiymanu, v'higiyanu lazman hazeh.*
> Blessed are you, Eternal our God,
> Ruler of the universe, for giving us life, for sustaining us,
> and for enabling us to reach this season.

> The Lubavitcher Rebbe, Menechem Mendel Schneerson, taught that birthdays are an opportunity to add one more mitzvah to our lives. That might mean, for example, adding a new element to Shabbat, a new aspect of keeping kosher, a new prayer each week, a new kind of tzedakah or *g'milut chasadim* (acts of lovingkindness).

Important Jewish Milestones

On reaching the age of 3: Among Chasidic Jews, a boy's third Hebrew birthday is celebrated with his first haircut and a festive meal. The origin of this custom is in Jewish mysticism. Man is likened to a tree, and biblical law forbids eating the fruit of a newly planted tree for the first three years (Leviticus 19:23).

On reaching the age of 5: The fifth birthday is traditionally the time to begin Torah study. Sometimes the five-year-old is brought to the cheder, the place of study, for the first time wrapped in his father's *tallith.*

On reaching the age of 13: The bar mitzvah at age 13 is a relatively recent ceremony in Jewish history; it began somewhere between the fourteenth and sixteenth centuries. The bat mitzvah at age 12 or 13 for girls is a modern tradition initiated in 1922 by the founder of Reconstructionism, Rabbi Mordechai Kaplan. The *Shulchan Arukh*, the Code of Jewish Law, tells us that we are closer to holiness on this special day: "The consummate indwelling of the holy soul in a person takes place on the thirteenth birthday for a male and the twelfth birthday for a female. For this reason they become responsible by biblical law to fulfill the mitzvot of the Torah" (Shulkhan Arukh Harav).

On reaching the age of 83: The eighty-third birthday is also associated with a Jewish custom. Many believe that a person has lived a full life when reaching 70. According to Psalm 90:10, "The days of our years are seventy years." If you reach 83, you have the right to celebrate your bar mitzvah all over again.

On reaching the age of 120: "Until 120!" is a traditional Jewish wish for long life and good health. Rabbi David Cahn-Lipman, in *The Book of Jewish Knowledge*, explains the custom this way: "In Genesis (6:3) God declares that humans will live only 120 years. According to the Torah, Moses dies at the age of 120. Because long life was viewed as a reward for righteous behavior, living to 120 became an idealized goal. It therefore became a European custom to greet someone on his or her birthday by saying in Yiddish: '*Bis hundert und tzvantzig*—until 120!' Not only are we wishing them long life; we are hoping that they will be, in some way at least, like Moses."

(Portions of this section originally appeared in *Apples and Honey,* a publication of the Robert E. Loup Jewish Community Center, 350 South Dahlia Street, Denver, Colorado 80222.)

Situations and Solutions

Q We have only recently started observing some Jewish customs in our home. Our son, who is into sports, resents what he sees as the imposition of religion onto him at every turn. His tenth birthday is coming up and we would very much like to do something Jewish but fear it may cause a backlash.

A It is difficult for children to understand spiritual evolution in their parents, and it can be particularly hard when the "goal posts" shift in the religious expectations of the family. Suddenly imposing your will is likely to turn off your son and create tension, so ease in new Jewish practices bit by bit over the years. His bar mitzvah is only three years away, so it is a good idea to add some Jewish observances each year.

Provide him with a list of Jewish sports players from the past. Your gift can be some harder-to-find baseball cards, like Sandy Koufax or Moe Berg. If you already celebrate Shabbat, you can also dedicate the Shabbat of his birthday to him without making it seem a stretch. Meet your child where he is and bring him along slowly. And celebrate your own birthdays Jewishly to set the standard.

Aleph, Bet, Starting Hebrew School

In the movie *A Stranger Among Us* tough cop Melanie Griffith goes undercover to solve a murder case in a Chasidic community, where she encounters strange yet compelling values and customs among the Jews. The Shabbat dinner with food, song, and dancing is a little overdone, but quite beautiful. At one point a young boy approaches the table, a rabbi takes the boy's finger and dips it in honey, and the boy tastes it. "So that the words of Torah will be sweet to you," says the rabbi.

Similarly, on an Israel tourism advertisement a child looks at a large, open scroll covered with Hebrew letters. Next to each letter is a drop of honey for the child to sample. Adding sweetness to the beginning of each Hebrew school is an old Jewish custom that can create meaningful associations over the years for you and your child. Preparing a gift bag with candy from Israel or a plate of honey with apples before the first day of school is a nice way of starting the year.

> " … as I started to grow up and have children myself, I began to look at the world differently…. I remembered the very warm and familiar way my parents and grandparents taught me during all those years of Hebrew school when I was a child. So I got really interested again, having made the decision to raise my children Jewish by re-educating myself."
>
> —STEVEN SPIELBERG
> Director

How to Choose a Hebrew School
by Ethan Feinsilver

THE SICKLY SWEET TASTE OF APPLE JUICE FROM A PAPER CUP. A stained ceiling, a dreary concrete building. Pent-up, hyperactive students

and a constantly strained expression on the teacher's face. The same dog-eared Hebrew workbooks year after year. And, of course, knowing the rest of the world is running free as the honk of the car pool beckons.

Like a dream image, each of these Hebrew school memories condenses volumes of commentary into a single, loaded observation. Jonathan Glick's is perhaps most succinct. "There's this one memory I have most clearly," he says, "of all the boys in the class climbing out the window."

In the event that this scenario has made you wonder what goes on after you drop your children off at their Hebrew school, here are some suggestions for finding a good school. Ask yourself these questions as you shop around:

1. Visit a synagogue service as well as the school. Is this place in harmony with your values?

2. Do the children look comfortable and happy? Or do they look tired and distracted? Does the teacher make you want to stay or leave? How is the discipline level?

3. Does the school have defined goals for students and a way to get there, such as Hebrew reading comprehension or community participation through junior congregation, charity work, or youth group activity?

4. Are parents involved in the school, or do they just swing through the parking lot?

5. Is there a sense of pride at the school? Is the staff eager to tell you how great the place is? Is student artwork displayed?

6. How do other parents feel about the school, its teachers, and its curriculum?

Before deciding on any school, you need to answer a few questions yourself. How will you respond when your child asks why you don't do such and such, which they are learning in class? Are you ready to make a commitment to take the educational voyage together?

Stimulating teachers and a relevant curriculum are important. But educators at the exceptional schools have their eye on a bigger picture. They see the students, but they are picturing the students' homes. Douglas Jones of Agudas Achim of Iowa City is troubled by parents who want Jewish education for their children "as long as it's not too much." He marvels at parents who are "willing to pay five hundred dollars a year for Hebrew school and schlepp kids to and from school three times a week, but who complain if their kid comes home and asks about Havdalah or wants to build a sukkah. They tell the rabbi they're feeling pressured to become more religious."

Committed parents are essential to a good Hebrew school. Parents who drop their children off at Shabbat services and then go shopping send an ambivalent message, and children are quick to sense it. A growing number of Hebrew schools are confronting this issue by planning events that involve parents as well as children. Parents are asked to participate in field trips to places like Ellis Island, to give book reports to their child's class, or to engage in tzedakah projects together with their child. Of course, those parents who volunteer their time are usually the ones who are already committed, and educators have to work hard to get reluctant parents involved.

At Beth El Synagogue in New Rochelle, New York, Jewish educator Ellen Burkovitch starts new parents off with the least threatening, most purely social activity she can find, like a family picnic for Lag B'Omer (33rd day of the counting of the Omer—the days between Passover and Shavuot). When she moves from there to putting on a Havdalah service, she does "a lot of hand-holding with the parents" to ensure that the religiously apprehensive will not be embarrassed by showing their lack of experience.

Ora Cohen-Rosenthal, Jewish educator of Bnai Jeshurun in Manhattan, says, "Flyers don't bring people in. When I want to get people to come in for one of these family education things, I call every family on the phone." When parents come to pick up their children at Manhattan's Town and Village Synagogue, teacher Wendy Seideman buttonholes every one of them, making sure to ask about family assignments she sent home.

Town and Village teacher Rina Cohen beams as her student, Miriam Jacobson, 8, explains the difference between Hebrew school and regular school: "We get to speak Hebrew here and we don't get to speak Hebrew there." The key phrase is "get to." Supplementary Hebrew

> "My children felt Jewish, but had little sense of being part of a historical constituency.... Like many of my anti-religion decisions, I have come to view this as a grievous error of judgment. Because I had a feminist axe to grind, I cheated my children out of a Jewish education and allowed them to reject a rite of tribal inclusion whose significance they were not equipped to evaluate."
>
> —LETTY COTTIN POGREBIN
> Author

> **"**Hillel used to say:
> 'The more schooling,
> the more wisdom;
> the more counsel,
> the more
> understanding.'**"**
>
> —PIRKEI AVOT 2:7

school is a tenable concept, according to Miriam Klein Schapiro of the Board of Jewish Education in Manhattan,"but only if it's not supplementary in people's heads. It has to be part of the tapestry of life."

Ethan Feinsilver is a New York-based writer whose stories have appeared in *The New York Times* and on National Public Radio.

Coming of Age: Bar/Bat Mitzvah

The Puzzle Place, a PBS children's puppet series, has an episode about coming of age, with a video recording of a bar mitzvah. The question that is being explored is whether a ceremony alone transforms a child into a grown-up. A pre-adolescent, preparing for the Big Day, is not always filled with a sense of holy transformation, but rather is often merely following the wishes of parents and is nervous about the "performance." Thirteen year olds want to be popular with their friends, so the party better be awesome. And then there are all those presents!

There is a joke that sums up much of what is wrong with many bar and bat mitzvah celebrations. One family wanted to outdo all their friends and have an unusual bar mitzvah. They told their son that money was no object and he should dream up his vision of a one-of-a-kind celebration. After months of plotting, he decided to have a safari bar mitzvah in the wilds of Africa. They rented a plane to fly all the guests to Kenya. The best caterer in Europe arranged to bring the food in. *National Geographic* sent a film crew. On the Big Day, they loaded up the elephants with food, guests, rabbi, and Torah scroll and proceeded through the bush for the half-hour trek to the designated spot. The caravan moved slowly, then suddenly came to a halt. There seemed to be a delay ahead. Guests became impatient. The rabbi went to check what was wrong. He came back and said that it looked like they would have to wait another hour—there was another bar mitzvah ahead of them.

There are understandable reasons why bar and bat mitzvahs have become such a big deal. And these have little to do with religion or the true purpose of a ceremony marking the beginning of adulthood.

1. Grandparents. Because Jews tend to marry later in life than most Americans, fewer of their parents are alive or healthy enough to attend the weddings of their grand-children, usually about 15 or more years after the bar/bat mitzvah. As a result, many families have a big fami-ly shindig with the hope of captur-ing this celebratory moment on video, and hoping that the experi-ence will bond the extended family together. Bar and bat mitzvahs have become as big, elaborate, and expen-sive as some weddings.

2. Status. After attending their fair share of elaborate bar and bat mitz-vahs, families feel the social pres-sure to conform to the stylish norm. Parents may use this opportunity to be in the spotlight for the first time since their wedding and to dis-charge their social obligations. Many parents just want to provide the "very best" for their children without realizing the discrepancy this creates between the price tag for the event and the Jewish values the day represents.

3. Social affirmation. Parents often worry about their children's social development, especially now that children start dating earlier and earlier. At 12 or 13, children may feel awkward interacting with peers, especially given their budding sexuality. A lavish bar or bat mitzvah party is often seen as a step toward greater peer acceptance.

Many Jews do not realize that one becomes bar or bat mitz-vah simply by turning 13 (for a boy) or 12 (for a girl). At that age a child is considered an adult for the purpose of privileges and obliga-tions within the Jewish community, such as being called to the Torah for an *aliyah* (the act of coming up to the Torah and reciting the bless-ing for the Torah reading). The ceremony merely marks and cele-brates the transition and demonstrates a desire to take this newly attained stage in life seriously as a Jew.

In addition to having a bat mitzvah for girls, some communi-ties have created rituals for a girl's first menstrual period. One of Susan's young congregants had such a celebration. A gathering of women and girls camped overnight by a river. Each brought a story, song, or ritual with which to bless the girl. At the end of the ceremo-ny they accompanied her into the river, which served as a mikvah (ritual bath), carrying candles in the darkness of the new moon.

> ❝For many years I was troubled that I did not have a bar mitzvah….Today, I…have had the gratification of seeing my own son, Sandy, enjoy a Jewish education and celebrate his bar mitzvah.❞
>
> —BUDDY HACKETT
> Veteran Comedian

In the years preceding a bar or bat mitzvah, it is important to think about your goals as a Jewish family. Where do you belong? What values do you associate with your family? What memories do you want your children to have of their special day? And is the bar/bat mitzvah an end in itself or a means toward a greater goal of religious and spiritual development?

Judaism teaches us to channel our impulses toward affirming a higher value. The likelihood of your child's understanding this way of thinking is significantly increased if you live as part of a larger Jewish community that supports your values.

Living in community is usually best expressed by, but not limited to, joining a worship community. About 85 percent of Jewish children celebrate their bar or bat mitzvah, which means that synagogues are filled with children learning the basics in time for their bar/bat mitzvah. Once that is over, many of them leave the school and often the synagogue. It becomes the last Jewish experience they will have until their marriage. Your worship community can be a decisive partner in educating your child and in forming a lasting bond.

If your involvement is currently limited to dropping off and picking up your children from synagogue so that they can learn the basics for their bar/bat mitzvah, then it is likely that Judaism and Jewish values will play a minor role in their lives. If, on the other hand, you participate in this Jewish community, take Jewish courses for adults, and reinforce learning and practice at home, then your child sees that you are serious about being a Jew. If you strive for an expansive model of parenting in the context of community, you will reap wonderful benefits.

Parenting can be a lonely and isolating experience. Our schedules are not our own. Our time is consumed by so many child-oriented activities, from doctors' visits to music lessons to car pooling. Becoming part of a loving community is a proactive step you can take to counteract that sense of isolation. Within the walls of your sanctuary are many others who are wrestling with the same problems, searching for nuggets of holiness in their lives. In a community of seekers and worshipers, you are likely to find like-minded people. Your children will benefit from meeting other children whose parents are doing the "Jewish thing." The community will reinforce what you are trying to do in your home and will make accessible to you resources, books, educators, and members of the congregation.

Planning for your son or daughter's bar/bat mitzvah presents an opportunity to make decisions about your life and role as a parent in the context of a larger community. Plan sensitively, deliberately, and well in advance.

Putting the 'Mitzvah' Back in Bar and Bat Mitzvah

by Suzanne Borden

EVERYONE HAS HEARD OF BAR AND BAT MITZVAH PARTIES where performers and people in costume are hired to entertain the guests, 12- and 13-year-old children arrive in limousines, and the mother of the bar mitzvah boy changes her outfit every time a new course of dinner is served. Although a certain amount of ostentation will always be with us, there is evidence that the days of splashy, flashy, flamboyant celebrations may be on the decline.

Tikkun olam, repair of the world, is now the buzzword circulating through bar and bat mitzvah celebrations. *Mitzvah,* after all, refers to our obligations toward God and toward other human beings. Believing that there is something special about becoming a bar/bat mitzvah—something bigger than the party afterwards—students across the country are taking on socially responsible community projects, such as collecting clothing or canned foods, giving money to charities, or planting trees in Israel.

> ❝Jewish tradition was always important to Alicia's (Silverstone) family. Her father…encouraged his wife and children to light Shabbos candles and make the blessing over the challah. From ages 5 through 13 Alicia studied Judaism three times a week. She describes herself as 'passionate about learning….' Despite the thrills and successes in her career, Alicia says the highlight of her life was her bat mitzvah. 'The light feeling I had during my bat mitzvah, I feel a lot. It's a connection to a positive force. I'm so grateful and appreciative to be part of this life and it's wonderful to feel genuinely connected.❞
>
> —LIFESTYLES MAGAZINE, vol. 26, no. 141

Profile

BEYOND A CONVENTIONAL
BAT MITZVAH

I N THE MIDST OF SHABBAT MORNING SERVICES, an expectant hush falls over the congregation of a small wood-paneled synagogue in a suburb of Boston. This is nothing uncommon at a bar or bat mitzvah. There is the eagerness and pride of family and friends, and of all who are gathered—a sense of awe in watching a young person publicly affirm a personal commitment to Judaism.

On this particular morning the hush is almost palpable as Devorah approaches the Torah. She is beautiful and poised, her face shining with accomplishment. As she begins chanting, those close to her understand that what they are witnessing has layers of meaning beyond a conventional bat mitzvah. Devorah's coming of age as a Jew comes in the context of the fact that she is also Korean. For her and her family, identity is fluid and complex.   And as the Korean dresses on the walls and dolls on the tables at the celebration to follow will indicate, all parts of her identity are being acknowledged and honored today.

When Lisa and Doug got married, they knew they would somehow have to merge her more traditional Jewish background and his more secular Jewish background. What they did not know was that they would also incorporate Korean and African-American cultures into their household. As their family expanded through four adoptions, so did their individual and collective identities, as well as the collection of life cycles that bind them together.

The adoption of Devorah's younger brother, Adin Benjamin Kim Tae Yung, also from Korea, is a perfect example. Doug and Lisa brought him home at age 13 weeks. "We had a traditional *bris*." Lisa explains, "In Korea they don't celebrate when a child is born. They wait until the child is 100 days old. And it so happened that his *bris* was on his hundreth day. We also spoke about who he was named for, his Hebrew and his Korean names." When Adin was five, he went with his family to the mikvah for a formal conversion ceremony.

"He was able to repeat the Rabbi's blessings himself," Lisa remembers enthusiastically, "and seeing that was really, really beautiful."

90

The impression the mikvah made on Adin was clear the following year, when he went to the civil ceremony to become an American citizen. Looking around intently, he tugged at his mother's hand.

"Mom? Am I going to have to get naked?"

"So he knew," Lisa laughs, "that the mikvah was something to become something."

She laughs often, but she is also intense and reflective as she shares these anecdotes of her family. Their spacious, uncharacteristically quiet living room (she suggested we talk during school hours!) contains objects pertinent to a Jewish home (a tzedakah box, several menorahs) as well as those related to the Korean and African-American roots of their children. She points out the articles of traditional Korean clothing gracing the walls, and the African naming book that they drew on for the adoption of their daughter Elana.

> "Gone are the days when I thought our hardest job would be to build a family around Doug's and my different Jewish backgrounds!"

"Gone are the days," Lisa says with a mock tone of resignation, "when I thought our hardest job would be to build a family around Doug's and my different Jewish backgrounds!"

She described an evolution in the covenant ceremonies and baby namings. No two were exactly alike, and through each one she and Doug learned something new that they would do for the next.

"We had Elana's, our third child's, baby naming at home, outside, with a lot of people from the adoption community—social workers, other adoptive parents—in attendance. Since Elana's was the toughest adoption, and the wait was the longest, I spoke about the people who were there and the role of each one in making the adoption happen. Then each of the adoptive mothers who were there read a portion of a long poem about adoption. Then my sister, her husband, Doug, and I sang a folk song about raising our children proudly, never turning back. And since Elana is African American, we read a poem about being an African woman.

Our youngest daughter, Rafaela, is also African American, and at her naming we added an African ritual in which we threw a sprinkling of water up into the air and whispered the baby's name into her ear. We gave her two African names, one from East Africa and one from West Africa, to symbolize the whole continent since we do not know where her ancestors came from —Ayana, which means "beautiful flower," and Kai, which means "lovable." We called Rafaela's birth mother to tell her the names, and it turns out that her middle name is Ayana! So at the naming we talked about that connection, and the importance of giving Rafaela an African name for precisely the purpose of connecting to her African heritage, and about the time of slavery in American history when you had to forget your African names.

We also did all the Jewish blessings, that she should have the blessings of Torah (learning), *chuppah* (the wedding canopy), and *ma'asim tovim* (good deeds). I amended the *chuppah* prayer to say, 'if she wants!'"

Doug and Lisa, like all parents, celebrate their children's birthdays, and they also celebrate the anniversary of the day that each child joined the family. Their tradition is a candlelight ceremony. There are two candles, representing the birth family and their present family, and also each child has her or his own candle. The birth family candle is in the shape of a man and a woman; the child celebrating the anniversary lights this candle first. Then that child lights his or her own candle from the birth candle. The child then lights the home-family's candle, comprised of many different shapes intertwined. Then the other children light their own individual candles from their family's candle and everyone talks about the anniversary child. They reminisce about the day the child came home and say other kind words about their sibling. They explain what they love about this child and make new memories. When their oldest daughter reached the age of bat mitzvah, it was natural that her ceremony would reflect the blending of cultures that her family affirms in the context of their Jewish life.

> ...the whole family honors identity as a multifaceted experience, strenghthened through Judaism and enriched by diversity.

Lisa and Doug work hard to make their family part of the Jewish community, of the adoption community, of the Korean community, and of the African-American community. But Judaism is their overarching identity. Within this framework, the whole family honors identity as a multifaceted experience, strengthened through Judaism and enriched by diversity.

Working to integrate all aspects of the children's identities in the family celebrations is exciting but at times also tense, Lisa acknowledges. "It brings up all sorts of questions about the mechanisms of cultural identity, about what it means to engage in another culture with respect. That tension feels essential to a process that touches who we are so deeply. With each life cycle we renew our commitment to learning about that process."

Shortly after her own adoption anniversary Devorah went on a special trip to the airport with her mother. They were meeting friends, a Jewish couple who were adopting a child from Korea. Devorah, who was taken off an airplane from Korea 14 years earlier, was to get on the plane and take their baby son off in her arms, beginning a new family cycle.

Here are a few ideas to help you get started with your mitzvah:

- Plant trees in Israel for each person who lights a candle on your cake.
- Donate leftover food to shelters.
- Donate leftover flowers to senior homes.
- Donate a portion of the gifts you receive to charity.
- Ask guests to bring canned foods or clothing for the poor.

Personal Experiences

When Michael Vidmar, of Gaithersburg, Maryland, became a bar mitzvah in 1993, he decided to give the money he received as gifts to the B'nai Brith flood relief fund. "I was sick about the materialistic greed surrounding my bar mitzvah and I was ashamed of it," he said. "I didn't think I deserved the amounts of money I was receiving, and I felt it was taking away from the religious experience." Michael did know that he wanted to help other people, and that is why he decided to donate his money to the relief fund.

Alison Stieglitz, now 22, became a bat mitzvah nine years ago. Instead of expensive flower arrangements, she placed baskets filled with food in the center of each table at her party. These baskets were then to be donated to the local United Way. "I thought that becoming a bat mitzvah was part of taking on adult responsibilities," Alison says. "Since my bat mitzvah was around the time of Thanksgiving, and I was receiving a lot of gifts, I wanted to give something back to the community. I wanted to contribute."

Ilana Gildenblatt, 14, from Cincinnati, Ohio, is also making a difference. Her synagogue, Temple Sholom, required her to participate in a family mitzvah project before she became a bat mitzvah last year. She knew she wanted to involve others and raise money for Cincinnati Dreams Come True (a program similar to the Make-a-Wish Foundation). So Ilana organized a three-mile "mitzvathon." Inviting family and friends to participate, she helped raise $1,500.

Alexandra Alper, 13, from Rockville, Maryland, says, "I felt that part of becoming a bat mitzvah meant doing a good deed." Alexandra collected close to 900 toiletry articles from neighbors, dentists, beauty salons, supermarkets, and hotels. All were donated to a women's shelter in Washington, D.C. Alexandra plans to continue her collections by placing a donation box in her synagogue for people to make contributions throughout the year.

> "For one whose good works exceed wisdom—the wisdom will endure. But for one whose wisdom exceeds good works, the wisdom will not endure."
>
> —PIRKEI AVOT 3:9

The World's Three Pillars

The bar/bat mitzvah program at Indianapolis Hebrew Congregation is based on the principle that the world stands on three pillars: Torah learning, divine service (worship and ritual), and deeds of lovingkindness. Students are expected to do 26 mitzvot that fall within these three categories.

Cantor Janice Roger wants her students to see the connection between these three pillars, and to have a full understanding of mitzvot. She points out that when you become a bar/bat mitzvah, you are declaring that you are a part of the Jewish community. So how can the community—other families and teachers—help bar/bat mitzvah students begin to see those connections?

Rabbi Jeffrey K. Salkin, author of the book *Putting God on the Guest List: How to Reclaim the Spiritual Meaning of Your Child's Bar or Bat Mitzvah*, recommends that in the planning stage parents ask, "What Jewish values do we hope this bar or bat mitzvah celebration will embody?" and make a list of them. The list may include compassion, dignity, justice, learning, social action, generosity, humility, moderation, a love for Jewish people and the Jewish homeland.

Plan your celebration around these values, and stick to them. "Jewish celebrations [should] celebrate Jewish values," Rabbi Salkin emphasizes. "The educational and spiritual part of bar and bat mitzvah can extend beyond the final hymn at the service. It can permeate the lives of our young, and it can enrich what they take with them into the world."

This is what happened for Alison Stieglitz, who is now working as a social worker in Pennsylvania. She says her bat mitzvah experience helped to guide her into her current career. "I learned how easy it is to make a difference," she stated. "It's important to try and make things better." Alison and her family and friends continue to assemble food baskets, which feed a family of four, every year. Currently they are making 200 baskets and feeding 800 people. All this from a small bat mitzvah project.

Suzanne Borden is program director at The Washington Institute for Jewish Leadership and Values, which sponsors Panim el Panim High School in Washington, D.C.

Situations and Solutions

Q We recently approached our local synagogue about having a bar mitzvah for our son. They said that we had to join and that our son would have to attend three years of their Hebrew school. He's already 11, and we don't like all this pressure and unexpected expense for getting ready for the bar mitzvah. What should we do?

A Your son will become an adult in the eyes of the Jewish community for the privileges allowed him and the obligations incumbent upon him just by turning 13. The reason we have the bar mitzvah ceremony and celebration is to make the statement that this life transition is not being taken lightly. It affirms in the eyes of the community your child's commitment to Jewish learning and obligations. If that is not the case, then a bar/bat mitzvah ceremony in a synagogue is unnecessary.

If you are reaching a point in your family life where a bar mitzvah would be meaningful, consider complying with the synagogue's standards. Your child will be learning with other children who are also preparing for their big event. Perhaps, to shorten the time span before the bar mitzvah, your son could take on additional studies to the regular course. Speak honestly with the rabbi about your approach to the bar mitzvah, and involve your spouse and son in this conversation. This is an important part of the process of learning about becoming an adult Jew. If money is a problem, remember that almost all congregations are flexible when it comes to families who cannot afford their membership.

Another option is to have your child tutored at home and to conduct a home ceremony. Or you could shop around. There may be a congregation that has different educational requirements for bar or bat mitzvah. But before you go looking for the most relaxed requirements, think about why you want this for your son. Talk to other parents with children of bar/bat mitzvah age about what they are doing—and what it means to them. You may be inspired by what you learn.

On the Road to Adulthood: The Driver's License

Perhaps one of the most important moments in the life of any teenager is receiving a driver's license, a license of freedom from the shackles of home and childhood—a ticket to a real social life, and a landmark on the road to adulthood. For all these reasons, don't miss the opportunity to instill a sense of Jewish responsibility when your teenager gets behind the wheel.

When your children pass the driver's test, hand them a set of keys that has a Jewish key chain. Some have the Shema prayer, others have a prayer for the road or even a mezuzah for a car. Place your hands on their head and give them a blessing for safety, asking for God's protective wings. There are times, especially during bad weather or long trips, that we would all appreciate an extra bit of heavenly protection.

The prayer for the road, *Tefilat Ha-Derekh*, is traditionally recited when one is journeying beyond the city limits, but feel free to say it every time you venture out of your driveway. Place it on your dashboard for easy reference.

> May it be Your will, our God and God of those who have gone before us, that You lead us toward peace and help us safely reach our destination for the sake of life, joy, and peace. Protect us from the hand of any creature who would harm us along the way, and save us from all forms of trouble and pain that appear among the goings-on of the world. Grant blessings upon all our handiwork, and look upon us with grace, kindness, and mercy, that all our earthly interactions may reflect Your light.
>
> *Barukh ata Adonai, shome'a tefillah.*
> Blessed are You, God, the One Who hears prayer.

Jewish Weddings

If bar and bat mitzvahs seem festive to you, a Jewish wedding is even more so. It is an unforgettable, uplifting experience with the power to create lifelong happy memories for the extended family. One way to help make the happy couple even happier is for the family to find meaningful ways to participate in the spiritual and symbolic details that will outlast the magical day itself.

Three of our most cherished family mementos are the *chuppah*, *ketubah* (marriage document), and Kiddush cup that were all used as part of our marriage ceremony. Our *chuppah* is made up of individual squares of cloth that we gave to family and friends to decorate. An artist sewed them together in a beautiful tapestry.

Our *ketubah* is a commissioned piece of art that hangs in our dining room. We wrote the text and sketched the initial design, which is of the old city of Jerusalem surrounded by the symbols of the Jewish holidays. At each gate to the old city is a different traditional quote that relays a value important in our home and lives. A talented *ketubah* artist brought it to life. Personalized *ketubot* can be expensive, so they make a wonderful cooperative gift. For one extended family we know, everyone chipped in to cover the $1,500 artist fee so the couple could dream of their perfect design. The *ketubah* now hangs prominently in their home.

At our wedding we received many of the Jewish ritual objects that now grace our home: the colorful Kiddush cup and a challah plate that we use every Shabbat, our Havdalah set, a ritual hand washer, a ring holder, and other items we use to enhance our celebration of the Jewish holidays. We think of the people who gave us these items every week as we use them, and we share with our children stories about these special people.

Another wonderful family gift to give a Jewish couple is the complete set of the *Encyclopedia Judaica*, a 23-volume collection of information on everything Jewish. Depending on where you buy it, it can cost as much as $1,000, so having several families chip in is a wonderful way for many different families and friends to be an ongoing part of the couple's Jewish life.

Children love to participate in family weddings. While walking down the aisle is still a preferred role for younger children, older children can hold candles (à la "Fiddler on the Roof"), hold the rings and/or *chuppah* poles, design the center pieces, or arrange a tzedakah project, such as finding a homeless shelter to which the leftover food can be donated.

More and more couples are having a wedding weekend, so that friends and family can become acquainted, celebrate Shabbat together, and help to prepare the couple for their special day.

Situations and Solutions

Q Our daughters have started dating in high school and we have been making the case to them not to date non-Jewish boys. We were recently invited to the wedding of our cousin Jennifer, who is marrying a non-Jewish man. Should we attend? Would our attendance make us hypocrites in the eyes of our daughters?

A Attending family events is an important part of life and we would encourage you to go to the wedding with your daughters. You need not do this in a vacuum. Discuss the situation with your daughters. Talk to them about your hope that Jennifer and her husband will choose to have a Jewish home, and about the sadness you will feel if Jennifer does not continue her own Judaism or raise Jewish children. This event provides an opportunity to talk about the reasons that you feel it is important to be Jewish, while also modeling respect for others and love of family. If your daughters think the reasons you don't want them to date non-Jews are shallow, racist, or meaningless, then you need a new approach to this issue. If, however, they understand that you wish for them a life partner who will develop and share with them a warm and vibrant Jewish home, and that there are real-life benefits of living a system that gives great meaning to life and brings change to the world, then Jennifer's wedding will not be so confusing to them. Your daughters can understand that Jennifer's wedding is a time to share love and joy with a cousin who is making a life choice different from the one you hope your children will make.

The Inevitable: Death and Funerals

Judaism views death as a natural part of life. God is evident in the process primarily through the loving acts of family and friends in the mourning and healing process. How a parent copes with the loss of a parent or relative will leave a lasting mark on children. It will teach them how to deal with tragedy, and ultimately, with your own death.

> **"**At the moment of a person's death, the deceased is not accompanied by silver or gold or precious stones or pearls. One is accompanied only by Torah and good deeds.**"**
>
> —PIRKEI AVOT 6:9

Helping Children Grieve

by Rabbi Rafael Grossman with Anna Olswanger

As a Rabbi, I often counsel families as they mourn the death of a loved one. One such family was Robert's. Robert was seven years old when his grandfather died. On the morning of the funeral, I overheard his mother explain to him, "This is a very sad time for Daddy and Grandma, and I need to give all my attention to them. You understand that, don't you?"

As I later discovered, Robert knew that people died, but he did not understand much else about death. He had questions about what might have happened to his grandfather, but there was no one to turn to. He wondered if death was a form of punishment. On television and in the movies he saw policemen shoot gangsters, and he assumed that the gangsters were killed because they deserved to die. With his friends at school during recess, he played games of "good guys and bad guys," and it was always the bad guys who fell down dead. But his grandpa was good and kind, so why did he die?

At the graveside service, the minister said that Robert's grandfather was resting peacefully in heaven. Robert thought to himself, "What's he talking about? I saw those men with shovels put Grandpa's coffin in the ground." After the funeral, one of his aunts put her arms around him and said, "Don't worry, baby. Grandpa is much better off now."

A few weeks later as Robert played in our den with my sons, he turned to me and asked, "How could my grandpa be better off lying in the ground? He can't do any of the things he used to do, you know, like playing checkers."

I frequently meet children like Robert whose parents fail to discuss death with them. That may be so for two reasons. First, as parents, we want to shield our children from sadness. We want to raise them in warmth and security so that they will enjoy their childhood and remember it as a happy time. Second, we want our children to perceive us as infallible. "My daddy can do anything," we hear them brag to their friends, or "I've got the smartest mommy in the world." If we tell our children that we will die, we risk shattering this image of infallibility.

So what do we do when our children encounter death? Some educators suggest sharing books in which one of the characters dies, but in most children's books the dead appear either as smiling angels who look down from heaven or as pale and troubled ghosts. A child might conclude that death is either a reward or a punishment. Neither of these explanations helps a child understand the feelings that occur when someone in the family dies.

I remember as a child feeling deep anxiety about death until my father revealed his own fears to me. He explained that he countered his fears with his belief in the eternity of the soul. Although I often use my father's spiritual approach with grieving children, I know that some parents are not comfortable with it. Here are five steps I developed that will help these parents relate death to objects in their child's environment.

1. Everything dies. I never hesitate to use the words death or dying in front of children. Even if you believe in a hereafter, as I do, the use of euphemisms such as "passed away" or "went to another world" make death even more difficult for children to grasp. They can only take the information we give them and reshuffle it according to their level of maturity. Instruction about death can begin when a child enters the first grade. I never say, "You're going to die someday," but neither do I beat around the bush. I use the image of a leaf which has fallen from its branch and is now dead. A cemetery is a place where dead people are buried. Accidents can cause death. I try not to emphasize the fearful aspects, nor deny that I am afraid.

2. What is death? When my children were young, a close friend of the family died. One of my sons had just entered elementary school, and when he came home, I told him that Mrs. Miller had died that morning in the hospital. I explained that we were sad and did not want her to die, just as we ourselves do not want to die.

"But why don't we want to die?" he asked, and I began to explain what death is. "You see," I told my son, "when we die, we can't do the things that the living do. We can't eat, drink, talk, laugh, or even cry." He seemed to understand that death is not a trip to a faraway place, and asked, "What happens to Mrs. Miller now?" I told him that in Jewish tradition we believe that there are two parts to each person: the body, which dies, and the soul inside us that lives forever.

My son then asked why people cry when someone dies. I explained that after the body is buried and can no longer be seen or heard, we can only remember how the dead person looked and sounded. I told him this makes us sad because we want to share things with the people we love. I reminded him of the time one of his little friends had moved away. "You were sad then, weren't you?" I asked.

With a nod, he admitted that he still missed his friend and was unhappy that he no longer lived in our neighborhood. "But you can still write to him or call him on the telephone," I said. When my son responded, "I guess you can't write to dead people or call them… since they can't see or hear anymore," I knew that he understood what death is.

3. Why? For several weeks thereafter, my son kept asking me, "But why did Mrs. Miller die?" Each time, I reminded him of the portable record player he had gotten for his birthday two years before. "It ran down and stopped playing, remember?"

"But you put in new batteries and it worked again," he said. "That's right, and sometimes doctors can do the same for us," I explained. "They can fix us with medicines or with an operation in the hospital, but there are times when something goes wrong and doctors don't know how to repair us." I mentioned the time his sister had dropped his record player and it shattered. "We didn't know how to put it back together, did we? Well, sometimes doctors don't know how to put people back together either."

"But why does God let things happen that doctors can't fix?" my son wanted to know. "Doesn't God love us and want us to live?" In my opinion, the answer to this question can be the deciding factor in a child's religious commitment.

"Of course God wants us to live," I told him. "In fact, it says so in the Bible."

"Do you remember the puppets in the school auditorium?" I asked. "Were they real children or animals on the stage?"

"No," he said, "they were made out of wood."

"I wonder how they talked and moved around."

"There was a man behind the curtain," my son answered. "He couldn't fool me. He did all the talking. I knew the animals and children were make-believe."

"That's right," I said. "The man was the puppeteer who pulled little strings and decided where the puppets would move and what they would say. Their words came from his mouth. But God doesn't want us to be like puppets," I said. "God wants us to make up our own minds and decide how we'll act. God wants us to love and take care of each other. Puppets aren't real, so they can't help each other, but we can."

4. Death is not the end. Children must be assured that one thing—love—never dies. A few weeks after his grandfather's funeral, Robert asked his father, "Do you still love Grandpa now that he's dead?" Wisely his father answered, "More now than before. All I have left of him is my love."

Children do understand feelings, and when Robert later asked me, "How can my daddy love Grandpa more when there's nothing left to love?" I explained, "Your daddy has a great deal to love. That's because feelings have nothing to do with objects. It's like music," I told him. "You like certain melodies, and you like them even more each time you hear them, but you never see the melodies."

> **"**In the daily bustle of life, we don't always realize that the values we hold dear are actually a vessel, filled by our parents and our ancestors. In my case, that vessel was filled not by empty words but by our family's view of the world, with its good-natured optimism and humor, its curiosity about people and events, and its constant readiness to face life's more difficult moments.**"**
>
> —NATAN SHARANSKY
> Russian Dissident, Israeli Politician

In addition to feelings, children can also understand memories. Whenever I officiate at a funeral, I pull aside the surviving young children and ask them to keep a part of their parent or grandparent alive through remembering. Children want to look back but are often afraid to because their parents or other adults will not discuss the person who died.

"That kind of talk depresses me," I sometimes hear a parent say, but this response denies the child a positive and healthy channel for grief and leads to the idea of death as something to be ashamed of, something that needs to be hidden.

Children need to be included in a family's grief when a loved one dies. And their questions need to be answered.

5. Reassurance. A child should share in an older person's grief. Sharing means that both are sad and are willing to talk about their sadness. It does not mean inflicting one's anger or hostility on the child. I know parents who openly make statements such as, "Your grandpa would have lived longer if he hadn't had to support that no-good sister of mine." Children should not be expected to serve as sounding boards for their parents' hostilities. A child does not have the capacity to shoulder an adult's emotions.

In Robert's case, his parents failed to realize that their seven-year-old son had suffered grief at the loss of his grandfather. Robert needed to mourn just as his own father did. He should have been given the chance to cry and been told that although his grandpa had died, his—Robert's—world would not fall apart.

Many parents tell me they prefer leaving their young children at home instead of taking them to the funeral of a family member. But I maintain that every child should be included in a family's mourning and not be left wondering what happens at a funeral. We need only imagine the ghoulish scenes that can go through a child's mind to understand how terrifying death can become.

Some parents, like Robert's, fail to include their son or daughter because they are preoccupied with their own mourning. They inadvertently ignore the child and play down the child's feelings. Other parents consciously conceal their grief. But I believe we should tell our children when we are sad and be honest about why we feel that way. If our sadness results from our own fear of death, then our fear should also be revealed. In this way, children will know that there is nothing wrong with being afraid of dying. They will watch an adult grieve and recover, and will learn that they too can recover.

Grieving children should be assured of their contribution to the life of the person who died. Almost every child enriches the life of a parent or grandparent, and surviving children need to know this. At funerals, I make a point of saying to them, "You made your grandpa (or grandma) very happy."

Sometimes a child has negative or hostile feelings toward the person who died. These feelings should also be expressed. We, as adults, can defend the dead person, but we must accept the child's anger. Unexpressed anger simmers and often turns to guilt. I once counseled a woman who, as a little girl, did not really understand what death meant but had wished her mother would die. At the time she whispered her wish, her mother had just scolded her. When her mother died in an automobile accident a few days later, the little girl believed it was the result of her wish, but she never revealed this fact to anyone. Her overwrought father and grandparents were concerned only with finding a relative to take care of the child while they concentrated on getting through the funeral and handling their own grief. Had at least one of them been concerned for her feelings, she might have been spared years of agonizing guilt.

Children often have hostile feelings toward a sibling who died. The surviving children should be made to understand that their hostility is normal. Even if the hostility is excessive, they should be persuaded that their thoughts are not the cause of their brother's or sister's death.

Exposing our children to death, the most painful of human experiences, is admittedly difficult. Parents like Robert's, who fail to do so out of misplaced love, are no different from those adults who will not allow a surgeon's scalpel to touch their child's skin. Caring parents will agree to submit their son or daughter to surgery and to any painful experience, including a frank discussion about death, if doing so is essential to the child's health. Then the child will not suffer needlessly when death strikes, but will grieve and recover.

Rafael Grossman is a rabbi and practicing psychotherapist specializing in grief. As president of the Center for Life, a national support program for grieving parents and siblings, he lectures widely on bereavement and other family issues. He is the author of *Binah: The Modern Quest for Torah Understanding* and writes a regular column for *The Jewish Press*.

Anna Olswanger adapted this article from Rabbi Grossman's book in progress on grief.

Jewish Rituals of Mourning

Jewish tradition acknowledges the need for family to mourn the loss of a loved one and has established rituals to assist in this difficult process.

We bury our dead usually within 24 hours, partly out of respect for the dead and also to enable the family to proceed through the various stages of mourning. Mourners wear a black pin with a black ribbon, which is then symbolically torn to show their agony. In ancient days, mourners would tear their clothing—a practice that continues in some communities today.

After the funeral, there is a seven-day mourning period called *shiva*. During shiva, friends and relatives visit the home of the deceased and give comfort to the family. A memorial candle burns for the week, although some Reform congregations have a three-day shiva tradition. Customarily, mourners (the term *mourners* refers to the immediate family, although other loved ones are certainly in mourning) sit on the floor or on low chairs or crates, the mirrors are covered, and people bring food baskets and prepared foods when they make the shiva call so that the family does not have to entertain guests. The first meal after the funeral usually consists of hard-boiled eggs, symbolic of the cyclical nature of life.

A daily service is often held at the home of the mourners, so that they have a loving community in which to recite the mourner's Kaddish, a prayer that is said for a year. Traditionally, mourners refrain from various celebrations for at least thirty days, called the *shloshim*, and some for a year. Yet the message of Jewish tradition is that your life must move forward. Therefore, even though you may be sitting shiva, you are obligated by Jewish law to celebrate Shabbat and every Jewish holiday as it comes along. If a holiday falls during the period of mourning, shiva is interrupted for the length of the holiday. We remember loved ones by observing their *yahrzeit*, the anniversary of their death; by lighting a memorial candle; by saying the mourner's Kaddish; and by holding special remembrance services (*Yizkor*) during the year. Often charity is collected in the name of the deceased for a cause that the family designates. Toward the end of the first year a tombstone is erected in a graveside ceremony called the "unveiling."

Situations and Solutions

 When Tiger died, we did not know what to do. Are there Jewish ways to observe and mourn the death of a pet?

This is a new question for Judaism, since the category of animal companion did not exist until fairly recently. Talmudic and rabbinic literature have much to say about care and compassion for animals that were used for work or for consumption, but not for those used for companionship. Laws relating to animals fell under the area of *tza'ar ba'alei chayim* (concern for animal suffering) or *shechitah* (laws of kosher animal slaughter).

Jewish tradition suggests that God's treatment of us is related to our concern for animals. Both Moses and David were chosen as leaders after they proved to be caring shepherds. The commandment to show sympathy for a mother bird sitting with its young in the nest (Deuteronomy 22:6) is like the one honoring human parents. Both mitzvot promise a reward of a good and long life.

The intimate connection between God and animals is expressed in our prayers. The daily liturgy includes Psalm 145: *V'rachamav al kol ma'asav*, "God's mercy is on all creation." The Shabbat liturgy says, *Nishmat kol chai t'varekh et shimkha*, "The soul of every living being shall bless Your Name." Though we may dispute whether animals have souls, there is general agreement that certain species have feelings and are capable of relationships with humans.

Grieving for pets does not receive sympathetic support from mainstream Judaism. There are books dealing with pet loss, pet bereavement counselors, pet loss support groups, and even pet cemeteries, but none of them is connected to Jewish sources and perspectives. Individual rabbis have conducted burial ceremonies for animals, but the responsa literature (modern rabbinic responses applying Jewish law and values to contemporary issues) of Conservative and Orthodox Judaism is silent on this issue, and the Reform responsum dismisses mourning for pets as a private matter "outside of the purview of Judaism." This means Judaism is not addressing a question of emotional and spiritual significance to large numbers of Jews.

In North America today, more than half of all families have pets and regard them as childlike members of the family. People talk to their animals and play with them. When pets are in a family for years, people often build deep attachments to them. Animal companions can contribute to mental and physical health. They can help to relieve loneliness, make people more mobile, enhance self-esteem, and increase contact with people.

When pets die, people may feel sad, empty, angry, depressed, and alone. They may feel the symptoms of grief normally felt at the loss of a human relative or friend. Their feelings are often complicated by a sense of guilt, particularly if they had to make the painful decision to euthanize. People who grieve for an animal often find that their feelings are not understood. When they try to tell of their own sorrow, they hear, "Oh, you'll get over it soon. Why don't you get another pet?"

Several people have told me they were unwilling to replace their animal because of fear of another painful loss. On hearing of a loved animal's death, a simple response such as "Tell me about [name of animal]" can be very helpful. A willingness to listen and a sympathetic ear can go a long way in easing grief.

The fact that Judaism sees animal life as of less importance than human life is not relevant. What is relevant is that a person is suffering and in need. Seeking to comfort such a person is an act of *g'milut chasadim*, of lovingkindness, an important Jewish value. Judaism should offer guidelines for a ritual of farewell and for tzedakah through deeds and/or monetary gifts. Synagogues ought to consider an appropriate way to acknowledge and support those grieving over the loss of animal companions. Judaism is weakened when people have to turn to outside support systems to meet their emotional and spiritual needs.

Rituals are best conducted by the family. If home burial is not an option (many locations prohibit it), a memorial service can be held. The following might be included: expression of gratitude for the relationship; acknowledgment of God's care for the animal; personal words about and pictures of the animal; readings associated with loss and comfort. This approach will comfort those experiencing loss while retaining the important distinction between a service for a human and a ritual for an animal. There are animal service organizations, religious and secular, that accept donations in memory of animal companions. Working for a group that cares for abandoned or mistreated animals will help transmute sorrow and bring blessing to other living creatures. The growing importance of animal companions in people's lives makes it imperative that Judaism offer religious guidance on grieving for them.

This response was provided by Rabbi Shohama Wiener, Executive Dean and Mashgiach Ruchani (spiritual director) of The Academy for Jewish Religion, a pluralistic rabbinical and cantorial seminary in New York City.

Chapter Four

LEARNING AS A FAMILY

HE RABBINIC TEXT *PIRKEI AVOT*, "THE ETHICS OF THE FATHERS," teaches, *Talmud torah k'neged kulam*, "The study of Torah is equal to all precepts of the Torah combined." What a powerful statement!

Among the obligations a Jew must fulfill are the pursuit of justice, helping the oppressed, seeking peace, never "standing idly by our neighbor's blood," loving our neighbors as we love ourselves (making their honor as dear to us as our own), honoring our parents, never worshiping idols—only God Who is One. How can we compare learning a text to even one of those values?

One rabbi recalls how, as a student in New York, she would pass many homeless people every morning on her way to campus—some sick, some drunk, some lying face down in the gutter. She sat in class, looking out of the huge windows and wondering why she was reading about ancient laws of mourning. It was not time to mourn, but time to act and prevent more mourning! She approached her teacher, who said, "Look at the soup kitchen we run. Every table has a pretty cloth and a centerpiece. Legal Aid assistants help people obtain housing, public assistance, and job training." The "legal aid" explanation made sense. According to the levels of charity set out by Maimonides, the great twelfth-century Jewish philosopher and legal thinker, the highest form of giving is that which results in the recipient's becoming self-sufficient. Legal Aid lawyers help people find housing and work. But tablecloths and centerpieces? What did they have to do with our learning?

Eventually she understood that it was a matter of human dignity and *tzelem Elohim*. Every human being is made in God's image and therefore deserves a dignified meal. One student was assigned simply to greet people, in the spirit of *ha-khnasat orchim*—making guests welcome—and others helped in various ways, from legal assistance to sewing buttons on torn coats and providing warm clothing. All these actions represented a practical application of the learning she did.

> ❝Intelligence plus character—that is the goal of true education. To integrate human life around central, focusing ideals and to supply the motive power as well as the technique for attaining these ideals—that is the highest effort of education.❞
>
> —ABBA HILLEL SILVER
> From *Religion in a Changing World*

In *Pirkei Avot* we also read: *Lo alekha ha-m'lakhah ligmor v'lo ata ben chorin l'hibatel mimenah*, "It is not incumbent upon you to complete the task, nor are you free to desist from it." This precept applies to both the vast amount of Jewish texts to learn and the vast amount of work to be done in the world. Maimonides taught that the study of Torah is equal to all other Jewish obligations *because it leads to them all.* Through study, we think about how the world should be—in grand terms as well as in every detail of life. However, we do not just run out into the world and "put out fires." We look at a time-honored map, get a sense of the whole picture and the goals we want to attain, as well as what our tradition views as right and wrong in a complex set of circumstances. This does not mean that we will always agree with the rabbis and their approach. Nor should it. Judaism thrives on new ideas and challenges. Learning enhances the chance of having a thought-out approach to the world that is based on the ethics and values of Judaism.

"Turn it, and turn it, for everything is in it. Reflect on it and grow old and gray with it. Don't turn from it, for nothing is better than it," teaches *Pirkei Avot.* This act of continuous learning is made clear in the Hebrew words for "learning" and "teaching," which have the same root letters. Teaching is closely entwined with learning and is the natural outgrowth of serious study.

Jews often refer to studying as learning because we take to heart what we study, because it is a lifelong pursuit, and because it is meant to be formative. Whereas "studying" implies a finite endeavor, "learning" suggests a lifelong process.. A college student may say, "I'm studying psychology." When asked about Jewish "text study," the same student may answer "I am learning Torah." (The term "Torah" designates the Five Books of Moses but is also used in a wider sense to encompass the breadth of Jewish texts and knowledge.) "Learning" implies that we are doing more than an academic exercise of committing information to memory.

As parents, we may learn with other adults or with our children in order to understand the values that underlie a text and to find ways to incorporate those values into our lives and homes—and even our communities. When we study Jewish texts, we ask: What truth does the narrative of this story embody? What ideas are the participants in this discussion trying to uncover? What can we learn about life and how to live it in relationship to our selves, our family, our community, the world, and God?

Learning in Jewish History

How did learning come to occupy such a central place in Jewish culture? In the days of the ancient Temple in Jerusalem, religious authority rested with the High Priest, and religion was largely a Temple cult. The priests were the sole interpreters of the Torah. They received the entire community of Israel during the three annual pilgrimage festivals (Passover, Shavuot, and Sukkot), and they performed all functions connected with sacrificial rituals central to worship.

The Pharisees ("separatists"), a group of reformers who may have been active several centuries prior to the destruction of the Temple in 70 CE, began to build a religious system based on scholarship rather than priesthood. In the years 66 to 70 CE, Jerusalem fell to the Roman army and the Temple was destroyed. The power that had been centralized in the Temple at Jerusalem for centuries now came to be localized in communities and academies that had been set up by the Pharisees. Learning, once the domain of the Temple cult, became the responsibility of the community, its rabbis, and the people.

In the absence of a Temple cult, the study and interpretation of texts gained great prominence and became an essential precondition for the continuity of the Jewish people and their traditions. Whenever a new Jewish community was established, a priority was to establish a *beit knesset*, a center of community and worship, and a *beit midrash*, a center of study. Torah learning and its application has consistently been the basis of Jewish communal life. The enormous body of traditional texts was transmitted from person to person, from generation to generation in the most far-flung places.

Learning the sacred texts is a communal goal but is accomplished for the most part in the personal relationship of teacher and student. The learner adds his or her voice to the body of sacred texts and thus Jewish tradition remains fresh and relevant to each generation.

In a beloved rabbinic story, God allows Moses into the future to observe Rabbi Akiva, an early second-century scholar, as he teach-

> **"**Great is the Torah, for it gives life to those who act according to it.**"**
>
> —PIRKEI AVOT 6:7

Maimonides taught that the study of the Torah is equal to all other Jewish obligations because it leads to them all.

"The complete education gives us not only power of concentration but worthy objectives upon which to concentrate; not only a critical faculty for precise judgment but also profound sympathies with which to temper the asperity of our judgments; not only a quickened imagination but also an enkindling enthusiasm for the objects of our imagination.**"**

—ABBA
HILLEL SILVER
From *Religion in a Changing World*

es his students. Moses is distressed when he is not able to follow their discussion. He is finally reassured when a student asks Akiva, "How do you know this?" and Rabbi Akiva replies, "It is a law given to Moses at Sinai."

Spirituality of Torah Learning

The importance of Torah learning and its spiritual power are great. This is expressed in a rabbinic text about the ancient rabbis discussing how many people must be present to say the introductory formula to *Birkat Ha-Mazon* (grace after meals). The answer is that three people must be present. However, if two people have been studying passionately together, they constitute three people for the sake of this blessing. Why? Because their study, which is *l'shem shamayim* (for the sake of heaven), evokes Shekhinah, God's presence, thus the requisite three for blessing. The power of serious and passionate study is so great that it elicits God's presence.

Families Learning Together

We might even say that the potential for eliciting God's presence through learning together has increased in our time. Until recently, it was for the most part only men who engaged in serious study of Jewish texts. Today, men and boys, women and girls all engage in serious text learning at all levels. The human experience that we bring to the study of sacred texts is broader now than ever before in our history. Sacred texts come alive, they bring God's presence closer to us to an extent that our sages barely imagined.

In our day, men find the meaning and joy in homemaking and raising children, and women are finding their place and voice in learning and interpreting Jewish texts. The consequent focus on home and on study for both sexes makes family learning a natural, compelling activity.

Your family can become a mini-learning community like the family of Harry and Janet, who study with their three children every Shabbat afternoon. They print out a weekly subscription to a study sheet from Jewishfamily.com that gives a summary of part of that week's Torah portion, commentary on the portion, relevant rabbinic texts, and a contemporary problem to which the texts may be applied. They then discuss the contemporary question as well as issues that have come up in their own lives, or a related subject.

"When I was growing up," Harry says, "I always felt very close to my father. I loved and admired him deeply. But it is only now, when I am myself middle-aged and he is almost 80, that I am really getting to know him. I never knew what was important to him, what he thought about different aspects of life. We talked to each other a lot about baseball and spent many, many happy afternoons in the stands together. But much of our love and connection was unspoken. With my kids, we use a language that is drawn from our very rich tradition and apply it to so many of the things in our lives and the world that are important to us. I'm establishing a relationship with my kids, and a whole family atmosphere in which we constantly learn about each other."

Some parents have found that learning with their children often brings out family issues that are otherwise difficult to broach. For example, many Torah stories contain topics that are relevant to at least one family member, or even the family as a whole. The discussions can serve to shed light on each other's concerns, joys, ways of thinking, and ways of relating to the world. Studying Jewish law or responsa (modern rabbinic responses applying Jewish law and values to contemporary issues) is an opportunity for family members to express an opinion and to grow in terms of their own and each other's values and ideas.

Sometimes family problems that have remained latent come to the fore through such discussions. Says Barbara, "In a way, by studying together we open up a parallel world in which many of the same life issues exist. We can walk in and talk about the problems and issues presented, many of which are relevant in our lives and the world around us, without feeling too defensive, threatened, or self-conscious."

Rather than simply turning the children's Jewish education over to "the experts," these parents teach by example that Jewish learning is the responsibility of every Jew. Parents become active participants in their children's education, and children see their parents as learners!

Profile

ONE FAMILY'S APPROACH
TO STUDYING

HE SINGERS COULD BE YOUR AVERAGE AMERICAN JEWISH FAMILY. Pamela, 17, subscribes to *Seventeen* and trades her copies with a friend for the latest *YM* magazine. Several earrings make their way up and around her right ear. Robert, 14, wears a Cleveland Indians baseball hat that hides a near-crew cut. He reads *Mad Magazine* and prizes his Sega video game. Both children have e-mail addresses and are on-and-off vegetarians.

Their parents, Simon and Audrey, have been married for 21 years and are both professionals; she is a psychologist and he is a scientist. After dinner most nights, they gather around the TV to watch *Seinfeld* reruns, and they watch *Seinfeld* and *Friends* on Thursday nights. On top of their television set is a rented video.

Yet the parents, both immigrants, have intense Jewish biographies. Simon was born in Jerusalem into an ultra-Orthodox family and has been ordained as an Orthodox rabbi. "Unfortunately," laughs Simon about his Orthodox ordination. He has since adopted more modern Jewish attire and practice, using electricity on Shabbat and wearing a yarmulke only during religious ceremonies. Audrey, who was raised in Australia, attended Jewish day school for 12 years and then several institutions of Jewish learning in Israel.

They now belong to a Conservative, egalitarian community, but Simon often sleeps on Saturday morning and misses services. "I don't think we had specific Jewish educational goals for our kids," says Simon. "We never had a plan, we just went along and tried to teach them what we thought they needed to know."

The Singers celebrate all the Jewish holidays but don't feel they do anything out of the ordinary. Pamela remembers one particular Hanukkah seven years ago when she was ten years old. "They gave me a big book. It was the new Steinsaltz Talmud. I was so excited!" She effortlessly recites several key passages in Hebrew and then explains them. Not to be outdone by his sister, Robert quotes other Talmudic passages that he has memorized. Both parents are clearly proud of their children's Jewish knowledge.

"When I hear my kids studying Jewish texts and doing things that I don't know, I love it," says Audrey. "I feel so happy that they have enough knowledge to go beyond the basic concepts that I have."

Studying as a family has meant different things at different times for the Singers. When Pamela and Robert were young, the parents placed Hebrew children's books around the common rooms of the house. Robert runs around the house to gather up some worn samples for a visitor. Pamela picks up an Israeli children's song book with 100 songs. "I still remember every song here," she says, leafing through the pages.

When the children were a bit older, the family would gather in the living room after Shabbat dinner and read stories out loud to each other. "Isaac Bashevis Singer is my favorite," says Pamela, pointing to a shelf of the Nobel-Prize-winning author's books.

One year Simon and Robert studied a chapter from the Book of Prophets every night before bedtime. "It was so cool!" says Robert. He then tells his favorite tales, which usually include some gory detail or military campaign. "Robert loved the story of King David and Batsheva the most," says Simon. "You know, the bathing beauty and all that." "I guess it was like a father–son bonding experience," says Robert of studying with his dad.

One year when Robert attended public school instead of Jewish day school, he would come home every day and study one portion of the weekly Torah reading with his mother. For each sentence he read correctly, he received a penny. "The amazing thing is that even though he wasn't in Jewish school that year, his Hebrew reading and comprehension improved," recalls Simon. After a year of study, they completed the Torah cycle with a party in their home. People brought Jewish books as gifts, which today rival Robert's sports books on his bedroom bookcases.

Both children studied for their bar and bat mitzvah with Simon. "Our attitude was that it's up to the kids to decide whether they want a bar or bat mitzvah celebration, what they would do to prepare, and what they wanted to study. So it all really depended upon their motivation," says Simon. While their children did not do anything out of the ordinary—chanted part of the Torah portion, chanted their Haftarah portion (a selection from the biblical prophets), and delivered a short speech—the parents left the choice up to them.

"There was no pressure to have their celebrations in a certain way," says Audrey. "I enjoyed watching my children struggle with the process of deciding what they really wanted."

Pamela's bat mitzvah was also a watershed event for Audrey. Audrey read Torah for the first time at her daughter's bat mitzvah.

> "When I hear my kids studying Jewish texts and doing things that I don't know, I love it. I feel so happy that they have enough knowledge to go beyond the basic concepts that I have."

When she was growing up, girls did not read from the Torah. Now Audrey reads Torah every two to three weeks at her congregation, but first she goes over the reading with Simon, who had taught his wife the special Torah cantillations.

When the children finished eighth grade in Jewish day school, both were given the option to attend public high school. "We didn't know if we could push Jewish high school," says Simon. "But the kids led the way." They both attend the Orthodox high school, even though they live a less stringent lifestyle at home.

> "Our attitude was that it's up to the kids to decide whether they want a bar or bat mitzvah celebration, what they would do to prepare, and what they wanted to study. So it really depended on their motivation."

Looking back with a degree of satisfaction that her children love Jewish learning, Audrey says that her immigrant experience was a key motivating force for making the time to learn with her children.

"I thought it was very important for me to inculcate Jewish values into my children in order to have a common language with them. I felt somewhat threatened by the big American culture that would swallow up my kids and make them strangers to the things that I hold dear. But I also wanted to make sure that Jewish values were transmitted to my children, because I saw intrinsic value in it. Their Jewish consciousness didn't just happen but took a concerted effort."

Simon, who still has ultra-Orthodox relatives in Jerusalem with whom he is close, says that the Jewish education he wanted his children to have was not religiously motivated. "Even though I've strayed quite far from my family of origin, my extended family, my tribe, I want my children to have a relationship and a common language with my parents and other relatives," he says. "It is very easy to get lost in the modern Western culture, and so I've always wanted my kids to have access to my Orthodox family as a kind of safety net. This has nothing to do with religion, it's just that the common language happens to be religion. It happens to be Judaism that binds them together."

David Epstein, author of *Torah with Love: A Guide for Strengthening Jewish Values Within the Home,* and his wife Ellen raised their children with Jewish study as a central element of Shabbat dinner. Everyone present would speak and have a chance to be heard. David says this tradition of presenting ideas in the home made his children good students: "In classes they were the first to raise their hands and voice their opinions, since they'd done so in the presence of adults their entire lives."

> **"**One who studies Torah becomes like "an ever-flowing spring, like a river that never ends."**
>
> —PIRKEI AVOT 6:1

Jewish Learning as a Participatory Sport

A text from the Kabbalah (Jewish mysticism) describes the Torah as the physical appearance of God's word. The Torah's narratives and laws are the cloak and the body respectively. What we need to discover is the soul.

Susan presented this text to a tenth grade class and asked, "Why didn't God just give us the whole Torah, including the deeper, inner meanings?"

One student replied, "Because if God just gave us the whole Torah, it would demand nothing of us."

Added another, "It would be as if life were a play and we were just reading a script. This way we have to put ourselves into it."

Rabbi Susan Harris says, "Our children need to participate in the extension of the rabbinic process of midrash. They need permission and encouragement to bring their lives and dilemmas to the text, to create friction and resolution, and to creatively and knowledgeably expand the conversation that has brought us thus far." She explains, "We need to expose our children to a wide variety of texts, sources, and interpretations. These will be where they begin to look for the answers to their own questions."

Through learning, we place our lives into the context of a millennia-old Jewish discussion. We, with our struggles, are not alone. If we as parents help our children see our sacred texts as eternally rich and responsive rather than one-dimensional and brittle, we do them a great service and provide them with another lifelong resource. As we grow up, we develop memories, skills, and insights on which we draw later in life. Learning enriches our lives. Together, parents and children gain insight into our people's history and values, into the rich and varied stories of our people.

> **"**[Daddy] said: 'All children must look after their own upbringing.' Parents can only give good advice or put them on the right paths, but the final forming of a person's character lies in their own hands.**
>
> —ANNE FRANK
> Holocaust Victim

Fixing a Time for Study

Shabbat is an excellent time to have a regular study session—around the dinner table or as an activity on Shabbat afternoon. Of course, if you go to synagogue you will hear the Torah portion and usually an interpretation or sermon connected to the text. This can form the basis of a later family discussion.

Many families use the Shabbat dinner as a study and discussion time.

In the Epstein home, Friday night dinner, with guests, is the main study time. For many years they went through the Torah, reading and discussing one line a week, without regard to the yearly Torah-reading cycle. David describes the Friday night ritual: "I read aloud a portion of Joseph Telushkin's book *Jewish Literacy*, usually selected at random by asking a guest to pick a number from 1 to 346 (the number of entries in the book). Then we would go around the table and break the ice by sharing a high point and low point of the week. Then each person was asked to add to the topic selected or ask a question about the topic. Our final discussion was on ethical issues. Guests were asked in advance to bring an ethical dilemma for discussion."

In addition to a weekly fixed time for study, there are other occasions that warrant learning at least a passage from tradition. Even just a quick reference to a Jewish text sets the tone for a meaningful holiday meal (even on national holidays such as Thanksgiving, the Fourth of July, Presidents' Day, or Martin Luther King's Birthday), a birthday or anniversary celebration, even a family meeting. Other occasions that can benefit from being placed in the context of Jewish values through text study include political demonstrations, volunteering to help the hungry and homeless, or traveling in the car to visit relatives. While discussing a political or social issue such as welfare reform, reach for a traditional text for insight, guidance, and stimulation.

Studying together as a family benefits both the family and the Jewish people as a whole. Family members can imitate the ancient rabbis by drawing on their diverse experiences and imagining situations to analyze through the lens of Jewish tradition. In this way families strengthen their understanding of traditional sources while seeking a higher truth.

Rabbi Susan Harris tells us, "We are challenged to include ourselves and our children in this shared memory as active participants. Or that is to say, to transmit a heritage that includes the actions, contributions, energies, and feelings of all Jews, including women, including girls. That means asking questions about our history that relate to the experience of the entire community—including girls and women. It means hearing and naming the silence, the people, mostly women, whose voices are unrecorded, even and especially when there are no obvious answers."

Creating a Library for Your Children

by Miriam Rinn

WHEN MY SONS WERE ABOUT TO ENTER PUBLIC SCHOOL, I had visions of their coming home pleading ceaselessly for baskets of Easter candy and a cozy chat with Santa at the mall. The suburban town we live in has a small Jewish population, and I knew that my boys would be among few Jewish children in their elementary school. What would happen in April and December? Would they wonder sadly why we weren't expecting a mob of gift-laden guests on Christmas Day, or why they couldn't gorge on Easter candy like all their friends? How could I teach them that, as lovely as these celebrations are, they aren't ours? How could I deepen their sense of Jewish identity?

My best ally, it turned out, was close at hand—heaped all over the house in fact. Like most young children, my sons loved listening to us read to them. Although they had their favorites, they were not very selective about the choices, as long as Mommy or Daddy took the time to read. I could easily introduce into our daily reading time books about the Jewish holidays, stories with Jewish characters, and tales of Jewish heroes and heroines. Without lecturing or preaching, or denigrating the beliefs of their friends and classmates, I could share with them the flavor and fun of Judaism.

So began a tradition of reading Jewish children's books in our home. It brought dozens of hours of shared learning and pleasure to our family. The presence of Jewish books makes your house feel like a

"I pray that I may be all that she [my mother] would have been had she lived to an age when women could aspire and achieve and daughters are cherished as much as sons."

—RUTH BADER GINSBURG
Supreme Court Justice

TEN RECOMMENDED JEWISH BOOKS
FOR CHILDREN OF ALL AGES

1. **God's Paintbrush** by Sandy Eisenberg Sasso. Ages 4 to 8.
2. **Why Noah Chose the Dove** by I. B. Singer. Ages 4 to 8.
3. **Miriam's Tambourine: Jewish Folktales from Around the World** by Howard Schwartz. All ages.
4. **Jewish Days and Holidays** by Greer Fay Cashman. Ages 6 to 10.
5. **All-of-a-Kind Family** by Sydney Taylor. Ages 7 to 10.
6. **The Book of Adam to Moses** by Lore Segal and Leonard Baskin. Ages 10 and up.
7. **The Jewish Book of Why** by Alfred J. Kolatch. All ages.
8. **The Other 1492: Jewish Settlement in the New World** by Norman H. Finkelstein. Ages 10 to 14.
9. **Fragments of Isabella** by Isabella Leitner. Ages 10 and up.
10. **Night** by Elie Wiesel. Ages 15 and up.

Jewish home. The books display the extraordinary 4,000-year-old saga of the Jews with color and drama. They can provoke discussion and argument, as well as shared laughter and tears. Books frequently express ideas about risk and moral courage and discipline that children often don't want to hear from their parents. So whenever your child pleads, "Read me a story," have a Jewish book handy. There are thousands of titles available for sharing with children, from tots to teens.

In addition to the many Jewish publishers who cater to every segment of the Jewish community, all major children's publishers publish Jewish books. Jews are known for being enthusiastic book buyers—not for nothing are we called People of the Book!—and publishers are eager to capture those dollars. Jewish book fairs are common events at community centers and synagogues.

An easy way to start is to buy an appropriate Jewish book

about a month before each Jewish holiday, or check one out from the library. If your children are preschoolers, choose one of the many holiday picture books available. Tell the children you want to read a story about Hanukkah, or Passover, or Sukkot. If they don't know or don't remember the holiday, tell them as much as you think they should know. Read the book several times before the holiday arrives, and refer to it as you make your holiday preparations. Purchase a Jewish children's cookbook, and use it to prepare holiday treats. Children enjoy making

With thousands of titles to choose from, there are Jewish children's books to suit all ages and interests.

potato latkes (potato pancakes) or hamantashen (a three-cornered pastry) or matzah brei (fried matzah and egg), and they get a kick out of following directions in their own cookbook.

Choose books for their entertainment value as well as for their Jewish content. Search out popular writers such as Barbara Cohen or Johanna Hurwitz. Hurwitz has written a series about a lively fourth grader called Ali Baba Bernstein. Although Ali Baba is clearly Jewish, Jewish content in the stories is casual rather than didactic.

For preteens and teens, just when they need to see their own concerns and lives reflected in what they read, Jewish junior-high students can be exposed to dozens of stories about the shtetl in Eastern Europe, tenement life of Jewish immigrants early in the century, or the Holocaust. Unfortunately, there are relatively few books about contemporary American Jewish youngsters for whom Jewish identity is a positive force. One solution is to have Jewish books available for your preteens to use for book reports or school projects. A seventh grader who has just remembered her book report is due in two days is not going to turn down your suggestion of a biography of Golda Meir or a novel about an immigrant teen. She may not be "choosing" these books, but she may still enjoy them and absorb what they have to offer.

Miriam Rinn is a freelance writer who writes about the arts and entertainment and who reviews children's books.

 Hands-On Judaism

1. Set a weekly time for study. Family learning is certainly not limited to sitting in a circle reading aloud! If you are reading the Bible, for example, each person can take a role or character in a particular passage and play out the scene.

2. Ask questions of the text. How did a certain character feel? What in his or her past motivated a particular behavior or action? What is missing in the text? Interview the characters. Encourage two characters to expand—or invent—a biblical dialogue.

3. Read parashat ha-shavua (the week's Torah portion). Use either the Bible or an abridged version for children. There are many wonderful books of commentary that work well in a family context. With older children, assign each child a commentary, with time to prepare an argument in favor of that interpretation. Take a look at books of modern responsa. Describe the issue presented, and then have each family member give his or her opinion in light of Jewish values. Then read the response.

4. Choose an article of interest from the newspaper. Discuss the article in light of Jewish values. How are certain words used? For example, if someone describes the merging of two companies as "good," does that mean that the employees are treated fairly? How does American culture define what is "good" or "bad" versus the way Jewish tradition would define the same instances?

5. Analyze current social problems. Share a problem that has come up in your family or community during the week. Explore how a solution could be reached from a Jewish values perspective.

6. Join a family education program. Family education programs are sprouting up in many communities across the country. These programs bring you together with other families who share an interest in living a fuller Jewish life, in learning, in discussing, and in applying Jewish texts to everyday living.

7. Gather information. Use a *parashat ha-shavua book,* fax service, or Jewishfamily.com to provide a summary of the portion as well as commentaries, questions for discussion, and relevant gems from other parts of tradition.

Situations and Solutions

Q My son goes to afternoon religious school three times a week. Often he comes home with questions that my partner and I do not know how to address. Is there a relatively time-efficient way to inform ourselves enough to have an intelligent discussion with our son?

A It is important for you to have religious discussions with your son. If you can't respond to his questions and comments, and consequently appear uninterested, he will wonder why you send him to religious school in the first place. You need to work together with your son to create, interpret, and shape important ideas related to the core of our tradition and human experience: ethics, values, roles, and obligations.

Talk to your son's teacher (or school director or rabbi). Explain your desire to reinforce your son's learning by being able to discuss it at home. There is nothing a teacher would like better than to hear of your interest! Ask the teacher to explain the curriculum, share the books used in class, or recommend any adult books that parallel your son's learning. Also arrange to sit in class periodically and get a sense of his overall experience. Use the texts related to the curriculum of your son's class in some of the family learning activities that are listed in this chapter.

You may also want to consider organizing a monthly parents' meeting, since you are probably not alone in your struggle. As a group you could develop creative ways to enrich your Jewish knowledge and share in your children's Jewish development.

Find an introductory course on Judaism in your area. Also, consider using family leisure time to participate in a Jewish family education program. These are frequently socially interactive and you may find this a good opportunity to learn together with your son, along with other like-minded families.

Q My wife is not Jewish, but we have agreed to raise the children as Jews. Since they have started religious school, we talk at bath time and bedtime about different religious issues, often using storybooks as a basis of our talks. My wife has recently requested that as a family we study not only Judaism but also Christianity. She does not want the children to be Christians, but she feels it is important that they know about the traditions of her half of their extended family. I think that doing so would be confusing to them.

A   First, it is important that there are no unspoken agendas on your part to discredit Christianity or on her part to undermine her agreement to raise a Jewish family. If these desires are present, they need to be worked out between the two of you, not in the presence of—or through—the children. If it is clear that you both want to raise Jewish children, remember that there will be times over the years when she will feel sad and have a sense of loss. Be sensitive and supportive of her.

It certainly is valuable for your children to understand the heritage, religious beliefs, and values of another part of their family. However, since you are raising Jewish children, these intimate talks should continue to focus on Jewish tradition, religion, and peoplehood.

Continue to present Judaism as normative (for your nuclear family) while responding to their inevitable questions about "Mommy's religion" with clear information and respect for Christianity. It is important not to treat Christianity or Judaism as "what the other is not," but as independent entities. Certainly, celebrating Christian holidays in your home would be inappropriate. When you go to a Christian family's home for a Christian holiday, be participatory but clear with your children that this is that family's holiday, not yours. Also, just by living in this country, the children will be exposed to Christianity. Keep the home discussions clear and focused.

Chapter Five

FOOD AND VALUES

T HERE IS A CHASIDIC STORY ABOUT ZUSYA, who appeared before his students greatly distressed. They surrounded him asking, "Zusya, why are you crying?" To which Zusya replied, "When I reach the gates of heaven the Holy One will not ask me, `Zusya, why were you not more like Moses?' But rather, I fear that the Holy One will say, `Zusya, why were you not more like Zusya?'"(There are many versions of this story.)

Zusya realized that he did not have to be the great prophet Moses. What he needed to be was fully himself. Similarly, the system of *kashrut* reminds us that human beings are not meant to be like celestial beings—who are merely spirits—and to deny our physicality. Nor are we meant to be like animals—who are just physical—and to make the fulfillment of physical needs the sole determinant of our behavior. We are meant to be fully human by honoring our physical needs, meeting them in a way that creates holiness. This idea applies to every aspect of our physicality. We honor and hallow our sexuality through committed relationships. We honor and hallow our relationship with food by eating selectively, by reciting blessings before we eat, and by maintaining a commitment to creating a world where all who are hungry may eat. Rather than denying our physicality, we celebrate and sanctify it in a Jewish context.

The special preparation of food, *kashrut*, occupies a central place in everyday Jewish living. For centuries kosher eating habits have been a marked distinction between Jews and Gentiles. The laws of *kashrut* state which animals are permitted to be eaten and which are not, and they specify how permitted animals are to be slaughtered. These laws are spelled out in the Torah and elaborated on in great detail in rabbinical writings. They transform and elevate the act of eating from a profane act of getting one's fill to a religious ritual in praise of God. From an early age Jewish children learn not to inhale their food the moment they see it, but to hold back until the appropriate blessing has been made. They also learn to look for special marking of *kashrut* certification, a ⓤ (Union of Orthodox Jewish Congregations) or a K, that is printed on many packaged food products found on the shelves of American supermarkets.

The Meaning of Blessings

Making blessings before we eat acknowledges our human need for food. It also affirms our human capacity to have control over our hunger. By blessing first and digging in second, we say, "Before I respond to the growl in my stomach, I am going to pause and bless the Source of this food."

With that acknowledgment we make a physical act holy by turning our attention to God at the moment we begin it, and at the same time we remind ourselves that no one person has a greater right to God's abundance than any other. With each meal we remember that it is incumbent upon those of us blessed with three meals a day to see to it that all receive that same blessing. By blessing, we acknowledge God and our partnership with God. We put our instinct-driven acts into a Jewish context, turning them into moral acts.

A blessing before every meal—even a picnic—offers the opportunity to acknowledge our partnership with God.

Here are some examples of blessings you can use for different kinds of food:

Blessing before eating bread:

> *Barukh ata Adonai, Eloheinu Melech ha-olam,*
> *ha-motzi lechem min ha-aretz.*
> Blessed are You, Adonai our God, Ruler of the universe,
> Who brings forth bread from the earth.

Blessing before consuming a tree fruit or juice:

> *Barukh ata Adonai, Eloheinu Melech ha-olam, borei peri ha-etz.*
> Blessed are You, Adonai our God, Ruler of the universe,
> Creator of the fruit of the tree.

Blessing before eating vegetables that grow from the ground:

> *Barukh ata Adonai, Eloheinu Melech ha-olam, borei peri ha-adamah.*
> Blessed are You, Adonai our God, Ruler of the universe,
>   Creator of the fruit of the earth.

Blessing before consuming a vine fruit or juice:

> *Barukh ata Adonai, Eloheinu Melech ha-olam, borei peri ha-gafen.*
> Blessed are You, Adonai our God, Ruler of the universe,
>   Creator of the fruit of the vine.

Maurice and Constance have two children. Constance says that food rules and rituals "make Judaism come alive." Maurice recalls a recent ice-cream trip: "When we go out for quick foods—desserts or beverages—it's not a tradition to say the blessings aloud in public. But when we sat down to eat, my son asked, 'Shouldn't we say the *brakhah?*' I was self-conscious, but I agreed. Even though I felt uncomfortable with so many strangers around, for the most part I marveled at my children's strong sense of Jewish identity. For them, it was the most normal thing in the world!"

A Holy Moment at McDonald's

by Eugene B. Borowitz

I DASH OUT BETWEEN CLASSES to grab a fried-fish sandwich at McDonald's. As I find a seat in the crowded, semi-greasy table area, I am quite preoccupied. I have to get back to class early because someone wants to see me and I'm troubled because I'm not sure I prepared adequately for the meeting I will be leading later. As I hastily unwrap the sandwich I remember—this time—my Jewish duty to say a Motzi before I eat. Something inhibits me from doing that in McDonald's...if I say the *brakhah* out loud, other people will feel uncomfortable. So, not wishing to be a public nuisance or because of my inhibitions, I say it to myself, silently—which, because of the tumult, isn't always easy. If I let all this overwhelm me, I know that saying the Motzi will not be very meaningful. So, hoping to let its spiritual purpose work, I must become dead still, take control of my frazzled self, center my soul for a precious minute, and only then say the *brakhah*.

The most important discipline of Judaism involves the blessing. When a blessing is recited before eating, then the act itself becomes a spiritual undertaking. Through the blessing, the act of eating becomes a contemplative exercise. Just as one can contemplate a flower or a melody, one can contemplate the act of eating. One opens one's mind completely to the experience of chewing the food and fills the awareness with the taste and texture of the food. One then eats very slowly, aware of every nuance of taste.

> Attributed to
> **RABBI ARYEH KAPLAN**, in
> *Jewish Meditation: A Practical Guide*

If I am to find the Transcendent even in McDonald's, I must do my part in seeking it—in this case by fighting cultural norms and my personal drive to get on with my work. Yet if I ignored my Jewish duty, I would come to most meals mired in the muck of using and being used. I make no claim that every time I follow this ritual I encounter the Transcendent.

Judaism rejects automatic means of summoning up God, as in magical religion, but that it does not happen every time does not mean it never happens. Although I have no special gift for spirituality, something does occasionally happen. Saying my Motzi amid the city rush, I sometimes again fleetingly but truly touch the Ultimate, reaffirming in this instant what I believe and must yet do. For all that these slight, intangible experiences pass quickly, few things are as precious, for they momentarily restore to me everything the metropolis seems organized to take from me.

From *Renewing the Covenant*, pages 111–12, by Eugene B. Borowitz. Philadelphia: Jewish Publication Society, 1991.

The Meaning of Kashrut

In listing animals and fish that are kosher for consumption, the Torah enjoins us to distinguish between pure and impure: *l'havdil bein tahor v'tamei.* "Pure" and "impure" are states of being that apply to humans, animals, and inanimate objects. In humans (as with objects) they are

BIBLICAL SOURCES:

"You shall not cook a kid in its mother's milk."

—EXODUS 23:19

"You are not to eat flesh that a beast has torn apart."

—EXODUS 22:30

"You shall separate the pure and the impure beasts."

—LEVITICUS 20:25

"You shall not eat anything that died a natural death."

—DEUTERONOMY 14:21

temporary and fluid. We move in and out of these states over time and/or through certain rituals. In animals, however, for the purposes of *kashrut*, purity or impurity is, for the most part, a permanent state.

We acknowledge a similar dichotomy during the Havdalah ceremony that concludes Shabbat. (Note the same Hebrew root letters in *havdalah*, "distinction," and *l'havdil*, "to distinguish.") In this ceremony we refer to God as the *Mavdil*, the One Who Distinguishes between *kodesh*, what is holy, and *chol*, what is profane. This dichotomy refers to matters of values and of time. For example, Israel is distinct among the nations of the world on the basis of its values, traditions, and history. The seventh day is distinct in the week for its holiness and peace. These are a different kind of dichotomy because they represent two ends of a continuum in which different levels of holiness and "everyday-ness" are present.

All that is "profane" is potentially holy. In contrast, meat that comes from a nonkosher animal will never be kosher. *Kashrut*, the traditional system of dietary observance, involves both the "purity/impurity" and "holiness/profaneness" dichotomies. It is an effort to transform the profane everyday activity of eating into a holy act. We acknowledge that the world's abundance is not simply ours for the taking. We may not hunt for sport. We may not eat the blood of an animal—for blood is thought to be symbolic of the animal's soul. And we may not wash down the meat from a calf (or any other type of meat for that matter) with a tall glass of its mother's milk.

TERMS

Fleishig (Yiddish); **Basari** (Hebrew): A meat product

Milchig (Yiddish); **Chalavi** (Hebrew): A dairy product

Parve: Nondairy, nonmeat products (includes fish and eggs)

Treife: Nonkosher food

WHAT'S KOSHER?

All fresh fruits and vegetables, grains, and cereals.

Milk and dairy products.(Cheeses made with enzymes or other nonmilk animal products are kosher by some standards, not kosher by others.)

Fish with fins and scales (no shellfish).

Eggs from kosher fish and fowl.

An animal that has split hooves and that chews its cud. (It must be slaughtered in a kosher slaughtering house.) Cows and sheep are kosher; horses and pigs are not.

Milk and meat are eaten separately. Some people wait three hours—others wait six hours—after consuming meat before consuming a milk product. Foods that are parve—neither milk nor meat—can be eaten with either milk or meat products. Fowl falls under the category of meat.

Profile

KEEPING KOSHER: AN AFFIRMATION OF BEING JEWISH

IFTEEN-YEAR-OLD MAYA WALKS INTO THE KITCHEN New Year's morning wearing jeans and a loose sweater, her hair in a ponytail.

"What time did you go to sleep last night?" asks her mother, Julie.

"Four," replies Maya as she heads for the refrigerator.

"We're *fleishig*, honey. Sorry," Julie calls after her daughter.

"Uggghhh!" Maya groans her resentment at the inconvenience and begins fixing herself a bowl of oatmeal and brown sugar.

Maya's father, Philip, is cooking a New Year's Day turkey dinner. The sink and the dishes in use are *fleishig* (meat). Therefore Maya may not take any milk products out of the refrigerator. A kosher kitchen has been part of the Carr-Greenberg household for only two years—two years to the day, in fact. It was on New Year's Day that they kashered (made kosher) the stove, microwave oven, and refrigerator and brought in new dishes and utensils.

Maya resents the sudden, and drastic, change in her lifestyle. For most of her life, Judaism did not pervade her home. It was a strong but private aspect of her father's life and an important but relatively unexplored part of her mother's life.

Julie recalls her early hopes for Maya in terms of having a Jewish life. "Because Maya was my first child, and I love her so dearly, when she was two or three years old I would think about what I wanted to say to her at her bat mitzvah. I would be jogging or vacuuming and formulating in my mind what I would say. One of the things was that I wished for her always to be sustained, strengthened, and enriched by her Jewish identity and her connections with Jewish community and observance. I wanted this to give her an anchor and a place in the world. Articulating that wish for her awakened a deeper awareness that this was something I was lacking. I knew that we had to shift a lot of things if we were to achieve that wish."

Philip and Julie decided to send their daughter to a Jewish day school, and Julie strove to include what Maya was learning into their family life. For example, before Passover, Maya would bring home a little matzah cover and an Elijah cup, and they would use both at their seder.

"There was a match between who we were at home and the world outside of the home, as opposed to a vague sense of alienation because of not completely fitting in anywhere," Julie says. "So that's when I first began to understand that if you happen to be Jewish in some way, you have a choice between feeling cut off from it or openly affiliating—living in a Jewish environment and behaving Jewishly."

When Maya reached third grade, she transferred to a public school. In the absence of the day school community, the family joined a conventional suburban synagogue, but they never felt completely comfortable there. When Maya approached bat mitzvah age, Philip and Julie began again to evaluate the role of Judaism in their lives.

"It was hard to shape the event in a way that felt natural," explains Julie. "We decided to stay where we were and have the bat mitzvah, since the time was upon us, but I wanted to do things in a way that felt more connected after that. We realized that we did not really have a community, or even family tradition, from which this bat mitzvah would emerge in an organic, meaningful way."

> "So that's when I first began to understand that if you happen to be Jewish . . . you have a choice between feeling cut off from it or openly affiliating—living in a Jewish environment and behaving Jewishly."

After Maya's bat mitzvah, Philip and Julie began shopping around for a Jewish community that would feel right to them. They found a traditional, egalitarian congregation that was led by its members. Everyone took turns leading services and sharing the more mundane aspects of synagogue leadership. They had found a home.

"Things sort of flowed from there," says Philip. "Julie stopped working on Saturdays and started to study Hebrew. We began to keep Shabbat. And the last thing we did was to go kosher. Julie was the driving force behind that, literally, and I'll never forget that day."

Maya offers in a tragic tone, "It was right after my bat mitzvah. We were on a long car trip to our cousin's for Thanksgiving, and completely out of the blue, Mom goes, 'Let's kasher the house.' If we hadn't been driving 70 miles an hour I would have jumped out of the car." Countered Philip, "It seemed as if it were coming out of nowhere at that particular moment in the car, but it did come from some place in Mom's life."

The transition turned Maya's life upside down. She could not eat freely in her own house and spent her Saturdays bored at home, since she did not wish to accompany her family to services.

Her father corrects her. "It wasn't that you did nothing all day. You were very busy being mad at us."

"For good reason! You guys did it all wrong. You should have

> "You guys did it all wrong. You should have eased into it. My whole life changed so suddenly. It wasn't fair. You can still be a good person and eat lobster."

eased into it. My whole life changed so suddenly. It wasn't fair. You can still be a good person and eat lobster. I don't need God's conceited rules. I have my conscience to guide me. Why bother following all these rules if there are other ways to be a good person?"

Philip and Julie think it ironic that the process of preparing for Maya's bat mitzvah led to a new, very fulfilling level of observance for them, but to a sense of resentment for Maya. Says Julie, "The thing that I feel saddest about in my whole life is that she feels the way she does. Since we did it as she was entering adolescence and dealing with all those difficult issues, it felt like an alien intrusion to her. If she had grown up with it, she'd be in a different place right now."

For their son, Jonathan, who is almost nine, it feels as if he had observed Shabbat and kept kosher all his life. He is shocked to hear that just a little more than two years ago he ate pepperoni pizza and cheeseburgers. He recalls eating a kosher hot dog he had brought from home last summer at his secular day camp and then being served ice cream. After taking a bite, he remembered that it was not kosher to have milk right after meat, and he threw the rest of the ice cream away.

But while it feels natural to him, he still does not understand why he keeps kosher. His parents are confident that the "why" will come in time, and for now the "what" and "how" should suffice. The "why" is very clear in their lives. Julie describes a number of ways in which keeping kosher is meaningful for her.

"For one, it enables us to live fully in our community because we can reciprocate other people's hospitality. It's also a way of creating boundaries. There are things I do and things I don't do, and in so living I affirm my being Jewish. That feels important and strengthening. Since there's a system of eating, a separation of milk and meat, there's thoughtfulness involved in all the daily food preparation and consumption. It's thinking about my place in the scheme of things and that this animal has been sacrificed in order to gratify me. After I eat the turkey, I'm not going to eat dairy for three hours, so I'm carrying that in my consciousness, and I think that adds thoughtfulness and balance to the world. It counters the mindless sort of consumption that troubles me in our society and that I think is troubling the planet."

At that point Philip gets up and puts the turkey in the oven. "It strikes me as very interesting," he notes, "that we are having this conversation about *kashrut* as we prepare for a New Year's Day festive meal. It symbolizes the balancing act that we've all experienced, in which we're trying to partake of the best that American culture has to offer while doing it in a way that is true to Jewish tradition."

How Jews approach the traditional values and make them a part of their lives differs greatly. Anita, who lives with her son Meyer in Arkansas, keeps a version of *kashrut* by refraining from pork and shellfish. "We do it for the sole purpose of reminding us that we are Jews," she explains, adding that in Arkansas that is a hard thing to do. "Everything has pork in it, from breakfast to dinner."

"*Kashrut*," says Gayle, "is a great way for kids to rebel against their parents. I'd rather my kids had a cheeseburger at the food court any day than engage in drugs, alcohol, or sex!"

Michael and Paula keep a kosher home. Getting to the point of having a kosher kitchen has been a gradual process, including doubts and questions. Paula felt at times that they should stop, but they just could not. "Every time you sit down to a meal," she says, "you are reminded that you're a Jew."

Says Lisa, "We keep strictly kosher at home. We eat nonkosher meat in restaurants, but not *treife* animals, and we don't mix milk and meat. For us, keeping kosher is about being thoughtful. We have to think and make decisions before we eat . The kids are, of course, very aware of which drawer to use for the silverware and which plates and pots to use. They do all that naturally. The tradition helps keep us connected to other Jewish people, and that's important. My children are constantly reminded of that connection because they go to public school and eat in cafeterias, so they're exposed to everything. They constantly have to make conscious decisions about acts that would otherwise be almost mindless, like standing in line and getting food in the cafeteria. Even if they eat *treife*, they're at least making a conscious choice. But if they do eat *treife*, they know that I don't want to know!"

Rina and Margot keep a kosher home, but the meat, while from a "pure" animal, has not necessarily been slaughtered in a kosher way. Rina explains, "For health reasons, our son must eat organic meat and that eliminated kosher meats." Still there is a kitchen drawer carefully marked "*basar*" (meat). Rina takes a fork from it when she empties a can of cat food into a bowl.

Becky and Paula have struggled to make keeping kosher "their own" as they raise their daughter Eliana. Says Paula, "Part of how you take something from the outside and make it your own has to do with both how you understand the utility of that thing for you and your identification with it. If a concept or an idea or a ritual feels useful in some way that would be spiritually elevating, or makes you think, or makes you feel good about yourself, or gives you relief, then you might try it, and if it works you keep using it."

Adds Becky: "I start with a sense of obligation to involve myself in Jewish tradition. Then from that premise, I ask what aspects

"In your young life, you rebel against values you think are square. After a while, you realize they are good values and there's a reason they've been around for thousands of years."

—BETTE MIDLER
Actress and Singer

One mother said that her daughter always wants to know if something is parve. "Is a milkshake parve?" or "I know something, Mama—cheese is not parve." She also wonders, "Does it hurt the animal when it's killed for food?" There is a heightened awareness of eating and consuming and an increased sensitivity to the experiences of all God's creatures.

For more information on eco-kashrut write: The Shalom Center, 7318 Germantown Avenue, Philadelphia, PA 19119.

of a certain observance I can emphasize and add my voice to so it makes sense and is meaningful to me. I ask what values are inherent in it and build around that."

Eco-Kashrut

The *kashrut* values of treating the world and its creatures with respect and of acknowledging the Creator as the true Source of Life extend far beyond the realm of food. The simultaneous resurgence of and constant challenge to dietary observance in the progressive streams of Judaism have brought a new insight into *kashrut*. Arthur Waskow, Jewish thinker and activist, describes in his book *Down-to-Earth Judaism: Food, Money, Sex, and the Rest of Life*, the concept of "eco-kashrut," a term coined in the late 1970s by Rabbi Zalmon Schacter-Shalomi. This modern construct acknowledges the halakhic (involving Jewish law) categories of *kashrut*—ritual slaughter, the separation of dairy products and meat, proper tithing of food—and both embraces and transcends them, expanding the concept of *kashrut*. Eco-kashrut looks at the existing Jewish laws and traditions and asks a number of questions. Is there a moral underpinning to those laws and categories? Within the laws are there guides to understanding the ideal relationship between a Jew and the earth? If so, Waskow asks, how would the laws guide us in answering questions such as these:

1. Are tomatoes that are grown by drenching the earth in pesticides "kosher" to eat, at home or at a synagogue wedding reception?
2. Should newsprint that is made by chopping down an ancient, irreplaceable forest be "kosher" to use in making a Jewish newspaper?
3. What about windows and doors that let the warm air seep out so that the furnace keeps burning all night? Are such doors and windows "kosher" for a home or for a Jewish Community Center building?
4. Is a bank that invests its depositors' money in an oil company that befouls the ocean a "kosher" place for me or for the United Jewish Appeal to deposit money?

(From *Down-to-Earth Judaism*, page 117.)

Or how about veal? A calf fits the traditional standards of *kashrut*, but mistreatment of animals is certainly forbidden. So how can an animal that is raised in painful, caged conditions be enjoyed by a Jew seeking to live in God's ways? How about food that is carcinogenic and harms our bodies? How about foods produced by companies that sell cigarettes? We might also ask new questions regarding the traditional laws of tithing. Is a meal kosher if we have not given a percentage of the cost of that meal to tzedakah?

Many Jews today interpret *kashrut* as God's way of gently leading us to vegetarianism. Torah, they argue, is a very practical document, so it did not seek to have Jews give up meat cold turkey (so to speak). Rather, the dietary laws were designed to help us move gradually in that direction. After all, the injunction "You shall not boil a kid in its mother's milk" forces us to realize two things. First, there is a limit to the extent to which we can use the earth and its fullness without becoming exploitative. And second, we have an obligation to be sensitive to the lives and relationships of all of God's creatures. Once we come to realize this, vegetarianism is a natural progression.

Jews incorporate *kashrut* into their lives in many ways, from simply cutting out pork to complete vegetarianism, from following the most traditional interpretations to embracing eco-kashrut. Many say blessings before eating, whether the traditional *brakhah* or a different one each time, sometimes offered in a child's own words. Many families already incorporate into their lives the values inherent in kashrut and blessings over food by expressing respect, appreciation, and responsibility for the earth

🌿 Hands-On Judaism 🌿

1. Assign values while shopping for food. When you take your children shopping, take a list of values with you (see below). Give each child a "value assignment" and allow them to choose a grocery item that is consistent with the value.

Bechirah chafshit (freedom of choice), the basic philosophical assumption that all human beings choose their actions and are responsible for those choices: Choose a dessert.

Chesed, rachamim (compassion), especially for those who are disadvantaged or vulnerable: Buy baby products to give to the poor. Consider this question with your children: If you are buying food explicitly to give it away, should it be kosher? Should it be eco-kosher?

Leket, shikhechah, peah (ancient agricultural laws guaranteeing a portion of privately produced agricultural products to be left untouched in the fields for the poor): Choose a can of vegetables for the local collection.

Tza'ar ba'alei chayim (prohibition of cruelty to animals): Choose products that are guaranteed not to have been tested on animals.

Bal tashchit (not to ruin the earth; protection of the environment): Choose biodegradable detergents and soaps. Choose products with recyclable or environment-friendly packaging. Reuse or return paper or plastic bags or use nondisposable shopping bags.

Tzedakah (righteous giving): Figure out 3 percent of the total cost of your groceries. (This is the percentage recommended by Mazon in *A Jewish Response to Hunger* as the amount to "tax" ourselves on *simchas*, joyous occasions.) Then put that amount in the tzedakah box at the store or at home. You might even have a special Mazon box for such food-related monetary contributions. Some supermarkets sell vouchers at the check-out counter from which they donate a percentage to an organization that feeds the hungry.

Ush'martem et nafshoteikhem (and you shall protect your health) or *sh'mirat ha-guf* (protecting the body): Find a healthy snack.

Arevut (a special bond to other Jews): Find a product, such as fruit, that is imported from Israel.

2. Draw pictures of kosher and nonkosher animals. Play a guessing game with your children: Kosher/NonKosher. The pictures can also serve as flash cards to learn what is and is not kosher. Some kosher animals and fish and insects—such as grasshoppers!—may be surprising.

3. Make up midrashim (stories that explain biblical texts). Have your children make up stories that give an answer to why some animals are kosher and some are not. This activity is open to creativity and imagination.

Situations and Solutions

Q The prohibition against combining milk and meat makes sense to me, but the prohibition against shellfish and pork does not. What is the relationship between those prohibitions, and why do some people who do not believe that the Torah was written directly by God follow them? We would like to raise our children with some sort of religious dietary structure but do not know how to justify these particular rules.

A The fact that you want to raise your children with some sort of religious dietary structure is an important part of the answer. Here in the United States it takes a conscious effort to find and eat what our tradition outlines for us. Doing so is a way of constantly recalling our relationship to God and our obligations that result from that relationship.

Most of the dietary laws do not seem to make scientific sense to us today, but unless they strike us as immoral or outrageous, it is worth giving them a try. In doing so, we set an example for our children of a day-to-day active tradition that sometimes makes sense to us and sometimes does not, but that is deserving of our consideration and efforts. Remember that your family's struggle with tradition will be enhancing and enriching. Keeping kosher is a system through which we affirm our Judaism every day in one of our most fundamental activities. After a while it becomes intrinsically meaningful. Our connection to other Jews is thereby affirmed in ways that are intellectually satisfying (being familiar with the same texts and prayers, holding similar values) and that make sense as marks of religious identity and communal identification. The laws of *kashrut* are a way of bringing holiness into the necessary daily acts of eating.

Q Our children go to a Jewish day school where keeping kosher is the norm among the students and their families. We also keep kosher but are more lenient than some other families. For example, we buy nonmeat food products that do not have a kosher certification. Recently our daughter came home upset that a friend was not allowed to eat dinner at our home. How should we respond to this?

A Speak to the child's parents to see what you can serve their child, and explain to your daughter that different Jews behave differently, and just as she does not eat certain things when she goes out, her friend is also bound by her family's understanding of *kashrut*.

In order to avoid any hurt feelings or embarrassment in the future, maybe the parents could meet and come to an agreement concerning food in each other's homes. For example, there may be certain practices on which all parents can agree, such as using reusable plastic plates and utensils that are used only for vegetarian kosher food. This need not involve a discussion on the validity of one person's *kashrut* versus that of another, but rather it sets up a system whereby the children can freely visit their friends.

Children will get the message that *kashrut* is something to be taken seriously along with the values of friendship and of not embarrassing someone. And it may provide an opportunity for a community to set up an educational program for people to get together and share their family's food values—why they observe the way they do and how they do it.

Q I'm a single parent with one daughter and a hectic schedule. Does it take more work to cook kosher?

A Preparation of a kosher meal is not more complicated than preparation of a nonkosher meal. Pick up a kosher cookbook and you will find that the recipes probably don't look "kosher." Try some kosher recipes, even in your nonkosher kitchen, and see how it feels.

Many people who decide to keep kosher begin by making their home vegetarian—only one set of dishes and utensils to start out. If you would like to have kosher meat but find it difficult to obtain in your area, check to see if your synagogue orders kosher meats in bulk, or contact a kosher meat mail-order service. If at some point you decide to make your whole kitchen traditionally kosher, then changing dishes, kashering ovens, and cleaning out your pantry and refrigerator may take a day or two of intensive labor. A good time to make the switch is around Passover, when you may be giving your kitchen a thorough make-over anyway.

PART II

HOLIDAYS

Chapter Six

FALL AND WINTER HOLIDAYS

FOR 4,000 YEARS THE JEWS HAVE BEEN WEAVING THE FABRIC of their religious life, expanding it, restyling it for the times, and adding new strands of meaning for each holy day of the year. The Bible and other sacred Jewish writings describe in detail how the holidays should be observed. Rabbis, sages, and ordinary people through the ages have sought to make each holiday speak to the sensibilities of their particular time while still leaving it grounded in its origins. Hanukkah, for example, has been reinvented and reformed numerous times. This flexibility of the Jewish holiday cycle allows Jews to introduce new holidays into the calendar or infuse secular holidays with Jewish meaning. In recent times, two new observances have been added to the Jewish calendar: Israel Independence Day and Holocaust Memorial Day.

American society's excitement about Christmas, Thanksgiving, Halloween, and Valentine's Day clearly expresses a human need to celebrate and commemorate. Two of these American holidays—Halloween and Thanksgiving—have been adopted by American Jews and endowed with Jewish meaning. Jewish families that partake of the full, diverse menu Judaism has to offer will have a rich and interconnected year of celebration. The cycle of Jewish holidays and Shabbat offers Jewish children a cornucopia of fun and spiritual nourishment.

Squaring the Home Calendar with the Jewish Calendar

The writer of a recent letter to *The New York Times*, commenting on an op-ed piece that compared Hanukkah to Christmas, observed that it was impossible to describe Hanukkah in a vacuum. She might have been writing about any of the Jewish holidays.

Hanukkah is not an isolated event. It is part of a yearly cycle, a spoke that turns with the whole wheel. The particular meaning of this and other holidays can be fully appreciated only within the wider frame of Jewish tradition and observance. Rabbi Susan Fendrick suggests that we should consider the holidays as a way of experiencing the different faces of God throughout the year—God as a judging, laughing, redeeming, comforting, creating, teaching being. With each new understanding of God, we also understand more about our own and our children's potential for being judgmental, humorous, redemptive, comforting, and creative, for teaching and learning. Recognizing those aspects of God and the Jewish tradition within ourselves increases our sense of purpose and leads us closer to spiritual fulfillment.

A good way to make Judaism a part of everyday family life is to use a Jewish calendar when planning family events. With a Jewish calendar on hand, you will be able to chart the important dates of the secular cycle—special events at your children's school, vacations, national holiday observances—and still keep track of the important high points of the Jewish year. In this way, the flow of the Jewish year becomes integrated with your family's life.

Three-Holidays-a-Year Plan

Like many American Jews, Brenda and Michael are "three-times-a-year Jews," meaning they step into a synagogue three times over the course of twelve months. They drag their daughter, Dina, to High Holiday services (the communal worship for Rosh Hashanah and Yom Kippur), where she fidgets in boredom while her parents spend most of their time trying to contain her.

"Every year it's basically a disaster," says Michael, "but my parents did it to me and I guess I'm just continuing the tradition."

If your experience as a family mirrors Brenda and Michael's attempt to do the Jewish thing, here's our advice to you:

Stop the madness!

If you are going to go to synagogue or temple three days a year, pick holidays that are family-friendly and free of guilt associations. Why drag yourself to Rosh Hashanah and Yom Kippur services? They are the longest services of the year, and the sermons are heavy. There are better holidays for children. So break tradition. We feel that our alternative three-day plan is the best way to introduce Judaism and synagogue life to your family. Here's the game plan:

Purim. *Purim*, which falls in early spring, is the wackiest Jewish holiday, a mixture of April Fool's and Halloween, but with issues of justice and tzedakah at its core. Jews celebrate their liberation from death at the hands of the evil Haman by giving tzedakah, exchanging food baskets, dressing up in costumes, reading the Purim story, and making a lot of noise.

Simchat Torah. Coming at the tail-end of Sukkot (a fall harvest festival), Simchat Torah is the time when Jews dance joyfully with the ancient scrolls, celebrating the end of the yearly cycle of reading a portion of the Torah each week. Children dance with makeshift Torahs, march with paper flags, and sing joyful songs.

Passover. The spring holiday marking the liberation of Jews from Egyptian slavery is filled with fun rituals, ancient stories, family traditions, exotic foods, and plenty of questions. A well-planned Passover seder can create warm memories and a real connection to Judaism.

Missing from our list is Hanukkah. We figured that if you have children, this one is already in your repertoire.

The Birthday of the World: Rosh Hashanah

In the movie *Groundhog Day*, Bill Murray is forced to live the same day over and over until he gets it right. Meanwhile, his life is on hold; it does not move forward. When he finally breaks the old pattern, he is reborn, free to enjoy and appreciate life anew.

In a way, Rosh Hashanah, the Jewish New Year festival, has a similar message. Participating in the holiday liturgy and ritual is a declaration of independence for your soul. You are freed from the shackles of the negative patterns and inclinations of the past year. Here is your chance to make a fresh start. Rosh Hashanah is a time for families to rededicate themselves to appreciating the life and home they have built and to making them better. It is the time when we face the mistakes we have made and the ways in which we have hurt others, and we ask forgiveness. It is also the time when we forgive others. As a community and as individuals, we pray to God for another year. Rosh Hashanah is the first of ten days of repentance culminating in Yom Kippur.

Rosh Hashanah is, of course, also a big birthday celebration, the birthday of the world. Whether it came about by Big Bang or God's handiwork or both, the universe, according to Jewish tradition,

When Gerri, a mother of five, jotted down the dates of her family's beach vacation on their calendar, she noticed that Tu B'Av (the "Jewish Valentine's Day") was during that week. Tu B'Av is the fifteenth day of the month of Av, which generally falls in July or August, and since the Hebrew calendar is based on the cycles of the moon, it would be a full moon that night. So she asked her teenagers to stay home that night and watch the younger children so she and her husband could have a long moonlit walk on the beach.

> **"**In the seventh month, on the first day of the month, shall you have a sabbath, a memorial blowing of horns, a holy gathering. You shall do no servile work. You shall observe complete rest, a sacred occasion commemorated with loud blasts.**"**
>
> —LEVITICUS 23:24

was created on the first day of the Hebrew month of Tishri. As we do on any birthday, we take stock of the past year, have a party, eat sweet foods, and look forward to a better year.

When you are traveling on an airplane, the flight attendant tells you, "In the unlikely event of an emergency, place the oxygen mask first over your face and only then attend to your child." As parents, we may feel a bit guilty to think of ourselves first and ignore our child's needs. But we need to breathe in order to help our children breathe.

The same is true for nurturing a spiritual life in our children. On Rosh Hashanah we draw in deeply from the divine breath; in other words, we reach as high as we can to attain spirituality that will make us effective spiritual guides to our children in the coming year. So if they are very young and they get in the way of your prayers, don't feel guilty about arranging adequate child care.

However, if your children are older, it may be advisable to shop around for a child-friendly synagogue, one that offers a family or children's service. If the only synagogue in town does not have such a service, approach other parents and suggest organizing one that will hold the children's attention and be meaningful.

For families, Rosh Hashanah can easily become a spiritual letdown if not planned wisely. If you drag your young children to a five-hour service, you had better be prepared with games, food, juices, a change of clothing, and other distractions. Even then, it is unlikely that they will let you listen to the rabbi's sermon. Leave very young children at home with a babysitter, or bring them to the shorter service in the evening. Either way, here are some survival strategies you may want to consider:

Find out in advance which High Holiday prayer book the congregation uses, buy several copies, and have everyone in the family make a special book cover of cloth or paper.

Look through the prayer book and, at leisure, familiarize yourself with the text and highlight words that speak to you. Some High Holiday prayer books come with audio cassettes, and you can play these while driving in your car. We have also found a children's High Holiday tape, which we play in the car while driving to and from school for several weeks prior to Rosh Hashanah. Aliza will sometimes sing one of the tunes to herself while she is playing with her blocks. As she grows up, she will become increasingly familiar with the prayers and will be more comfortable when she attends the services.

Rosh Hashanah is also a great time for home and family celebrations. It is customary to prepare festive meals, often with fish as the main course. Jewish tradition tells us that at the time of Noah, before

Sweet foods at Rosh Hashanah signify the desire for a sweet year.

the great flood, fish were the only animals free of sin, so they were allowed to live and flourish during the downpour that destroyed the world. In some traditions the fish is served with the head on, signifying the *rosh* or "head" of the new year.

On Rosh Hashanah we eat symbolic foods: Round foods represent the yearly cycle and time without beginning or end, and sweet foods embody our desire for a sweet, delicious year. The special bread, the challah that we eat every Shabbat, is not braided as usual but is shaped in a round twist. The recipe for the Rosh Hashanah challah is the same as for Shabbat challah, but sweet raisins are added to the dough. Other symbolic foods eaten on the holiday are apples dipped in honey. For a mouth-watering treat spread the challah with honey too. In fact, honey goes on or in just about everything. The wine we drink is sweet, and for dessert we eat honey cake.

One "heretical" idea is to split your observance of Rosh Hashanah. On the first day, go to synagogue, have the festive meals, and participate in the traditional customs of the New Year. On the second day, however, celebrate the "birthday of the world" with a hike in the mountains or by the seashore. Your children will appreciate the beauty of nature and the majesty of our Creator. Since Rosh Hashanah always falls in September or early October, try to go somewhere that is resplendent with colorful leaves. Pack a picnic of fruits and other sweet foods—although you may want to defer the honey until you get home, to avoid the insects.

RULES AND REGS

Rosh Hashanah is observed by most Jews as a two-day holiday, although many Reform congregations celebrate one day only. The general rules for Shabbat apply here also: no school, no work, no television, no e-mail, no voice mail. Every adult is obligated to hear the sound of the shofar (ram's horn) and to participate in prayer. As on all holidays, we light candles—a symbol of God's presence—and say the appropriate blessings:

Barukh ata Adonai, Eloheinu Melekh ha-olam,
asher kidshanu b'mitzvotav v'tzivanu l'hadleek ner shel yom tov.
Blessed are You, Adonai our God, Ruler of the universe,
Who sanctifies us with commandments and
commands us to kindle the holiday lights.

Barukh ata Adonai, Eloheinu Melekh ha-olam,
shehecheyanu v'kiymanu v'higiyanu lazman hazeh
Blessed are You, Adonai our God, Ruler of the universe,
Who has given us life, sustained us, and
brought us to this moment.

Hands-On Judaism

1. Apple picking. We emphasize the roundness of the year by picking, eating, and baking the round fruit of the season. Apple picking before Rosh Hashanah is a great family activity, especially if it is followed by making apple pie. If you don't have much time, buy apples in a store and dip them in honey.

2. Shopping for clothing. Rosh Hashanah is about starting anew, renewing ourselves, our souls. Clothing is often an outward reflection of what is going on inside. Since the Jewish New Year frequently coincides with the beginning of the new school year, you are probably already searching for several new outfits for your growing children.

Turn shopping for clothes into an opportunity to help them renew themselves inside and to affirm how special they are. For example, it is a Jewish custom to say *titchadesh* (to a male) or *titchadshi* (to a female), meaning "May you be renewed," to someone who has gotten something new, such as clothing or a haircut.

3. Rosh Hashanah cards. Just before Rosh Hashanah, call the family together and sit everybody down with stamps, envelopes, and cards (either bought or self-made) and prepare New Year's cards to be sent out. Your children will learn about the importance of family relationships for family celebrations. The card you send to your old college roommate, who lives across the country, shows them the value of building lasting friendships. Then save the cards you receive, laminate them if possible, and decorate your sukkah (see "Dwelling in Huts for Sukkot" later in this chapter) with them in two weeks.

4. New Year's resolutions. At the beginning of the secular year, you may make resolutions regarding losing weight or learning a new skill. On the Jewish New Year it is appropriate to make resolutions relating to the way we treat each other, our contribution to society, our spiritual growth, observing a new mitzvah (commandment) or a new ritual, or reading more books on Jewish themes. Post these resolutions on your refrigerator as a friendly reminder.

5. Tashlikh ("You will cast out"). On the first afternoon of Rosh Hashanah, it is traditional to go to a body of flowing water—a brook, a creek, a river, an ocean, a lake— with other Jews and symbolically cast out your sins while saying a special prayer. You usually do this by tossing bread crumbs into the water.

Tossing breadcrumbs into water symbolizes casting out your sins.

Situations and Solutions

Q I'm one of those Jews who never walks into a synagogue except on the first day of Rosh Hashanah. I'm not sure why I do, but I always leave feeling more alienated from the faith of my parents than I felt before I arrived. Should I just bag the whole experience, or are there other ways of celebrating this holiday without the heavy stuff?

A You are trying to plug into a community that you are not a regular part of, on one of the most intense days of the year. Of course you are going to feel alienated! Try to find some like-minded Jews (interested but uninitiated). Then during the month before Rosh Hashanah, get together and read through the prayer book and have discussions about the themes and purpose of the High Holy Days. (Prayer books have sections devoted to short readings and poetry that could serve as a basis for discussion.) After the High Holy Days you may want to become part of a Jewish community where you can comfortably explore your own Judaism. Then by next Rosh Hashanah you will have a better context for your worship.

Wiping the Spiritual Slate Clean: Yom Kippur

For most people Yom Kippur, the Day of Atonement, is the day when Jews fast and go to services all day. In fact, this "day of atonement" is rich with meaning and heavy with awe and even fear, especially if you believe literally that this is the day when God decides who shall live and who shall die in the coming year. This may not, therefore, be the easiest holiday to make into a family experience, if your children are very young. There are no special foods, no silly costumes, and no upbeat songs. Yom Kippur is a solemn time of soul searching, asking for forgiveness, pleading for Divine mercy, and turning inward.

The ten days of repentance—from Rosh Hashanah to Yom Kippur—is a time that lends itself to serious family discussion. During that time, we face each other and ask for—and grant—forgiveness. This period of time culminates on Yom Kippur with a heightened sense of truly pleading for life. We experience the power of the

> **"**Throughout my life, when I was moving farther and farther from Judaism, I always clung to a single thread—Yom Kippur. On that one day I fasted. I might be shooting it out with Burt Lancaster or John Wayne, or battling Laurence Olivier…but I always fasted.**"**
>
> **—KIRK DOUGLAS**
> Actor

questions we have been asking for the past ten days: What is the nature of our family relationships? What would we like to change in the way we relate to one another? How can I grow as a person? How can I better live in relationship to God? How can I bring *tikkun olam* (repairing the world)?

These questions are important because Judaism teaches that we cannot attain Divine forgiveness until we have seriously and with integrity sought forgiveness from the wronged party in the community, at work, at home. There are two ways Jews seek forgiveness: the traditional way, and what might be called the "wimpy" way. Either you can go up to your father-in-law and say, "I'm sorry for the time I broke your computer," or you can take the easier route and say, "Please forgive me for anything that I may have done intentionally or accidentally, that you may or may not know about." It is the custom in our extended family to take the wimpy path—which, frankly, is hard enough. Either way, Jewish wisdom holds that because you know you will eventually have to come face to face with those you have wronged, you should look them in the eye, and ask for forgiveness. The hope and the intention is that in the future you may alter your behavior.

Once, in a pre-Yom Kippur rush, Yosef tried to ask forgiveness from a colleague by e-mail for a specific action, and did not hear back. Did this act count as a serious attempt? It lacked the human touch, which is a cornerstone of Jewish living. If someone does not forgive you, you have to go back and plead sincerely at least three times. If they still stonewall, our tradition teaches, then you are off the hook.

Yom Kippur, unlike most Jewish holidays, has few home ritu-als. It is made for communal worship. There are no meals, except for the breaking of the fast at the end. Even so, for children to see their parents engaged in serious prayer and reflection sets an important example for them. We pray for our collective redemption as a people as we recite each possible sin committed by any Jew. And the day ends with the triumphant blast of the shofar, which is heard with great relief by the entire congregation.

> **"**I was schooled in the religion, but I'm not what you call a practicing Jew. The only thing I do is fast on Yom Kippur. That holiday has some resonance for me.**"**
>
> —JERRY SEINFELD
> Comedian

RULES AND REGS

This is holiest day in the Jewish year, the Shabbat of Shabbats. Like all Jewish holidays, it runs from sunset to after sundown (when there are three stars in the sky). A Jewish day runs from evening to evening. The holidays always begin the evening before the first day of the holiday and end the evening of the last. As on Rosh Hashanah, we light candles and say the blessings. No work on Yom Kippur. No food or drink except for pregnant or nursing women and those who are ill. No school for the children. No wearing of leather shoes or clothing made of leather—one reason given is to discourage ostentatious status symbols on a day when we emphasize that we are all equal before God. And no sex.

This is a day for the soul and the spirit. This is the day when you deprive your body in order to experience your physical vulnerability and, you hope, to rise to a higher spiritual and ethical level. Yes, you may read. But don't open your mail. Try instead to read Jewish material relating to repentance and spirituality.

Go to synagogue. Hear the shofar. Attend the Yizkor Memorial service for those who have passed away. Then break your fast in the company of family and friends. (All the preparation for breaking the fast is done before the holiday begins.) And try to be a better person in the coming year. There are actually dozens of more detailed rules, but these are the basics.

Hands-On Judaism

1. **Write a letter to yourself.** On the day before Yom Kippur, gather the family in the living room, hand out paper and pencils, and have them write a letter to themselves. Choose a topic that is appropriate for the holiday, such as "What I would like to do to be a better, more sensitive person in the coming year."

Have each person write a letter, seal it in a self-addressed envelope, and put a stamp on it. Someone should then mail the letters in six months or so, or just prior to the next Yom Kippur. You and your family members will enjoy receiving these annual private letters, which can then be collected in a scrapbook.

2. Break the fast. While there are no special foods for Yom Kippur, a meal is certainly a necessity at the beginning and end of the holiday. People often gather in the synagogue or at the home of friends for breaking the fast. Choose one item to make or bake with your children. It is traditional to eat challah and cake, but you need not limit yourself to these. Avoid meat dishes, since they are difficult to digest after fasting.

A Daughter and a Shofar

by Mitchell Eisen

THE CANTOR CHANTS THE FINAL MOURNER'S KADDISH as another Yom Kippur comes to a close. I am standing in the rear of the shul staring at the swaying bodies in front of me. I stand there holding my baby daughter, as the weight of her body presses on my arms and shoulders.

I hear her breathing—almost, it seems, in perfect rhythm with the cantor's voice. The cantor finishes and the congregation waits for the sound of the shofar to signal the end of the holiday.

Children begin to gather on the bimah (the raised platform at the front of the sanctuary), and I slowly begin my journey with my infant daughter toward the front of the shul. As we pass the other worshipers, I feel all eyes upon us. I sense people can see what I am feeling—a tremendous sense of pride and emotion.

It is a symbolic journey for both of us as I carry my little girl forward into our heritage. For her it is a first step on what I hope will be the long and fulfilling road of Judaism. For me it is the beginning of a new chapter as a Jewish parent. The rabbi slowly removes the shofar from its protective covering. He inhales deeply, puts the ram's horn to his lips, and produces the high-pitched, shattering sound that has moved the Jewish people for thousands of years.

As the sound breaks the silence, I see my daughter's eyes wider with amazement. I gently kiss her forehead and whisper in her ear, "May you always be inscribed in the Book of Life. I love you."

Mitchell Eisen is a freelance writer based in Washington, D.C.

Situations and Solutions

My Christian friends speak of redemption. I don't remember that word being used in my Jewish education. How do Jews find redemption?

We are all created in God's image, but we are also endowed with inclinations for both good and evil. The Jewish way is to modulate our patterns of behavior and thought so that we will more naturally gravitate toward doing what is good and right. And when we transgress, we seek forgiveness from those we have wronged. Then we seek God's forgiveness. Individuals find redemption through *t'shuvah* (from the word meaning "returning"), the act of repentance. *T'shuvah* is done not only by asking for forgiveness, but also by correcting past mistakes. Redemption is most often spoken about in large-scale terms in Jewish tradition: the world will be redeemed in a messianic era of peace and harmony. We are commanded not to wait passively for redemption to happen, but rather to work for it actively through the way we raise our family, conduct our business, treat others, and strive for justice.

Dwelling in Huts for Sukkot

How fragile are our lives? One minute life is good and secure, and then, without warning, tragedy strikes. A lump is found, a drunk driver strikes. Suddenly life is turned on its head. Our personal and family existence is so easily altered, fractured, broken. So little is really in our hands.

Judaism wants us to experience the negative in life as being finite and manageable. Thus we express our vulnerability that rain may not fall this season and then we celebrate when it pours. Our joy is ever so much greater when our fragility is confirmed in a healthy way.

Five days after the terror of the Day of Atonement, when we hope and pray that God may have granted us life and renewal, we are commanded to build little huts outside of our homes, booths called *sukkot* in the plural (singular: sukkah). Some Jews sleep and eat in the sukkah, others limit their time there to meals. Often people get together for a festive meal in a sukkah.

The festival of Sukkot symbolizes temporality; living in huts gives us a sense of the fragility of life. As we build a sukkah, we fulfill God's commandment to remember that the Jews first lived in sukkot when they were brought out of slavery in Egypt (Leviticus 23:33-36). In a larger sense, the sukkah enables us to touch on our people's history of wandering, of making their home wherever they found themselves. While we may be fortunate enough not to experience homelessness in an interminable, life-altering way, celebrating Sukkot marks our collective passage from vulnerability to renewed strength.

Three thousand years ago we were an agrarian people. The livelihood of the Jewish community was intertwined with the seasons and the elements. Would the skies open and pour out much-needed rain or would our fields lie parched? Sukkot also celebrates the fulfillment of the annual agricultural season, and at its end, on Sh'mini Atzeret, Jews around the world begin to pray for rain to fall on Israel. Between Passover and Sukkot not a single raindrop graces the Holy Land, but on Sukkot, as we dwell in our fragile huts, the first sprinkles can often be felt, bringing relief and exuberation.

Even though most Jews are no longer farmers, much of the Jewish calendar still revolves around the agricultural calendar. In a world that is increasingly removed from nature, celebrating festivals like Sukkot gives us a grounding in the natural world, in God's world.

Becoming attuned to nature in Israel is a wonderful way to introduce your children to the Jewish state. And finally, agriculture means food! Experiencing Jewish life through food is good family fun.

Our friends Jacob and Haviva packed up their children to celebrate Sukkot with Jacob's parents. Michal was two and little Adin was just a few weeks old. He was strapped into his car seat. At the end of the 45-minute drive, Haviva noticed that Adin's face was blue and that he had stopped breathing. They quickly pulled into the driveway and Jacob administered CPR until the ambulance arrived. Sukkot was spent in the hospital, where Adin made a full recovery. "For the first time in my life, I understood what Sukkot was all about," says Haviva. "I profoundly felt the vulnerability that Sukkot symbolizes."

> **"**You shall live in huts seven days; all citizens of Israel shall live in huts, in order that future generations may know that I made the Israelite people live in huts when I brought them out of the land of Egypt, I Adonai am your God.**"**
>
> —LEVITICUS 23:42-43

RULES AND REGS

These festival days are in many ways like Shabbat, especially in the requirement to refrain from all work, but there are special legal provisions for cooking. At the beginning of Sukkot, light candles and say the blessings. Just as at Passover and Shavuot, Yizkor, a memorial service for those who have passed away, is held on the last day.

Traditionally, children do not go to school on the first and last days of the festival (Yom Tov). The days in the middle are called *chol ha-moed,* and restrictions and obligations are somewhat relaxed. During Sukkot you will want to eat in a sukkah, unless it's raining. And you will want to shake the *lulav* (a bundle of palm, willow, and myrtle branches) and the *etrog* (a citron, a lemonlike, fragrant fruit indigenous to the Holy Land) and say the blessings once a day in the sukkah. You can order the *lulav* and *etrog* set from your synagogue or local Jewish bookstore, although shopping for your own "perfect" *etrog* and *lulav* can be a great family expedition.

SEVEN VS. EIGHT DAYS

Reform and Israeli Jews celebrate as Yom Tov the first and last day of seven festival days; others celebrate the first two and last two of eight festival days. (Yom Tov literally means "good day," but here it means holidays.) The days of Yom Tov—one at the beginning and one at the end of each seven-day festival—are extended to two days at each end for Jews outside of Israel (making it an eight-day festival). This is done because in ancient times the date of a holiday was determined in Israel. When the holiday arrived, it was announced by the blowing of the shofar from mountaintop to mountaintop, originating in Jerusalem and moving outward to the diaspora communities. Therefore these communities outside Israel added an extra day of observance in order to be sure to observe on the correct day. Now with standardized calendars we are not in need of such a buffer day, but in non-Reform diaspora communities the tradition remains.

 Hands-On Judaism

by Julie Hilton Danan

Here are some tips for a great sukkah and Sukkot celebration at home:

1. Simple sukkah set-up. There are at least two ways to build a sukkah. The first is to purchase a sukkah-making kit. Most of these kits include a step-by step assembly guide and all the necessary hardware. You will need to buy the lumber, standard two-by-fours, locally. The kits are generally "klutz-proof." All that is required is a screwdriver and a few reasonably energetic people.

For the hopelessly screwdriver-shy, or those just too busy to do a real building job, there is a simpler, albeit more expensive, option. Instant reusable sukkah kits consisting of a tubular frame, canvas walls, and sometimes bamboo poles for the roof covering are available from some Jewish gift shops, bookstores, sukkah markets, or by mail order. Most instant sukkot will set you back at least a few hundred dollars, but if you imagine the amortized cost over many years and figure in the accrued savings in time, it may be the best real-estate investment you ever make.

According to Jewish law, a sukkah may incorporate a standing wall, such as the side of the house. It must be at least 3 feet high and no taller than 30 feet!

2. Finding material for the roofing. The roof, called *s'khakh*, is a crucial part of the sukkah. One tradition holds that it represents the "clouds of glory" that billowed atop the Israelite camp during their desert sojourn. The *s'khakh* must provide more shade than sun, yet must allow the sky to peek through. It must be made of natural items in their natural state (boards from the lumber yard won't do), cut rather than growing (don't train a vine to grow over your sukkah roof or build under a tree). The type of *s'khakh* you will select will depend on what is available in your area. In southern locations, there is nothing like palm leaves, while up north evergreen pine boughs may be the more logical pick. Bamboo (fresh with leaves, or smooth and dried) and rushes can also be used. If you live in a large Jewish community, *s'khakh* may be available for sale at a sukkah market. Otherwise, check well in advance with a local gardening service or parks and recreation department for trimmings.

3. Decorations. Decorating the sukkah is the really fun part, especially for children. Set up a table with colored paper, colored cellophane,

or mylar wrapping paper, glue, scissors, and glitter, and let everyone's imaginations run wild. Because the sukkah is an outdoor space exposed to the elements, fragile decorations won't keep well. Flat creations can be laminated and reused every year.

Here are a few ideas:

- Display laminated Rosh Hashanah cards on a string stretched along a wall of the sukkah.

- Make a chain or a paper lantern from construction paper.

- Decorate with fresh or artificial fruit. Dried gourds, Indian corn, and miniature pumpkins are ideal and readily available at this time of year. Or go Israeli and decorate with the seven kinds of produce for which Israel is famous: dates, almonds, pomegranates, figs, olives, wheat, and barley. You may also include the greenery that makes up the *lulav*: palms, myrtles, and willows.

- Cover the walls with posters or calendar pictures of Israel, particularly of sacred sites. Save last year's calendar pictures with Jewish themes or have the children draw pictures of Jewish themes.

- Hang mobiles from the roof. You can make these by hanging lightweight objects from clothes hangers, or from a simple strip of poster board stapled into a circle with holes for stringing objects punched at even intervals around the circle. Hang your mobile with plastic fruit, or cutouts of holiday symbols.

4. Put out the welcome mat. Sukkot is a holiday associated with hospitality. It is traditional to invite guests, and the sukkah is a fun and easy place for a meal with friends or even an open house. Put a sign above the sukkah entrance with the words *B'rukhim Haba'im* (Welcome).

5. *Ushpizin*—**mystical guests.** It is also customary to invite mystical, celestial "guests" to the sukkah each night: Abraham, Isaac, Jacob, Joseph, Moses, Aaron, and David are regulars. Today many people also include Sarah, Rebecca, Leah, Rachel, Miriam, Deborah, and Esther, as well as other persons from Jewish history. This can be a great opportunity to discuss your personal Jewish heroes and heroines with your children.

6. Light up the night. There are many options for lighting your sukkah. The holiday and Shabbat candles will add a special glow in the sukkah, although some people prefer to light these in the house. Electric light can come from an outside house light or from a light bulb attached to an extension cord. Camp lanterns or votive candles are other options, but they should be used only with great care and supervision. Citronella candles, the kind that repel bugs, are a good idea in mosquito-ridden climates.

SUKKAH MEMORIES by Julie Hilton Danan

My family built its first sukkah when I was a teenager. My parents rigged walls out of colorful, batik-style cloth, and we hung the leafy roof with fresh fruit. I ate all my meals in our sukkah, including breakfast on some uncharacteristically frosty Texas mornings.

Since then I've enjoyed many diverse and wonderful sukkot, including a simple wilderness sukkah made of fallen branches; a penthouse sukkah overlooking the Mediterranean; and a romantic, candlelit sukkah on a hillside deck. Looking back, our first sukkah was a turning point in my family's Jewish life, a sign of intensified interest and involvement in our Jewish roots. Building that first sukkah is a hands-on, holistic Jewish experience that creates magic and memories for the entire family.

Julie Hilton Danan is the author of *The Jewish Parents' Almanac* and spiritual leader of Congregation Beth Am in San Antonio, Texas.

A SUKKOT THEME DINNER by Carol Goodman Kaufman

Your sukkah is built. Now what? Here are some ideas for foods with a Sukkot theme.

Sufferin' Sukkah-tash: 2 cups frozen corn; 1 cup frozen lima beans; 1 cup frozen green beans; 3 tablespoons margarine or butter; 1 teaspoon salt; 1/2 teaspoon pepper; 3/4 cup milk. Combine all ingredients in a pot and heat. Serve hot.

Hearts of Lulav (Palm) Salad: 2 cans hearts of palm, chilled and cut into 3/4-inch pieces; 1 head romaine lettuce; red, yellow, and green peppers; black and green olives. Dressing: 2 tablespoons lemon juice; 4 tablespoons olive oil; 3 cloves garlic crushed; 1 teaspoon sugar; 1/2 teaspoon cilantro; 1/2 teaspoon cumin; 1/2 teaspoon dry mustard; 1 teaspoon salt; 1/2 teaspoon freshly ground pepper. Arrange pepper rings and olives around palm pieces on large platter. Pour dressing over all.

Carole Goodman Kaufman is a freelance writer who lives in Worcester, Massachusetts.

Situations and Solutions

Q I enjoy having meals in a sukkah, but the custom of shaking the lulav and the etrog seems almost pagan.

A All religious systems are influenced by the societies and cultures in which they flourish. The Sukkot festival is in part an agricultural festival that may have some roots in pre-Israelite society. But as often happens with rituals that are "imports" from another religion, our sages have taken foreign ideas and Judaized them. For example, Jewish mysticism has interpreted the commandment of taking the *lulav* (palm, myrtle, and willow branches) and *etrog* together as representing our worship of God using our whole bodies. The palm branch is likened to the spine or backbone of a person, the etrog to the heart, the myrtle leaves to the eyes, and the willow leaves to the mouth. Rabbinic tradition understands the lulav as representing different kinds of Jews, united in worship and service of God. To modern, often urban, sensibilities, the "earthier" rituals through which ancient peoples found meaning may seem foreign or even primitive. Yet if we try, they may give us a way to connect with past generations of Jews and may teach us something about the timeless themes associated with Sukkot, such as our physical dependence on, and inextricability from, the earth.

Dancing the Night Away: Simchat Torah

Nothing in Jewish life symbolizes Judaism as does the Torah. Nothing is holier than the Torah, except human life. If you drop a Torah scroll, tradition maintains that you must fast for 40 days— the number of days Moses remained on Mount Sinai to receive the Ten Commandments. Needless to say, people are extremely careful with a Torah scroll. It is handled with the care accorded an infant, held against the shoulder or cradled in the crook of the arm.

Simchat Torah, which follows Sukkot, celebrates the completion of the yearly cycle of Torah reading in the synagogue and the beginning anew. On Simchat Torah, grown-ups and children parade around and dance in the sanctuary. Adults carry the Torah scrolls, children wave flags, and everybody sings. This is a communal festival that takes place entirely in the synagogue. The celebration begins in the evening with parading, dancing, and singing. The next morning the rejoicing is followed by Torah readings and many people have the opportunity for an *aliyah*—the going up to the Torah and saying the traditional blessings before and after a section is chanted.

In some congregations the adults form a long line and extend their arms to hold the scroll, which the rabbi unrolls completely to give the children a guided tour, section by section. This is a wonderful, unforgettable experience for a family. Find out if there is a temple in your area where this is a practice, or encourage your rabbi to try it.

Teaching reverence for the Torah can begin very early. We bought stuffed toy Torahs for our children even before their first birthdays. They carry them around the house, and hug and kiss them. Halleli sleeps with her toy Torah. When we go to synagogue, Aliza and Halleli are eager to give the real Torah a kiss as it passes by in the procession before and after the Torah reading. When Aliza was three, we bought her a printed Torah scroll with a red velvet cover for Simchat Torah.

Simchat Torah is a good starting point for attending weekly services or having home study sessions. The weekly readings of the

annual Torah cycle begin with familiar stories your children will enjoy. At the very beginning is the story of how God created the world and the first human beings who lived in the Garden of Eden. The following week we hear the exciting story of Noah and the Flood and how God destroyed an evil world. For several weeks after that the Torah recounts the lives of the first Jews: Abraham and Sarah. And on it goes to Isaac and Rebecca, their son Jacob, the sisters Leah and Rachel, and the dramatic stories of all their children.

RULES AND REGS

The same rules apply as for Shabbat: no work, no school. It is customary to dance with a Torah scroll and hear the reading of the Torah in synagogue.

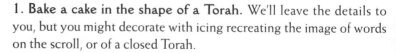 Hands-On Judaism

1. Bake a cake in the shape of a Torah. We'll leave the details to you, but you might decorate with icing recreating the image of words on the scroll, or of a closed Torah.

2. Make a mini-Torah. Take two empty paper towel rolls and chopsticks or something with a similar shape. Staple pieces of paper together and attach to the ends of the holders. Have the children decorate the paper with words, stories, and/or pictures related to Simchat Torah or being Jewish.

3. Make a flag. Flags for parading and dancing in the synagogue can be bought, but you can involve your children by making them yourself at home. Have your children draw Jewish artwork, such as a Star of David.

4. Start reading the Torah portion weekly. Explain to your children that the Torah tells a long story, which we read a portion of every week. On Simchat Torah read the last few lines of the last chapter of the last book (Deuteronomy) and then turn to the first few lines of the first chapter of the first book (Genesis). This act gives the children a sense that Simchat Torah celebrates the completion and the beginning of a cycle. Stop at an interesting point and discuss, ask questions, improvise. Start each week with a lively recap of the preceding week's chapter (which can be downloaded from Jewishfamily.com).

Situations and Solutions

Q When I was a little girl, women were not allowed to dance with the Torah. I understand that this is now permitted in some congregations. How did Jewish law and practice change in this regard?

A Judaism has always responded to the thoughts, ideas, and passions that arise in each generation. Since the beginning of the Common Era, rabbis have interpreted our sacred texts, weighing the wisdom, ideas, and politics of their time in relationship to Jewish sacred texts. Through this process, and over the generations, the laws, customs, and traditions have progressed and evolved.

In more recent years Jewish feminism has affected all branches of our religion. Women are now ordained as rabbis and invested as cantors in three of the four religious streams (Conservative, Reconstructionist, and Reform). In the past, few women had the opportunity to study sacred Jewish texts; now women across the theological spectrum are engaging in the study and interpretation of our texts.

> **❝**Jews are known for their generosity. It's no accident that there are so many Jewish hospitals, so many Jewish people in the helping professions, so many Jewish teachers. Jews give because it's a part of our culture…My ability to be a role model is based on who and what I admired in my formative years, and I have to say that my father was my role model. If I'm passing on my father's values, I'm very glad about it.**❞**
>
> —WILLIAM SHATNER
> ("Captain Kirk")
> Actor

Orthodox women are also making great strides now—studying, interpreting, and even serving in many leadership capacities within their communities. The transformation of women's roles in Jewish communal life has greatly invigorated rituals and theology. The changing status of women, like all evolutions in Jewish law, has been an incremental process strongly connected to ancient sources and experienced—then accepted or rejected—by thoughtful community. In the past, women did not touch, read from, and celebrate with the Torah. But today women dancing with the Torah is accepted—and encouraged!

The Festival of Light: Hanukkah

The best-loved of Jewish holidays in America is actually a minor festival in the Jewish calendar. Children go to school and adults go to work, just as on any ordinary day. In fact, there are really very few religious obligations associated with Hanukkah other than lighting the candles in winter's dark evenings and saying the blessing over them; this is done each evening, beginning with the evening before the first day.

We recall the Hanukkah story. A small band of Jews, led by the Maccabees, triumphed over the Assyrians and reclaimed the Jerusalem Temple. The Temple had been defiled, and much cleaning and purifying needed to be done. The Jews relit the eternal light, but there was only enough oil to last a day. Miraculously the oil lasted for eight days—enough time to replenish the supply and keep the eternal light lit.

The meaning of Hanukkah has changed over the centuries and varies from place to place. In Israel, it celebrates the military victory of the underdog Jews over the superpower Syrian Greeks. It has also taken on an athletic theme: the Maccabee Games, in which Jews from all over the world compete in Israel, parallel the Olympic Games. In the United States, we emphasize the struggle for freedom of religion, and gift giving has gained great importance.

The story of Hanukkah, the miracle of the light that lasted for eight days, attunes us to the contrast between darkness and light, in a physical, metaphorical, and spiritual sense.

RULES AND REGS

Normal school and work hours. Before lighting the candles in the Hanukkiyah (special Hanukkah candleholder), say the appropriate blessings. The first night, light the candle farthest to the right. The second night, light the two candles farthest to the right—but light them from left to right. Continue to add one candle each night, moving leftward (but light them from left to right). The *shammas* is the candle used to light the others and remains lit along with the rest. On the Friday night during Hanukkah, light the menorah before the Shabbat candles. Shammai, a first-century rabbi, advocated lighting eight candles on the first night of Hanukkah and decreasing the number by one each night down to a single candle on the last night of the festival to represent the decreasing amount of oil that miraculously lasted for eight days. However, today Jews follow the practice of Hillel, another first-century rabbi, whose rulings generally prevailed over those of Shammai: we add a candle each night for eight nights. This lighting symbolizes the spreading of light and faith and our ability as Jews to continue the legacy of Hanukkah, with the hope and freedom it implies, and to carry it forth into the world.

In fact, the Hanukkah lights should be put in a place where they can be seen by passers-by in the street, proclaiming the miracle of the lights to all the world.

Profile

CLOSE ENCOUNTER WITH STEVEN SPIELBERG

by Tom Tugend

VEN THE MOST SUCCESSFUL FILMMAKER IN THE HISTORY OF MOTION PICTURES has to relax. So twice a week Steven Spielberg makes matzah brei. Does this unusual hobby hold any deep, symbolic significance for the creator of *Schindler's List, Jurassic Park,* and *E.T.*? Not really, he says. "It's just that my mom used to make it when I was growing up, so it reminds me of home. My mom used to make salami and eggs one day, and matzah brei the next day. I make matzah brei very dry, without grease. It's actually better greasy, but I'm on a diet. My mom makes it great."

Spielberg's Mom is Leah Adler, a petite, irrepressible, 76-year-old woman who is the ultimate authority on Steven Spielberg, the boy and the man. She recalls the celebration of Hanukkah when Steven, her eldest, and his three sisters were children. "Everything in our household was exciting, everything had an edge of hysteria. One Hanukkah I decided to do what normal people do and give one gift for each night. It was a fiasco, because the first night was the big present, but the next night it was a box of crayons. Steven was so disappointed. From then on, we went back to just giving one big present the first night."

Now Spielberg and his second wife, Kate Capshaw, have their own blended family of five children, ranging in age from two to eighteen, including Theo, a young boy whom the couple adopted. Spielberg lights the menorah and the whole family joins in the songs. Presents are still a problem, but now it's because "the kids are just inundated with toys," says their grandmother. "At that point Kate takes charge. She sees to it that the kids aren't overly indulged."

An equally happy holiday is Purim, over which Bernard Adler presides. Leah divorced Steven's father more than 30 years ago, but she credits Bernard with instilling her and her family with a strong religious feeling. "Bernard reads the megillah to the kids, who are all in costume, and to their parents," says Leah.

Ask Steven Spielberg to define himself as a Jew, and he pauses for a moment. "I think I have always been private in my practice of Judaism," he responds. "I don't keep kosher, but I observe the holidays. I would characterize myself as being a private individual with a strong faith in God. I have a very strong personal belief in Judaism, but I had to get through anti-Semitism before I could take pride in being Jewish.

"It wasn't something to write home about when I was a child in the affluent Gentile areas where my parents brought us up," Spielberg continues. "There was no place to practice being a Jew, except at home or shul."

Spielberg grew up in Scottsdale, Arizona, where one set of neighbors took joy in standing outside the family's home, chanting, "The Spielbergs are dirty Jews!" But Spielberg's bitterest memories are about Saratoga, an affluent northern California community, where the family moved when he was sixteen. During his last year in high school, he was physically abused and beaten up. He recalls, "In study hall I would have pennies tossed at me, which made a lot of noise when they hit. And that happened to me almost every day."

> "I have a very strong personal belief in Judaism, but I had to get through anti-Semitism before I could take pride in being Jewish."

Some journalists have suggested that the experience of making *Schindler's List* represented a kind of reimmersion into Judaism for the director. Spielberg himself, however, credits two earlier events. One was the birth of his first child, Max, in 1985. "I had to make a decision on how I wanted to raise him," Spielberg says. "When I began reading books to him, I had to make a choice. Do I read books about Santa Claus or do I read books about Moses and Abraham and Isaac? I made a very strong choice to raise him Jewish with Amy Irving." Irving, Spielberg's first wife, had a Jewish father.

The second decisive factor was his marriage to Kate Capshaw, whose own immersion in the study of Judaism spilled over onto her

Spielberg's Matzah Brei

6 eggs, beaten
2 cups half and half
4 whole matzahs, broken into pieces
4 tablespoons vegetable oil

INSTRUCTIONS
Soak matzah in half and half for two minutes. Remove matzah and soak in eggs. Fry in oil until golden brown.

husband. "I studied along with her," Spielberg explains. "I was the beneficiary of everything she was learning and I had forgotten."

When Spielberg proposed to make *Schindler's List*, an executive at Universal Pictures suggested that he just make a donation to a Holocaust museum and save the studio a lot of grief. Spielberg persevered, and he had enough clout to see it through. But even he expected the film to have a limited audience and lose money. Instead it has become an international cultural and educational phenomenon that has helped shape the views of a new generation toward the Holocaust and the fate of the Jews.

> **When Spielberg proposed to make "Schindler's List," an executive at Universal Pictures suggested that he just make a donation to a Holocaust museum and save the studio a lot of grief.**

The film has also had a profound impact on its creator, who has established two foundations to extend its message. One is the Survivors of the Shoah Visual History Foundation, which uses cutting-edge video technology to preserve the testimonies of 100,000 survivors. The other is the Righteous Persons Foundation (RPF), which will distribute all of Spielberg's personal profits from the film, an estimated thirty to forty million dollars, to Jewish causes.

Asked to describe the impact of *Schindler's List* and its phenomenal success on himself, as a man and a Jew, the filmmaker responds, "For one thing, I came out and stated for the first time in my life that I'm proud to be a Jew. That was something that Hollywood had never heard from my lips. It was a wonderful second bar mitzvah to have been able to do *Schindler's List* and start the two foundations. It's my second coming out. I was able to say, 'Today I am, yet again, a man.'"

> **"For one thing, I came out and stated for the first time in my life that I'm proud to be a Jew. That was something that Hollywood had never heard from my lips."**

 Hands-On Judaism

1. Making latkes. One way of commemorating the Hanukkah miracle, primarily in the European tradition, is to fry potatoes in oil. Another Hanukkah favorite is a deep-fried, jelly-filled doughnut rolled in sugar. In Israel, these are called *sufganyot*, and they are most scrumptious right out of the hot oil.

LATKE RECIPES by Faith R. Corman

Looking for a change from the traditional potato and apple latkes? Try these.

Carrot and Zucchini Latkes: 6 large carrots, grated; 3 medium or 4 small zucchini, grated; 2 eggs, lightly beaten; $1/2$ cup flour; 1 tablespoon dill; $1/2$ tablespoon chives; $1/2$ teaspoon nutmeg; oil for frying; salt and pepper to taste.

      Combine grated vegetables and squeeze out excess moisture (very important). Add beaten eggs, seasonings, and flour. If mixture is too wet add a little more flour. Fry in oil and drain. Serve with sour cream dusted with chives or dill. Makes 30 small pancakes.

Sweet Potato Latkes: Four large sweet potatoes, peeled; 1 peeled apple; 2 eggs, lightly beaten; 2 tablespoons flour (approximately); 1 teaspoon brown sugar; 1 teaspoon cinnamon; $1/2$ teaspoon nutmeg; $1/4$ teaspoon ground cloves; $1/4$ teaspoon ground ginger; oil for frying; salt and pepper to taste.

      Grate potatoes and apple. Mix well with remaining ingredients. Fry in oil and drain. Serve with apple sauce. Makes 30-36. For Pumpkin Latkes substitute 3 $1/2$ cups of grated pumpkin flesh for the sweet potatoes and increase brown sugar to 1 tablespoon.

Faith R. Corman is the editor of *Holistic Living* magazine.

A LATKE PARTY PLAN

Invite friends to bring the main ingredients: potatoes, onions, apples, and so on. Have the remaining recipe ingredients measured and ready to assemble. Try different types of oil—corn, peanut, safflower, vegetable, or olive oil—in which to fry the latkes. Add a tossed salad, some pita bread, a good wine, and a dessert, and voilà! You have a perfect meal for your latke party.

Situations and Solutions

 What harm is there in celebrating both Christmas and Hanukkah, especially since my wife and I come from two different religions?

Celebrating both holidays might seems like an enjoyable way to avoid the question of who is going to give up their childhood traditions, and the children would enjoy a gift bonanza. Resist the temptation. Your children look to you for direction. Your example of cherishing traditions, believing in God, or attending a house of worship sets a standard for your children and helps them define themselves in this chaotic world. A child wrestling with two religious identities may gain the ethics and identity of neither. In choosing one religion over the other—as they are likely to do—they will be faced with a sense of divided allegiance toward their parents.

If you decide to raise Jewish children in a Jewish home, you can still go to the home of the Christian grandparents and celebrate their religious holidays with them. Your children will understand that they are celebrating someone else's holiday with them—the way one might celebrate another person's birthday. Build your Jewish home with commitment and a spirit of enthusiasm.

A Party for the Trees: Tu B'Shevat

As the Once-ler chops down a truffla tree for his new industry in Dr. Seuss's *The Lorax,* a fuzzy little man appears on the stump and cries, "I am the Lorax, I speak for the trees!" He pleads for the Once-ler to stop destroying the earth.

This same message of preserving and respecting the earth was formulated thousands of years ago in ancient Israel. The fifteenth day of the Hebrew month of Shevat (Tu B'Shevat), which usually falls in January, is Jewish Earth Day.

Now in January in America, you are still probably watching out for the next winter storm, your child has the flu, and your back aches from shoveling snow. But in Israel the days are beginning to warm and clouds of white and pink are appearing around the near-bare branches of the almond tree, called the *sh'kediya.* The blooming of the *sh'kediya* heralds the coming of spring in the Holy Land and the rejuvenating miracle of nature.

Since the sixteenth century, Jews have celebrated Tu B'Shevat with a seder, a communal meal with a set order as on Passover. But instead of celebrating redemption from slavery, Tu B'Shevat celebrates, yes, another birthday—the birthday of the trees! Tu B'Shevat is the New Year of trees. A lovely Sephardic folktale relates that at midnight of Tu B'Shevat the trees stretch out their branches and embrace each other, wishing each other a good new year.

Today Tu B'Shevat directs our attention toward the earth, the land of Israel, and the way we treat nature. Trees, after all, are dependent upon the biblically ordained custodians of the world—meaning us. Judaism not only enjoins us to take stock of our human relationships, as it does on the birthday of the world, Rosh Hashanah, it also wants us to examine our relationship with the wider world of God's creation. Instilling these values in our children will help them become moral, sensitive, and thoughtful young adults who care about people and the world around them.

In preparation for Tu B'Shevat, it is fitting to review your recycling habits and look for ways to improve them. Allow your children to take charge and recommend even better ways to handle the recycling in your house.

One way of sensitizing your children to the wonders of God's creation is by making blessings a part of everyday life, not only Shabbat. Each category of food has its specific blessing that teaches us to appreciate the diversity of foodstuff on our planet, and our beautiful, intricate ecosystem. (See Chapter 5, "Food and Values.")

RULES AND REGS

At the seder or at meal times, eat fruits you have not eaten since before Rosh Hashanah and say the corresponding blessings. Normal school and work hours.

There are two traditional ways of observing Tu B'Shevat. The first is to plant trees in Israel by donating money to an organization that plants trees and/or protects the environment in Israel. The second way is to plant trees locally. By doing this we can experience "suspended exile." Through the magic of the ceremonial moment, we transcend time and place and reach a level of holiness that parallels Israel's holiness. Tree-planting ceremonies at your synagogue, at school, or even in your home can become spiritual experiences, especially if they are conducted with song and prayer. Another way of observing Tu B'Shevat is to arrange a seder that mirrors the Passover seder.

Unlike for Passover, there are few books or haggadahs that tell the story and list the blessings for Tu B'Shevat. The following section outlines a basic ritual order of foods, blessings, and readings. This may be amended and adapted, individualized and expanded.

Hands-On Judaism

The Tu B'Shevat Seder: Set up your table as for Passover: white or other nice tablecloth, good dishes, flowers, wine, and juice. There is no requirement to light candles, but scented candles add a nice touch and a festive glow.

Either one person can lead the seder, reciting each reading and making the blessings, or everyone can take turns. The directions concerning which fruit to locate and the mix of the wines should be read aloud. As each piece of fruit and each cup of wine is being considered and blessed, that object is held by the reader. After each blessing, the participants taste the fruit or sip the wine.

Hand washing. Fill a large bowl with flower scented water and float a small cup in it. Carry the bowl from person to person or set up a washing station in a corner. Feel how nice it is to place your hands over the bowl and have someone pour warm water over your fingers. Have towels ready!

Say this blessing:

Barukh ata Adonai, Eloheinu Melech ha-olam,
asher kidshanu b'mitzvotav, v'tzivanu al netilat yadayim.
Blessed are You, Source of all life,
Who commands us to ritually wash our hands.

Reader: And God said: Let the earth put forth grass, herb-yielding seed, and fruit-tree-bearing fruit after its own kind, wherein is the seed thereof, on the earth. (Genesis 1:11)

Reader: In the sixteenth century in northern Israel, in the spiritual town of Tzfat (Safed), the Jewish mystics created the Tu B'Shevat seder. They recognized the many and varied dimensions of God's creation and used the fruits of Israel to symbolize their existence.

The first cup of wine. This cup of white wine or juice symbolizes winter and the mystical dimension of atzilut, or emanation, at which God's energy infused the creation process with initial life.

Barukh ata Adonai, Eloheinu Melekh ha-olam borei peri ha-gafen.
Blessed are you, Source of all life, Creator of the fruit of the vine.

Reader: For Adonai your God is bringing you into a good land. A land of brooks of water, of fountains and depths springing forth in valleys and hills, a land of wheat and barley and vines and fig trees and pomegranates, a land of olive trees and honey, a land wherein you shall eat without scarceness, you shall not lack anything in it; a land whose stones are iron and out of whose hills you may dig brass. And you shall eat and be satisfied, and bless God for the good land which is being given unto you. (Deuteronomy 8:7-10)

The first fruit. Fruit that is hard on the outside and soft on the inside such as walnuts, coconuts, or almonds. The hard shell symbolizes the protection that the earth gives us and reminds us to nourish the strength and healing power of our own bodies.

Barukh ata Adonai, Eloheinu Melekh ha-olam, borei peri ha-etz.
Blessed are You, Source of all life, Creator of the fruit of the tree.

The second cup of wine. This cup of wine or juice is mostly white, with a little red mixed in, to symbolize the passing of the seasons and the mystical concept of formation and birth, often associated with water.

Barukh ata Adonai, Eloheinu Melekh ha-olam, borei peri ha-gafen.
Blessed are You, Source of all life, Creator of the fruit of the vine.

Reader: Blessed shall you be in the city, and blessed shall you be in the field. Blessed shall you be in the fruit of your body, and the fruit of your land, and the fruit of your cattle, and the young of your flock. Blessed shall you be in your basket and your kneading trough. Blessed shall you be when you come in and blessed shall you be when you go out. (Deuteronomy 28:3 6)

The second fruit. This fruit is soft with a pit in the center— olives or dates—and symbolizes the life-sustaining power that emanates from the earth. It reminds us of the spiritual and emotional strength that is within each of us.

Barukh ata Adonai, Eloheinu Melekh ha-olam, borei peri ha-etz.
Blessed are You, Source of all life, Creator of the fruit of the tree.

The third cup of wine. This cup of wine is mostly red with a little of white mixed in and symbolizes once again the change of seasons and the mystical concept of b'riyah, or creation.

Barukh ata Adonai, Eloheinu Melekh ha-olam, borei peri ha-gafen.
Blessed are You, Source of all life, Creator of the fruit of the vine.

Reader: Then God formed the human from the dust of the ground, and breathed into the nostrils the breath of life; and the human became a living soul. (Genesis 2:7)

The third fruit. This fruit is soft throughout and is completely edible, such as figs, grapes, and raisins. This type symbolizes God's omnipresence and our own inextricable ties with the earth.

Barukh ata Adonai, Eloheinu Melekh ha-olam, borei peri ha-etz.
Blessed are You, Source of all life, Creator of the fruit of the tree.

Serve a vegetarian dinner here. A favorite is vegetarian lasagna and noodle kugel with fruit. Eat other exotic fruits that are placed around the table.

The fourth cup of wine. This cup is all red, symbolizing the mystical concept of fire and the idea that within all living things dwells a spark of God.

Reader: And the angel of God appeared to him in a flame of fire out of the midst of a bush; and Moses looked, and behold, the bush burned with fire and the bush was not consumed. (Exodus 3:2)

The fourth fruit. This has a tough skin on the outside but sweet fruit within—mangos, bananas, avocados, or sabra, a desert pear— and symbolizes the mystery of the world and our study of Torah. We are constantly seeking to uncover her secrets, and are continually nourished by her fruits.

> *Barukh ata Adonai, Eloheinu Melekh ha-olam, borei peri ha-etz.*
> Blessed are You, Source of all life, Creator of the fruit of the tree.

At the end of the seder, ask everyone to plant parsley seeds in a pot with soil. The parsley will be fully grown in time to be dipped in salt water at your Passover seder.

> Read *The Lorax* by Dr. Seuss and show the children the pictures.

Situations and Solutions

Q A birthday for trees? You must be kidding. Next there will be Jewish birthdays for who knows what. Shouldn't we just say what Judaism is and not try to add to it or jazz it up for the kids?

Q According to the Mishnah, there are actually four new year festivals in the Jewish tradition. Each one draws our attention to different aspect of creation and humanity. The first day of the Hebrew month of Nissan is the new year for kings, when they must take stock of their rule. The first day of the Hebrew month of Elul is the New Year for tithing—ancient Israel's tax day. The first day of the Hebrew month of Tishri is Rosh Hashanah, the birthday of the world, when we take stock of our lives and relationships. And the fifteenth day of Shevat is the birthday of trees, Tu B'Shevat, when we evaluate our relationship (and the human relationship in general) with the earth.

Chapter Seven

SPRING AND SUMMER HOLIDAYS

Celebrating Life: Purim

IT MAY BE CONFUSING TO YOUR CHILDREN THAT THERE ARE TWO HOLIDAYS in which they dress up in costume: one American, the other Jewish. But there are important differences. Halloween focuses on death; Purim celebrates life. Halloween is about taking; Purim is about giving. Halloween is fun; Purim is fun *and* meaningful.

The Festival of Purim, the most joyous of Jewish holidays, is a good opportunity to affirm the uniqueness of being Jewish, the values that we cherish, and the values that set us apart. So, even in the midst of raucous good cheer, we remember our obligation to do good deeds and to stand up to tyranny.

At Purim we read the story of the Jewish Queen Esther, who saved the Jewish people from the evil designs of Haman, the vizier of the King of Persia. We celebrate this come-from-behind (probably fictitious) victory over our enemies with costumes, cookies, reading of the Megillah (the scroll of the book of Esther), festive meals, gift baskets, and perhaps a little schnapps.

On Purim eve, the synagogue is the place for the whole family, with the children in full costume. It is permissible to bring your camera on this holiday that has no prohibitions. As the Megillah is being read, you are expected to make a lot of noise at every mention of Haman in order to drown out his name.

Even in the chaos, however, some staples of Jewish observance remain. We have a festive meal, we give tzedakah. In addition to the normal monetary tzedakah, there is a special Purim custom of mishloach manot, or gift baskets filled with food, which we give to family, friends, and those in need.

RULES AND REGS

Normal school and work hours. Attend the reading in the synagogue and hear every word of the Megillah read; drown out the name of the bad guy with really loud noises. Eat a festive meal; drink and be merry; give charity; and exchange baskets of goodies. (Most forms of headache relief are kosher and are encouraged for adults.)

Seven Silly and Serious Suggestions for Purim

by Julie Hilton Danan

PURIM IS THE TIME, as one Jewish educator has put it, for some "serious partying"—having a wild and crazy time for significant spiritual reasons. A carnival atmosphere prevails, even as we recall serious themes.

Purim commemorates the rescue of the Jews from genocide in ancient Persia, thanks to the intervention of the brave and beautiful Queen Esther and her righteous Uncle Mordechai. It is traditional to celebrate the day-long festival by reading the story aloud, feasting, sending gifts of food, giving charity, and generally making merry.

In modern-day America, Purim has acquired the reputation of a children's holiday, but in many parts of the world, and throughout Jewish history, it has been a time of masquerades, satire, and feasting for adults that included at least a little tippling, if not intoxication (the latter custom has been called into question in an age of sensitivity to the hazards of alcohol). Here are the ingredients of a traditional Purim celebration.

1. Meaningful Megillah. The story of Purim is recorded in the biblical book of Esther and is inscribed on a long parchment scroll, the Megillah. Traditionally, the Megillah is read in the synagogue on the eve of Purim and again on Purim day.

This story of Esther and how she saved the Jewish people combines high melodrama of court intrigue, treachery, and redemption with reflection on good and evil. Although the name of God is never explicitly mentioned, Jewish sages have always seen in the story God working behind the scenes and guiding the human interactions. (Interestingly, "Esther" connotes "hiddenness" in Hebrew.) The vulnerability of diaspora Jews (Jews outside of Israel) as "a certain people" different from the majority is contrasted with their eventual success and celebration of community at the story's end.

Depending on the setting, the entire Megillah may be read in the original Hebrew, with English translations provided to follow along, or selections may be translated and even dramatized. The Megillah reading is often followed by eating, drinking, and entertainment, such as carnivals, live music, or a Purimshpiel, a play reenacting the story.

To really appreciate the reading, review the book of Esther with your family in advance. Adults may be in for a surprise if they are acquainted only with a watered-down or cleaned up "Sunday School" retelling of this classic tale; the rating for the uncut biblical

version would definitely be "R"! Read a simplified, illustrated version to the children so that they will understand what the fuss is about when you get to synagogue. For grade school and up try *The Whole Megillah* by Shoshana Silberman; younger children will enjoy *A Purim Album* by Raymond Zwerin and Audrey Friedman Marcus. Check your Jewish bookstore or synagogue library for other editions and commentaries.

2. Colorful Costumes. Dressing up is a must for most Purim celebrations. Children dress up as characters in the story—Mordechai and Queen Esther are favorites—or as anything brave, beautiful, or ridiculous that they choose. You can search through your closets or through rummage sales, or buy Halloween costumes on sale on November 1. At least do some face painting or make funny hats.

A serious message behind the costumes is that "all the world's a stage;" all our precious personas are bit parts in a bigger production, and behind the scenes is a Director guiding the dramas and actions we think are ours. The mystics say that everything in the world is only a mask hiding an inner divinity.

3. Great Groggers. How often do we get to ask our children to "please raise a ruckus?" Kids love the Purim tradition of making a lot of noise every time the name of Haman is said aloud during the Megillah reading. Although most synagogues supply noisemakers, it can be a fun family project to make your own. My favorite easy version is to put a marble, jingle bells, and/or beads, and lots of glittery stuff in an individual-sized plastic soda bottle (glue the top on if small children are around), decorate with some stickers or ribbons on the outside, and shake away! Challenge your children to invent a truly original grogger.

How often are children actually encouraged to make noise? Small wonder that Purim is a favorite holiday.

4. Delicious Delights. The next three customs emulate the actions of the Jews of ancient Shushan, Persia, in celebration of their redemption: sending food to friends, feasting, and giving gifts to the poor.

Mishloach manot (parcels of portions) are gifts of food presented to friends on the day of the holiday. At least two types of food are sent to at least one friend, but families often make up several goody baskets to distribute. This is one of those great family activities that can be as simple or as elaborate as your energy and budget allow.

To hold the goodies, you can decorate gift bags, paper plates, inexpensive baskets, food boxes, or "recycled" clean containers. Fill them with your choice of delicacies—fresh or dried fruits, snack foods, nuts, candies, bottled or canned juice, or baked goods. Recipes for hamantashen, the traditional filled three-cornered Purim pastries, can be found in many kosher cookbooks. Kids love the sticky fun of filling the dough with pastry filling, jelly, or dried fruit before baking.

Delivering *mishloach manot* is a great way to share the joy of the holiday. Try to include among the recipients some friends or neighbors who have never experienced this custom before.

5. Fabulous Feasts. Although most of us think of the Passover seder as the quintessential Jewish dinner party, for centuries Jews regarded the Purim *seudah* (meal) as a major occasion for feasting at home. Today many Jews have forgotten this custom, and the observance is more public. It seems that any celebration that centers on the family table deserves to be revived.

> **"**... because Haman, the enemy of all the Jews, had schemed against the Jews to destroy them and had cast Pur (that is, the "lot" a lottery with which they determined the date to kill the Jews) to consume them and to destroy them; but when Esther came before the king, he gave orders in writing that his wicked scheme, which he had devised against the Jews, should return upon his own head....Therefore, they called these days Purim after the name of Pur....The Jews ordained, and took upon them, and upon their seed, and upon all who joined themselves to them, that they should unfailingly keep these two days according to their writing, and according to their appointed time every year; and that these days should be remembered and kept throughout every generation....**"**
>
> —ESTHER 9:24-28

The Purim *seudah* traditionally takes place on Purim day (not eve), usually in the late afternoon. Unlike in the Passover seder, there are no formal rituals beyond the Motzi, the blessing over bread, and the birkat Ha-Mazon, grace after meals. Some people also do a kind of spoof Kiddush for fun.

6. Gracious Giving. *Matanot la'evyonim* (gifts to the poor) is a Purim custom that symbolizes the human role in redeeming and perfecting the world in partnership with God. It is customary to give donations to at least two needy individuals or worthy organizations. Take up a collection of cash and perhaps also food and clothing at your Megillah reading, party, or *seudah*. Get the children involved so they learn that true rejoicing can take place only in the context of sharing with others.

7. Silly Spoofing. The custom of putting on a *Purimshpiel*, a farce in which the Purim story is reenacted, began in the Middle Ages and today has extended to satirical or April Fools-style skits, publications or—in the case of modern Israel—even media broadcasts. Enter the spirit of the day by staging a family farce, creating a satirical Family Newsletter on your PC, or inserting a spoof page in the synagogue or *havurah* bulletin.

"Nahafokh hu," all was reversed, according to the Megillah, and this phrase has granted license to all manner of jokes and parodies over the ages. By making fun of ourselves on Purim, we can inject a little humor into our sometimes overly serious family and congregational life. By taking Purim seriously as well, we take our Judaism a bit more seriously and prove to ourselves, and to our families, that Judaism can be downright, outright fun!

Julie Hilton Danan is the spiritual leader of Congregation Beth Am in San Antonio and the author of *The Jewish Parents' Almanac*. She and her husband, Avraham, are the parents of five children.

✿ Hands-On Judaism ✿

1. Design and deliver gift baskets.
This is the tradition, known as *mishloach manot,* or *shaloch manot,* of sending baskets of food to the needy. Today *shaloch manot* can be sent both to the needy and to friends in general. A typical *shaloch manot* plate or basket may consist of fruit, one or more baked goods (such as hamantashen), a few hard candies, coins, and wine or grape juice. This aspect of Purim holds a wealth of opportunity for your aspiring artists! You can decorate a basket using crayons, markers, glitter, or just about anything else. Encourage your children to draw Purim symbols or characters. You can also make designs on paper plates to be used for *shaloch manot* or you can buy special cardboard *shaloch manot* boxes and fill them with goodies of your choice. Some synagogues assemble and deliver baskets for you as a fund-raiser.

2. Bake hamantashen. An excellent recipe for hamantashen can be found in *The Jewish Holiday Kitchen* by Joan Nathan.

3. Design a costume. While children may choose to dress up as anything they want for Purim, the story itself offers a wealth of costuming options. There are Queen Esther and Mordechai, of course. Or for children who want to explore their villainous side, there is always Haman. (On the Purim when she was three years old, Yosef's sister stood out amid a sea of Queen Esthers as a blond, bedeviled Haman complete with three cornered hat, a kaftan made of a white sheet, and an eye-pencil beard!)

4. Contribute to the Purim Fund. This fund helps provide for the needs of low-income women and their families, such as affordable housing and childcare. The fund also gives grants to community organizations working to combat poverty at a grass roots level, and provides resources for Jewish women's groups who want to take action on these issues. (For more information contact Jewish Fund for Justice, 260 Fifth Avenue, Suite 701, New York, NY 10001. Telephone (212)213-2113.)

Situations and Solutions

Q I have a hard time explaining to my co-workers why I need to take Purim as a religious day off, even though work is permitted according to Jewish law. My boss says he heard Purim is a holiday celebrating how Jews killed a lot of non-Jews. Is this true, and do you have any suggestions to help me celebrate with my family without getting in trouble at work?

A If Purim is an important enough holiday for you to miss work, then take it as a vacation day. While there is no prohibition against working on this day, it is hard to do so if you are planning a midday *seudah*, or if you plan to deliver baskets of goodies to your friends and family or to take clothing and food to a homeless shelter.

Your boss is half right about the nature of the holiday. Purim is about the saving of the Jews from a decree that would have killed them, a clear cause for celebration. (By the way, most scholars believe there is little historical basis for these events.) The story of Purim does end with the Jews taking revenge on their enemies. (An example of how the moral of the story has been misinterpreted is provided by terrorist Baruch Goldstein, who killed 29 Moslems on Purim in 1994 in Hebron, claiming that he was acting in the spirit of this fanatical tale.) Modern Jews struggle with this part of the story, and in some congregations the last part of the story is read in a hushed tone, to express its problematic nature. The holiday, however, is really about the saving of Jews and the party that follows. There should be no shame in sharing this holiday with your co-workers and celebrating it with your family.

The Festival of Freedom: Passover

Passover is the preeminent Jewish home holiday (although going to synagogue the first and last days is also traditional). Passover is the holiday that commemorates our redemption from slavery and our exodus from Egypt. Moses the shepherd is chosen by God to confront Pharaoh and demand freedom for the Israelites. Pharaoh refuses. After ten now-famous plagues, the Israelites are allowed to go. They leave in haste and arrive at the banks of the Sea of Reeds (commonly referred to as the Red Sea) as Pharaoh changes his mind again. The final chase ends dramatically when the sea splits in two and the Israelites walk through the sea bed to safety. The Egyptian army, in hot pursuit, drowns as the suspended waters close over horses and riders.

The ritual most observed by American Jews, according to surveys, is not lighting Hanukkah candles or fasting on Yom Kippur, but attending a Passover seder—a festive spring meal full of symbolism and good food. The Passover seder has endured and evolved, carrying with it some ancient symbols, ethnic foods, and bold declarations wrapped in the particulars of the Jewish experience. It also has remained, in the mind of most Jews, as the nostalgic centerpiece of memories of warm Jewish family gatherings.

Perhaps the leading factor for Passover's preeminent status is—what else?—food. More than on any other Jewish holiday, on Passover we have a complete melding of food, ritual, and symbolism, and thus of body and soul.

The center of the celebratory table is the round seder plate on which are traditionally placed five items: (1) the shank bone, symbolizing the "strong hand and outstretched arm" with which God redeemed the Israelites from bondage; (2) the roasted egg, symbolizing fertility and continuity; (3) the bitter herb, symbolizing the bitterness of slavery; (4) the parsley, a symbol of spring and rebirth; and (5) the charoset (a mixture of apples, nuts, cinnamon, and wine), symbolizing the mortar with which our ancestors in Egypt laid bricks.

A Haggadah (literally, "telling"—a script of the seder) is read aloud, usually with each participant taking turns. The Haggadah guides the rituals and narrates the story. It is often interrupted by relevant questions and discussion.

In the course of the seder we drink four cups of wine or grape juice. There are different understandings of what the four cups symbolize. One common interpretation is that they represent the four phrases used by God in promising to free the Israelites from bondage: "I will bring you out." "I will rescue you." "I will redeem you." "I will take you (to be my people)." (Exodus 6:6-7)

As we recite each of the ten plagues that God sent against the Egyptians, we remove a drop of wine from our cups to decrease our joy since God's creatures suffered in the process of our liberation. Similarly, we read in the Haggadah that when the angels rejoiced at the Israelites' safe passage through the Sea of Reeds, God reprimanded them saying, "My children [the drowned Egyptian soldiers] have suffered, and you rejoice?"

> 66Thou shalt keep the feast of unleavened bread: thou shalt eat unleavened bread seven days, as I commanded thee, in the time appointed of the month Aviv; for in it thou didst come out from Mizrayim [Egypt]; and none shall appear before me empty-handed.
>
> —EXODUS 23:15

A visitor to jewishfamily.com reports:

"A story we like to tell in my family is of the seder when my uncle was nine or ten. When he was sent to open the door for Elijah [the biblical prophet who is said to visit each and every seder], there stood (about to knock) a very surprised evening paper boy! Years later, we had a very dear friend who is not Jewish at one of our seders. She asked questions about everything very seriously, and about a week later we received a thank you note with a P.S.: 'I do have one last question. What happens if you open the door and Elijah is standing there?'**"**

Everybody has a role at the seder, which occurs on the first two evenings of the eight-day holiday. Actually, there is no prohibition against having additional seders on Passover, so new seders are constantly proliferating. In our family, we have three seders. The first two are for immediate family and the third is for our extended family.

There are also feminist seders, peace seders with Arab Americans, freedom seders with African Americans, interfaith seders with Christian groups, gay and lesbian seders, and seders for vegetarians. Seders like these often highlight the parallels between the Passover story and modern struggles for justice and liberation from various forms of oppression. Regardless of who is in attendance and what common interests brought them together, each seder is conducted according to a particular version of the Haggadah.

Children have a special role in the seder. One child recites the Four Questions. Also the children search for the *afikomen*, a piece of matzah (unleavened bread) that was hidden by one of the adults, to be ransomed off by the children when it is found. The evening can be a long one, though, so if you have children under ten, you might want to get a babysitter or assign an adult to put the children to bed as they begin to tire out. Too many seders end early, or never start up again after the search for the *afikomen*. Even though your children may not make it past the meal, they should see that it is important to you to complete the seder. Allowing them to retire also gives you an opportunity for uninterrupted adult questions and discussions.

In many homes the Passover seder concludes with singing that can go on for hours. Many of the best-known Jewish songs are Passover songs. For example, "Dayenu" lists the miracles God performed, each of

which is affirmed by a rousing chorus of *Dayenu* (it would have been enough). Some families conclude their seder by reading parts of the biblical Song of Songs.

The four questions are traditionally asked by the youngest child who is able to present them.

1. On all other nights we eat either leavened or unleavened bread. On this night, why only unleavened (matzah)?
2. On all other nights we eat all kinds of herbs. On this night why only bitter herbs?
3. On all other nights we do not dip our herbs even once. On this night why do we dip them twice?
4. On all other nights we eat sometimes sitting and sometimes reclining. On this night why do we all recline?

These questions are not answered directly in the Haggadah to teach that every question lends itself to many answers and interpretations.

RULES AND REGS

Passover is the strictest of holidays when it comes to food. Regular kosher food is not enough. Passover foods are labeled Kosher for Passover, although most nonprocessed fruits and vegetables are permissible. When the Israelites had to pack their things quickly for the long trek in the desert, they did not have time to let the bread rise. So in memory of their hasty exodus, we eat unleavened bread (matzah) for eight days and we abstain from *chametz* (literally "vinegar" but used to refer to all foods not kosher for Passover such as bread products and foods made with yeast). To prepare for Passover we rid our homes of any items that are not kosher for Passover. This is usually done by cleaning out the refrigerator and the entire kitchen and putting many dry items in an out-of-the-way cabinet which is then taped up. The custom is to "sell" anything that would represent a major financial loss (ranging from your liquor cabinet to your family bakery) if you had to get rid of it. These items are "sold" to a non-Jewish friend or neighbor for a nominal fee, so even though it is on your property, it is not technically yours. Then after the holiday, you "buy" it back.

Then you clean, clean, clean. The kitchen gets most of the attention, although we have a pious friend in Israel who airs out every book in her home in case there should be any bread crumbs in them. In the kitchen, the stove usually gets a lot of extra scrubbing. Special pots, pans, dishes, and utensils that are used only on Passover are brought out (once the kitchen is ready) for use in preparation for and throughout the eight days.

The day of Passover is filled with preparing and cooking, a strain at any time. On this day also it is traditional for the firstborn in a family to fast in memory of the firstborn Egyptians who perished in the final and most perilous plague. For Yosef, this is the hardest of the fasts because he is cooking all day.

Then, finally, the seder. Light two candles and say the candle lighting blessing for the holiday. It is an oblig-

ation to drink four cups of wine or kosher grape juice, read the Haggadah, dip various vegetables in salt water, partake of the *afikomen* that had been hidden, and recline comfortably at the seder table.

In a custom that sadly is not widely followed, the poetic biblical book of Songs of Songs is read out loud in synagogue. This scroll of erotic poetry is often read as an allegory of the union between God and the newly liberated people Israel, but its verses are among the most beautifully poetic descriptions of love between a man and a woman in all of literature.

There is no schoolwork or business the first two and last two days of Passover because it is a major eight-day festival. The days of *yom tov* (*yontif* in Yiddish) are like Shabbat, and the chol ha-moed (middle days) of the holiday are regular days except for the food regulations. It is also customary to attend a *Yizkor* (memorial) service in synagogue on the last day of Passover.

COUNTING THE OMER

On the second night of Passover, many Jews begin to count each of the 49 days until the night before Shavuot. Each day is recognized by recitation of a blessing:

Barukh ata Adonai, Eloheinu Melekh ha-olam,

asher kidshanu b'mitzvotav, vitzivanu al sfirat ha-omer.

Blessed are You, Adonai our God, Ruler of the universe,

Who sanctifies us with mitzvot and commands us regarding the counting of the omer.

Ha-yom yom _____ ba'omer.

Today is the [number] day of the omer.

If we forget to count the omer one night, the law is to resume counting the following night but without saying the blessing.

This daily ritual brings to our consciousness the important link between Passover and Shavuot. On Passover we celebrate our people's freedom from slavery. On Shavuot we recall the very purpose of that freedom: to be a holy nation in covenant with God.

Ten Tips to Enliven the Seder

by Ron Wolfson

Some innovative ways to hold people's interest
and delay that Fifth Question, "When do we eat?"

IN OUR FAMILY, THE PASSOVER SEDER is a dress-up affair: suits and ties, new clothes for the children. So imagine our surprise when one year we arrived for the seder at the door of our friends David and Shira in our dressy clothes, and they greeted us in long, flowing Bedouin robes!

"Welcome to our seder!" they exclaimed. "Please take off your shoes before you come in." We dutifully took off our shoes and entered their home. On the right we saw the formal dining room, the table set with fine china and crystal, seemingly ready for the seder guests. David and Shira led us right past the dining room, however, and into their family room.

We should have expected something unusual from our hosts' desert garb, but we were hardly prepared for the sight that greeted us. Large white sheets were draped from the beams of the vaulted ceiling, forming a tent-like structure in the center of the room. The only furniture was a few beanbag chairs and overstuffed pillows scattered about the floor. And in the center of the "tent" was a low coffee table on which was placed the seder plate.

"Welcome to our home in the desert," David and Shira explained. "The seder is a simulation of what really happened on that night of the Exodus from Egypt, so we've decided to conduct our seder in this tent. Please make yourselves comfortable. Take off your ties and jackets, and recline with your kids on the floor."

You can imagine what followed! Everybody enjoyed a delightful, relaxed telling of the Passover story. Once we completed the *maggid* [storytelling] section of the Haggadah, we moved to the dining room for the seder meal. After opening the door for Elijah, we returned to the tent to complete the seder.

It was a seder we will always remember. That, in a word, is what the seder is designed to help us do: *remember* the story of Exodus, and, more important, our place in it. The most important words of the Haggadah are: "All people, in every generation, should see themselves as having experienced the Exodus from Egypt." The seder is much more than a history lesson; it is our yearly reenactment of the liberation of the Jewish people and a celebration of its continuity.

Although the seder is the most observed Jewish holiday of the year among North American Jewish families, many of us base our conduct of the seder on a model we knew as children: Each person takes a turn reading a paragraph from the Haggadah. In some families that is considered a "participatory" experience. It might be, but it is not always very engaging.

Here are ten suggestions for ways that you may liven up your seder:

1. Assign homework. When the Weber family invites us for the seder, we are asked to prepare a presentation on some aspect of the ceremony. Over the years our presentations have taken the form of plays, songs, or a takeoff on a game show. There is no better way to encourage participation than by asking people to prepare something in advance.

2. Buy time. The seders of my youth never lasted more than 20 minutes. That is how long it took to say Kiddush, do *karpas* (the dipping of the "greens" that represent spring, usually parsley), break the matzah, and fight over who was the youngest grandchild who could say the Four Questions. For a few minutes everyone took turns reading a paragraph, then my Uncle Morton would ask the famous Fifth Question: "When do we eat?" End of ceremony.

One way to buy time so you can dwell on the story is to offer your guests something to nibble on between the vegetables of *karpas* and the meal. My wife, Susie, often prepares an edible centerpiece.

She and the children slice jicama (a vegetable variety) very thin and with Jewish cookie cutters they stamp out Stars of David, Torah scrolls, and Kiddush cups. The shapes are placed on shish kebab skewers and inserted into a head of red cabbage in a wicker basket. Susie adds florets of red and green pepper, carrots, celery, and other vegetables. The result is a spectacular centerpiece on the seder table. After *karpas* we invite our guests to eat this centerpiece by dipping the vegetables into saucers of salad dressing. Another idea is to serve each guest a whole artichoke and have bowls of butter or sauce for dipping.

3. Tell the story. The core of the seder is the telling of the story of the Exodus from Egypt. The traditional text of the Haggadah contains four different tellings, each one beginning with a question, a response, and praise for God. Think of ways to tell the story that supplement the Haggadah.

One year we were invited to a seder where the host family put on a skit. Another family we know uses puppets and storybooks. The most unusual telling, however, had to be the family who presented a magical version of the Ten Plagues in costume. The father played Pharaoh, who, after complaining how thirsty he was, asked one of the children to fetch him some cool, clear water from the Nile. The child left the room and returned with a pitcher of water and an empty glass. As "Pharaoh" poured the clear water into the glass, it turned red! The father was an amateur magician.

4. Ask questions. The Haggadah invites questions. Encourage your guests to liberate themselves from the book and discuss what it is that the Haggadah is trying to tell us. A favorite point at which to do this is after the recitation of the Ten Plagues. "What are ten things that plague us today?" is a question anyone, no matter what their level of Judaic knowledge, can answer. What are we doing about Jewish continuity in our family? In our community?

5. Have fun. Having family fun is serious business, especially at the seder table. The seder was never meant to be dull. Quite the contrary, it is to be a relaxed, informal educational experience. Some families add favorite songs that children learn in religious school: "Go Down, Moses," "One Day When Pharaoh Awoke in His Bed," and others. A favorite parody is "Only Nine Chairs" by Deborah Uchill Miller, a hilarious account of a family seder.

6. Be inclusive. Inside most Jewish adults is a child who was upset at not finding the *afikomen*. We have created a way to include everyone in the *afikomen* search. We make a chart with the order of the seder (*kadesh, urchatz,* and so on) and select one letter from each word that will combine to make a word or short phrase. We put these fourteen letters on cards and hide them around the house. We tell the children that each must find at least one of the cards for us to find the real *afikomen*. When the children have found all the cards, they bring them to the table. Then we ask the adults to figure out the jumbled two-word clue from the letters. In one case, for instance, the letters spelled "at refrigerator." Once the clue is deciphered, everyone runs to the location and finds the real *afikomen*. Everyone who participates in the search gets a prize.

7. Use materials. One of the problems in keeping young children interested in the seder is that most Haggadahs are not designed for them. When our children were in nursery school, Susie created a *Pat-the-Bunny*-type Haggadah using the coloring sheets sent home from class. She added tactile materials to the sheets where appropriate: cotton balls on pictures of sheep, sandpapers on pictures of bricks of the pyramids, grape scratch and sniff stickers on pictures of the Kiddush cups. Susie also gave each child a "goody bag" filled with Passover symbols, a bookmark, even moist towelettes for the inevitable spills of wine.

8. Chiddushim (Innovations). Each year, experienced seder leaders look for new ideas to incorporate into the ceremony. Here are a few of my favorites.

Instead of filling Elijah's cup with wine at the beginning of the seder, wait until just before opening the door and pass Elijah's cup to each participant to pour some of his or her wine into it. This is a demonstration of the need to act in order to bring in the Messianic Era.

The Sephardim pick up the seder plate and place it over every person's head during the recitation of *Ha lachma anya*—this is the bread of affliction—the invitation to participate in the seder.

Miriam's cup is set beside Elijah's. Instead of being filled with wine, it is filled with water. This symbolizes the miraculous well that, because of Miriam's merit, followed the Israelites throughout their desert wanderings until her death. A well is also a symbol of sustenance, Torah, and God.

9. Choose a good Haggadah. There are 3,000 editions of the Haggadah catalogs in the library of the Jewish Theological Seminary. Jews have always put together Haggadahs that reflect their particular slant on the seder. So we have the *Haggadah for the Liberated Lamb* (a vegetarian Haggadah) and *The San Diego Women's Haggadah* (a feminist Haggadah). Choose a Haggadah that fits your family's needs.

10. Prepare. The ultimate Haggadah may be one you put together yourself. With desktop publishing software and inexpensive printing widely available, it is not difficult to produce your own Haggadah text. You can include modern interpretations, readings, songs, and information. Doing this will take some time, but the reward will be a meaningful and memorable seder experience.

One father goes to the mikvah before Passover each year. **"**It commemorates the crossing of the Red Sea, and I symbolically purify myself of the *mitzrim* (narrowness—the same root as *Mitzrayim*, Egypt) within—my personal inner oppressions.**"**

Hands-On Judaism

1. Making a matzah cover. Much like a challah cover but used only during the seders, a matzah cover is distinguished by having three internal layers and a decoration that is appropriate for the holiday. As a family activity, have your children decorate a piece of cloth with markers, glue and sprinkles, or anything else fun that will dry or stay on. Preparing the three-layered cloth can be as simple as cutting out four equal squares of material, about a square foot each, and stitching together three of the four sides on your sewing machine. Gently sew on the decorated cover your children made, and you have an instant matzah cover.

2. Cleaning the house. This might not seem like an enjoyable activity, but it is a good way to get a taste of slavery. "We were once slaves in Egypt … ." It is traditional to clean like crazy for Passover, making sure all the *chametz*—the breadcrumbs and Cheerios between the couch cushions or in the car—are removed. Make a list of all the cleaning chores that need to be done, then take volunteers for individual assignments. Start organizing a month before the holiday and post the list in a prominent place. The work will be made easier if you choose a week when everyone will scrub, wash, sweep, and so on to the tune of Passover music blaring from the stereo.

3. Searching for the chametz (*b'dikat chametz*). Children love this activity! On the night before the seder, families make a symbolic search in the house for *chametz*. Before the activity, place a bagel or cracker or something similar in an obvious place in each room in the house. Then turn out all the lights; everyone must be silent for the search. The family goes room to room looking for the *chametz* with a lit candle (make sure an adult is holding it). Give one child a big paper bag and another a feather, the *lulav* from Sukkot, or a stick; when some *chametz* is found, the one with the feather (or other object) gently sweeps it into the bag. The point is to not actually touch the bread. When all pieces are found, the bread, candle and feather/*lulav* are placed in the bag. The next morning they are safely burned outside. Most Haggadahs contain the appropriate blessings for the "search-and-burn" operation.

Situations and Solutions

 This is a meaningful, festive holiday, but does it have to be observed so strictly? In recent years we've relaxed the bread ban and it feels fine. Are we missing something?

Traditional laws about food on Passover are indeed strict, although most American Jews pick and choose among them for what fits their lifestyles and value systems. Personal autonomy is an important part of being Jewish, but it is in the context of community and continuity.

We rid our homes of *chametz* in an effort to connect with our ancestors who fled Egypt. The act of burning the *chametz* also symbolizes our desire to liberate our souls from unwanted negative character traits that enslave us. Through ritual and recounting the exodus story perhaps we can free ourselves, in every generation and every year, from our modern-day Pharaohs. The more authentic the recreation of the original exodus, the stronger we are in confronting our "slavery" to modern-day vices such as alcohol, consumerism, or selfishness. The power of Passover observance is that it serves as a constant medium for internalizing this central story. Although Judaism values words, we also know that some things are best learned through ritual and symbolic acts. Ridding our homes of bread for a week is a creative way to remind ourselves annually that we can and must liberate ourselves and the world in new ways.

Breaking Bigotry: Holocaust Memorial Day

When Steven Spielberg accepted the Oscar for his film *Schindler's List,* he challenged the world to seek out survivors to hear their stories. Your children will be the last generation to hear the stories directly from survivors.

While in some ways the mass murder of the Jews stands out as an isolated event, it was the culmination of a long history of European and German anti-Semitism. Germany's defeat in World War I and recurrent economic crises in the postwar years prepared the ground for a political and social climate that fostered virulent outbreaks of anti-Jewish sentiments and gave widespread popular appeal to the Nazi ideology. Immediately after Hitler's accession to power in 1933, the new regime instituted systematic measures to exclude all Jews from German public life and placed escalating restrictions on their lives and freedom.

The outbreak of World War II in 1939 and the German conquest of most of Europe provided the opportunity for putting into effect the "Final Solution," Hitler's plan for the destruction of European Jewry. Although the exact way in which it was carried out varied somewhat from place to place, the basic plan involved the deportation of millions of Jews from all over Europe to ghettos and mass extermination centers in the East, primarily in Poland. Among the methods used to murder the victims were starving, mass shootings, forced labor under brutal conditions, and the most inhuman tortures. However, the most effective and systematic killings, which included one and half million children among the victims, took place at specially constructed gas chambers, the most notorious of which were at Auschwitz-Birkenau and Treblinka. The Shoah, or Nazi Holocaust, claimed the lives of some six million Jews and virtually brought to an end Jewish life in Europe as it had existed for more than a thousand years.

Yom Ha-Shoah is a day set aside in the late spring for the commemoration of the murder of the European Jews. Although this is a workday, not a religious holiday, it is an appropriate time to read and discuss with your children some of the individual stories of survivors.

In Israel, a siren is sounded for two minutes on this day. Motorists stop their cars, get out, and stand in silence. For a few minutes all activity in the country ceases and people engage in solemn meditation. In the United States, hundreds of commemorations are held at Holocaust museums and memorials as well as at synagogues and Jewish centers. Jews in the United States remember the Holocaust, perhaps dwell on it, not only because of the biblical commandment to remember. By observing this holiday, we also remind ourselves and all people of the dangers of bigotry unchecked, of the need for tolerance and pluralism.

RULES AND REGS

Since Yom Ha-Shoah is a recent addition to the Jewish calendar, the traditions surrounding it are still forming. While most Jewish holidays are joyous celebrations, Yom Ha-Shoah, as one would expect, is low-key, similar in tone to Tisha B'Av, the commemoration of the repeated destruction (586 BCE and 70 CE) of the Temple in Jerusalem. Synagogues usually have special services or programs for this day.

Talking to Your Children About the Holocaust

by Ann Moline

WHEN CHARLENE SCHIFF TURNED 11, she had survived three years on her own, living in a forest in the Ukraine. By night she foraged in nearby barns for food; by day she hid in shallow holes she dug, covering herself with leaves. At 11, Charlene was a veteran of the forests, maintaining a routine that ultimately saved her life. For those three years she lived by her wits, eating anything that came to hand, worrying about what happened to her family, constantly moving from one hiding place to the next in a frantic race to evade the German armies who patrolled the countryside. She forgot the sound of her own voice, for she never spoke, not even to herself.

When Jewish-American children turn 11, they stand on the threshold of independence, looking ahead with excitement to the wonders of middle school and the bar and bat mitzvah. They forage in the refrigerator for snacks, and hide from their siblings in their rooms. At 11, our children are veterans of Hebrew school and soccer fields, maintaining a routine of activities which will ultimately be listed on college applications. They worry over changes in their bodies. They constantly move from one best friend to the next. They are in a frantic race to keep up with their own busy lives.

Our children's lives are far removed from the terrors of the Holocaust. Many of them have no firsthand knowledge of survivors. Indeed, many have never been touched directly by anti-Semitism. As Americans, our national passion is to prolong our children's childhoods; as Jews, our natural instinct is to protect our children from the existence and history of anti-Semitism. How, then, do we address with them an event of such enormity as the Holocaust, and when do we start?

While no one set of definitive answers exists, there is a general consensus among Holocaust educators. "Teaching about the Holocaust before the age of eight is counterproductive. Children will only come away with nightmares," says Shari Werb, an educator with the U.S. Holocaust Memorial Museum in Washington, D.C. "Even eight is very young, unless the family has firsthand experience and there is a reason to talk about it."

Ms. Werb says that most of the Holocaust material for schools is designed to begin at sixth or seventh grade, when children are 11 or 12 years old. Tying in discussions at home with school lessons—either Hebrew school or public school—is a very effective approach.

Presenting the material gradually, with a generalized overview, and then adding more details as the children get older will help them develop a context through which to filter the information. An initial discussion might begin with an example from the child's own life in which the child or a friend was treated unfairly because of skin color, religion, or mental or physical disability. After relating the idea of prejudice to the child's own world, the talk can center on the importance of speaking out against injustice.

"A child can relate to 'Let's talk about why the kids in the class shouldn't make fun of Bobby because he talks differently.' A child can also understand 'It might be hard to stand up to your friends and ask them to stop making fun of him, but here is why that is important.'" Ms. Werb says that from this type of conversation, a first, nongraphic description of the Holocaust can help demonstrate why we should not stand silent when confronted with unfairness.

For more information, bibliographies, and other related sites, go to the U.S. Holocaust Memorial Museum Home page: http://www.ushmm.org. For more information on the ADL and its programs, go to http://www.adl.org. If you are interested in helping your local school with a Holocaust education curriculum, call or write Facing History and Ourselves, 16 Hurd Road, Brookline, MA 02146. Telephone (617)735-1625.

What the Experts Say

According to Ms. Werb, whose specialty is elementary and middle school educational programming for the U.S. Holocaust Memorial Museum, a child's sense of historical perspective does not become fully developed until seventh or eighth grade. Before that time, children tend to view the past as a flat plane rather than a moving time line. In their minds, events separated by hundreds of years—the discovery of America, the Civil War, or the invention of television—all seem to have occurred in that same murky distance of "a long time ago."

If there is a specific reason to begin discussing the Holocaust at an earlier age—for example, if a grandparent is a survivor—the conversation must be steered away from the graphic details. "Young kids can't separate then from now. Giving them the full picture is too scary," says Ms. Werb.

Charlene Schiff agrees. For the past 15 years she has spoken about the Holocaust at dozens of schools. "I don't think children younger than fourth grade should be hearing this. And older than that is even better. I don't want to send kids home with nightmares. I paint a picture that is historically accurate, but I leave out the graphic details." Mrs. Schiff believes that children are exposed to too much sadness at too young an age. "I don't want my young grandchildren to watch Bambi, for example. If I were the child, I would always be afraid that I would lose my mommy. And, speaking as one who really did lose her mommy, why expose a young child to something he doesn't have to experience?"

With the younger children, Ms. Werb says, it is important to focus not just on the idea that something bad happened to the Jews, but on survival under the most horrible circumstances.

"I always talk about what I call spiritual resistance. I ask the children what they think people did in the ghetto to while away the time. It is an interesting exercise for kids who are never without video games or Walkmans to try to picture a world in which they must use their imaginations instead of a piece of technology for amusement. I tell them about the stories and games that kids came up with. I talk about the schools and newspapers that were established." Ms. Werb believes that this type of discussion can encourage children to find their own inner strength to help them through difficulties in their own lives.

As children grow older, they are ready to confront the cruelty of the events as well as the moral issues. Lesley Weiss, Assistant Director of the Washington, D.C., branch of the Anti-Defamation

League, targets most of her organization's educational efforts at high school students and their teachers. "We try to present the Holocaust as a culmination of 3,000 years of antisemitism. We talk about other types of prejudice, such as racism, and use the Holocaust to demonstrate what happens when prejudice is allowed to dominate a society."

"Parents must do what they feel comfortable with. Don't say anything that will traumatize the children. Children hang on to terrible details," says Ms. Werb. Both Ms. Weiss and Ms. Werb recommend adding more detail each year, as the child matures. Allow the child to ask questions, and give honest answers, but don't give any more information than is asked for.

Why Do We Agonize over Teaching This History?

Few topics spark greater debate and controversy than when and how to introduce the Holocaust curriculum in school. In Hebrew schools across the country, debate rages over the right time to begin instruction. Jewish day schools wonder about including the youngest children in schoolwide Holocaust Memorial Day observances. In the public schools, civic-minded parents fight to have the topic included as a standard part of the high school twentieth-century history curriculum, while others argue that it does not belong.

Why does this topic stir up so much emotion? Michael Platt, principal of Salisbury High School in Allentown, Pennsylvania, believes that parents are generally uncomfortable talking about difficult issues with their children. "To make a rather unusual analogy, talking with your kids about the Holocaust is a little like talking with your kids about human sexuality. Most parents would prefer that the schools take care of it." Platt says that parents want to remain an all-knowing force in their children's lives. "When the kids ask questions for which there are no answers, like 'Why did God let the Holocaust happen?' parents may feel that they are diminished in their children's eyes. That is not the case, but it is a presumption on the part of many parents."

Another factor may be the desire to protect our children. As Jewish parents who are well entrenched in American life, we have worked hard to create an idyllic world for our children. Most are third- or fourth-generation Americans, far removed from the traumas of the immigrant experience. They lead privileged lives, knowing that their path will probably take them to college and on to graduate school or into business. They can achieve whatever they want in an environment that is largely without overt prejudice.

We are the ones who have worked to establish this world for our children. And we constantly try to ensure that nothing will puncture the safety of that world. Can it be that we are afraid of introducing the Holocaust into that picture-perfect world? Will telling our children that six million Jews died terrible deaths while the world stood by shatter the world we worked so hard to create?

Lesley Weiss, the daughter of an Auschwitz survivor, spends her days teaching about the Holocaust. She is also the mother of two children. "My choice of career was very much dictated by my exposure to the Holocaust. My mother spoke to me about her experiences from the time I was very young." She sees groups of children of all ages, all the time, and speaks about the results of injustice and intolerance. And yet she has not discussed the Holocaust in detail with her older son, ten-year-old Adam. "Adam sees his grandmother every day. He knows that something bad happened to her when she was young. But I haven't told him the whole story. I am really struggling with when and how to tell him."

Ms. Weiss sees the contradiction in her own life. She makes a distinction between teaching other people's children and her own. "I'm certainly not uncomfortable with the subject matter, but teaching other people's kids is different from teaching your own." Although she herself was not spared the details of the Holocaust as a child, she worries for her own children. "I guess I just want to protect them as long as I can."

"Protecting our children" is a watchword of our lives. We live in the suburbs where there are "good" school districts. We make sure that our children will not be penalized for missing school on the Jewish holidays. We bring our little ones to story hour at the library, and we read all the parenting books. We are room parents, scoutmasters, and PTA presidents, to ensure that we are involved in our children's lives. But when we finally begin to talk about this horrible chapter of our recent collective history, we are acknowledging that we can no longer completely shield them from the evils of the wider world outside.

Ann Moline is a freelance writer and journalist living in Alexandria, Virginia. She and her husband, Jack, are the parents of three children.

Hands-On Judaism

1. Set the mood. There are no religious requirements for Yom Ha-Shoah, but some customs have been developing. Instead of a full dinner, plan a bland meal of bread and weak soup. Don't let the children watch TV except for age-appropriate videos related to the Holocaust. Discourage the playing of music and dressing in bright colors. Most important, this is a day to talk to your children about a painful topic.

2. Tell family stories. If you have family members who perished in the Holocaust, take out the photo album and tell their stories. Older children can research the family names, gathering information in advance about the Jewish communities in which the families lived, and can make presentations on that day.

Planting yellow tulips is a good way to mark Yom Ha-Shoah—the commemoration of the Holocaust. Yellow symbolizes the yellow star that Jews were forced to wear.

3. Light candles. It is customary to light a special *yahrzeit* candle when the commemoration begins and to keep it burning in a prominent (and safe) place in your home. Some special candles for Yom Ha-Shoah are colored yellow.

4. Plant tulips. The color yellow also plays a role in commemorating the anniversary of Kristallnacht, the "Night of Broken Glass." Kristallnacht occurred on a November weekend in 1938, when mobs incited by the Nazi Party burned synagogues and smashed the windows of Jewish businesses throughout Germany. More than 150 Jews were killed and thousands were arrested and sent to concentration camps in a brutal prelude to the Final Solution. Plant yellow tulip bulbs in your garden. Yellow reminds us of the yellow star Jews were forced to wear. The flower should bloom in time for Yom Ha-Shoah.

Situations and Solutions

 Death, death, death. Why do we Jews always dwell on tragedy and oppression? Isn't it time we moved past this horrible period in our history?

We learn in the biblical book of Ecclesiastes that there is a time for everything—a time to celebrate and a time to mourn. Both are necessary expressions of the human experience and of the Jewish experience. It may be true that Jewish organizations have focused too much on the Holocaust to the detriment of teaching about Judaism, but this practice is in many ways understandable. We are the last generation to have direct contact with survivors, and they (and we) are deeply fearful that, once they are gone, the events and lessons of the Holocaust will fade from the consciousness of the world and that the Jewish people or other nations may once again be victims of terrible hatred. While the situation of Jews today throughout most of the world is remarkably different from what it was 60 years ago, a nuclear, chemical, or biological attack on Israel is still conceivable, with a similarly disastrous and murderous effect.

Most people who, year in and year out, insist on Holocaust commemorations do so with a universal message in mind. Prejudice unchecked can lead to hate, violence, death, and genocide. Even in the shadow of the Holocaust, other populations in other places have since been targets of mass destruction. Remembering and honoring the victims is a mitzvah; preventing future mass murders is part of our mission as Jews. A world that is sensitive to the lessons of the Shoah will be a better world for all people. But Holocaust sensitivity should not overshadow, in our own homes and communities, the joy and meaning of Judaism and Jewish life.

A National Birthday party: Yom Ha-Atzma'ut

"Abba!" Aliza is trying to get my attention as I'm reading the newspaper. "Abba!"

"Yes, sweetie."

"I want to go to Israel to Jerusalem. Okay?"

For someone who grew up in a Zionist youth movement and who lived in Israel for eight years, having my three-year-old daughter proclaim in no uncertain terms her desire to go to the Jewish homeland made my heart beat faster. We must be doing something right, I thought. Maybe it's the smattering of Hebrew words we use or the Israeli flag in her bedroom. Maybe it was having an Israeli nanny for a couple of months. Either way, I was very satisfied to note that my little one was a Zionist. Beaming, I asked her why she wanted to go to Jerusalem, sure she would say something like "It's the homeland of the Jewish people" or "Because Ha-Shem promised Israel to the Jews."

"Because I want to see Kippy," she says matter-of-factly, as if the answer were obvious. Kippy is a big porcupine, the equivalent of Big Bird, on *Shalom Sesame*, a Hebrew-English co-production of the Children's Television Workshop and the Israeli version of Sesame Street, *Rehov Sumsum*. Even though Aliza's answer was not what I had hoped for, I accepted it. We now call it Sesame Street Zionism. Phase one of our Zionist indoctrination program is complete. *Mazal tov!* Phase two is much harder.

Yom Ha-Atzma'ut, Israel Independence Day, is another recent addition to the Jewish calendar. It celebrates the founding of the modern Jewish state in the ancient Jewish homeland and the fulfillment of a thousand-year-old Zionist dream.

Modern-day Zionism is the national liberation movement of the Jewish people. It was founded in the late nineteenth century, in the wake of the Dreyfus Affair in France (in which a Jewish officer in the French army was falsely accused of treason), by Theodor Herzl, who sought to realize the Jewish yearning for a return to Eretz Yisrael. Herzl was convinced that Europe would never accept Jews, even those who were assimilated or had converted to Christianity. Jewish children, especially those in Eastern Europe, quickly understood the need for a Jewish state as they were taunted in school by antisemitic classmates and heard stories of persecution and pogroms.

Today the existence of a strong, vibrant Jewish state challenges us to define ourselves as Jews and to determine what being Jewish stands for. There are many questions we must ask ourselves as Jews. Do we feel in any way like an outsider in our community? Do our children have difficulty being different from their neighbors when it comes to religion? Or, more importantly, on the flip side, if we weren't "different," how would we define ourselves? What does it mean to be Jewish? What should a Jewish society do that is different? How would we like to see Israel change and evolve? Yom Ha-Atzma'ut is an opportunity to affirm a positive Judaism in the context of world politics. No longer are we focused solely on combating anti-Semitism; we are celebrating what it means to live fully and in relative freedom as Jews.

Hands-On Judaism

1. Join the community. The local Jewish community center or synagogue will likely have an outdoor Israel fair or concert. These are always family-friendly events.

2. Prepare special foods. Make a theme dinner with your children on Yom Ha-Atzma'ut with traditional Israeli fare such as pita, falafel, hummus, and Israeli salads. Play Israeli music in the background as you prepare and eat the food.

3. Blue and white everything. From streamers to flags to the clothing your children wear to school, instilling pride with these national Jewish colors can be exciting and fun.

4. Practice Hebrew. Children can learn to develop a love for Israel and a familiarity with some Hebrew words. Show them the natural beauty of Israel by viewing color photograph books and travel videos. Collecting Israeli stamps and coins is also a way of introducing Israel to your children.

Situations and Solutions

Q Without a long history lesson, can you explain why American Jews should be celebrating the independence of another country? It brings up the confusing issue of dual loyalty and, frankly, Israel has little to do with my day-to-day life as a Jew in the United States.

A The rebirth of the state of Israel, and its victories over the enemies who sought repeatedly to destroy it, is a modern-day miracle for those who lived through this darkest time in Jewish history. Today, with Israel's survival all but assured and its place in the world community firmly established, many American Jews feel less need for emotional and spiritual investment in Israel. Yet we should remember that it is still the land where our kings and prophets walked, where Jewish history lives and is being made. It is the place where the majority of Jewish children in the world are being raised.

The fact that so many American Jews are moved by their visits to Jerusalem indicates a spiritual attachment that is not in conflict with being an American. There can be a difference between a spiritual homeland and a place of citizenship.

Israel is the place where Jewish spiritual and social possibilities are endless. The relevance of Jewish teachings and values can be tested on a national front. Through our relationship with Israel, we are able to dream about what an ideal, Jewishly based society would look like and then explore that vision. The idealism and inherent optimism that Israel can represent to our children, and especially our teenagers—most clearly manifest by a visit—are characteristics that will serve them well in life. Furthermore, to be a Jew in Israel is to bestow a sense of normalcy and calm in the hearts of the American Jewish visitor, who may not usually be aware of the sense of "otherness" to which they have become accustomed and, therefore, did not even know existed in their American lives. We in America have generally lost the national aspects of being Jewish, of being part of a people; we focus mostly on the religious or cultural dimensions of Jewishness. Israel challenges us to think of ourselves as part of one people, one nation. This national consciousness among our people has worked to create the miracle of the rescue of Jews from oppression in far-flung areas of the world. The challenge is to wrestle and redefine the relationship of the diaspora with Israel in each era so that it can be mutually beneficial and inspiring.

Haircuts, Weddings, and Rabbi Akiva: Lag B'Omer

It is traditional to let a child's hair grow until his or her third birthday. This practice is an outgrowth of the prohibition against picking the fruit of a tree until it is three years old. We interpreted this hair cutting custom as a reminder to ourselves, as parents, that as much as we are obligated to teach—even train—our child, we wish also to preserve the child's spirit and uniqueness.

So when Aliza turned three, she had her first haircut. And it is one she will never forget. She was surrounded by about 20 people who love her; everyone gave her a blessing and then cut off a section of her long hair. By the time the last person was finished, most of us were crying and all of us were singing as Aliza danced around the room, shaking around her new hairstyle.

We gave her this haircut on Lag B'Omer, the 33rd day of the counting of the omer, about a month after the last Passover seder. According to tradition, people do not have their hair cut during this 49-day period, as a sign of mourning for the death of thousands of the disciples of Rabbi Akiva, the great scholar who lived from about 40 to 135 CE. Because of this tragedy, no weddings take place during this period, except on the new moon and Lag B'omer, which is the day when the plague that is believed to have decimated the followers is said to have ceased.

In Israel, the holiday is commemorated by games with bows and arrows, in remembrance of a temporary military victory over the Romans by Bar Kokhba, a contemporary of Rabbi Akiva. Israeli families also go on outings and have picnics on Lag B'Omer.

There are two rabbinic stories about Lag B'Omer which speak to two different approaches to handling conflicts. In the first, Rabbi Akiva anointed Bar Kokhba as the Messiah in the hope that his doing so would inspire the people to rise up and fight the occupying army of Rome. Although at first there was a resurgence in Jewish victories, it was short-lived. The story ends in tragedy: exile, martyrdom, mass executions, and more devastation of the land.

The second story is about Rabbi Simeon bar Yochai and his son, who hid in a cave for 13 years and studied Torah every day, waiting out the Roman occupation. A carob tree at the mouth of the cave miraculously fed the scholars. When the Romans finally left Judaea, Simeon and his son emerged as heroes and teachers who brought light and teaching to the Jews.

The rabbis were clearly uncomfortable with Akiva's call for armed resistance and tried to temper it. This problem brings up the question of how we should approach conflict. Should we fight? Should we wait it out, or should we try to find a peaceful solution? Under what circumstances is each of the two approaches called for, if any?

Rabbi Akiva did not even know the Hebrew alphabet until he began to study after the age of 40. How many of us simply feel overwhelmed by Hebrew and liturgy? At this stage in our lives can we really begin learning a new language? Can we really make the time to start reading Jewish books? Akiva's example teaches that learning is essential—and possible—at any stage of life.

Rabbi Akiva is also famous for having reemphasized the biblical golden rule: Love your neighbor as yourself. He interpreted this rule as meaning that we should treat other people the same way we want to be treated.

Some 24,000 people are said to have perished during the days of the Omer. Some attribute the cause to a plague and others say they died in an uprising led by Bar Kokhba against the Romans. The deaths ceased on the thirty-third day of the Omer-Lag B'Omer, which then became a holiday. All traditional restrictions that apply during the Omer on haircutting, weddings, and other forms of enjoyment are lifted for that one day.

Hands-On Judaism

1. Picnic! Spring is a wonderful time for outdoor activities, and planning an annual Jewish family picnic is a good way to introduce Lag B'Omer. Plan an ethnic food menu, maybe something Middle Eastern. Say the appropriate blessings over food. And in the spirit of being kind to others, have each person give words of blessing or a compliment to each member of the family.

2. Bonfire! In Israel, it is customary to sit around the fire, roasting onions and potatoes, singing songs, and dancing. In the United States, Lag B'Omer presents an occasion to go on a camping trip with the family.

3. Haircuts! Explain to your children that today is a special day when Jews around the world get their hair cut. Have you been thinking about getting a perm? Dying your hair? If you are going to do it, do it on this day and connect your family life to the Jewish calendar.

Situations and Solutions

Q Which model of Jewish leadership are we to revere: that of the mighty warrior Bar Kokhba or that of the learned sage Rabbi Akiva? What should we be teaching our children?

A Our choices of role models say a lot about our values and the society in which we live. The Jewish view is that it is appropriate to wage battle in certain, very restricted instances—mostly in self-defense. But our peacemakers are even greater heroes. Who is mighty? our rabbis ask in *Pirkei Avot* (Ethics of the Fathers), found in the Talmud. *Pirkei Avot* is a collection of wise sayings and adages of the early rabbis (300 BCE to 200 CE). The answer may surprise you. A mighty person is someone who conquers his or her own evil inclinations. Someone like that, teaches *Pirkei Avot*, is stronger than one who conquers a city. Killing in self-defense is a Jewish obligation but a regrettable action. When children play with guns or other toy weapons, they are acting out and testing models of behavior. You may not be able to stop them once they have begun (we simply don't have any toy weapons in our home), but you may be able to temper this activity by emphasizing the limits of force, by trying to redirect their play to reconciliation and cooperative efforts, and by talking about how sad it is when one of God's creatures dies.

Renewing the Covenant: Shavuot

In the 1960 Hollywood epic *The Story of Ruth* the never-to-be-forgotten Elana Eden makes a vow to her husband through which she joins her fate to that of the Jewish people.

In the biblical (and, original!) version of the story, Ruth's vow is made not to her husband—who is dead—but to her mother-in-law, Naomi. Through her commitment she helps to renew the Jewish people; tradition honors her action by declaring her the grandmother of the great King David and, therefore, a forebear of the Messiah. For that reason, when we go to synagogue on Shavuot, we hear the reading of the book of Ruth.

Shavuot, meaning "weeks," comes exactly seven weeks after Passover (49 days of the Omer, remember). It originated as a harvest festival, but in the period of rabbinic Judaism the focus of the holiday shifted to commemorating the giving of the Torah to the Jewish people at Mount Sinai. Hence the importance of the story of Ruth, a woman who accepted Judaism and its covenant with God of her own free will, without having been born into it.

One midrash (rabbinic story) about the giving of the Torah has God offering the Torah to different nations. Each turns it down for some reason. Finally God turns to the Jews and asks if they will take the Torah. Without even asking what is in it, they say, with one voice, "We will do and we will listen."

The order of their words of acceptance has been the topic of rabbinic discussion for generations. First, the Israelites say they will do. Before even knowing what is involved, they agree to do God's will. Then, only after accepting the Torah, they say, "We will hear"—we will now find out what it is we agreed to do. This is interpreted as a sign of the great faith the Israelites had in God. After all, who would agree to a contract before reading it?

Another midrash is not as flattering. In this version God lifts Mount Sinai over the heads of the petrified Israelites and asks them if they will accept the Torah. Under such overwhelming duress, they hardly have a choice.

The Torah itself is quite unequivocal in its description of the Sinai scene. It states very clearly and unambiguously that the Torah was given to all generations of Jews. Much like renewing wedding vows, we read the book of Ruth and renew our commitment to the Torah and to our covenant with God. Shavuot is also a day to honor the converts to Judaism who so inspire and renew us. Some converts go to the mikvah (ritual bath used for many purposes) every year on Shavuot to commemorate their conversion to Judaism. Also on Shavuot it is common for synagogues to have confirmation ceremonies for teenagers who have finished two years of post bar/bat mitzvah Jewish education, and consecration ceremonies for children beginning their religious studies.

RULES AND REGS

Although it lasts only a day for Israeli and Reform Jews and two days for non-Reform diaspora Jews, Shavuot is one of the major ancient pilgrimage festivals. In ancient days of the Temple, Jews would ascend to Jerusalem three times a year—on Passover, Shavuot, and Sukkot—to present offerings and to receive the priestly blessings. As on the holidays, no work is done on Shavuot, nor is there school or day camp. A *Yizkor* (memorial) service ends Shavuot, as it does on Yom Kippur, Sukkot, and Passover. On this particular holiday, it is also traditional to refrain from eating meat. For three days the Israelites purified themselves in preparation for receiving the Torah at Mount Sinai. Part of that purification involved refraining from slaughtering animals; thus the importance of dairy products on the Shavuot table.

Hands-On Judaism

1. Study together into the night. According to the Jewish mystical tradition, it is customary to stay up all night on Shavuot to prepare for the revelation of the Torah. Some people spend the night studying at the synagogue. While it may not be possible for a family with children to do this, you can recreate that sense of urgency and holiness

Cheese blintzes are ideal for Shavuot, a time when it is traditional to refrain from eating meat.

by studying together at home. Going a little past the children's bedtime can add to the sense of specialness and mystery. Many communities combine this evening study session with a dessert potluck.

2. Making cheese blintzes. A favorite dairy food is crepes filled with a cottage cheese mixture, called blintzes. Homemade or frozen, they are wonderful with jam or sour cream.

3. Make fruit baskets. Like Sukkot, Shavuot is a harvest festival, the harvest of *bikkurim*, the first fruits. The pilgrims would carry baskets full of the seven species of fruit for which the holy land is famous to Jerusalem as an offering at the Temple. Decorate your dining room table with a colorful fruit basket that symbolizes the harvest season.

Situations and Solutions

Q I remember a story from Hebrew school that God tried to give all the nations the Torah, but no one but the Jews wanted it. That's not true today. There are many people of many faiths that subscribe to the Ten Commandments. What does it mean to be a "chosen people" in today's society?

A Chosenness, within our tradition, is a function of knowledge and perspective. We, as Jews, know that every human
being is created *b'tzelem Elohim* (in the image of God) and that
we are interpreters of the Torah and active participants in a tradition
that teaches of the potential for a perfected world, of what that
means, and of what we have to do to get there. Once we accepted
our partnership with God in *tikkun olam* (repairing the world) we
became chosen. (In fact, each person in each generation must accept
that mission.) In our contemporary society, especially post-Holo-
caust, some Jews are uncomfortable with the idea of being chosen.
Michael Lerner, in his book *Jewish Renewal*, writes, "…one reason why
Jews in the contemporary world do not take kindly to Jewish renewal
[is] because it puts us back into a position of vulnerability that many
Jews have been trying to escape by covertly telling the world, 'Don't
worry about us, because we are no longer into advocating a God that
would challenge your political and social arrangements.'" Chosenness
means challenging that which our tradition and communities teach
us are unjust.

Destruction of the Temple: Tisha B'Av

The ninth day of the Hebrew month of Av, Tisha B'Av, commemorates
the destruction of the Temple in ancient times, as well as a whole series
of misfortunes that are said to have befallen the Jewish people on the
same day over the centuries. Here's a partial list of bad things that,
according to tradition, have happened to the Jews on this jinxed day:
destruction of the First Temple in 586 BCE; destruction of the Second
Temple in 70 CE; expulsion of the Jews from England in 1290 CE; expulsion of the Jews from Spain in 1492 CE; outbreak of World War I in 1914.

With a record like that, why would we even want to think
about this day? A major theme of Tisha B'Av is the need to heal internal rifts among fellow Jews. Tradition ascribes the destruction of both
Temples not to the obvious overwhelming force of our historical enemies, but to constant internecine feuds. Jerusalem was destroyed,
holds this tradition, because the elders of the city did not intervene
to save the honor of one of its citizens against the verbal attack of a
wealthy leader.

This is a day of mourning and fasting that does not lend itself
easily to family activity, especially since it falls during summer vacation. In some sense, the best thing to do is to send the children to a

Jewish overnight camp, like those affiliated with Young Judaea or one of the religious movements. At camp the children usually have an outdoor evening ceremony. They read parts of the biblical book of Lamentations, and they conduct bunk discussions on contemporary issues that divide us. Before you enroll your child at a camp, ask if the program includes a significant, dignified observance of Tisha B'Av.

Adults can attend a synagogue or a community commemoration of Tisha B'Av, which will usually include the reading of Lamentations and a study session. In general, however, this is not a holiday for home ritual. Because it is a day of mourning, it is customary not to conduct business on this day nor to take long trips.

Being in Jerusalem on this day and visiting the Western Wall is one of the most moving experiences. In the evening, tens of thousands of mourners fill the plaza before the Kotel (the remains of the Western Wall of the ancient Temple), many of them sitting on Yemenite prayer rugs, wailing and praying.

Rabbi Simeon ben Gamaliel says, anyone who eats or drinks on the Ninth of Av is as if he or she ate and drank on the Day of Atonement. Rabbi Akiva says, anyone who does work on the Ninth of Av will never see in his or her work any sign of blessing. And the sages say, anyone who does work on the Ninth of Av and does not mourn for Jerusalem will not share her joy.

TALMUD TA'ANIT 30B

RULES AND REGS

Traditional Jews fast for 25 hours, from sunset the night before until three stars appear in the sky at the conclusion of the day. The biblical book of Lamentations is read. Avoid activities that give pleasure, including sex, watching TV, or listening to upbeat music. As on Yom Kippur, wearing leather is prohibited as a way of discouraging displays of wealth or being comfortable.

Hands-On Judaism

1. **Hold a slumber un-party.** Traditionally, Jews sleep on the floor on this day to express their sorrow and discomfort. If you set the example in your room, your children are likely to try it. Maybe on this occasion they would choose to give up sleeping with their favorite stuffed animal so they have a hint of what it is like not to have something you care about anymore, at least for a night.

2. Study Jerusalem. If you have older children, have them research an aspect of Jerusalem's history to present to the whole family. This project can also focus on current events in the Holy City.

Situations and Solutions

Q I thought Yom Kippur was the saddest day of the year. Why would the destruction of Jerusalem a long time ago still be a day of mourning, especially since Jerusalem is now rebuilt and in Jewish hands?

A From a historical perspective, no day is as terrible to Jewish people as Tisha B'Av. Yom Kippur is certainly the most contemplative, especially if you believe you are being judged by the Sovereign of Sovereigns, but it is actually viewed as potentially uplifting. The day the first and second Temple were destroyed is also the anniversary of national catastrophes, ending national Jewish life, sending us into slavery and exile, and resulting in many deaths. The only other Jewish holiday where these themes are echoed is Yom Ha-Shoah, Holocaust Remembrance Day.

The fall of Jerusalem, first to the Babylonians and then to Roman legions, has been used by our rabbis to highlight the danger of internal divisions. Jerusalem fell, our sages teach, because people were dishonored in their everyday affairs and because of *sinat chinam*, "baseless hatred." What we mourn on Tisha B'Av is not only Jerusalem's history, but the divisions that separate the Jewish people. This idea serves as a warning against the forces that even today have the potential to cause irreparable harm to Jews, Israel, and Jerusalem once again.

All You Need Is Love: Tu B'Av

The walls of the ancient city of Jerusalem have historically been a source of inspiration for romance and love. Thousands of years before anyone ever heard of St. Valentine or Sadie Hawkins, the Jewish people created a Jerusalem-centred love festival for couples. This custom is quite in keeping with the sensuous poetry of the Song of Songs, canonized in the Hebrew Scriptures.

In the glow of a full summer moon, young women, robed in white, would dance in the fields outside the walls of Jerusalem. The men would follow in hopes of finding a bride. This ancient Jewish love festival is called Tu B'Av because it was celebrated on the 15th day of the Hebrew month of Av (the Hebrew letters for "Tu" equal the number 15). Coming one week after Tisha B'Av, the saddest day of the Jewish year, Tu B'Av is celebrated outside of the walls of the city, away from the Temple Mount, the site of the destruction.

Whereas Tisha B'Av is the day when God declared that the Jews would wander 40 years in the desert (until the generation that knew slavery died out), Tu B'Av is the day when, 40 years later, the remaining 15,000 Israelites of the desert generation were told they would be able to enter the Promised Land. God was able to forgive the Jewish people on this day, even for the sin of having built and worshiped a Golden Calf.

In the Talmud (*Ta'anit* 4:8) we read that Rabbi Simeon ben Gamaliel said there never were in Israel greater days of joy than the 15th of Av and the Day of Atonement. On these days the daughters of Jerusalem used to walk out in white garments that they borrowed in order not to put to shame anyone who had none. The daughters of Jerusalem danced in the vineyards exclaiming, "Young man, lift up your eyes and see what you choose for yourself. Do not set your eyes on beauty but set them on good family. Grace is deceitful and beauty is vain. But a woman that fears G-d, she will be praised."

Rabbi Simeon's linking of Tu B'Av and Yom Kippur is at first disturbing. Why does the Jewish year end with a celebration of love? The answer says a lot about Judaism's unique perspective on relationships, a perspective that could enhance courtship today. Tu B'Av, like Yom Kippur, is about introspection and new beginnings concerning our relationships and personal values. How courting was done is indicative of this view. The young girls borrowed white dresses so that the young men could not choose among them according to materialistic concerns. The Talmud teaches that women set the rules; the women admonish their suitors to pick not according to beauty, but by the good name of the women's families and by their fear of God. Today we live in a world that is status- and fashion-conscious, a world of beauty pageants and beauty ideals set by television and movies, and some synagogues are even described as "meat markets" where one goes to look over the unmarried merchandise.

Tu B'Av tells us to look beneath the surface when looking for (or at) a life partner, just as Yom Kippur forces us to look deep into ourselves before God grants us life anew. Like Yom Kippur, Tu B'Av is a time for reflection and introspection. But instead of being an individual process, it is a mutual, shared experience between two people.

Tu B'Av is a great day for weddings, commitment ceremonies, renewal of vows, or proposing. It is a day for enhancing current relationships or defining anew what you are looking for in a partner. It is a day for romance, explored through singing, dancing, giving flowers, and studying. The rabbis teach that on Tu B'Av one begins to set more time aside for studying Torah as the High Holidays approach.

RULES AND REGS

Only two: The sexual satisfaction of both partners should be attended to, and the object of your desire should be your spouse (one of the top Ten Commandments).

 Hands-On Judaism

1. Who do we love? If you are like us, we always remember much too late to prepare Rosh Hashanah cards. Instead of waiting for the last minute, gather your family together on Tu B'Av, make a list of all the people whom you love and who love you, and address the Rosh Hashanah card envelopes together.

2. Arrange to be alone together. Get a babysitter, rent a hotel room nearby, and go swimming (or skinny-dipping!) together in a nearby stream, river, lake, or ocean.

3. Give flowers. A rabbi we know always brings home a bouquet of flowers on Tu B'Av for his wife. Sounds like a good example to follow. It would be nice if florists received thousands of Tu B'Av orders or if Elit (an Israeli chocolate company) made a special chocolate Tu B'Av rose or wall of Jerusalem.

4. Teach children about true beauty. Since Tu B'Av falls in the summer, Jewish camps could use this festival as an opportunity to teach children to look beyond physical beauty to seek partners with strong Jewish values.

5. Food for love. For lovers and vampires, eating garlic is the kiss of death. Jewish sources, however, have other ideas. Lacing a dish with garlic increases sexual desire in a man, according to nineteenth-century doctor and Talmudic scholar Julius Preuss. In his book *Biblical and Talmudic Medicine*, he claims that not only garlic, but fatty meat, cheese, eggs, mustard seed, fish brine, wine, and milk are aphrodisiacs. It is for this reason, he writes, that high priests were not allowed to drink milk before the Day of Atonement.

Mandrake is also a good aphrodisiac to serve to your lover, according to the Bible. The only problem is, Preuss writes, no one is quite sure what a mandrake is. So finding this item in the supermarket might be difficult. It's possible, Preuss writes, that according to the rabbinic midrash, mandrake is an ancient name for barley.

Making Time for Togetherness

by Debra B. Darvick

Is romance still possible even amid toddlers and teens?

"I am my beloved's and my beloved is mine." (Song of Songs 6:3)

CHILDREN HAVE A WAY OF LANDING BETWEEN COUPLES like a seven-ton octopus. My husband and I have been married for 16 years and have been parents for 12. Long gone are the days of uninterrupted conversations or nights in a bedroom whose door has no lock.

Our children's presence in our lives is constant and we do what all good parents do—we give. We give time, our hearts and souls, advice, and concern. But we've also learned when to stop giving, when to say, "Bye, sweetie. Daddy and I are going out. For a walk. To dinner. Away for the week." They've learned not to protest—too much.

When my son was small, I would put him to bed only to hear, "Me with you and Daddy." I launched into a pep talk, more for my benefit than his: "Elliot, I love you, but I also love your daddy. I'm with you all day. Now it is time for you to go to sleep, time for me to be with Daddy." It was hard to resist those outstretched arms; more than once I wondered if I was harming my son by turning my back on him. But in some corner of my sleep-deprived brain I knew that I must reserve some time for my husband and me.

Because I was a full-time mother in those days, separating from my son was easier. Twelve solid hours of parenting was plenty. When both spouses work outside the home, the tendency is to spend every spare minute with the children. But working couples need to focus on the "couples" part of their equation too. Setting aside time to reestablish ties with one another is important, even if it means grabbing an hour a week for an ice cream cone. Jewish tradition recognizes the importance of a married couple's relationship. A Jewish husband is responsible for providing his wife not only with food and clothing but with the satisfaction of her sexual needs as well. Some years ago my husband and I decided to incorporate *Eyshet Chayil* (the Woman of Valor prayer from Proverbs 31 that is traditionally sung by a husband in honor of his wife on Friday night) into our Shabbat dinner ritual. I revel in the space created when he honors me by reading it. Beyond creating space for us, it shows our children that we value our relationship, and so does Judaism.

Really getting away takes some planning but it is well worth the effort. Can your evening sitter stay for a weekend or longer? Is there a child care service in your area that provides part-time sitters? Trading children with another couple is a good option and not as costly as hiring someone to care for your children while you're gone.

Two couples we know have had this arrangement for years. They each get away four weekends a year. If you're uncomfortable about leaving your children with someone new, the friend option may make the separation easier on everyone. And if a week or long weekend isn't in the cards right now, steal away for a night for some R & R (romance and reconnecting), and go away for longer when time and money permit. Children grow up so fast, but a marriage must also be enriched with experiences independent of the children.

The Jewish community should also take an active role in supporting parents. Synagogue youth groups could add baby-sitting to their list of mitzvah projects. Many young parents and empty nesters live far from family. Why not create a Borrow-a-Bubbe (grandmother) program? Jewish communal organizations should call an occasional moratorium on meetings for the express purpose of returning spouses to their families and/or each other.

For my husband and me, the issues have shifted as our children have gotten older. They are nearly 12 and 9 now. They know that if we leave on Friday we'll return by Sunday. We can leave them at home and take a walk. But there is a downside as well. Gone are the days when our children were in bed by 7:30. Just last week it was close to 10 P.M. and my son wanted me to look over his report "one last time." I found myself saying, "Elliot, not now. I've been available to you since 4 P.M. Now I want to be with Daddy. It's our time to be together."

After twelve years of parenting, the guilt is gone, but not the thrill. My beloved is mine and I am his.

Debra B. Darvick is a freelance writer from Michigan. A recipient of a Simon Rockower Award for Excellence in Jewish Journalism, she has had articles and essays published in *The Jewish Women's Journal*, *The Jewish Parent Connection*, and various major city newspapers.

Situations and Solutions

Q I always thought that Christianity, and not Judaism, emphasized love. Isn't revitalizing this holiday moving Judaism closer to Christianity, especially closer to St. Valentine's Day?

A The Jewish mystical tradition teaches that God created the world out of love, that God physically withdrew from a small segment of space to make room for humanity, a concept called *tzimtzum* (contraction). Creation, like deciding to marry or have a child, is an act of love that requires increased limitations and obligations on oneself. Love does not negate the role of commandments, or mitzvot. Rather, love enhances the mitzvot. Because we love God and God loves us, we try to act accordingly. Doing so includes bringing sanctity into our romantic relationships.

A rabbinic story tells of a discussion between a Roman and a prominent rabbi. "What does your God do that is so great?" the Roman challenged. "Our God makes marriages," the rabbi replied. "What is so great about making marriages?" asked the Roman. "I could make marriages as well." The Roman summoned a thousand slaves, half of whom were men, half of whom were women, and paired them off and married them. The slaves returned the next day with complaints, bruises, black eyes. When the Roman saw her failure at making marriages, she conceded that making couples is indeed the work of the Divine. And then the Roman converted to Judaism.

Chapter Eight

NON-JEWISH HOLIDAYS

"Who is wise? The one who learns from every one."
(*Pirkei Avot* 4:1)

IN ADDITION TO THE DOZEN OR SO JEWISH HOLIDAYS, the calendar is peppered with many secular celebrations that offer Jewish parents opportunities to affirm Jewish values. At one time most American Jews, especially the traditionally religious, felt as if they were living between two separate worlds—one American, the other Jewish. The early immigrants tended to downplay their Jewishness because they thought it would impede their integration into American society. Children were frequently embarrassed by the foreign accents and traditions of their parents and grandparents as they embraced American customs and culture. Today, however, we are comfortably part of the American mosaic.

Since the late 1960s, a growing movement among American Jews has sought creative ways of combining the unique Jewish culture and religious heritage with full participation in American public life. So we celebrate American holidays such as Thanksgiving, Martin Luther King Jr.'s Birthday, July 4th, and Halloween. But celebrating these holidays outside the context of our Jewish values, ritual, and history may give children the misleading message that Judaism is merely an activity that we can begin and end rather than being a total identity and way of life.

Do not stand idly by or be too busy while your children internalize who knows what! Use this basic precept: Never miss an opportunity to affirm your Jewish values and be a moral teacher to your children.

Our look at non-Jewish American holidays is a mixture of fun, learning, and values, and it includes features, personal experiences, and selected responses from our website.

Ghosts, Witches, and Demons: Halloween

This American version of an old Celtic end-of-summer observance may be the most difficult to endow with Jewish values since it seems the very antithesis of all that Judaism stands for. But it may also be the most difficult to draw your children away from, since it is geared almost entirely toward children. The question that is often raised is what harm is there in having a Jewish child dress up as a goblin or fairy and go trick-or-treating.

Is Halloween a Jewish Holiday?

by Ted Roberts

HALLOWEEN IS NOT A JEWISH HOLIDAY. You should go to work as usual. And don't fast. However, I have just thoroughly researched both the Jerusalem and Babylonian Talmud and I cannot find a single prohibition against Jews engaging in trick-or-treating activities. So, it's okay according to Jewish law, as long as your neighbors don't distribute pork chops or bowls of young stewed goat in mother's milk sauce. If they do, cite Exodus 23:19 and ask if you could have a Hershey bar with nuts instead.

Doctrinally Halloween games are okay, but philosophically they are very un-Jewish because the air is full of witches, spooks, and spirits. And they are not singing Hebrew songs either. Witching didn't get very good press in our Bible, because basically, it was a heathen occupation. In the Bible, statements about witches are usually linked with stones—as in "She shall be stoned to death."

But if you let your kids loose on Halloween, I suggest that you balance the evening with a reading from Samuel, the prophet, after they come home with bulging pillow cases. King Saul is preparing to fight the Philistines at Gilboa. He needs all the help he can get. He goes to a witch at Endor (remember Endora from the television show *Bewitched?*), even though Saul had banned the practice of witchery, the only profession open to women except for that other one. The witch conjures up Samuel's spirit, who tells Saul that the day of battle will be disastrous. And so it is. Saul is killed. But then David becomes king. Why not have your kids dress up as King David?

Ted Roberts is a humorist who resides in Huntsville, Alabama.

Jewishfamily.com Cyber Discussion: Should Jewish Children Trick-or-Treat?

Pro

YES. IT WAS QUITE TOUCHING TO SEE HORDES of parents and children walk along Central Park West in Manhattan, dressed up in everything from Woolworth's cheap-o costumes to some really inventive homemade stuff. I complimented a group of boys on their Marilynesque blond wigs. One boy turned to me and said in perfect falsetto, "Oh, this is not a wig. This is my real hair. And my real hair color, too." Needless to say, everyone around cracked up.

Moving northwestward, it was interesting to observe the changing demographics of the city. While most trick-or-treaters on Central Park West were white, those on Columbus Avenue in the high 90s were primarily black and Hispanic. And their parents were every bit as caught up in the fun of this child-oriented spirit of the holiday, if not more. It was that child-centeredness that really caught my attention; now how often does one see that in Manhattan?

The real danger of Halloween, I believe, is if trick-or-treating is the only memorable ritual you give your Jewish child. But guess what! This year it is on a Friday afternoon, so my Jewish children who "celebrated" Halloween will, G-d willing, come home to a kitchen redolent with wonderful smells, to the sacred hustle and bustle of the making of Shabbat. The ritual celebration that takes place 52 times a year will hopefully override the memories of one that takes place only once a year.

Con

NO. Pagan, pagan, pagan. A holiday that celebrates and glorifies death, fear, and witches is not in the spirit of Judaism, which is life affirming. We don't believe in magic, but in G-d's miracles. And the hunt for candy sends the message to our children that greed is all right. A real mitzvah would be to turn on your porch light and have your children hand out candy to their Gentile neighbors. This teaches tolerance, both ways, and is the *menschlich* [Yiddish for kind] thing to do; but it also teaches that we ARE different.

Hands-On Judaism

1. Encourage costumes that don't symbolize death. Consider having your children dress up as Jewish characters. Some families use the same costumes for Purim and Halloween.

2. Practice tzedakah. Ask your children to choose a charity box to take from door to door when they go trick-or-treating. One mother who e-mailed us has an agreement with her children that after trick-or-treating, they can pull out ten candies that they can eat over the next week or so. She gives them a nickel for every left over candy, and the proceeds are split between their savings account and the tzedakah box. The leftover candy goes to a food pantry for the poor.

3. Separate kosher from nonkosher. After trick-or-treating, sit down with your children and separate out the candy that is kosher from the candy that is not kosher. Give the nonkosher candy to a food pantry, or buy it from your child. Then put half the money in a savings account and give the other half to charity.

4. Read Jewish stories. After trick-or-treating, sit down with your children and read some Jewish mystical or magical stories by candlelight. We recommend: *Lilith's Cave: Jewish Stories of the Supernatural* by Howard Schwartz, *The Four Who Entered Paradise* by Howard Schwartz and *The Golem* by Isaac Bashevis Singer.

Pilgrims, Indians, and Turkeys: Thanksgiving

Thanksgiving is a uniquely American family holiday. It is also a holiday that can be easily incorporated into Jewish family life. Most American families get together for the traditional turkey dinner because it is nice for everybody, even those who live far away, to return home at least once a year. The story of the pilgrims and their plentiful harvest that was followed by a feast with the Indians is part of American folklore, but it is not recalled at the dinner table the way we recall the story of Exodus at the Passover seder.

We have the model of storytelling with which generations of Jews have taught and renewed our values and commitments. We can apply that model to the Thanksgiving meal. At Thanksgiving we can recall the good and the bad in American history. We remember the suffering and displacement of the indigenous people, and other shameful oppressions such as slavery, as well as the refuge the United States provided for so many people, and the on-going revolutions such as civil and human rights.

Thanksgiving day is an opportunity for a living Haggadah ("telling"—the book used at Passover), an opportunity to take stock of the country and give thanks for its blessings and for the opportunity here to work for and create change.

 Hands-On Judaism

1. **Bake a challah for Thanksgiving dinner.** Try one with a Thanksgiving theme, such as cornmeal or cranberries. Say the motzi (the blessing over bread) before eating.

2. **Recall the history of this land.** Go around the table and have everyone participate in recalling the history of the land since the pilgrims arrived. Each person can continue where the one before left off.

3. **Answer questions.** Allow each person an opportunity to respond to questions such as these: What are we personally thankful for? What are we thankful for as American Jews? What do we wish to contribute to this country? What do we believe are the highest ideals and best values of the United States? Have we, as a nation, lived up to those ideals and values in the past year?

4. **Read aloud great quotes.** A great example of something you can read aloud at Thanksgiving is the Emma Lazarus poem that is inscribed on the base of the Statue of Liberty:

Not like the brazen giant of Greek fame;
With conquering limbs astride from land to land,
Here at our sea-washed sunset gates shall stand
A mighty woman with a torch, whose flame
Is the imprisoned lightning, and her name
Mother of Exiles. From her beacon-hand
Glows world-wide welcome; her mild eyes command
The air-bridged harbor that twin cities frame.
"Keep ancient lands, your storied pomp!" cries she

With silent lips.
"Give me your tired, your poor,
Your huddled masses yearning to breathe free,
The wretched refuse of your teeming shore.
Send these, the homeless, tempest-tost to me,
I lift my lamp beside the golden door!"

5. Conclude with a blessing. Here's an example of a blessing you can say before you conclude with the grace after meals: "God, Source of life, compassion, and justice. Grant us wisdom and strength that we may lift our lamps for freedom, justice, and compassion. Amen."

The December Dilemma: Christmas

While it may be possible to compromise on Halloween since it is a folkloric observance rather than a religious one, Christmas simply cannot be reconciled with being Jewish. There is no way around it, Christmas celebrates the birthday of the Christian savior. That theology is in no way conducive to our own. It is therefore important to explain this fact to your children at an early age to fortify them, so to speak, against the annual bombardment in public places, on television, and so on. As for the nod toward Hanukkah which has become a custom in recent years in the media, schools, and even public places—although motivated no doubt by a well-meaning desire to be equitable if not a giving in to pressure from Jewish groups—it tends to create the impression of Hanukkah as the "Jewish Christmas." Jewish parents thus find themselves truly on the horns of a dilemma that requires patience and firmness, especially with very young children. In a family where there is a clear consensus between the parents, the conundrum is fairly easy to overcome. The real problem arises in interfaith families in which parents are indecisive and pulled in conflicting directions.

Schools have become more sensitive to Jewish holidays, but most parents still have to deal with the "December dilemma" and the media blitz that accompanies Christmas.

Interfaith Families and the December Dilemma

by Nancy Mades

THEY CALL IT THE DECEMBER DILEMMA and it usually goes something like this:

She: "Well, should we have a Christmas tree or a menorah?"

He: "If we have both, will it confuse our children? If we have neither, are we depriving our kids of their history?"

She: "What will our parents think?"

Making room for two traditions under one roof is never more of a challenge than during the holiday season, when differences that seem inconsequential during the rest of the year suddenly become acute.

"The holiday season calls to the surface tensions, struggles, and issues related to the intermarriage," says Rabbi David Abrahamson, former spiritual leader of B'Nai Abraham in Beverly, Massachusetts. "They're more acutely felt during the holidays. Issues of how children will be raised or how a childless couple is going to conduct their religious life need to be talked about."

December is not the best time to start talking, because emotions are so intense. The intensity of feeling catches a lot of people by surprise.

It certainly was a surprise for Margie Benea of Peabody, Massachusetts, who was raised in a traditional Jewish family and has been married for 20 years to Frank Benea, who grew up in an equally traditional Catholic family. Margie remembers their first Christmas together, when she went out and bought a tiny six-inch Christmas tree for her new husband. "The tree didn't last very long in the house because it made me feel very uncomfortable," says Margie.

"I think that the Christmas tree in an interfaith home very tangibly brings out that whole question of the religious future or religious identity of the family," says Rabbi Abrahamson. "Also, even for a Jewish family—two Jewish parents with Jewish children—a Christmas tree is a stereotypical symbol of assimilation."

Today, Margie and Frank raise their 10-year-old daughter and 14-year-old son as Jews. They don't have a Christmas tree at home, but they still celebrate the Catholic holidays with their father's family. "The kids always give him a present on Christmas morning too, because they understand that it is Dad's holiday," says Margie.

"Our kids really look forward to going to their grandparents' house to help decorate their tree," Margie says. "It's a very special night for them. It isn't difficult for them because it's all they've ever known. We told them that Dad's family believes in God in a different way."

The bright lights of a Christmas tree can be a hard thing for the more low-key Hanukkah menorah to compete with, says Lauren Gaudette of Peabody, Massachusetts. "When my children saw my in-laws' Christmas tree last year, they immediately wanted one of their own," says Gaudette, a Jewish mother of three toddlers, whose husband was raised Catholic. "It was very difficult to explain to my three-year-old twins why they couldn't have the beautiful tree. Kids are impressionable, and the tree, lit up, was impressive."

Gaudette says she strives to play up the Jewish holidays for the children so that they won't ever feel that they are missing out on something. The family practices only Judaism at home and the children attend preschool at a Reform synagogue. Allowing a Christmas tree in the house, Gaudette says, would send a confusing, mixed message to the children.

Explains Dr. Samuel Migdole, a psychologist in Beverly, Massachusetts, "No matter how you think about Christmas, it is a religious holiday with special significance for Christians. If you've grown up Christian, it has tremendous meaning for you."

Hanukkah comes at about the same time of year and is a festive holiday with gift giving, but there is a major difference. Hanukkah is a minor holiday in the Jewish calendar that has taken on major proportions because of its proximity to Christmas.

Marriages between Christians and Jews have been steadily increasing since the 1950s. "The fear of estrangement from community and family may have been an effective disincentive to intermarriage a generation ago," says Abrahamson. "As recently as 25 years ago, it has been estimated that only one Jew in ten married someone who was not Jewish. Now some estimates are as high as 50 percent."

Migdole agrees that the social stigma attached to interfaith marriage has lessened considerably. But, he says, there are still important issues a couple and their extended families need to work out well before that first holiday season comes around.

"It is very important that a couple be united in their decisions about their religious home life," says Migdole. "The trouble starts when a couple says, we're in love and it doesn't matter, because it really does matter."

At the very least, says Migdole, a couple should come to a decision about religion at home before they have children. "Within the boundaries of the nuclear family, a child may clearly understand that he or she is Christian even though one parent is Jewish," says Migdole, "but the child will still have an extended family of Jewish relatives."

"Even when the parents decide to go one way with their children, you cannot pretend that an interfaith marriage is not an interfaith marriage," says Migdole, adding that parents need to explain the differences in a gentle and respectful way. "You can say to your child, 'We're Jewish and we don't have a Christmas tree, but Grandma and Grandpa are Catholic and we respect that. Let's help them celebrate their holiday,'" says Migdole.

For couples who are experiencing tension from one or both sides of an extended family for not living up to certain holiday traditions, a united front is an absolute must, Abrahamson says. "You won't dictate to the extended families what they should do, but you have to decide where you will draw certain lines in terms of your own children's involvement. As with any other aspect of relationships—you have to negotiate."

Nancy Mades lives near Boston with her husband, John Alabiso, and their two children.

'Tis the Season…for Jewish parents to become advocates in the schools

by Ann Moline

TWO TALES FOR THE HANUKKAH SEASON. Nine years ago, near the end of President Reagan's term in office, my family was invited on a tour of the West Wing of the White House. My oldest, Jennie, was six and a first-grader at Gesher Jewish Day School. Our visit happened to coincide with Hanukkah. When we were shown the Oval Office, where the president conducts official business, we were all struck by a large, ornate *hanukkiyah* (a Hannukah menorah) sitting prominently on a window sill behind the president's desk.

The next morning I spoke to Jennie about her reactions to the visit. "What did you like best about the White House?" I asked.
"I thought it was really beautiful," she replied. "But you know what I thought was the most amazing thing of all, Mom? I had no idea that President Reagan was Jewish!"

Living close to our nation's capital affords us opportunities that people living outside the D.C. area do not have. My father, for example, volunteers once a week, answering telephones at the White House. Many of my children's friends' parents work in government jobs. The children, therefore, understand the ways in which the nation conducts its business and the avenues one must take to pursue something one believes in.

One winter night, when my middle child, Julia, was nine, she was absolutely distraught as I put her to bed. When asked what was the problem, she explained that she was thoroughly disgusted with her favorite television shows because all of them were airing Christmas specials, and none of them so much as mentioned Hanukkah. I was a little shocked at how upset she was. After all, she attended a Jewish day school, and our home emphasizes all the richness Jewish tradition offers. I didn't think the Christmas blitz would really bother her. Because I was so surprised, I didn't quite know how to respond. I needed to stall for time to think of an appropriate response, and so I turned it back to her. "I can see that you are really angry about this. What do you intend to do about it?" I asked.

Through her tears she responded. "Well, I thought about calling President Clinton to complain, but then I figured it would just be Grandpa who answered the phone. And I can talk to Grandpa anytime."

I believe these stories highlight the importance of this season in our children's minds. We cannot pretend that the national emphasis on Christmas will not affect them, even if they are from the most Jewishly educated backgrounds. And we also cannot pretend that our children do not notice the symbols of the season.

National Guidelines for Holiday Education

In our age of political correctness, much confusion surrounds the types of religious activities that are permissible in schools and other public places. These battles become more emotional around the holiday season, when Jewish parents worry about the impact of the inundation of Christmas on their children. Recently the U.S. Department of Education issued guidelines designed to clarify things for parents and public school officials. Based on a directive from President Clinton, Education Secretary Richard Riley met with diverse religious organizations and subsequently released a document entitled "Religious Expression in Public Schools."

Rabbi Charles Feinberg, chairman of the Social Action Committee of the Rabbinical Assembly, was one of the national religious leaders invited to Washington to meet with Riley. Afterwards, Riley asked the leaders to distribute the new guidelines among their constituencies. Although Rabbi Feinberg did what he was asked to do, he is skeptical about the efficacy of the document. "It is not helpful," he says. "There is too much gray. They leave so much up to the discretion of the individual school district."

A source at the Department of Education disagrees with this characterization. "Since these guidelines were published, we have heard from the National School Board Association that the number of calls asking about what is permissible in schools has dramatically decreased." The source explains that the guidelines were a distillation of the current laws on the issue of prayer in public schools.

Organizations ranging from the American Jewish Congress to evangelical Christian groups, not to mention countless constitutional law experts, participated in the discussions while the document was written. The U.S. Department of Education source says that the primary problem most people have with the issue is that of confusion. "There was a tremendous knowledge gap ever since the Supreme Court decision thirty years ago to allow students their constitutional rights." The

For information from the U.S. Department of Education, including Secretary Riley's letter to public school superintendents and the document *Religious Expression in Public Schools*, go to the Department's homepage: http://www.ed.gov.

For a copy of *A Parent's Guide to Religion in the Public Schools*, go to the Freedom Forum's First Amendment Center homepage: http://www.fac.org.

The Anti-Defamation League also maintains a database of helpful information on the subject: http://www.adl.org.

Your branch of the Community Relations Council (CRC) will be aware of local issues and will have a listing of experts who will assist in any problem.

First Amendment to the Constitution allows for religious freedom of expression, which includes the right to voluntary prayer in school.

While the larger issue of prayer in school will continue to be debated, the immediate problem for Jewish parents is the December holiday sensation. Does your child have to participate in the singing of Christmas carols? No. Can you demand of the school choir not to sing those songs? Again, the answer is no.

The Jewish Perspective

Rabbi Feinberg, spiritual leader of Temple Beth El in Poughkeepsie, New York, believes that Jewish parents must take the lead in confronting issues before they become problems. "Once November rolls around, things escalate quickly. The issue of Christmas-tree projects and holiday concerts must be discussed before this time period. You cannot have a rational discussion on this subject during the Christmas season."

The rabbi recalls a comment made in a Wisconsin town where he headed a congregation some years ago. After Jewish parents protested the inclusion of Christian religious songs in a holiday concert, the word on the street was "The Jews are trying to take Christmas away."

Rabbi Feinberg recommends approaching local school officials with an outline of positive steps for a district to follow which will meet the needs of Jewish children. If you want to sensitize school officials, start early, and arm yourself with as much practical information as possible. Bring along a copy of the federal guidelines issued to school superintendents, in case your district does not have a copy. Also have a copy of a Jewish perpetual calendar, which your local rabbi can provide. Highlight the dates for Rosh Hashanah and Yom Kippur, since school districts are notorious for starting school on these days. Don't have unrealistic expectations, and be sure that what you are asking fits within the federally mandated guidelines.

A Grass-Roots Effort in Florida

For the past few years the State of Florida has been embroiled in a massive political battle, pitting religious conservatives against liberals. Last year the Republican majority in both houses of the state legislature succeeded in passing an amendment to a bill that would allow student-led prayer at school functions such as football games and assemblies. A coalition of Jewish legislators and community leaders led an extensive grass-roots campaign, ultimately convincing Democratic Governor Lawton Chiles to veto the amendment.

Robert Wexler, newly elected democratic member of Congress, was a state senator at the time, representing parts of Palm Beach and Broward County. He led the fight, delivering a series of fiery speeches on the floor of the Senate which were later used as text for full-page ads in local papers to counter the letter-writing campaign, marches, and candlelight vigils of the religious right.

Congressman Wexler said that local rabbis were asked to encourage congregants to write letters, and local newspapers endorsed the position in editorials, encouraging readers to write to the governor.

The bill, according to Congressman Wexler, called for students to vote on whether or not they wanted some type of prayer at a school function. "That absolutely flew in the face of everything I believe this county stands for," he explained. "That a majority vote would determine whether a prayer was said—who do you think would win—certainly not a Jewish minority!" The congressman also said that the issue was of concern not just for Jewish children, but for any family that did not want other beliefs foisted upon them.

Although the bill's proponents claimed that prayers would be nonsectarian, enforcement would be up to the faculty, and faculty involvement was specifically prohibited by federal guidelines. The only solution, therefore, was to defeat the bill through a grass-roots campaign. Wexler encouraged parents to alert their local legislators and enlist the support of organizations should a school prayer issue arise in their community.

Ron Klein, a state representative who won Congressman Wexler's vacated seat in the state Senate in November 1996, says, "The moral of this story is that individuals, working together, can make a difference. I totally believe that if we had not had all of those ordinary citizens writing letters to the governor, we would have lost the fight."

In this season of rededication (remembering the rededication of the ancient temple in Jerusalem), the message rings loud and clear.

Ann Moline is a freelance writer and journalist living in Alexandria, Virginia. She and her husband, Jack, are the parents of three children.

> **"**The Southern
> Christian Leadership
> Conference has
> expressly, frequently,
> and vigorously
> denounced anti-
> Semitism and will
> continue to do so.
> It is not only that
> anti-Semitism is
> immoral—though
> that alone is enough.
> It is used to divide
> Negro and Jew,
> who have effectively
> collaborated in the
> struggle for justice. It
> injures Negroes
> because it upholds
> the doctrine of
> racism which they
> have the greatest
> stake in destroying.**"**
>
> —DR. MARTIN
> LUTHER KING, JR.
> in a letter to Jewish
> leaders, October 1967

Repairing the World: Martin Luther King, Jr.'s Birthday

The World Jewish Congress, in a meeting with Coretta Scott King in 1994, declared Martin Luther King, Jr.'s birthday an international Jewish holiday. The widow of the slain civil rights leader spoke movingly of her husband's commitment to equality, his support of Soviet Jewry and Israel, and his rejection of antisemitism. "It is the fulfillment of a dream to have Martin's birthday become an international holiday," she said, thanking the representatives of Jewish communities from around the world.

It is not the custom of most Jewish communities to celebrate the birthday of their leaders, be they kings, prophets, or prime ministers. Jewish holidays revolve around the events in the history of a people and not around a person. Yet Dr. King's birthday has been an exception because of his unfulfilled prophetic mission which found great support in the Jewish community.

The pursuit of justice and peace are fundamental themes in Jewish text and law. In Genesis we are taught that men and women are created in God's image. The Exodus story of the freeing of the Israelite slaves has been an inspiration for all oppressed groups. In Deuteronomy (16:20) we are commanded, "Justice, justice shall you pursue." Coming from a long history of persecution and discrimination and a tradition that emphasizes human dignity, Jews understood the work of Dr. King and rallied behind him.

While children will learn about Dr. King and what he stood for in public school, his sensitivity to Jewish issues and his echoing of the biblical prophets is something that you can teach your children at home.

In introducing Dr. King to the Conservative movement's Rabbinical Assembly, Rabbi Abraham Joshua Heschel said, "Where in America today do we hear a voice like the voice of the prophets of Israel? Martin Luther King is a sign that God has not forsaken the United States of America. God has sent him to us. His presence is the hope of America. His mission is sacred.... I call upon every Jew to hearken to his voice, to share in his vision, to follow in his way. The whole future of America will depend upon the impact and influence of Dr. King."

Hands-On Judaism

1. Volunteer. Martin Luther King's birthday is not only a time to rededicate ourselves to his dream of equality and justice, but could also be a day for volunteering. As a family, choose a location for volunteering where your children will see for themselves how much work still needs to be done to accomplish Dr. King's dream.

2. Talk about racism. Your children have no doubt heard racist or anti-Semitic remarks or jokes or have encountered instances of prejudice and discrimination over the past year. Ask them about what they have seen and heard and role-play situations to help them combat stereotyping and prejudice.

3. Participate at school. Does your child's school have a celebration of Martin Luther King Day? Are your children involved as participants or organizers? Encourage them to assume leadership positions.

4. Demonstrate for good causes. Take your children out of school on any days throughout the year when there are demonstrations about issues you care about passionately. Just as it is a religious obligation not to go to school on certain Jewish holidays, our tradition also mandates involving ourselves in important social issues as religious obligation.

> **"**My people were brought to America in chains. Your people were driven here to escape the chains fashioned for them in Europe. Our unity is born of our common struggle for centuries, not only to rid ourselves of bondage, but to make oppression of any people by others an impossibility.**"**
>
> —DR. MARTIN LUTHER KING, JR.
> in an address to the American Jewish Congress, 1958

Situations and Solutions

Q I feel very self-conscious about this holiday. On the one hand, I want my children to celebrate Dr. King's legacy. On the other hand, we live in the suburbs far from the plights the Reverend King challenged so well. Am I a hypocrite?

A Your feeling of awkwardness is a sign of sensitivity. Having your children come to this same somewhat uncomfortable understanding might help them think about questions of racial and economic barriers that are often left unchallenged in their daily lives. Living in the suburbs, however, does not preclude you or your children from activism. In fact, we set a very powerful and important example for our children if we work for social justice, even when the injustice does not directly affect us. Through your actions, you model a belief in Dr. King's teaching that "injustice anywhere is a threat to justice everywhere."

The Fourth of July

To Americans it may seem natural that Jews should be treated as equal citizens. However, the Jewish experience for thousands of years has been a very different one. In every society in which we have lived we were outcasts and were subject to discrimination and oppression. In the course of our 4,000-year history, we have constituted a nation that has periodically been banished from its homeland and been dispersed among many nations. Under Muslim rule, we were by and large tolerated in most places. Under Christian rule, we were often lucky to be permitted to earn a livelihood, and then only in exchange for exacting taxes.

Part of the reason for this fear and oppression of Jews may be that the Jews have long defied a clear model of classification. The development of the modern, secular nation-state brought the promise of equal rights for individuals rather than specific rights and privileges for people of certain classes or religions. Yet the question of who and what the Jews are is still sometimes debated, often by Jews themselves. Yes, Jews are a religious group, adherents of a religion called Judaism. But the Jews are also a people bound together by a common history, and even those born of Jewish parents who do not practice or who reject Judaism are still Jews. A third dimension is that Jews are a nation, having reestablished the modern State of Israel in the ancient Jewish homeland. And no, Jews are not a race—a fact made evident by looking at the rainbow of faces of the Jews in Israel.

With which aspects of Jewish life do you and your children identify? Surveys indicate that most Jews classify themselves as cultural Jews or religious Jews. Others say their Jewish identity has a national component. In fact, they react when other Jews are threatened—you may recall how you felt when Israel was under SCUD attacks during the Gulf War.

As proud citizens of the United States, Jews run into no conflict or religious dilemma when celebrating the birthday of the United States on the Fourth of July.

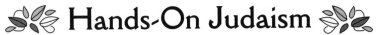 # Hands-On Judaism

1. **Discuss loyalty and patriotism.** For families with teenagers, the case of Jonathan Pollard—a civilian Navy analyst who in 1986 was convicted of spying for Israel and has been sentenced to life imprisonment—is a challenging question to consider on the Fourth of July. Is there a limit to our patriotism? What about recurrent charges of dual loyalty? Pollard believed that Israel had a right to the information under a strategic alliance agreement and that Israeli lives would be saved. Should Jewish intelligence agents have the same access to classified materials about Israel or the Middle East as other agents? Should Jews in government be involved in decision making when it comes to Israel? What would your children do if they ever found themselves in Pollard's shoes? Is Pollard's sentence, as some critics contend, unduly harsh? (Your children can write to him at this address: Jonathan Pollard/09185-016, P.O. Box 1000, Butner, NC 27509-1000.)

2. **Discuss what it is like to be Jewish in America.** Is there a special role for us here? What makes us different from other Americans?

3. **Have a Fourth of July party with a Jewish theme.** Perform songs, skits, or recitations by or about famous American Jews, from Emma Lazarus to Steven Spielberg.

PART III

VALUES

Chapter Nine

LOVINGKINDNESS AND ACTS OF JUSTICE

TWO MEN ARE WALKING DOWN THE STREET. They have equal incomes and expenses. A man comes up to them and says, "Please help me. I have no money and have to feed my family and get medicine for my sick child." The first man is visibly moved by the story. "Oh, you poor man! Let me help you. Here is five dollars and may God be with you." The second man is unmoved. "Okay," he says, "my religious obligation is to give at least 10 percent of my income. Since I made a thousand dollars this week I have to give a hundred. Here's a hundred dollars. Goodbye."

Dennis Prager, a contemporary Jewish thinker and writer, routinely presents a version of this story to high school students across the nation. He asks them, "Which man did the better thing?" Almost unanimously, the students respond that the man who gave five dollars with kindness and love did the better thing than the one who curtly gave one hundred dollars. Then Prager suggests that the students put themselves in the position of the man asking for money. He asks them whether they would rather bump into the man who kindly gave five dollars or the man who matter-of-factly gave one hundred dollars. Again the students invariably answer in an almost unanimous voice. But this time they answer, "The man who gave one hundred dollars."

Tzedakah (Righteous Giving)

The Hebrew word *tzedakah* contains the same root letters as tzedek, "righteousness," and is most accurately translated as "righteous giving." It is most commonly translated, inaccurately, as "charity." "Charity," from the Latin word *caritas*, or "unselfish giving," suggests that the giving is done out of the goodness of one's heart. The Jewish concept of tzedakah is obligatory giving. Of course, it would be better still if the man who gave a hundred dollars did it lovingly and with good wishes. But tzedakah is not dependent on one's desire to give. It is a religious obligation and must be done regardless of sentiment. It is not about the feelings of the giver, but about contributing to the common good and helping fellow human beings.

During a recent election primary, a voter who supported a version of welfare reform that cut off benefits from many recipients was debating with a rabbi who was protesting such sudden cutbacks. The voter argued that there are plenty of people in the private sector who will help their neighbors and that it is not the job of an overtaxing government to fight against poverty. "The difference between you and me," he concluded, "is that I believe that people are basically good. Therefore," he argued, "government intervention is not needed to provide food and housing to the poor."

The rabbi paused, then replied, "I'm not sure what you mean by 'good' when 40,000 children die of hunger every day, and one quarter of the children in the wealthiest country in the world live in poverty. So you're right. I don't believe that people are basically good —or bad. In fact, I'll take it a step further. To me, whether people are basically good is not even the question. It is a non-issue. What matters is that we act to solve the problems we face."

Tzedakah is a social obligation incumbent upon everyone. If we were to depend on everyone to have giving hearts, we would first have to work to change attitudes and feelings, and then hope that

Moses Maimonides (known as "Rambam"), a twelfth-century scholar and philosopher (as well as a medical doctor), who is the most authoritative commentator on Jewish law in the last millennium, determined that there are eight degrees of tzedakah:

1. The person gives reluctantly.
2. The person gives graciously, but less than his or her means would designate.
3. The person gives the appropriate amount, but only after being asked.
4. The person gives before being asked.
5. The person gives without knowing the recipient, but the recipient knows the identity of the donor.
6. The person gives without making his or her own identity known.
7. The person gives without knowing the recipient and without making his or her own identity known.
8. The person helps another by enabling that person to become self-sufficient through a gift or loan, or help in gaining a skill or finding employment.

those feelings would lead to sufficient giving. Judaism is very practical and very clear about our ethical obligations in this realm. "Give 10 percent of your net income to those in need. It would be nice if you did it joyfully. But do it."

The section of the Torah that is called "the holiness code," found in Leviticus, begins with the words *k'doshim tib'yu ki kadosh ani Adonai Eloheikhem,* "You shall be holy, because I, the Eternal your God, am holy." Humanity is holy because God is holy—but our expression of that holiness is not, for the most part, through our actions toward God, such as worship, meditation, or sacrifices; the holiness code focuses on our responsibilities toward other people.

One of the first declarations of the holiness code reads, "When you reap the harvest of your land, you shall not reap the corners of your field, or gather the gleanings of your harvest. You shall not pick your vineyard bare, or gather the fallen fruit of your vineyard: you shall leave them for the poor and the stranger: I am Adonai your God." We are not permitted to consider profit as the sole purpose of God's land. We are merely custodians of the land, even if the "title" is in our name. If we take all the profit without leaving "the corners" and "the gleanings" for the poor, we are stealing.

Judaism applies this same value to all of our income. Our tradition supports the desire to make a good living. Life should be comfortable and joyful, and personal financial stability helps us achieve those ends. But we must remember that in some sense, all the resources we use to make our living, from paper products to our intelligence and our physical strength, come as divine loans. We are borrowers, and as such we have an obligation to share the products of that abundance.

> "Spare Me the sound of your hymns, And let Me not hear the music of your psalms. But let justice well up like water, Righteousness like a mighty stream."
>
> —AMOS 5:23–24

G'milut Chasadim (Acts of Lovingkindness)

G'milut chasadim is the doing of acts of kindness. The rabbis equate *g'milut chasadim* with all the other commandments combined, and there are many rabbinic sources that depict doing *g'milut chasadim* as directly imitating God. One text points out that the Torah begins and ends with lovingkindness: at the beginning God made clothing for Adam and Eve, and at the end God buried Moses. These examples of God's performing acts of lovingkindness point to another quality of *g'milut chasadim*: it is done with no expectation of being repaid.

Giving for its own sake begins in our own home and extends into the community. We do acts of lovingkindness when we visit the

> "When lovingkindness and truth have met together, then righteousness and peace have kissed each other."
>
> —PSALM 85:11

A SHINING EXAMPLE

Elka and Charlie Kuhlman have made a determined effort to educate their daughters Ruth and Eleanor about the importance of giving back to their community. "I felt like they never felt needed by our community. It was important to me that they know their role in the community. The world needs them for daily survival," Elka explains. In Austin, Texas, where the family lived before they recently returned to New England, they volunteered as a family at a local food bank. "When they would see homeless people on the streets in Austin, they knew the role they were playing. They knew that there was a way to help and be a part of the solution," says Elka.

sick, bury the dead, comfort mourners, and rejoice with a bride and groom. Of course there are many more examples of *g'milut chasadim.*

Tradition teaches that if you live in a community for 30 days, you take on the responsibility of contributing to the kitchen that feeds the poor. If you live there for three months, you become responsible for giving to the communal fund for tzedakah. Once you are there for six months, you are also responsible for giving to the clothing fund. Once you've been there for nine months, you also become responsible for giving to the burial society. Once you have lived in a community for twelve months, you must also assist in the repair of the community walls. One's responsibility begins with the most pressing needs and leads to those that are less urgent.

When Jews lived in shtetls, or self-enclosed European villages, it was always known when an act of *chesed* (kindness and compassion—the singular of *chasadim*) was needed. Everyone was expected to respond. Today our communities are spread out in cities and suburbs, so the need to be organized for the purpose of giving is all the more pressing. Some congregations have *g'milut chasadim* committees who are responsible for coordinating the efforts, carrying on the tradition of special societies in the Jewish communities of Eastern Europe, each devoted to a particular kind of *g'milut chasadim*—visiting the sick, caring for mourners and the dead, assisting brides and grooms. Through *g'milut chasadim*, our human interactions are made holy because we treat each other with the kindness that God has modeled for us and expects of us. The way we treat each other in our interpersonal relations and through social policy even has the power to affect our relationship with God. Rabbinic tradition teaches that tzedakah and *g'milut chasadim* create shalom (peace) between Israel and God.

Shalom (Peace)

Jewish tradition both sets peace as a goal and sets forth principles to guide and limit our actions in war. For example, we may not wage a war of aggression merely to impose our views or to acquire land, although we must enter into a war of self-defense. In war of any kind, the wanton destruction of trees—an act that would harm generations to come—is forbidden. The ultimate goal is to prevent the kind of conflict that can lead to war. The Psalmist instructs the person who treasures life to *bakesh shalom v'rodfehu*, "seek peace and pursue it." We must actively preserve and consistently work for peace.

The Hebrew word for peace, *shalom*, contains the root letters *shin*, *lamed*, and *mem*. These letters also form the word *shalem*, which means "wholeness." There are so many parts of our world that need to be made whole: the lives of many people we know and love (and many we do not); fractured communities in need of repair; raging illness and rampant hunger. Peace and wholeness are connected at their core. Peace is a natural result of tzedakah (righteous giving), *tzedek* (justice), and *g'milut chasadim* (acts of lovingkindness).

> **"**God says to Israel, 'My children, whenever you give sustenance to the poor, it is as though you gave sustenance to Me.'**"**
>
> —MIDRASH TANNA'IM

Judaism encourages us to strive for *shalom bayit*, peace in the home.

> **"**The sword comes into the world because of justice delayed, because of justice perverted, and because of those who render wrong decisions.**"**
>
> —PIRKEI AVOT 5:11

> 66 Mere praise of peace is easy and ineffective. What is needed is active participation in the fight against war and everything which leads to it. 99
>
> —ALBERT
> EINSTEIN
> Scientist

Perhaps the most elusive peace that Judaism encourages us to strive for is *shalom bayit,* peace in the home. The value of peace in the home is so great that for its sake God lies! When God told our matriarch, Sarah, that she would bear a child, Sarah laughed and made a reference to her own and her husband's advanced age. In reporting the story to Sarah's husband, Abraham, God tactfully reported that Sarah laughed only at the idea of having a child in her own old age. From this story, the rabbis tell us, we learn that peace within a family is so important that God may be less than truthful in order to maintain family harmony.

Our liturgy and home rituals seek to strengthen peace in the home. Lighting candles brings light into our lives and calm into our hearts. Shabbat and other holidays present opportunities to connect with loved ones, affirming human dignity. Peace is so great that God is called *Oseh Shalom,* "Maker of Peace." Your home is the sanctuary where you invite the Maker of Peace to dwell.

The Power of One

by Ann Moline

AS A YOUNG GIRL IN ANN ARBOR, MICHIGAN, Janet Green contributed a portion of her weekly allowance to charity. Just before candle lighting each Friday night, Janet placed some of her hard-earned coins in the family tzedakah box. At Shabbat dinner her parents discussed responsibility to the community. And each Passover, her father recounted the Exodus from Egypt while connecting the plight of the ancient Hebrews to a pressing modern issue, taken from the front page of the newspaper.

> 66 Judaism has had a very profound effect on me. Jews believe you can't have justice for yourself unless other people have justice as well. That has motivated much of what I've done. 99
>
> —BELLA ABZUG
> Former
> Congresswoman

Today, Green is deputy chief executive officer of the 1996 Democratic National Convention. Prior to this appointment, she served in the White House as special assistant to Eli Siegal, creator and first director of AmeriCorps, President Clinton's community youth service initiative. She attributes her career in public service in part to the foundation laid in her childhood. "My Jewish values are absolutely interconnected with my belief in the power of public service," she explains. "The emphasis on tzedakah and on giving to the community was as natural as brushing your teeth in my house. It was just something that you did."

Green's parents' active support of political candidates who were pro-Israel and who stood for other values they shared also influenced the course of her professional life. Her family's belief in the electoral process was so great, in fact, that when Green went away to college, her parents made sure that she exercised her rights as a citizen. "My mom always sent me my absentee ballot, because she was afraid I wouldn't make the effort to vote on my own," Green recalls with a laugh.

Get Involved! Some Practical Hints for Budding Activists

by Ann Moline

1. *Talk about the issues of the day.* Have your children each select one article from the newspaper that interests them, and discuss them at dinner. For families whose midweek dinners are rushed, Shabbat dinner may be the best time to discuss current events.

2. *Hold regular family meetings to discuss important (and sometimes not so important) family matters.* Doing this teaches children about negotiation, participation, and involvement.

3. *Make tzedakah decisions as a family.* Discuss which organizations should receive what portion of the family's tzedakah budget. Encourage older children to gather information on groups they are interested in supporting and to make presentations to the rest of the family.

4. *Volunteer.* Show your children that one person can make a difference. When you take on a project, be sure to talk with them about why you believe in its importance, and bring them along to help.

5. *Watch televised political debates as a family, if the children are old enough.* Discuss and debate the campaign issues and the stands of the candidates. If you don't like any of the candidates, discuss this fact too, being sure to emphasize the importance of the process.

6. *Vote!* That means always, even when the choices don't excite you. Take your children with you when you go to the polls. Even toddlers will understand if an explanation is framed in simple terms. Watch the election results as a family.

7. *Believe that you have the power to effect change, and show your children how.* If you are angry about a local regulation, do something about it. If your school year always begins on the Jewish holidays, mount

According to Jewish tradition, "the world stands on three things: on truth, on justice, and on peace, as it said, 'Execute truth, justice and peace, within your gates.'" (Zechariah 8:16) These three are interlinked: when justice is done, truth is achieved and peace is established.

—PIRKEI AVOT 1:18

By volunteering you show your children that each person can make a difference.

a petition drive to change the school calendar. Don't simply accept the status quo. If you do, your children will, too.

The Role of Parents in Creating Young Activists

by Ann Moline

THE LESSONS OF CIVIC RESPONSIBILITY must be taught at home, experts agree. Claire Scheuren, board member of Project Vote Smart, a non-partisan, nonprofit voter education organization based in Washington, D.C., says that the decline in voter turnout over the past years is symptomatic of a less involved society. "Young people are not responsive because parents are not. People don't think involvement can make a difference. This is the message they pass along to their children."

One cause of this communal disengagement is the increasing disillusionment with public figures and government in general, says Scheuren. Issues that once seemed clear-cut are no longer simple. Politicians have begun to sound alike. And there is a mean-spiritedness to the public debate that appalls many citizens.

Precisely because the issues are more complex, parents must renew their efforts to get involved and teach their children that one person's efforts can matter. Gordon Freeman, a rabbi in Walnut Creek, California, believes that Jewish parents should begin teaching their children civic responsibility through family dynamics. At the most fundamental level of interpersonal relationships, says Freeman, an associate of the Jerusalem Center for Public Affairs, lies the basis for political discourse. "Any time there is authority and power, there is the opportunity for politics," he says. "At the highest levels this means government. At the lowest levels, it means learning to negotiate within a family, and helping your children develop the ability to resolve conflict through discourse."

Political and civic involvement are inherent to the Jewish tradition. "Even in ancient Rome, Cicero complained bitterly about the impact of Jewish pressure groups on the Roman senate," Freeman notes. The covenantal nature of the Jewish people served as the model for modern democracies. The family unit is the most basic form of covenantal relationship, Freeman believes, and parents must teach their children lessons of participation, accountability, and responsibility through the give-and-take of family life.

Parents must also help their children look outward, expanding the lessons of family life to involvement in the greater community. This turning outward can take many forms. Claire Scheuren recom-

---

For more information on community activism:

- **Project Vote Smart.** Information on local and national political candidates, free voter's guides. Call 1(800) 622-7627 or check out the PVS website at http://www.vote-smart.org.

- **Exercise Democracy.** For free copies of Doing the Right Thing, a coloring book that deals with volunteerism and activism, write to 2636 North Venice Avenue, Tucson, AZ 85712 or call (520) 327-4824.

- **League of Women Voters.** Find out about Mr. and Mrs. Potato Head's plans to vote! Learn how to start a voting drive in your neighborhood. Write to them at 1730 M Street NW, Washington, DC 20036, or call their voter hotline, 1(800) 249-VOTE.

- **Beacon Press.** For a list of titles about teaching ethical imperatives, or stories of children who have made a difference in their communities, call (617) 742-2110.

mends finding a project to which the entire family will become committed, whether a neighborhood cleanup, collections for a local soup kitchen, or stuffing envelopes for a candidate.

"Children learn by doing," explains Scheuren. "Children are natural idealists, so if they see that their participation in a cause directly changes something related to their own world, it will make them believe in the process. It might also re-instill the value of activism into jaded and cynical parents."

Scheuren admits that political shenanigans can be depressing. "I'm a veteran community activist and true believer in the process, but even I get disillusioned sometimes." To combat the disillusionment, she suggests that parents redouble their efforts at the grass-roots level, working not necessarily to change the world, but to make their own corner of it a better place. And while they are at it, they should bring the kids along, so that some day, those children will know how to pass the tradition on to their own children.

Jeremy Feit, Student Activist

Joe Feit, an attorney in New York City, who has been an active supporter of the rights of Soviet Jews since the 1970s, brought each of his three children to the Soviet Union for their bar mitzvahs to visit Refuseniks. "He wanted to use our bar mitzvahs as an educational tool rather than just a milestone in our lives," said Jeremy Feit, now a 22-year-old student and activist at Columbia University. "I really learned from my father and my bar mitzvah experience that insurmountable problems can be solved by individual efforts."

This past year at Columbia, Feit was instrumental in working out the differences that erupted between African-American and Jewish students when an African-American student made derogatory remarks about Jews in a front-page article in *The New York Times*. "No one was trying to work out the problems," Feit said.

Using his connections on the student council and with university administrators, Feit organized several projects, including a bone marrow drive for an African-American and Jewish child, to improve relations between the African-American and Jewish students at Columbia. "Our interests don't coincide very much, and one way to approach the problem was to work together on a project that was beneficial for us both."

Ann Moline is a freelance writer and journalist living in Alexandria, Virginia. She and her husband, Jack, are the parents of three children.

> **"**And as much as I learned from my father, I learned about compassion and family values from my mother, Lillie Specter. It was my mother who would tell me that in America I could be anything I wanted to be—even president. And I listened to her, and I am still listening to her.**"**
>
> —ARLEN SPECTER
> U.S. Senator

How to Raise Moral (and Jewish) Children

by Helen Mintz Belitsky

WHEN MY SON, AARON, WAS LITTLE, we would sometimes find ourselves stuck in a line at the supermarket behind an elderly woman slowly counting out her change. A superactive child, my son would chew his fingernails and mutter impatiently to himself, making it plain he had no sympathy for her slowness.

Does Judaism have something to say about how to behave in such a situation? Does Judaism challenge us to teach our children moral behavior? It does. At the heart and soul of Jewish moral values is the duty to remember our obligation to others. "Let the dignity of other people be as important to you as your own," teaches Ethics of the Fathers (*Pirkei Avot*), a portion of the Talmud. Since Judaism is about deeds, parents should emphasize this basic value by regularly showing how it translates into everyday actions.

Even the two loaves of challah on the Shabbat table have a lesson to teach us. Why, ask the rabbis, do we cover them? To save the bread the "embarrassment" of being blessed last, after the wine. If our rituals teach us compassion for the feelings of a loaf of bread, how much more so must they teach us about caring for the feeling of other human beings!

The Hebrew word for parents is *horim*, which means "guiding." To raise a moral child, you have to accept yourself as a guide to moral values. Parenting is not only about techniques, it's a matter of passing on to children values inherent in the Jewish tradition.

Reflecting on how your own actions are guided by Jewish values is a first step. Understanding your profound influence on your children is the second. Children watch you intently. Your choices and deeds build ethical memories within them. These memories, more than anything else they learn, will guide them as they choose between "What is the decent thing to do?" and "What's in it for me?" Your example empowers them and helps build a safe and secure family life.

You may not have a clue that your child is tuning in to your behavior, says Gene Ridberg, a psychologist in Kensington, Maryland, whose practice includes many children. When you engage in even the smallest dishonesty—cheating on a restaurant bill, or keeping the extra change a store gives you—you're passing along a message about values.

"When your message is not consistent with the values you preach," Ridberg explains, "a child feels vulnerable, making it harder to have the courage or the incentive to make moral choices later on in life." Ridberg's counsel caused me to think about my daily actions—replacing an item that I knocked off a store shelf or passing over a handicapped parking space. "We build memories in our children," says Richard Joel, father of five and international director of the B'nai B'rith Hillel Foundation, "by seizing the moment and drawing a lesson from it."

For my parents, the rabbi and rebbitzen (wife of a rabbi, often with many unofficial responsibilities) of a large synagogue in Flatbush, conscience and the "rightness" of things were important in human relationships. I grew up with a strong sense of morality about being a friend. I still remember my father taking me to task about the hurt I was inflicting on my best friend when we fought and I encouraged our classmates to be on my side. "All right," I remember saying as a 10-year-old, "I'll forgive her." He made it plain that forgiveness was not the issue.

The arbitrary canceling of plans with friends, to me, is hurtful and even immoral. I taught my son such a lesson when as a first grader he invited his best friend for a sleepover on a Saturday night. Aaron spent the day in high anticipation. The phone rang after Havdalah (the end of Shabbat), and his friend's mother told me that her son had changed his mind. Aaron was crushed, and at that moment we began to talk about what it means to be a good friend. Blu Greenberg, author of *How to Run a Traditional Jewish Household*, saw a lesson to be learned from her daughter's slumber party when she insisted that a classmate not be excluded. Peer pressure made the battle tough, but Greenberg was firm—being a *mensch* (a good person) overrides being popular.

Ethics in all things was Judge Abner Mikva's credo. The judge recently retired as White House counsel after a distinguished career as a congressman and an appeals court judge. His daughter Rachel, now the rabbi of a Reform congregation in Chicago, recalls standing with him at a bank's ATM machine when she was a child. "That day he tried to withdraw $25," she said. "To his surprise, out came $400. My father returned the cash immediately, and he also used the situation as a way to talk to me about honesty."

Winning is appealing, sometimes making decency a hard choice. As a 15-year-old, Rabbi Neil Gillman, associate professor of Jewish philosophy at the Jewish Theological Seminary of America, found it hard to make the moral choice when, as a Color War (all-camp competition) captain, he always used a one-armed member of his team last. "I remember telling him not to swing, to take a walk on balls," Gillman admits. As a father, Gillman created a set time for talking about ethics with his chil-

dren. "Sara and I used our Friday night table to air our own conflicts and ethical dilemmas, creating a setting in which kids could bring their problems to us for feedback."

Encouraging children to reach out to others, as these children visiting a seniors' center are doing, helps them develop a values system that recognizes the needs of others.

Building ritual and observance into family life helps children feel secure. "Explaining the meaning of Jewish rituals to children," says Rabbi Yitzchak Breitowitz, "teaches them a lot about the moral values inherent in Judaism. Sabbath candle lighting taps into a child's need for continuity, predictability, and safety." When mitzvot (good deeds or commandments) are intimate and personal they have power, and prayer suffuses a home with safety and peace.

Tzedakah, a central precept in Judaism, teaches compassion for others. Rabbi Nina Beth Cardin, editor of *Sh'ma*, says there are wonderful ways parents and children can work on a tzedakah project. Every parent, Cardin says, knows how children, surrounded by torn gift paper, high-tech games, and sports gear, are often dazed by the sense of plenty at their birthday party. "We wrap the duplicate toys and games and bring them to a shelter in our area. Because the children are sharing what belongs to them, they are doing their own tzedakah, not mine."

Ridberg sees tzedakah as creating inner strength and well-being in a child, who learns to share without feeling deprived. Rabbi Avis

Miller of Adas Israel Congregation in Washington, D.C., believes that observing mitzvot shows children that some responsibilities must be taken care of immediately and cannot wait. When the sun sets, it's time for Shabbat. When someone is bereaved, there are a prescribed number of days in which to pay a shiva call.

Greenberg used the mitzvah of visiting the sick to teach her children about the Jewish concept of *z'man kevua*, or set time. "When one of my children was sick, it was the rule in the house that when the other kids came home from school, they would pay a visit to the sick room. It had to be before their snack, TV, or a game."

Bedtime prayer is another example of a ritual performed at a set time. Reciting the Shema together creates a quiet, intimate moment of family closeness, love, and a feeling of inner strength. "When I finish reading to my children," Cardin says, "I recite the portion of the bedtime Shema having to do with the angels and God standing guard over us. I bless my children, touch them, and hold them, invoke God's presence, and create in them a sense of self-worth."

As our children grow up, we tend to blame ourselves for their failures and attribute their successes to destiny. Learn to take credit for what you succeed in teaching them as role models. I'm slow to admit I had anything to do with it, but Aaron is one of the most empathic people I know. Last summer, for example, he experienced the violent death of three friends and their father, who were murdered in their home. In becoming a reliable anchor for the mother, Aaron showed that he had learned from lessons of compassion we taught him. He visited her every day during the week of shiva. For many weeks after, he called her every day, and now, months later, he remains in touch with her through visits and phone calls. If you asked him about it, I'm sure he would say it would never occur to him to do otherwise.

Helen Mintz Belitsky is a freelance writer in Washington, D.C., who specializes in the Jewish community.

Chapter Ten

TALKING TO YOUR KIDS
ABOUT SEX

HERE IS A SCENE IN ALICE WALKER'S ACCLAIMED NOVEL *The Color Purple* in which two women are discussing sex. Shug Avery matter-of-factly informs her disbelieving friend Celie that "God love all them feelings. That's some of the best stuff God did." Most of us assume that Western religions view sex either as shameful or as a "necessary evil" for procreation. You may be surprised and heartened to find that Judaism's attitude is consistent with Shug Avery's: simply put, Jewish tradition both acknowledges the pleasure inherent in human sexuality and honors it as a means of sanctifying our lives.

The Bible and halakhah (traditional Jewish law) contain many sexual prohibitions, among them adultery and incest. One outgrowth of these and other laws is a disapproving attitude toward nonmarital sex (although the offspring of a nonmarital union bears no halakhic shame, while the offspring of an adulterous union does). It is also forbidden for a couple to have sex while the woman is menstruating. This prohibition is the basis for marital purity laws called *nidah*. Today some couples do observe these laws, citing their potential to keep the rhythms of marital life organic and exciting. Others struggle with the implication of a woman's impurity. Finally, Judaism is replete with references to both partners' obligation to respect and attend to each other's sexual satisfaction, with emphasis on the husband's obligation to his wife. Some modern *ketubot* (Hebrew marriage contracts) include this as one of the marital vows.

The concept of sanctity elevates the mundane in our lives to the holy. This is true of our sexuality as well. It is forbidden to have sexual relations on the solemn holidays (Yom Kippur and Tisha B'Av), and by the same token, it is considered a mitzvah to honor God by making love on Shabbat. In the Jewish view, sex is part of a world created in God's image and thus has an inherent goodness and beauty.

This is certainly not to imply that sex should be treated in a cavalier manner. The Bible and rabbinic texts are at once stringent and very open concerning sexual relationships. Sex should be

> **❝** Sexual intimacy is valued for the pleasure partners can provide each other, separate from the value of procreation. **❞**
>
> —TALMUD
> PESACHIM 72B

engaged in by a man and a woman who are married, and only at certain times of the month. But within that context, sex should be enjoyed fully. (We should note, however, that there are a few rabbinic voices that view sex as necessary simply for procreation.)

Evolving Attitudes Toward Sexuality

Today many Jewish communities expand the definition of sacred sexual relationships to include committed homosexual partners. This inclusion is based in part on the idea that everyone is made in God's image and that to deny the sexual orientation of God's creatures is to deny God's creation. Also our tradition teaches that failure to experience sexual pleasure is seen as a rejection of God's command. There is also the issue of family. Gay and lesbian lifetime partnerships can be the foundations of valuable Jewish homes and families.

One of Judaism's greatest strengths is its capacity to evolve and expand in response to the challenges of contemporary life. The full involvement of gay and lesbian families in our midst can more fully invigorate our communities with a sense of respect for and excitement about Jewish life. To honor the spectrum of loving, consensual, adult sexual relationships is to keep faith with our moral imperative to treat each other with the honesty and respect with which we ourselves want to be treated. Judaism strives to temper joyful and fulfilling sexual relations with mature responsibility. In practical terms, this means that sex best fulfills its Divine purpose when it is in the context of a caring, committed relationship.

Sex is a touchstone for intense questions about freedom and responsibility, passion, and sanctity. How do we wish to be treated in our sexual relationships, and in the rest of our lives? How are we to treat others? Can sexuality be a way for us to cement our inner truths of respect and compassion? What does it mean to engage in sex not only as an expression of love between two people, but also as a powerful, spiritual way of being in the world? For many of us, the process of asking these questions may bring us to a meaningful understanding of how we may live fully Jewish lives.

> **❝** Failure to experience sexual pleasure is seen as a rejection of God's command. **❞**
>
> —TALMUD
> KETUBOT 47B–48A

The Jewish standpoint on sexuality provides us with a lens into the whole of Judaism. Like all Divine blessings, it is something that can intensify our relationship to God, the earth, and each other. And like all blessings, sex is something we are meant both to rejoice in and to treat with care.

Talking to Kids About Sex

by Rahel Musleah

ZINA RUTKIN FOUND THE FOLLOWING ADVICE in a parenting book at her library: "On your child's eighth birthday, both parents should take the child out to dinner and have material ready that will explain the facts of life." Rutkin's daughter, Ariella, had turned eight three months earlier.

"I came home and told my husband, 'I blew it.'" Rutkin says. Later, she decided it was still important to have "The Big Talk." "I sensed there was a lot going on at school that I was shying away from," she says. "The book lit a fire under me."

Ariella had been hounding her parents to have another baby, so when she broached the subject again, Rutkin launched in. "I asked her if she knew how we'd go about having a baby," Rutkin recalls. "She started to wriggle and look embarrassed and said she didn't want to talk about it. I said, 'Let me tell you what I want to tell you.' After I was finished, she looked at me and said, 'I know that!'

"I thought, 'Whoa!' It was enlightening for me to find out how much she knew. But I was disturbed that she was embarrassed. I said, 'It's more than okay to talk about this. I'd rather you come to me if you have questions than get information or misinformation from your friends.'"

Rutkin says her training as a psychologist with a specialty in child and family counseling didn't make her any less nervous. "This is still sex, and this is still my kid," she says. "I wasn't sure what was the right amount to say so she would get the message that Mommy's here anytime you want to talk to her, but not overwhelm her with information."

Rutkin's story reflects common worries among parents in talking to their kids about sex. When should I start? How should I start? What should I say when they're 4? 8? 12? 15? How much information should I give? What Jewish values can I convey?

"There's no one correct way to talk about sex," says Dr. Daniel Gensler, director of the Child, Adolescent and Family Clinic at the Postgraduate Center for Mental Health, located in Manhattan. "There's a huge range in terms of what's normal that varies according to people's religion, their culture, their socioeconomic class. It's important for parents to act in accordance with how they feel."

> **❝**Part of my being able to talk about issues of sexuality has to do with my being so Jewish. Because of us Jews, there's never been a question of sex being a sin, but of sex being a mitzvah and an obligation. **❞**
>
> —RUTH WESTHEIMER (DR. RUTH)
> Sex Therapist, Media Personality

> **❝**The act of sexual union is holy and pure…whatever [the Holy One] created cannot be shameful or ugly.**❞**
>
> —NACHMANIDES
> Thirteenth-century talmudist, kabbalist, and Bible commentator

> Life companions
> who love each other
> as they love them-
> selves and honor
> them more than they
> honor themselves,
> lead their children in
> the right path.
>
> Based on
> —TALMUD
> SANHEDRIN 76B

"It's more how you act than what you say," notes Paulette Bourgeois, a Toronto-based author who wrote *Changes in You & Me: A Book about Puberty Mostly for Girls* (Andrews and McMeel) and a parallel title for boys. "If you have parents who are comfortable with their own sexuality and their own bodies, who are comfortable showing affection to one another, you're already ten steps ahead."

Dr. Bernard Novick, author of *Making Jewish Decisions About the Body* (United Synagogue of Conservative Judaism), agrees. "Children learn how to treat the opposite sex from how parents treat each other. Parents should set a model of love and respect."

Touching, hugging, and cuddling children from babyhood on helps children become comfortable about their bodies, Bourgeois says. As they grow and begin to ask questions, find out what they really want to know, she notes. She recalls a five-year-old child who asked, "Dad, what's sex?" Dad took a deep breath and delivered The Big Talk. The child took the identification card out of a wallet he had received as a gift. "So Dad," he asked, "do I write M or F?"

Too Much Openness?

Despite the positive values in talking about sex instead of treating it as a taboo, the pendulum has swung toward too much openness, says Dr. Samuel Klagsbrun, psychiatrist, executive medical director of Four Winds Hospitals in Katonah, New York, and chairman and professor of pastoral psychiatry at the Jewish Theological Seminary of

America. "To prove they are up-to-date, parents feel pressured to be far too informative at too young an age for the child. It's confusing, overstimulating, and unnecessary. The key is to deal with children in age-appropriate ways and not read into a child's curiosity adult sexuality concepts. That's self-evident yet amazingly overlooked."

When children are little, answer the question that's asked only, Gensler suggests. "Between ages three and five, kids ask why. That curiosity is a cognitive achievement that includes where babies come from. Where does a baby come from? It grows in its mother's uterus. Don't go into a long lecture about how a baby gets in there or what it grows out of. Let the child take the answer in and let it perk around. When there's another question, the child will ask it. This is not about withholding information. The same thing applies to nonsexual questions. How does a car go? You put gasoline into the fuel tank and the gas works inside the engine to make the car go. The child is not asking about combustion engines."

Why do parents feel they have to give the whole lecture? "Parents are nervous," Gensler says. "When you talk about sex, your own attitudes are right on the line. In parenting, you learn as you go along. How many times in your life has a three-year-old asked you where babies come from? You have to grow into a comfort with the subject." Parents who cannot overcome their discomfort with sexual discussions can offer their children a range of books on everything from how the body works to AIDS, he says.

Use Appropriate Language

Using physiologically appropriate language also sets an important tone. "Instead of using euphemistic or pet names for genitals, say vulva, vagina, penis, testicles," Bourgeois advises. "When parents teach their kids about parts of the bodies, how many add penis and vagina to the list of ears, nose, eyes, toes? It's important to teach that those are parts of the body that children can feel as good about as their big brown eyes. If kids don't know the appropriate terms, later on, when you need to give information, they will have trouble."

Recognize that inappropriate language can be an invitation to sexual exploitation as kids grow into adults, Klagsbrun says. Talking about "scoring" with a girl, for instance, can contribute to developing unhealthy relationships.

Dr. Pamela Shrock, a sex therapist and clinical psychologist, suggests that parents clarify for children what constitutes appropriate and inappropriate touch. If your child explores his or her own body or likes to play doctor, don't punish or react with fear or panic, she says; those are normal ways for children to discover their own bodies. "Tell the child, 'The body feels good and it's okay to touch, but there are some things we don't do in public.'"

A Gift of Knowledge

Between the ages of 6 and 10, provide kids with factual information about puberty. It's especially important for girls, because some begin menstruating as early as the age of 8.

"It's a gift of knowledge," says Gensler. "It can be empowering to a child for a parent to tell him or her the whole story. Try to wait for natural contexts rather than deciding that at 4:00 tomorrow we're going to talk about the birds and bees." Bourgeois, for instance, recalls talking to both her son and daughter about menstruation while watching tampon ads on television. She points out that television and movies, with their open treatment of sexuality, provide good openings for talking about sexual issues. "Let kids know they're normal," she adds, "that what they're going through is part of growing up, that it's scary and weird, but also quite wonderful."

Parents can demystify a lot of sexual nervousness and clarify misconceptions if they can keep the lines of communication open. While fathers often feel more comfortable talking to sons, and mothers to daughters, it's also important for parents to talk to children of the opposite sex, experts say. And, they add, boys and girls need to have an understanding of each other's anatomy. Mothers can talk to sons about menstruation. Fathers can talk to daughters about ejaculation and wet dreams.

Bourgeois, who is now separated from her husband, recalls that her daughter got her period when she was with her father. "When she called to tell me, she said she'd be embarrassed to tell her dad," Bourgeois says. "I spoke to my husband and told him what to buy at the drugstore. Later he gave her a big hug and said, 'You're growing up. Let me know what I can do.'"

For kids to feel comfortable with their own sexuality, parents need to go beyond the facts, Shrock says. "Sexuality is how we feel about ourselves as male or female. Part of that is to have an awareness of feelings, that it's okay for girls to get angry and for boys to cry. Tell kids that there are different ways of expressing sexuality—holding hands, touching, and kissing—long before sexual intercourse. Stress that intercourse is done between two loving, caring, and committed people."

Parents may have trouble explaining the facts of life, but often they have even more difficulty explaining that sex is part of an intimate relationship, Bourgeois says. Clarifying family values and setting standards is crucial. Talking about sex provides an opportunity to transmit values such as responsibility for one's own body, respect for another person's body, privacy, and commitment. Many of the values are also Jewish values.

"In Jewish tradition, respect for the other person is paramount," says Klagsbrun. "Don't be insulting, abusive, or exploitative of another person, especially your mate. You can teach sex in a moral and religious context that preaches relationships as opposed to sex as a goal." As kids move into the preteen and teenage years, he adds, parents must "shift gears from watching and being available to influencing and directing."

Parents who are comfortable with their own sexuality will communicate a positive message to their children

Teaching Teens to Make Decisions

One of the most important things parents can teach teens about sex is how to make decisions, says Bernard Novick. "Teenagers are moving from dependence to independence. They are trying to figure out who they are and what they stand for. For kids to be raised to be independent they need information about the facts of life, about where Judaism stands, and where the family stands. But they also need to learn the skills of making decisions using those standards as criteria. My concern is that kids don't know how to process the information they have. It's left to chance."

Parents need to provide information for teens too—on sexual responsibility, contraception, abstinence, sexually transmitted diseases, and AIDS, Shrock says. Once, she recalls, she couldn't find her copy of *The Joy of Sex* that she used in teaching classes about sexuality. She found it on her 15-year-old son's bed. She took the book away and replaced it with a book about contraception, along with a note that read, "When you understand all the facts in this book, you may have the other book back." Shrock explains: "Contraception is a responsibility. It teaches that sex goes beyond what I want for me. You never coerce anyone."

Depending on their religious outlook and family values, parents should share their views on abstinence or safe sex. One parent interviewed for this article says she gave her 16-year-old son a package of condoms before he left for summer camp. Sharon Kalker, a social worker and an Orthodox mother of four, says her children know the facts about safe sex, but they also know that their parents do not believe in sex before marriage. Whatever you choose to teach your children, Kalker says, don't be afraid to make mistakes. "If they didn't hear what you said in the way you wanted them to hear it, you can always find another appropriate time," she says. "There are lots of moments for important conversations."

The Jewish Perspective on Sex

Once, when Rabbi Michael Gold was invited to speak on sexual ethics, he recalls being told, "Rabbi, religion belongs in the synagogue or church, but please keep it out of the bedroom." "Many modern Jews feel that sex is too private and too physical to be the concern of religion," says Gold, who set out to prove otherwise in *Does God Belong in the Bedroom?*. Children, too, need to understand that Judaism has a specific attitude toward sex, he stresses: "Judaism says sex is more than biology. The same biological act in one context can be a way of serving God and in another context can destroy a family. Sex within marriage is holy. Casual sex detracts from holiness."

"If sexuality is a way toward holiness, the ultimate decision-making criteria in sexual issues are what will result in more God-like behavior or goodness," says Bernard Novick, whose text, *Making Jewish Decisions About the Body*, is widely used in Hebrew high schools. He points out that parents may not be aware of how different Jewish, secular, and Christian views of sex are. "The secular attitude is that we're animals, so we do natural things, and sex is natural. Christianity looks at sex as the source of original sin and a necessity for procreation. In Judaism, we find that everything God created was good. If sexuality was a part of creation, then sexuality is good also."

Wide Range of Opinions

The Jewish community includes a range of opinions on sexuality, notes Novick. Sharon Kalker and Arthur Waskow exemplify that diversity. "The key for us has always been that a child is the product of a mother, father, and God," says Kalker, a social worker and Orthodox mother of four children, ages 14, 11, 8, and 6. "We told our kids that God was part of the process because He enabled us to conceive and have a child." Kalker says she taught her children that "sex is a wonderful thing that has its proper place, like eating delicious food and making a blessing over it. Every act has a physical and spiritual component." Her 14-year-old daughter has known about modesty and the laws of family purity for many years, she says, and understands that there are people with different lifestyles "but it's not right for us." Her younger ones know that "first you get married, then you have babies." "We have a system that we try to adhere to in all aspects of our lives," Kalker says. "Sexuality fits into that system."

Waskow, author of *Down-to-Earth Judaism: Food, Money, Sex and the Rest of Life* and one of the founders of Jewish Renewal, a dynamic, neo-Chasidic trend in American Judaism, says that because he believes it's unhealthy to remain celibate until the age of 25 or 35, he told his own children, now 32 and 29: "Sex is very powerful. It engages very powerful emotions. I urge you to approach it with care and I hope you won't wait until you get married to have a serious sexual relationship." "Some people think it's outrageous," he says, "but I think it's insane to pretend otherwise." While "it's correct that compared to most of Christianity Judaism is more pro-sex," Waskow argues, "it is also true that the mainstream Jewish definition is in terms of the narrow bed of heterosexual marriage, and not for two weeks out of four because of the laws of requiring distance during and after the menstrual period.

"One of the most alienating elements of American Judaism is that we know what Judaism says about sex and we ain't going to live that way. In one of the most important areas of our lives, we wall Judaism out. We have to reopen the sense that sexuality is sacred.

"The Song of Songs," he says, "is a good way to introduce teenagers to the concept of sex as a loving, pleasurable, and spiritual act." Waskow's practical suggestions include welcoming a girl's menstruation as a celebratory moment in a community of women, and introducing boys around the age of 16 to a condom as "a sacred tool as much as tefillin [phylacteries]." Parents don't have to be soaked in Jewish knowledge to open discussions of sexuality based on the numerous Bible stories with archetypal and universal themes that raise questions about the intersection of sexuality, ethics, and spirituality. "Kids will come up with expressions of their own conflicts and can deal with them in safe contexts," he says.

Books on the Jewish attitude toward sex are good resources for parents who want to deepen their knowledge. For the many parents who fall somewhere between Kalker and Waskow, the conflict between what Jewish tradition teaches, what society encourages, and what makes sociological and psychiatric sense is hard to bridge, acknowledges Samuel Klagsbrun. "If you live in both camps, finding a level of permissible sexual behavior in modern society is quite a task. It's a serious issue that I don't have an answer to."

Parents should not feel they have to bend their values to accommodate what others feel is appropriate, Klagsbrun says. "Parents not only have the right but the obligation to set standards, including standards within the tradition. Kids need to live within a familiar structure. If they want to rebel against it, so be it, but parents do not have to apologize or soft-peddle their rules or regulations."

He points out, however, that excessive fear of sexuality can be repressive, destructive, and guilt-provoking. "Explain your standards from a positive point of view," he suggests, "stressing that the level of behavior that differentiates us from others leads to a deeper and more satisfying life."

Author's note: One day, soon after I had completed this article, my three-year-old was pretending a piece of cloth she had rolled up was a baby. "Mom," she asked. "How do you make a baby?" Having learned to find out exactly what my child was asking, I answered, "You mean, how can you roll this cloth back up into a baby?" "Yes," she nodded. I smiled.

Parents' Guide to Talking About Sex

1. *Deal with children in age-appropriate ways.* Don't read adult sexuality concepts into a child's curiosity.

2. *Find out what it is your child wants to know, then answer that question only.* Don't feel you have to give the whole lecture.

3. *Use appropriate language for body parts and sexual acts.* Euphemisms and slang terms will communicate discomfort or shame.

4. *Clarify for your children what constitutes appropriate and inappropriate touch.*

5. *Give factual information about puberty when your daughter is between the ages of 6 and 10, so that when she reaches menarche she already knows what is happening in her body.*

6. *Keep the lines of communication open.* Talk to all of your children; don't leave it up to your partner to talk with children of the opposite sex.

7. *Go beyond the facts.* Talk about values, including responsibility, respect, privacy, and commitment. Stress relationships, rather than sex, as the goal.

8. *As children become teenagers, shift gears from being available to influencing and directing.* Teach your teenager how to make decisions.

9. *Give teens information about sexual responsibility, contraception, and sexually transmitted diseases.* Depending on your religious outlook, share your views on abstinence or safe sex.

10. *Don't be afraid to make mistakes.* There will be opportunities to clarify your views in the next conversation.

The Jewish View of Sex

by Dr. Ruth Westheimer and Jonathan Mark

IN THE JEWISH MARRIAGE CEREMONY, sexual satisfaction is part of the contract. Under the wedding canopy, a groom promises his bride that he will provide her with comfortable standards of food, shelter, and sexual gratification. The holiest men are required to marry. Celibacy is not a virtue—orgasms are.

Judaism is intensely sexual. Ramban [Nachmanides, a medieval rabbi] taught in *Igeret Hakodesh* [The Holy Letter]: "When sexual inter-

259

course is done for the sake of heaven, there is nothing so holy and pure....God did not create anything that is ugly or shameful. If the sexual organs are said to be shameful, how can it be said that the Creator fashioned something blemished?"

Adds the *Zohar*, the main Jewish mystical text: "The Divine Presence rests on the marital bed when both male and female are united in love and holiness....After the destruction of the Jerusalem Temple, the bedroom in each home was considered as an aspect of the once glorious and sanctified Holy of Holies."

How is a young religious couple to know how to go about having good sex? There's a story in the Talmud about a rabbi (known simply as Rav) who was having sex with his wife on Friday night, after a very good Shabbos meal, when he suddenly had a strange feeling that there was a third person in the room. He got up, looked behind the curtain, in the closet, under the bed, and lo and behold, there was his favorite student (Rabbi Kahana) hiding under the bedsprings. Rav said:

"Is this proper behavior, for a yeshiva boy to be under the rabbi's bed while the rabbi performs the mitzvah (God's commandment) of intercourse?"

The yeshiva boy answered: "Rabbi, what you are doing is a mitzvah from the Torah, and I must learn from you!"

What is interesting here is Judaism's braiding of sexual openness and sexual modesty. The yeshiva boy convinces the rabbi that his audacity is legitimate because knowing how to perform intercourse is a legitimate part of his religious and spiritual education. Nevertheless, the boy understands that he must hide. This dialectic is ongoing, not only within the tradition but within each of us who seeks to balance our need for modesty and privacy with our need for sexual education.

Sex, in and of itself, has never been a sin for Jews, or something not to discuss. Within Sinai's conventional boundaries, it is a mitzvah, religious commandment. And what is a mitzvah except a blessing, or a guide on how our lives can be more heavenly?

In the Jewish tradition, sex is very much in the mind of the beholder, in the mind where a healthy approach to sex made good sex possible for Jews in the most trying of circumstances and situations. As the Talmud teaches us in tractate Sanhedrin: If a man and a woman are truly lovers, they can make their bed on the edge of the sword; if their love goes bad, the best bed in the world is not big enough.

Reprinted from *Heavenly Sex: Sexuality in the Jewish Tradition* by Dr. Ruth K. Westheimer and Jonathan Mark, © 1995, New York University Press.

Chapter Eleven

RESPECTING THE HUMAN BODY, EARTH, AND NATURE

The earth and all its fullness belongs to God.
(Psalm 24:1)

IN THE BIBLICAL ACCOUNT OF CREATION, AS GOD MADE THE EARTH and all the life on earth, God found each new creation "good." The physical world came into being in six days and is described one day at a time: light and darkness, the separation of heaven and earth, gathering waters so that there is dry land and its vegetation, sun and moon, creatures of the sea and sky, and creatures of dry land, including humans.

God created humans in God's own image and blessed them and said to them, "Be fruitful and multiply, fill the earth and master it; and rule the fish of the sea, the birds of the sky, and all the living things that creep on earth." At the end of the sixth day, when God saw all of creation, God found it "very good."

This "very good" world is the vehicle through which we are able to see God's presence, which is otherwise palpable but invisible to us. So it's impressive (and maybe a bit surprising) that God seems to hand this holy creation over to humans to rule. The gift of the earth is testament to the fact that God sees us as partners in the continuing creation of the world. There is still a great amount to discover, create, fix, and improve, and we are empowered to do that work.

Later in the same biblical portion, God gives basic parameters within which humans are to do their work, making clear that although we have domain in the world, we are not owners of it. There are rules by which we must abide. God puts Adam, the first human, in the Garden of Eden to "work" the land and "guard" it. We may extract our livelihood from the earth, but we must also protect it.

This paradigm of using the physical world for our needs while carefully preserving it also applies to the human body. Bodies are holy because they are part of God's creation and thus "on loan" to us. The earth is seen as "God's body," in the sense that through it, along with our own innate sense, we are able to experience God. Similarly, the human body is the only way to experience the soul as well as the rest of God's world. The human body and soul are partners in being a person, created in the image of God. Therefore we are obliged to protect and nourish our bodies.

There is a Jewish concept of a messianic age at which time all the righteous will be bodily raised from the dead. Rabbi Neil Gillman of the Jewish Theological Seminary teaches that the myth of bodily resurrection in the messianic age serves less to provide an image of what this age will bring, than to validate the essentialness of the bodies in which we live our lives now. There is a Jewish notion of afterlife, but we understand death in its finality. We have the notion of a future redeemed world, but we protect the one we have because it's the only one we've got!

Our bodies (created by God) and the rest of the natural world (God's creation and dwelling place) deserve utmost care. The rabbinic notion of *sh'mirat ha-guf* (protection of the body) teaches that we must take care of our bodies and not wantonly damage them. Similarly, the biblical notion of *bal tashchit* (you shall not destroy) teaches that we must not wantonly destroy the natural world. It is interesting to note that *bal tashchit* is taught in the context of war: We may not destroy fruit trees for the sake of battle. Even though we have less than perfect ways of being human, we must keep sight of the dignity and sanctity of all life.

The rabbis teach: "At the moment when the Holy One created Adam, the first human, God said, 'See My works, how fine and excellent they are! All that I created I created for your benefit. Think upon this and do not corrupt and destroy My world. For if you destroy it, there is no one to restore it after you.'"

Custodians of Creation

by Sharon Goldman Edry

It's not easy getting kids to eat right. Shira Dicker, a mother of three and a self-described "health-food mom," has experienced this challenge firsthand.

"I worked at a sleepaway camp several years ago, where my son Adam attended," she explains. "Adam was so excited to be in his own bunk, out of my jurisdiction. He said, 'I'm going to eat anything I want, whenever I want,' particularly the fluffernutter sandwiches he heard everyone eats at camp. So I said, 'Fine, go ahead.'"

But by the second week of camp, Adam was at his mother's side, telling her how disgusting the food was, and that he wanted to eat healthy food again. "Eating in a healthy way and taking care of my body is just an outgrowth of my Jewish outlook on life, and I guess I've passed it along to my kids," says Dicker.

Teaching our children Jewish ethics and morals comes with the Jewish parental territory. Honesty, charity, kindness, and doing good deeds—to offer a few examples—are concepts that usually receive regular attention throughout childhood.

But there are other important ethics, and one of Judaism's central tenets is the importance of protecting God's creations. Helping children to understand that we need to care for everything on the earth, including the health of our own bodies, is as vital a task for parents as teaching children the importance of helping the needy.

"We try to teach our children a sense of awe and wonder at the greatness of God," says Rabbi Wayne Dosick, author of *Golden Rules: The Ten Ethical Values Parents Need to Teach Their Children*. "We want to respect everything around us, including our own physical needs."

Three Jewish values are central to this entire concept, and they all revolve around the ethics of gratitude and compassion. The first is *bal taschit*, a prohibition against destruction and wastefulness, encouraging us to take care of the earth around us. The second is *sh'mirat ha-guf*, which literally means "defending our bodies" and which emphasizes the importance of eating right, exercising, and not taking excessive physical risks. Jews are also not supposed to tattoo or maim their own bodies or to abuse drugs or alcohol. The third value is *tza'ar ba'alei chayim*, which prohibits cruelty to animals.

> 66 All that [we] see—the heaven, the earth, and all that fills it—all these things are the external garments of God. 99
>
> **REBBE SHNEOUR ZALMAN**, Belorussia, 1745–1813

Vegetarianism is a perfect blend of everything in this chapter. It encompasses Jewish dietary practices, which symbolize the fact that we are holy like God. It promotes healthy eating habits, which are in line with the religious obligation to treat our bodies well. It addresses the commandment to not be cruel to animals by not killing them. It means eating in a way that doesn't consume too many resources, treating the natural world with care and respect, and helping care for other human beings by addressing hunger issues. All of these things serve to express our sense of connection to, not separateness from, the natural world.

> ❝ The world is a tree and human beings are its fruit. ❞
>
> **RABBI SOLOMON IBN GABIROL**,
> Malaga, Spain,
> c. 1020–c. 1057

Not take excessive physical risks? Eat right? No tattoos? Many parents will laugh, thinking of their rebellious, risk-loving teens. How can this issue be explained in terms young people understand? And while taking care of the earth is a concept that may be taught on Earth Day or Recycling Week in a child's regular school, how can parents impress upon young children and self-absorbed teens the importance of caring for nature in Judaism?

Some Advice from Experts and Parents

"We come from a tradition that is profoundly connected to the earth," says Rabbi Bradley Artson, author of *It's a Mitzvah! Step-by-Step to Jewish Living*. "Judaism sees God as the creator and creation, as something beautiful and worthy of protection. It is important to bring back that part of Judaism that was so connected to seasons and cycles and nature. And our bodies are part of nature, connected to the larger physical world."

Showing children the world and helping to develop in them a sense of wonder and gratitude will help them to appreciate the importance of taking care of nature and their bodies. "If we see God in everything—in every leaf, in every tree, in the earth, in butterflies, and in our own body—you begin to have a great sense of awe and respect," says Rabbi Dosick.

> ❝ My daddy said that if you think you're too big for your britches just go stand in the ocean and feel how small you really are. I always remember that. ❞
>
> —**GOLDIE HAWN**
> Actress

Talking About Care of Nature

Start simple, suggests Shira Dicker. Even a trip to the beach can be exciting to a child and help him or her to feel the wonder of creation. "Kids pick up the seashells, watch the waves, see the tide changing, see the horizon—it's a wonderful thing," she says.

Children can be shown the power of nature just by taking a walk, says Dosick. "And if a walk is good, a hike is even better," he says. "Just by walking, you can see the greatness of the universe and attribute it to God."

Naomi Danis is a mother of three and author of the children's book, *Walk with Me*, about a mother and child taking a walk together and exploring along the way. Danis says she has utilized the walk as a way to connect with her children.

❝ Master of the Universe, Grant me the ability to be alone. May it be my custom to go outdoors each day among the trees and grasses, among all growing things, and there may I be alone and enter into prayer, to talk with the One that I belong to. **❞**

REB NACHMAN
OF BRATSLAV,
1772–1810.

Something as simple as a walk in the woods helps children appreciate the wonders of nature.

"It's great as a sort of cooling-off time with young children," she says. "You can make observations on things that they see. And if you see the child paying attention to something, even if they're too young to describe what they're seeing, you can share their experience."

Make the best of your situation, even if you live in a city where natural wonders seem hard to come by. "It doesn't matter if you are viewing the grandeur of the Grand Canyon or a sliver of sun through a sea of skyscrapers," says Dosick. "It's still the greatness of God."

❝ The best remedy for those who are afraid, lonely, or un-happy is to go outside, somewhere where they can be quite alone with the heavens, nature, and God. Because only then does one feel that all is as it should be and that God wishes to see people happy, amidst the simple beauty of nature. As long as this exists, and it certainly always will, I know that then there will always be comfort for every sorrow…. And I firmly believe that nature brings solace in all troubles. ❞

—ANNE FRANK
Holocaust Victim

Dicker admits that most of her spiritual experiences have happened in more rural settings. "During the summers, we head up to a cabin community on a lake. It's a perfect time to go climbing, sleep under the stars, run barefoot, and go to country fairs. We try to spend as much time outdoors as possible."

There are other ways, of course, to show children how to show respect for nature. Recycling, composting, and buying environment-friendly items are all ways to care for nature and show children that we should not be wasteful.

The everyday act of cooking, too, can show children the importance of eating right and not wasting food, says Danis. "My kids have each cooked one night a week for several years," she says,

Recycling is just one of many ways you can show children how to respect nature.

adding that she usually serves as the child's 'assistant.' "I think it's an important way of teaching them to take care of their bodies and what they eat, and how to be independent."

The Jewish holiday of Tu B'Shevat, which celebrates the New Year of Trees, is another good time to involve children in the act of growing things. Eating different types of fruit at a Tu B'Shevat seder or planting a tree is a good way to spend this holiday with a child.

Nurturing a garden can be great fun for children, says author and psychotherapist M. Gary Neuman, a father of five. "Kids like herbs, tomatoes, cucumbers, things that you can use." With that kind of activity, he says, a child comes to respect his or her environment.

Talking About Care of the Human Body

"People are made in God's image," says Rabbi Artson, "and how we treat our bodies is very much of an expression of our love for God." But in an age when esthetic beauty seems to take precedence over health, things such as clothes and dieting can appear more important than eating right and exercising.

First you need to get children to understand the importance of the body, explains Artson. Parents need to communicate to children that their bodies require a balance. "The Jewish balance is one of modesty and of caretaking. We treat ourselves in a healthy way because we are made in God's image."

There are special blessings for many things having to do with the body: after washing the hands and after going to the bathroom, for example. "Those kinds of *brakhot* can make children conscious of the fact that appreciation for the functioning of the body is a mitzvah," says Artson, who says that he tacks up translations of such blessings in the bathroom of his home.

But teaching children to care for their bodies needs to be understood within the context of their emotional well-being as well, says Neuman. "Your soul and your body go together," he says. "A lot of kids with low self-esteem think they don't deserve to look great or feel good."

Try to figure out what a child's motivation is when dealing with some of these issues, recommends Neuman, particularly with teenagers who may begin to experiment with smoking, drugs, body piercing, or other things that parents consider unhealthy (or just unattractive). "Instead of just presenting kids with facts like, 'This is bad for you' or 'Judaism says this is wrong,' try to find out what's

> **"**What poverty surrounded my youth, what trials my father had with us nine children. And yet he was always full of love and in his way a poet. Through him I first sensed the existence of poetry on this earth. After that I felt it in the nights, when I looked into the dark sky.**"**
>
> —MARC CHAGALL
> Artist

Children who understand the importance of the body are more likely to treat it with respect.

going on," says Neuman. "Find out what is attracting the child to smoking, for example. Does he think it looks cool? Is it peer pressure? Then you can deal with that."

Talking About Care of God's Creatures

If you want your children to see a miracle of God's creations, have them witness a birth, says Rabbi Dosick. "If they don't have the opportunity to see the birth of a human baby, or perhaps a puppy or kitten, even seeing a seed growing in a cup can help them to see the power of creation."

Even if your children do not have the opportunity to see how animals come into the world, caring for an animal can help children become more responsible and sensitive. "There's a great line from the Talmud that says, 'When you get home and you're hungry, you feed your animals before you feed yourself,'" Dosick says. "That shows compassion."

Even feeding the pigeons in the city or the seagulls at the beach can help children become exposed to animals, says Neuman. "It's a matter of helping your kids become connected with things on the earth." Give them the opportunity, he says, even if you just take them to the zoo.

The Importance of Modeling

The most important way for parents to impart the concept of caring for the earth, its creatures, and our own bodies is by setting a good example, say many experts and parents. "It's like anything else," asserts Rabbi Dosick. "If you don't want your kids to smoke, don't smoke. If you want your kids to exercise, you exercise."

That is, of course, easier said than done. Many parents find it hard to stay focused on health and well-being. As much we try to eat right, exercise, and stay away from bad things, it's hard to be perfect. "But we all make our choices, and it is important for children to understand that," says Dosick.

Shira Dicker admits fudging the truth on certain occasions, particularly on the subject of drugs. "It gets sticky there," she says. "I had access to recreational drugs when I was young, but I don't want my kids doing that. So I have never told the full truth about that part of my past, because I don't want to set the wrong example."

There is also the thorny issue of witnessing other people doing what you are trying to tell your children is wrong. Dicker recalls her children coming to her after seeing a religious man who was overweight and smoking. "They said, 'Why doesn't he understand that God wants him to preserve his own body?'"

But not everyone sees Judaism in the same way, and children should also be taught not to stand in judgment of others, says Artson. "I tell my kids not to worry as long as they are doing as well as they can be doing."

 # Hands-On Judaism

1. **Go to the beach.** This can be exciting for the child and help him or her feel the wonder of creation. Watch the waves, feel the sand, and see the horizon.

2. **Take a walk or a hike with your child.** No matter if you see the grandeur of a mountain or a sliver of sky through a skyscraper landscape, you can point out the greatness of the universe.

3. **Recycle, compost, and buy environment-friendly items.** These are all ways to care for nature and show children how to avoid waste.

4. **Have the children cook dinner.** The everyday act of cooking can teach children how to eat right, not waste food, and become independent.

5. **Celebrate Tu B'Shevat, the New Year of the Trees.** Eating different kinds of fruit or planting a tree are good ways to spend this day with a child.

6. **Have your children nurture a garden.** Let them grow herbs, tomatoes, cucumbers, or carrots. Not only will they enjoy the act of growing the produce, but they'll get to use the fruits of their labor as well.

7. **Say blessings.** There are blessings to say after going to the bathroom, when you wash your hands, when you eat, when you see thunder or lightning. These can help make children conscious of the fact that the functioning of both the body and nature is a blessing.

8. **Witness a birth.** If the opportunity to show your child the birth of a human baby does not present itself, then perhaps the birth of a puppy or kitten will. Even showing a child a seed growing in a cup will help him or her see the power of life.

9. **Let your children take care of a pet.** Doing this can help them learn respect for animals and life, as well as responsibility.

10. **Show by example.** Face it, if you don't want your children to smoke, you shouldn't smoke. If you don't want your children to litter, don't litter.

Chapter Twelve

THE VALUE OF MONEY

Who is wealthy? One who is happy with what they have.
—*Pirkei Avot*

ON MANY PEOPLE'S LIST OF UNCOMFORTABLE TOPICS, money ranks higher than sex. In our culture, it is considered boorish to ask people how much money they make or how much they paid for their house. This discomfort is apparent in public discourse as well. Conversations about minimum wage and welfare reform rarely focus on how much money people actually have to live on; instead they focus on issues such as the effect on the greater economy, the undeserving nature of the worker or welfare recipient, and corporate well-being.

Not all cultures have these limits on discussions about money. When Yosef was a college student in Israel, his group of American students was given an assignment. They were to go out on the street and ask strangers three questions: How much money do you make? How much do you pay in rent (or how much did you pay for your home)? How much money do you give to tzedakah? The students were shocked and afraid they would give Americans a bad image. But they were assured that no one would be offended. And no one was. Every Israeli who was approached on the street responded to the questions with ease and in detail.

Money in the Minds of the Rabbis

The culture of the rabbis of the Talmud that informed the regulations concerning business, financial dealings, personal wealth, and tzedakah certainly did not have the baggage and self-consciousness

> **❝**There are eight things that are harmful in large quantities but good in small quantities. They are: traveling, sexual intercourse, wealth, work, wine, sleep, hot baths, and blood-letting.**❞**
>
> TALMUD *Git-tin* 70A

"Were you honest in your business dealings?" This question teaches that business is not separate from life, is not accountable only to rules of profit and financial gains as is suggested in the motto, "business is business" and in the idea that the "bottom line" is financial and not ethical.

that we do concerning the issue of money. The rabbis had a solid self-understanding in terms of their relationship with God and their subsequent obligations. One of the ways this understanding of their covenant with God manifested itself was through the role of money in their lives and how money fit into their world.

The rabbis viewed the tools and objects used in our lives as value-free. Things such as weapons, alcohol, and money were not seen as inherently good or evil. All three have the abilities to perpetuate evil and to accomplish holy ends. Guns in the hands of peace-keepers or police can save lives, but in the hand of a criminal or dictator, weapons are instruments of violence. Jewish tradition teaches the concept of *taharat ha-neshek,* the "purity" of weaponry, sensitizing soldiers and their commanding officers to the potential for good and evil within each bullet.

Drunk drivers cause death and injury in the United States every year, and alcohol abuse is often connected to domestic violence and financial decline. Yet alcohol itself is not viewed as inherently negative or positive by Jewish tradition. We are instructed to use wine to sanctify nearly every holiday and life-cycle event.

When we allow weapons, alcohol, or money to have power over us, we don't use them in ways that reflect a consciousness of holiness. When we exercise control over them, we can use them in ways that honor our values. As Joshua Steinberg wrote at the turn of the twentieth century, "Money is a difficult master but an exceptional servant."

Money provides opportunities to enjoy God's world, to give tzedakah, to provide an interest-free loan, to be honest and fair in business dealings. As Abravanel, the fifteenth-century commentator said, "Although wealth is not a virtue, it is an instrument toward virtue."

Reb Saphra had wine to sell. A customer came in to buy wine at the time when Reb Saphra was saying the Shema, which cannot be interrupted. The customer said, "Will you sell me the wine for such an amount?" When Reb Saphra did not respond, the customer thought he was not satisfied with the price and raised his bid. When Reb Saphra had finished his prayer, he said, "I decided in my heart to sell the wine to you at the first price you mentioned; therefore I cannot accept your higher bid."

SHE'ILTOT, PARSHAT VAYECHI,
as found in *Judaism and Global Survival*, Richard Schwartz

There is a rabbinic teaching that the first question one will be asked in the "world-to-come" is, "Were you honest in your business dealings?" With money, as with other aspects of life, the way we behave can create holiness. The rabbis say that one who wishes to become wise should study the Jewish monetary laws, for in those they will learn about relationships, temptations, honesty, and ethics. The world of financial dealings is a microcosm for the whole range of human experience.

Money and Living a Good Life

The Jewish understanding of God is of One who wants us to enjoy life. In fact, as we've mentioned before, it is even sinful not to share in God's bounty and enjoy all the beauty and physical pleasures we can, in a moral and measured way. Our desire to live comfortably and well, to eat good foods, to sleep in comfortable beds, to travel, and to learn are acknowledged and even honored. In fact, the rabbis teach that one should give poor people who were once rich extra tzedakah so that they can get closer to the lifestyle to which they had become accustomed.

Wealth is a potential contributor to the value of enjoying life. Enjoying life includes interacting in the world with honesty and integrity. Therefore, money must also be a tool for fairness. For example, according to Jewish tradition, parents have the obligation to make sure their children learn a trade so that they will not become thieves. Workers must be paid a fair wage and must receive it in a timely manner. Our weights and measures must be accurate because we must be honest in our business transactions. The Bible states that we are obligated to let our land lie fallow every seven years as a reminder of our ultimate dependence on God for our wealth and well-being, and every fifty years we are obligated to return all land to its original (human) owners. This concept of a "jubilee year" is supposed to prevent all the land from becoming the property of a few.

Many Jews in Israel observe the commandment to let the earth rest one year out of every seven (sh'mitah), either symbolically or in reality. In markets, there are special areas for fruit and vegetables that meet the requirements of sh'mitah, such as crop rotation or transferring of ownership of the land for one year. Some tracts of land are simply left alone and are overtaken by weeds as the land rejuvenates itself.

Some of these laws may no longer be possible to follow in our own culture, but the underlying values can be applied to the current

> "Lending [money to a poor person] is greater than giving tzedakah (because the person receiving the money can do so with greater dignity); and putting [money] into a common fund [to form a partnership with a poor person] is greater than either."
>
> BABYLONIAN TALMUD *Shabbat* 63A

> **"**The rabbis taught: Who is wealthy? Whoever takes pleasure in their wealth"—these are the words of Rabbi Meir. But Rabbi Tarfon said: "Whoever has one hundred vineyards, one hundred fields, and one hundred slaves working in them." Rabbi Akiva said: "Whoever has a spouse who is pleasant in deeds [not necessarily appearance]." Rabbi Yose said: "Whoever has a bathroom right next to their table (indoors).**"**
>
> **BABYLONIAN TALMUD** *Shabbat* **25B**

reality. We are obligated to give 10 percent of our money (based on the after-tax figure) to tzedakah. Giving an interest-free loan to help someone start a business is considered a greater act than tzedakah.

The rabbis discussed this topic extensively, and many rabbinic stories were written about people who gave generously, creatively, and with modesty. As with all other aspects of money, and other "living tools," it all comes down to Jewish obligation. What does God expect of us? What will bring *tikkun olam* (a repaired world)?

The Jewish View of Money in Today's World

It's not easy to figure out the place of money in today's world. Sports figures earn millions of dollars a year; annual bonuses on Wall Street are six-figure sums; and Hollywood stars can retire on their share of the profits from one movie. Meanwhile, one quarter of our children live in poverty, some teachers are struggling to make ends meet, and many parents must take precious time away from raising their children in order to make enough money to pay the bills.

"You would think I was curing AIDS or educating children," says Susan's sister, actress and comic Sarah Silverman, reflecting on the money she makes in Hollywood. In a society that prizes wealth and status, how can we live by a system that defines the "value of money" so differently than does our Jewish culture? For Jews, the value of money is related not to how much one can acquire, but to how it can be used to live an enjoyable and meaningful life.

For example, attending the Wharton Business School may be a modern expression of the value of learning a trade in order to become a productive member of society. A Wharton education is inherently neither a good or bad tool. How graduates apply their business school training, and what they do with the large income they may earn, will depend on their value system.

On a smaller scale, the money a teenager makes from a summer job can all go toward buying a high-status sports car—or it can be distributed among savings, some "toys" and socializing, education, travel, and tzedakah.

Money, from the perspective of Jewish tradition, has an important place in our lives and in society. It can be a support for living an enjoyable and meaningful life in which the true meaning of "value" emerges.

An Allowance Is Not a Bribe

by Allan Gonsher

ALLOWANCE. The word is enough to make kids squeal with glee and send parents into panic mode. Parents know that children need money, and children expect to receive an allowance. But parents have many questions. At what age should a child begin to receive his own spending money? How much should she get? What expenses should he be expected to cover with allowance money?

I believe there is only one way to give children an allowance, what I call the "I Love You Allowance." Children get an allowance not because they're good or bad, not because they have done their chores, but simply because their parents love them. The amount of the allowance is predetermined and doesn't vary according to a child's behavior during the week. The allowance is not a reward for chores well done, and it isn't withheld as a punishment. When you

> **"**Abayye said: We have a tradition that one is not poor unless he lacks knowledge.**"**
>
> **BABYLONIAN TALMUD** *Nedarim* **41A**

One purpose of an allowance is to teach financial responsibility. So let your children make their own decisions.

give your children an allowance without any strings attached, you're saying, "I love you unconditionally."

Why is it so important to keep an allowance independent of your child's behavior? I have found that an allowance connected to conduct or to the performances of chores seldom works. You may tell your daughter she has to do five chores each week to get her $3 allowance. If she does only two chores, does she get $1.20? If she does six chores, does she get $3.60? The reward allowance can lead to disagreements between parents and children. Your children should have a list of chores they need to do simply because they live in the house.

When my three boys cleaned their rooms for Shabbat or set the table for a meal, they were thanked for their efforts, nothing more. They received their set allowance whether they did their chores, behaved at school, or attended junior congregation on Saturday mornings. If they misbehaved or failed to complete assigned chores, they received an appropriate punishment such as going to bed early or not being able to watch television.

You might want to provide a list of chores for your children to do to earn extra money. For example, cleaning the kitchen cupboards for Passover might be worth $10, raking the leaves in the yard might be worth $2, and so on. Post the list on the refrigerator where it's readily available for your children to see and choose from.

You determine how much allowance to give your child and whether part of the money goes into a savings account. It will be difficult to watch your children spend their money playing video games or buying candy. You might be tempted to manage your children's money so they don't waste it. But remember that one purpose of an allowance is to teach financial responsibility. This can be accomplished only if your child has the freedom to spend some money without your guidance.

Who controls the savings account? Before the account is set up, you need to determine whether you or your children control this money. Parents should control the savings account of a child under five. For older children there are other options: parents can continue to decide how the savings are spent; the decision can be made jointly by you and your children; or your children can decide for themselves.

You do need to be careful not to "bail out" your children by giving them extra money. As my boys got older, they wanted to visit friends they had made at *shabbatonim* (weekend youth programs) or summer camps. They had to save their own money to pay for the trips. From experience they learned that if they spent money on video games or going out with their friends, it took longer to save for a plane ticket. They also discovered that they could save money faster if they did the extra chores posted on the refrigerator.

An allowance helps children learn to make choices. For example, suppose you and your daughter go shopping at the mall, and she asks you to buy her a new doll. You respond that she needs to use her allowance, or a portion of it, to buy the doll. She must choose between the instant gratification of buying the doll now, or the delayed reward of saving for the new bike she wants.

Many parents wonder how much money they should give their children. There is no standard amount for allowances. You need to decide what will work best for you and your children. You could give a larger amount of money and expect the children to buy their own clothes and entertainment. Or you could give a nominal amount of money to spend for incidentals such as gum, candy, or comic books while you pay for the other expenses.

Children can learn at an early age to save part of their allowance for tzedakah.

The older the child, the greater the allowance should be. Periodic increases in the allowance can be negotiated, but parents must have the final say. As your children get older, you want to encourage them to seek other sources of income so that they know they can't always depend on you for all their money.

Children need to learn at an early age to help people who are less fortunate than they are. Teach your children to use their allowances to help others and to save part of their allowance for tzedakah. You might have a *pushke* (charity box) in your home, but you can also give children one of their own. However, putting money in the *pushke* is very impersonal. You might want to encourage hands-on giving as well. For example, when a *meshulach* (collector) comes to the door, involve your children in making him feel at home and giving him money. Or, when you are at the grocery store, encourage your children to buy a can of food to put in the food bank cart.

Here are a few more tips for helping your children learn how to handle money:

- Don't use money as a bribe to change your children's behaviors.

- Don't bail out your children after they have made bad financial decisions.

- Teach by example. Show your children how you manage the family finances, including saving for future expenses such as yeshiva, college, or a trip to Israel.

- Help your children invest their money so they see financial rewards for delaying gratification.

- Teach your child to give tzedakah.

Allan Gonsher is a father, rabbi, and therapist based in Omaha, Nebraska. He is writing a book on Jewish parenting.

Chapter Thirteen

INTERFAITH DATING AND MARRIAGE

HEN PARENTS ARE ASKED ABOUT THE QUALITIES they would want in a spouse for their child, we might hear words like *loving, honorable, kind, bright, sensible, funny*. The parents might describe this person as someone with whom their child laughs, or as a partner in building a meaningful and joyful life, or as someone with whom their child will become a fulfilled adult.

Some Jewish parents might also list "Jewish." There is so much involved in choosing a life partner, and the role that Judaism plays in that decision varies. The question of whether one chooses a Jewish spouse comes back, inevitably, to the importance of Judaism in an individual's life. If Judaism is nominal, then it may be difficult to see the value of having a Jewish household. If the language and structure that mark life and make it holy and meaningful are Jewish, then choosing a partner who builds with Jewish tools and honors Jewish goals makes sense.

For many Jews, however, this is not a cut-and-dried decision. A Jew may marry a non-Jew, and in the context of that relationship have a Jewish home and raise Jewish children. This type of union can lead to serious thought about what it means to be a Jew, and ultimately to a committed Jewish household. Two nominal Jews who marry might never engage in a serious discussion about religion, whereas somebody entering into an interfaith marriage may feel forced to examine his or her values. It is not uncommon in synagogue interfaith groups, for example, to hear a Jew articulating, for the first time, why it is important to be Jewish.

Interfaith Relationships in History

The tension between condemning interfaith marriage as a threat to the future of the Jewish people and seeing it as an opportunity to expand and strengthen the community is mirrored in the Bible. On

What has God been doing since creation? Making matches of loved ones, for making matches is as difficult as dividing the Red Sea.

Based on
GENESIS RABBAH
68:4

"Your tent is in peace..." refers to those who love their spouses as themselves and who honor their spouse more than themselves, and who guide their sons and their daughters in the right path.

TALMUD *Yebamot* **62B**

the one hand, in the book of Numbers, Pinchas is praised for taking a spear and attacking a Jewish man and a non-Jewish woman who are making love. He is rewarded by having a portion of the fourth book of Moses named for him because of his leadership in opposing Jews marrying non-Jews.

On the other hand, Jews historically consisted of a family, then a tribe, then a people, who grew in part by individuals marrying outside of the Israelites and bringing non-Jewish spouses into the Israelite community. No less a figure than Moses married Tzipporah, the daughter of a Midianite priest. When Moses's sister Miriam and brother Aaron criticized Moses—God's appointed leader—for his marriage to a black non-Israelite, Miriam was punished by God with leprosy. Later in biblical history, King Solomon married women of various nations to increase his influence in the region. Yet when the Jews returned from their Babylonian exile, the prophet Ezra decreed that all Jews should divorce their non-Jewish partners and rebuild the devastated nation through Jewish family units.

The most powerful story of interfaith marriage is that of Ruth. Naomi, her husband, and sons left Canaan in the Holy Land for Moab, where her two sons marry Moabite women, Ruth and Orpah. Upon the death of all three men, Orpah returns to her place of origin, but Ruth joins Naomi in returning to Canaan. Her words to Naomi have reverberated through the centuries: "Wherever you go, I will go. Wherever you lodge, I will lodge. Your people shall be my people; and your God, my God." A woman from an enemy people created the first formal conversion ritual and became the great-grandmother of King David, from whose lineage, the rabbis teach, will come the Messiah.

In the Bible and in rabbinic literature, there are many laws concerning who may marry whom. For example, incest is forbidden (although marriages between an uncle and his niece and between cousins were permitted). A man may not remarry his wife after he divorces her if she has been married in the interim. A man may not marry his brother's ex-wife, although if she is his childless brother's widow he must marry her and have children, unless he is ritually released from this obligation.

In rabbinic literature, there is no legal category for an interfaith marriage. In fact, it is completely unrecognized from the perspective of Jewish law. There is, however, a discussion of interfaith offspring: If the mother is Jewish, so are they. From the Middle Ages to the modern era, there were in fact very few marriages between Jews and non-Jews. When Jews did marry partners of the majority faith, they were usually obligated to convert to Christianity or Islam.

Interfaith Relationships Today

Interfaith dating and marriage used to be taboo in the American Jewish community, but that is no longer the case. Americans today are generally more tolerant of interfaith marriages, and Jews have followed the same trend. As interfaith marriage has become more common, children have increasingly been raised in two faiths. Only about a quarter of the children of interfaith couples are raised as Jews, a fact that has provoked Jewish leaders to call for increased conversion efforts directed at the non-Jewish spouse, Jewish education for the children, and other efforts to encourage interfaith couples to have a Jewish home.

Interfaith marriages present special challenges that require honest communication between the partners.

> **"** If husband and wife are worthy, the Shekhinah (God's presence) is between them. If they are not worthy, there is fire between them.**"**
>
> TALMUD *Sotah* 17A

One such effort has been to amend the 1,800-year-old Jewish tradition of matrilineal descent, which states that religion is passed from the mother to the children. The Reform and Reconstructionist movements both now accept patrilineal descent, provided the child is raised as a Jew. The Orthodox and Conservative movements still require formal conversion for children born to non-Jewish mothers. Many Jews hope that religious leaders from across the denominational spectrum will eventually find a creative and respectful way to acknowledge the Jewish status of individuals whose mothers are not Jewish.

For interfaith couples to choose Judaism as their system of living, they need to find an open door to the Jewish community. If this happens often enough, according to this line of thought, interfaith couples will add numbers and energy to our people. Then we will be able to have a communal discussion that reflects the many individual discussions that are happening across the country: What does it mean to be a Jew?

> **"** One who marries a person who is not an equal, Elijah shall tie him up and the Holy One shall lash him.**"**
>
> TALMUD *Kiddushin* 70A

What do Paul and Jamie Buchman (*Mad About You*), Fran Fine and Maxwell Sheffield (*The Nanny*), Dr. Joel Fleischman and Maggie O'Connell (*Northern Exposure*), and Michael and Hope Steadman (*thirtysomething*) have in common? They are all examples of television romantic relationships in which a Jewish character is partnered with a non-Jewish character.

"Hollywood writers have wrestled with their own personal life-choices on screen," says Dr. Jonathan Pearl, of the *Jewish Televimages Report*, a newsletter that monitors Jewish images on the small screen. "There are almost no Jewish-Jewish couples on television shows because there are so few Jewish writers who live a religiously based life with another Jewish person."

Can Love Conquer All?

A group of teens from a Reform synagogue in Boston tell how they feel about interdating and intermarriage.

Betsy Stein, 18:

"I don't think religion can dictate whom you fall in love with. Having a boyfriend is pretty much like having a best friend. When I become friends with people, it doesn't matter to me what faith they are. It's the same with a guy. It's important to me that my children be Jewish, but I think if I were really in love with someone there would be a way to work around it."

Max Shulman, 15:

"Personally, I have had very few Jewish relationships. I don't see it as an important thing and I don't think that is something that you think about when you're looking for someone. Love is love. Especially in a school like mine, where there are very few Jewish people. If you try to say, 'I will only date Jewish people,' you are cutting out a lot of people. If you date someone who is Jewish, it's just another topic, another thing you have in common. It's not like you go home and quote Torah together."

Daniel Older, 16:

"As long as it's a good relationship, it shouldn't matter what faith they are. I wouldn't pick or ditch someone because of Judaism. How someone looks at their faith does matter, like whether they completely resign themselves to it or whether they are passionate or questioning."

Alex Sunshine, 16:

"My sister is in an interfaith relationship. It's a burden on the whole family. In the past I've dated people who aren't Jewish and I've had great relationships. Now I want to meet a wide variety of people. I hope to marry someone who is Jewish. If I don't, I want to raise my children in one religion. I'd rather have them be Christian than half and half, but I hope that's not what it would come down to."

Joanna Sandman, 15:

"There are so many interfaith couples in my school. No one cares. As a teenager, interfaith dating is fine because I'm not going to get married at this stage. None of my friends discuss it. It's not an issue. Judaism has always been a part of my life. No matter whom I marry I will still practice it. Maybe it's not so important that I marry someone Jewish, as long as I can continue my Jewish life and have a child that is Jewish."

Ann Fishman, 16:

"Interfaith dating is an okay thing to do. Dating is just practice for getting married, for meeting the right person. When you're younger you are just trying out different things, to see whom you want to spend your life with. If you only date people of your own religion, you limit yourself to such a narrow field. What's really important is being happy. I think when I get older, I'm going to want to start looking for a Jewish man to marry. It's hard to raise an interfaith family. The kids don't know what they are, and they don't have a religious identity."

> **❝** [I converted to Judaism] because I wanted to be part of that strong and steadfast tradition that withstood and overcame thousands of years of bigotry and persecution. **❞**
>
> —SAMMY DAVIS, JR.
> Entertainer

Interfaith Dating

by Helen Mintz Belitsky

HEATHER LEVY, 17, A MERRY, SELF-CONFIDENT SENIOR, dates primarily non-Jewish boys and believes that religion should not get in the way of falling in love. She acknowledges that when children come along in an interfaith marriage "it gets really hard," but she sees herself as many years away from marriage.

Heather, who recently broke up with a non-Jew she dated for more than two years, says, "I find dating only Jews too limiting." Her mother, Bev, sees the handwriting on the wall but fears that to raise objections would reflect badly on her non-Jewish son-in-law, Pat, who is married to her older daughter, Laura.

Bev is struggling with conflicting emotions as she strives to balance the desire to keep peace in the family with a commitment to perpetuating the Judaism that was at the heart of her own upbringing. Jewish grandchildren is an assumption she has not relinquished. "As long as Pat respects our religion and allows and encourages Laura and their future children to practice Judaism, that's all I ask." She admits that her wish for a Jewish son-in-law is implicit but has not been articulated directly and unequivocally.

With Jewish intermarriage at the 50 percent mark and rising, it's obvious that the message "I expect you to marry a Jew" is not getting across in many Jewish homes around the United States. In the overwhelming majority of these intermarriages, the non-Jewish partner does not convert to Judaism, and in nearly three-quarters of these interfaith homes, the children are not being raised as Jews.

Through the years, the Levy home was warmed by Passover and High Holy Day celebrations and by the girls' childish bat mitzvah chants learned at Hebrew school. Still, a generation and a world of divergent values separate Heather and her mother. Heather is growing up in an open society that extols individuality, perplexes young people with choices, and offers the freedom to adopt new belief systems. Her parents belong to a generation that assumed from the "givens" of their own upbringing that their children would make the same choices they did regarding dating and marriage.

"I grew up in Baltimore, two blocks from the synagogue," Bev reminisces. "My friends and I walked to shul every Shabbes. The whole world was Jewish around me, so it was easy. I was naive enough to assume that it would be that way with my children."

Bev's father was Orthodox, and plain speaking characterized his message to her about marriage. "The bottom line was intermarriage was unacceptable," she recalls, "and I couldn't have thrived in such a marriage. Even now he lectures me about Heather." Bev thinks aloud about what she would do differently if given a second chance. "I'd choose a close-knit Jewish community in which to raise the kids. I'd send Laura to a college with a large Jewish population instead of Georgia Tech. I'd try to create a home with extended family close by, where Yiddish was spoken in front of the children."

In the Levys' neat brick home on a quiet suburban street, family life has gone smoothly over the years. The family had no magic formulas, but love, harmony, respect, good friends, and hard work graced their lives. Says Laura, "My sister and I grew up knowing our parents would love us and support us in our choices. They did, and it has made a lot of difference to us. I told Pat I wanted him to meet my family. 'If you meet my family, I told him, you'll know what I want out of life.'"

Pat and Laura respect each other's traditions. They make a seder and light Hanukkah candles. They celebrate Easter and have a small Christmas tree. Laura misses the large family celebrations. "Pat has learned that my identification with Judaism is less with the ritual and more with the traditions we celebrate as a family."

Bev Levy's sincere joy in her daughter Laura's marriage to Pat, who is a Catholic, has been mixed with regret. "When Laura met him I was troubled," Bev recalls. "I lost sleep. Steve and I didn't say much to each other. Neither of us was thrilled, but we didn't want to wind each other up." Later, drawn to Pat and convinced that Laura had found the man who would make her happy, Bev was reluctant to say a word to destroy her daughter's happiness or drive a wedge in the relationship between them.

Bev recalls: "It never occurred to me to date a non-Jew. It didn't occur to me Laura would marry one. But when Pat first got off the plane, it was as if we had known him all our lives. There was no doubt in our minds about why Laura fell in love with him, and he adores her."

Jewish memories, Bev believes, are part of what makes a person who they are, and Pat and Laura are trying to create their own Jewish memories. When Laura didn't get home in time to light the Hanukkah candles last winter, Pat did it himself, reading the blessings on the box as best he could, Bev says proudly.

"I expect you to marry someone Jewish" is one of the ten things Rabbi Jack Moline of Agudas Achim Congregation in Alexandria,

---

TIPS FOR PARENTS

Here are five suggestions for helping your children recognize the importance of religion when they start dating:

1. If you expect your children to marry someone Jewish, explain why.
2. Let them know that this standard applies to dating.
3. Talk about this issue when they are very young. Don't wait until their first date.
4. Create a strong, positive Jewish environment at home that supports your position on dating.
5. Enroll your children in Jewish activities, such as youth groups and summer camps, so that they have the opportunity to meet Jewish peers. This is especially important if you live in an area where your child is one of the only Jewish children in his or her class at school.

Virginia, believes parents should say more often to their children. Say it before they begin dating, Moline urges in a forthcoming book, *Tomorrow's Harvest: Planting Seeds of Jewish Renewal*. After that, it comes out like a judgment.

"What do you say after you've said 'No, you may not marry a non-Jew'?" asks Dr. Egon Mayer, professor of sociology at Brooklyn College, director of the Center for Jewish Studies at the Graduate Center of the City University of New York, and author of numerous studies on Jewish intermarriage, outreach, and conversion. "Because the no expresses a wish more than a powerful affirmation. Once it becomes an issue, saying no is a weak response," says Mayer. For parents anxious about the future Judaism of their grandchildren, the wisdom inherent in all parenting advice applies: consistent articulation of values without apology.

Parents heed this advice when it comes to teaching children about hard work, honesty, compassion, and loyalty. Yet somehow, plain talk about religion seems awkward to some parents, a contradiction of American values of tolerance and equality. Yet psychologists, educators, and rabbis underscore the value of religion in guaranteeing a child's security, sense of well-being, and rootedness.

Religion emphasizes a vocabulary of values, says Rabbi Alan Silverstein, former president of the Rabbinical Assembly of Conservative Judaism, in his book, *It All Begins with a Date*. "Religion is a way of teaching morality. It's a way to define yourself. It gives people a common history, values, traditions, rituals…in short, an identity."

Creating and sustaining Jewish identity in a family requires concrete daily reminders to children about what it means to be a Jew, says Rabbi Moline. "Say more often to your child: give tzedakah, be

Teens are at an experimental stage in their life. Interfaith dating during the teen years does not necessarily predict an interfaith marriage later.

at the Shabbat table, come to the synagogue, Jewish education is the most important part of your education, it's important to pray, this is what I believe about God, you have a home in Israel."

Put simply by David Epstein, the father of five children and an Orthodox Jew living in Maryland, "Guaranteeing Jewish identity is the sum of everything you do when you raise your children. It's not just telling them *don't*."

In the Epstein home, Jewish values of study, charity, and observance are creatively integrated into family life. The Epsteins eschewed anniversary gifts, choosing instead to buy a handcrafted mezuzah each year. The mezuzahs now hang on their dining room wall, one for each year of marriage. Shabbat dinners have always been the focal point of family life. "When the children were growing up," Epstein says, "we used to choose an episode from the Torah portion and assign roles." The family opted out of large bar mitzvah celebrations and turned such events into an opportunity for a unique experience—a theme trip of their children's choice. Son Jeremy visited his grandparents' birthplaces in Lithuania and Poland.

For Ellen and Roy Rosenthal, Reform Jews who gave their three girls a Hebrew school education but sent them to secular schools, Jewish identity is a matter of pride, comfort, and self-esteem. Their oldest daughter, Dayna, is married to a Jew, and Roy believes that a potential husband's religion places high on his daughters' list of priorities.

Says Ellen, "I've always been proud to be Jewish, without apologies. We opted for public schools, but I always thought of my kids as little ambassadors, good examples for people who didn't know much about Judaism." Adds Roy, "We told our kids from the beginning that marriage is tough. Choosing a non-Jewish mate simply adds problems down the road."

Asking young people to look down the road often brings the answers, "It's just a date," or "I won't be getting married for years," or "We'll bring up our children with no religion/both religions." In a group setting at Ohr Kodesh Congregation in Chevy Chase, Maryland, teens in grades 8 through 12, most of whom attend a multiracial and multireligious public high school, are being given the chance to wrestle with these issues among their peers. "We plan to ask the kids to role-play—pretending they are the parents explaining to their children the advantages they've experienced in being married to a Jewish mate," says Rabbi Lyle Fishman. "Listening to their peers downplay some of the difficulties may give them pause. They may end up turning to their friends and reminding them that there are problems."

Parents who engage their children in discussions about interfaith dating often confuse a frank and clear articulation of their values with seeking to win an argument, says Rabbi Alan Silverstein. "The absence of immediate victory," he cautions, "should not be mistaken for failure."

For Aileen Cooper of Washington, D.C., such discussions challenge parents to guide their children, respectfully, to articulate values without angry prescriptions. "Judaism was always a strong underpinning for me and for Dave, who had a strong religious education. There was never a question about whether I would marry a Jew. It was never an issue."

Cooper raised her children, Mitch and Amy, in Minnesota, where they were the only Jews in their elementary school classes. She and her former husband, Dave, were active in the Reform synagogue, and the children went to Hebrew school at different stages of their lives. The family later moved to Alexandria, where the schools had a larger population of Jewish children. "I never explicitly told my children not to marry a non-Jew," Cooper says. "I've tried not to undermine my kids' ability to make their own decisions, especially by the time they reached college."

When her daughter's relationship with a non-Jew was getting serious, she sat down with her and turned the discussion to consequences. "Believe it or not," she says, surprise still lingering in her voice, "Amy and Carter had not talked about children. When they did, it turned out he didn't want his children to be Jewish. The relationship ended."

Diane Radin of Austin, Texas (with a Jewish population of just 6,000), laments the small pool of Jews her daughter, Sarah, 18, has to choose from. "Sarah attended Hebrew school and belonged to Kadimah and United Synagogue Youth as she was growing up. But the Jewish kids she knows, she's known since she was two. I don't want her to interdate, but for years she was the only Jewish kid in her class." Radin looks forward to Sarah's attendance next year at the University of Texas, which has a strong and active Hillel (Jewish student organization).

Parents can open new doors for their children outside of their own communities. The Stein family of northern Virginia looked to Jewish camping as a way of providing their three children, each usually one of ten or twenty Jewish children in a high school class of 500, with a new network of friends and day-to-day experiences in Jewish living. With some financial sacrifice, they enrolled their children in Ramah Camps, which are sponsored by the Jewish Theological Seminary of America. The summer program is based on intense daily Jewish experience, including study, rituals, and travel to Israel. This camping experience changed the course of Jewish experience in the Stein family.

Says mom Evelyn, "The Jewish friends they made, they made at Camp Ramah. They learned more about Judaism and Jewish living in two months at Ramah than they did all year at Hebrew schools. Home observance changed. We began to make Havdalah on Saturday nights. We sang the Eyshet Chayil (Woman of Valor) before Kiddush on Friday night. I asked my husband to begin praying every morning."

Humility must temper predictions about interfaith marriages, and there are no permanent guarantees, only a lessening of probabilities. Parents do their best and fail, and regarding the unique dynamic between parent and child, it has been said, "We do not know what we do not know." The imponderables of Jewish identity and parent-child relations raise questions about the future of every young person.

The story is hardly over for young people who interdate, says Aileen Cooper, reminding herself and others that teenagers need to stretch their wings, to experiment. "Interdating need not be a predictor for lifelong patterns of living."

Heather Levy, who dates primarily non-Jewish boys and who dropped out of B'nai B'rith Girls with the first press of high school activities, is a case in point. Powerful emotional connections link her to her early traditions. The satisfaction of working toward her bat mitzvah and the flickering *yahrzeit* candle her mother has lit annually for her grandmother are among her cherished Jewish memories.

As she looks toward the time when she leaves the warm embrace of her home and departs for the University of Delaware, she pictures herself going to temple, "this time by my own choice," she says. Out on her own for the first time in her life, she plans to seek a place where everyone has a common history, value system, traditions, and yes, even stories and jokes. In a synagogue, she believes, she will find the community she all but deserted after her bat mitzvah.

Helen Mintz Belitsky is a freelance writer living in Silver Spring, Maryland.

Ten-Year Holiday Calendar

Jewish holidays begin the previous evening. When holidays are traditionally celebrated more than one day, Reform, Reconstructionist and Israeli Jews usually subtract one day from the observance.

Sukkot (7 or 8 days)

1997	Oct 16
1998	Oct 05
1999	Sep 25
2000	Oct 14
2001	Oct 02
2002	Sep 21
2003	Oct 11
2004	Sep 30
2005	Oct 18
2006	Oct 07
2007	Sep 27

Tu B'Shevat (1 day)

1997	Jan 23
1998	Feb 11
1999	Feb 01
2000	Jan 22
2001	Feb 08
2002	Jan 28
2003	Jan 18
2004	Feb 07
2005	Jan 25
2006	Feb 13
2007	Feb 03

Rosh Hashanah (1 or 2 days)

1997	Oct 02
1998	Sep 21
1999	Sep 11
2000	Sep 30
2001	Sep 18
2002	Sep 07
2003	Sep 27
2004	Sep 16
2005	Oct 04
2006	Sep 23
2007	Sep 18

Simchat Torah (1 day)

1997	Oct 24
1998	Oct 13
1999	Oct 03
2000	Oct 22
2001	Oct 10
2002	Sep 29
2003	Oct 19
2004	Oct 08
2005	Oct 26
2006	Oct 15
2007	Oct 05

Purim (1 day)

1997	Mar 23
1998	Mar 12
1999	Mar 02
2000	Mar 21
2001	Mar 09
2002	Feb 26
2003	Mar 18
2004	Mar 07
2005	Mar 25
2006	Mar 14
2007	Mar 04

Yom Kippur (1 day)

1997	Oct 10
1998	Sep 30
1999	Sep 20
2000	Oct 09
2001	Sep 27
2002	Sep 16
2003	Oct 06
2004	Sep 25
2005	Oct 13
2006	Oct 02
2007	Sep 22

Hanukkah (8 days)

1997	Dec 24
1998	Dec 14
1999	Dec 04
2000	Dec 22
2001	Dec 10
2002	Nov 30
2003	Dec 20
2004	Dec 08
2005	Dec 26
2006	Dec 16
2007	Dec 05

Holocaust Memorial Day (1 day)

1997	May 04
1998	Apr 23
1999	Apr 13
2000	May 02
2001	Apr 20
2002	Apr 09
2003	Apr 29
2004	Apr 18
2005	May 06
2006	Apr 25
2007	Apr 15

Israel Independence Day (1 day)

1997	May 12
1998	Apr 30
1999	Apr 21
2000	May 10
2001	Apr 26
2002	Apr 17
2003	May 07
2004	Apr 26
2005	May 12
2006	May 03
2007	Apr 23

Shavuot (1 or 2 days)

1997	Jun 11
1998	May 31
1999	May 21
2000	Jun 09
2001	May 28
2002	May 17
2003	Jun 06
2004	May 26
2005	Jun 13
2006	Jun 02
2007	May 23

Passover (7 or 8 days)

1997	Apr 22
1998	Apr 11
1999	Apr 01
2000	Apr 20
2001	Apr 08
2002	Mar 28
2003	Apr 17
2004	Apr 06
2005	Apr 24
2006	Apr 13
2007	Apr 03

Tisha B'Av (1 day)

1997	Aug 12
1998	Aug 1
1999	Jul 22
2000	Aug 10
2001	Jul 29
2002	Jul 18
2003	Aug 07
2004	Jul 27
2005	Aug 14
2006	Aug 03
2007	Jul 24

Lag B'Omer (1 day)

1997	May 25
1998	May 14
1999	May 04
2000	May 23
2001	May 11
2002	Apr 30
2003	May 20
2004	May 09
2005	May 27
2006	May 16
2007	May 06

Tu B'Av (1 day)

1997	Aug 18
1998	Aug 07
1999	Jul 28
2000	Aug 19
2001	Aug 04
2002	Jul 24
2003	Aug 13
2004	Aug 02
2005	Aug 20
2006	Aug 09
2007	Jul 30

Resource List

Compiled by Lynn Golub-Rofrano

ANNOTATED BIBLIOGRAPHY

Why Be Jewish?

Fink, Nan, *Stranger in the Midst,* Basic Books, 1997.
Subtitled "A Memoir of Spiritual Discovery," this is the memoir of a woman who converted to Judaism. The author is a co-founder of Tikkun magazine and writes informatively about the difficulties she has experienced, both inside and outside the Jewish community.

Gordis, Rabbi Daniel, *God Was Not in the Fire,* Charles Scribner's Sons, 1995.
This book is considered a "why-to" be Jewish rather than a "how-to." It suggests that the religion of one's youth can and should deepen in adult life. Rabbi Gordis argues that it is not through blind faith that Jews come to understand the world around them and their place in it, but through "spiritual discipline" and a ceaseless round of investigations.

Grishaver, Joel Lurie, 40 *Things You Can Do to Save the Jewish People,* Alef Design Group, 1993.
This book is full of practical suggestions for raising Jewish children in a secular world. It is very readable and is sure to become well worn and dog-eared. Joel Grishaver's vignettes illustrate important considerations in raising Jewish children who will be "good enough."

Kushner, Rabbi Harold S., *To Life!,* Little, Brown and Company, 1993.
Subtitled "A Celebration of Jewish Being and Thinking," this book describes the traditions and practices of Judaism in an accessible and inspiring way. Rabbi Kushner explains the importance of prayer, holiday observances, lifecycle events, dietary laws, and so on.

Kushner, Lawrence, *God Was in This Place and I, I Did Not Know: Finding Self, Spirituality and Ultimate Meaning,* Jewish Lights Publishing, 1993.
Rabbi Kushner gathers together an inspiring range of interpretations of Genesis 28:16 as given by sages, scholars, and commentators. Through a fascinating new literary genre, Kushner's creative reconstruction of the teachers' lives and times, we enter their study halls and learn from these spiritual masters. This book is about discovering God's place in the universe and in your life.

Lerner, Michael, *Jewish Renewal,* Grosset/Putnam, 1994.
This book provides insight into the process of Jewish renewal that is bringing thousands of Jews back to a Judaism that they are both discovering and helping create.

Levin, Sunie, *Mingled Roots,* B'nai B'rith Women, 1991.
This book, subtitled "A Guide for Jewish Grandparents of Interfaith Grandchildren," offers suggestions to strengthen the connection between grandparents and grandchildren.

McClain, Ellen Jaffe, *Embracing the Stranger,* Basic Books, 1995.
Ellen McClain is an observant, intermarried Jewish woman who rejects the popular myth that intermarriage will lead to the death of American Jewry. She encourages the Jewish community to reach out to intermarried families and include them in community activities.

Petsonk, Judy, *Taking Judaism Personally,* The Free Press, 1996.
Interesting story, written in beautiful language, of one woman's search for spirituality, and the development of the *havurah* movement.

Silver, Abba Hillel, *Where Judaism Differed: An Inquiry into the Distinctiveness of Judaism,* Jason Aronson, 1987.
A lively account of Judaism, its distinctive traits, and its revolutionary message of unity, freedom, and compassion. The reader will find that the history of Israel is not a mere succession of events, but an unfolding moral process.

Stein, Rabbi David, ed., *A Garden of Choice Fruit,* Shomrei Adamah, 1991.

This little book consists of 200 classic Jewish quotes on human beings and the environment categorized by contemporary topics. A wonderful source for combining traditional Judaism with modern living.

Telushkin, Rabbi Joseph, *Jewish Literacy,* William Morrow & Co., 1991.

Written in a scholarly yet readable format that contains facts as well as anecdotes, stories, and humor, this book covers all the essential areas of Judaism, providing a basic foundation for families.

Umansky, Ellen M., and Dianne Ashton, eds., *Four Centuries of Jewish Women's Spirituality,* Beacon Press, 1995.

Every time you pick up this collection of memoirs, essays, poetry, and stories, you will find something new and wonderful in it.

Waskow, Arthur, *Down-to-Earth Judaism: Food, Money, Sex, and the Rest of Life,* William Morrow & Co., 1997.

Waskow explores the four areas of our lives mentioned in the title as they have evolved over the past 3,500 years, and includes suggestions for egalitarian ceremonies, prayers, and celebrations.

Wolpe, Rabbi David J., *The Healer of Shattered Hearts,* Henry Holt, 1990.

In this book Rabbi Wolpe offers a Jewish view of God. Using traditional text as well as midrash, this book examines God's place in the lives of modern Jews. This is a truly spiritual book that will be treasured for years as a guide for forming a personal relationship with God.

Wouk, Herman, *This Is My God: The Jewish Way of Life,* Doubleday, 1992.

An introduction to Jewish history, faith, customs, and law.

Making Your Home Jewish

Diamant, Anita, *Choosing a Jewish Life,* Schocken Books, 1977.

Anita Diamant, in a gentle, respectful way, provides information and guidance for those on the journey to conversion. She addresses "how-to" issues, from selecting a rabbi to participating in conversion celebrations, and helps people explore ways of integrating Judaism into their lives. She also deals with personal issues, such as some converts' difficulty in putting aside Christmas.

Donin, Hayim Halevy, *To Be a Jew: A Guide to Jewish Observance in Contemporary Life,* Basic Books, 1991.

This book covers many aspects of observance, including Shabbat, the holiday cycle, life-cycle events, dietary laws, and so on. The information is based on halakhah (traditional Jewish law) and provides a rationale for the laws and traditions. Often used in conversion classes, this book is a excellent resource for families looking for material relating to tradition.

Epstein, David, and Suzanne Stutman, *Torah with Love: A Guide for Strengthening Jewish Values Within the Family,* Simon & Schuster, 1986.

Geared toward family study and discussion, this book explains how to use the process of discussion and Torah commentaries to strengthen Jewish values, and is considered a classic.

Falk, Marcia, *The Book of Blessings,* HarperCollins, 1996.

This compilation of new prayers, blessings, poems, and meditations can be used to help create a more personal, spiritual life and to enhance the sacred potential of our moments and days.

Golub, Jane Ellen, and Joel Lurie Grishaver, *Zot ha-Torah: This Is the Torah,* Torah Aura Productions, 1994.

This book, great for family study, offers a guided exploration of the mitzvot found in the weekly Torah portion followed by insights and questions for discussion.

Greenberg, Blu, *How to Run a Traditional Jewish Household,* Simon & Schuster, 1985.

This well organized book describes in detail the way a traditional modern Orthodox Jewish household is run. Among the topics covered are the observance of Shabbat and *kashrut,* Jewish education, life-cycle events, blessings, and Jewish attitudes toward sex, birth control, and abortion.

Olitzky, Rabbi Kerry M., and Rabbi Ronald H. Isaacs, *The How To Handbooks for Jewish Living,* KTAV Publishing House, 1993.

This concisely written book contains the bare facts of basic Jewish living. There are two volumes dealing with everything from braiding challah to tying tzizit! An excellent resource set for every Jewish family—particularly when you don't want long explanations.

Stern, Chaim, ed., *On the Doorposts of Your Home,* Central Conference of American Rabbis, 1994.

This excellent reference, written in gender-sensitive language, contains a variety of prayers dealing with holidays, festivals, life-cycle events, and life-changing moments.

Strassfeld, Michael, and Richard Siegel, *The First Jewish Catalog: A Do-It-Yourself Kit,* Jewish Publication Society, 1989.
Strassfeld, Michael, and Sharon Strassfeld, *The Second Jewish Catalog: Sources and Resources,* Jewish Publication Society, 1989.
Strassfeld, Michael, *The Third Jewish Catalog: Creating Community: With a Cumulative Index to All Three Catalogs,* Jewish Publication Society, 1989.

These books were written over twenty years ago and are now considered to be classics. The first catalog contains basic information for such activities as building sukkot, blowing a shofar, Jewish symbols, and most other aspects of Jewish living. The second contains a directory of Jewish sources and resources. The third examines the Jewish community throughout the world. A must have for any Jewish library!

Syme, Daniel B., *The Jewish Home: A Guide for Jewish Living,* UAHC Press, 1988.

Rabbi Syme's book gives clear and explicit definitions and descriptions of home items, rituals, and holiday observance. The book is written from a Reform perspective in a question-and-answer format. It addresses questions concerning the reasons for, or origins of, an object or holiday. An excellent resource for spot-checking information.

Raising Jewish Children

Beiner, Stan J., *Bible Scenes: Joshua to Solomon,* Alternatives in Religious Education, 1988.

This book, written in a dramatic format, focuses on Jewish history from the period of Joshua through the time of Solomon. Parents and children can act out the different scenes together and then discuss them. The issues covered have many relevant contemporary applications.

Chubara, Yona, Miriam P. Feinberg, and Rena Rotenberg, *Torah Talk,* Alternatives in Religious Education, 1989.

Although intended for teachers, this book is an excellent resource for families with young children because it tells the stories of the Torah in a way children can understand, and includes discussion ideas and useful craft and game suggestions.

Coles, Robert, *The Spiritual Life of Children,* Houghton Mifflin, 1990.

This non-denominational book explores children's faith development and their different levels of spiritual growth. It is an excellent resource because it helps families understand how children relate to God and the Bible.

Danan, Julie Hilton, *Jewish Parent's Almanac,* Jason Aronson, 1993.

A complete guide book to raising Jewish children from birth through the teen years. It is appropriate for families of all backgrounds.

Frankel, Ellen, Ph.D., *The Five Books of Miriam,* Grosset/Putnam, 1996.

This is a great book for family study. It includes a brief description and commentary on each Torah portion followed by the "women's voices" of the past and present questioning and discussing Torah.

Gellman, Rabbi Marc, *Does God Have a Big Toe?,* HarperCollins, 1989.

A wonderful collection of "modern midrash" that children of all ages enjoy as they learn to look at biblical text through creative eyes. Great for family discussions and as a jumping-off point for family-created midrash.

Gellman, Rabbi Marc, *God's Mailbox,* Morrow Junior Books, 1996.

This very funny book of midrashic stories, known to make children laugh uncontrollably, is a guaranteed hit for the entire family.

Greenberg, Melanie Hope, *Blessings: Our Jewish Ceremonies,* Jewish Publication Society, 1995.

This children's book is written in simple language and explains to children the meaning of prayers and ceremonies. Children are introduced to the ways we thank God for God's gifts, and there are blessings for life-cycle events and everyday occurrences.

Groner, Judyth, Shelly O. Haas, and Madeline Wikler, *Thank You, God!: A Jewish Child's Book of Prayers,* Kar-Ben Copies, 1993.

This is a beautifully illustrated book of prayers for young children. Included are Shabbat blessings and blessings for food, health, holidays, and life. The prayers are provided in simple Hebrew with transliteration and English translation.

Kushner, Harold, *When Children Ask About God: A Guide for Parents Who Don't Always Have All the Answers,* Schocken Books, 1995.

Rabbi Kushner explores the many images of God people have and how best to translate these images into concepts accessible to children. The book is aimed at children ages 4 to 14 and relies heavily on the teachings of Rabbi Mordecai Kaplan.

Ramsfelder-Levin, Miriam, *In the Beginning,* Kar-Ben Copies, 1996.

This is a cute story that tells of creation from the viewpoint of a little boy who wakes up to his messy room and creates order in a sequence that follows the creation of the world. Children probably won't realize this connection until it is pointed out to them, but it is a great discussion point for the story of our world's origin.

Sasso, Sandy Eisenberg, *But God Remembered,* Jewish Lights Publishing, 1995.

Children's stories about women who lived between the time of creation and the arrival in the Promised Land. The book is introduced with a wonderful conversation between God and the angels about remembering and forgetting and proceeds to relate midrashic tales that discuss Lilith, Serach, Bityah, the Pharoah's daughter, and the five daughters of Zelophechad.

Sasso, Sandy Eisenberg, *God's Paintbrush,* Jewish Lights Publishing, 1992.

This is a wonderful nondenominational, interactive book for children that provides families with the opportunity to discover how we think about the world around us.

Sasso, Sandy Eisenberg, *In God's Name,* Jewish Lights Publishing, 1994.

This wonderfully illustrated children's book tells the story of the search for God's name. It provides a great opening for parents to discuss with their children their names for God.

Singer, Isaac Bashevis, *Stories for Children,* Farrar Straus Giroux, 1984.

Share the warmth and humor of these stories with your children by reading them aloud. The stories bridge the generation gap because they are loved by all ages. The collection includes such classics as "Why Noah Chose the Dove," "Zlateh the Goat," and "The Power of Light."

Wolpe, Rabbi David J., *Teaching Your Children About God,* HarperPerennial, 1993.

This is a wonderful book that deals with many aspects of teaching children about God and religion. The book helps us answer the tough questions children ask as it enables us to explore our own spirituality.

Lifecycle Traditions

Brener, Anne, *Mourning & Mitzvah: A Guided Journal for Walking the Mourner's Path Through Grief to Healing,* Jewish Lights Publishing, 1993.

An excellent resource for someone who is mourning. The book offers 60 guided writing exercises to help in the healing process, and includes an explanation of the different customs connected with mourning.

Diamant, Anita, *The New Jewish Wedding,* Summit Books, 1986.

The authorative guide, informative and well written, is for modern couples seeking to mix contemporary sensibilities with Jewish tradition.

Fuchs, Rabbi Nancy, *Our Share of Night, Our Share of Morning,* HarperCollins, 1996.

Relating interviews with over a hundred parents, Rabbi Fuchs eloquently evokes the powerful spiritual nature that is found in the everydayness of parenting.

Gallant, Janet, *My Brother's Bar Mitzvah,* Kar-Ben Copies, 1994.

This is a nice children's story dealing with bar mitzvah preparations from a kid sister's point of view. It helps us remember the others who are affected by preparations for the big day.

Goldin, Barbara Diamond, *Bat Mitzvah: A Jewish Girl's Coming of Age,* Viking Children's Books, 1995.

This book, written for the upcoming bat mitzvah, gives a brief history of women in Judaism from the time of the matriarchs to the modern era. The planning of, preparation for, and significance of the bat mitzvah ceremony are discussed.

Grode, Phyllis Agins, *Sophie's Name,* Kar-Ben Copies, 1992.

This is a wonderful story about a young girl who decides she hates her name and wants to change it. However, as she begins to learn about the people she was named after, she realizes how much her name really fits her.

Kolatch, Alfred J., *The Complete Dictionary of English and Hebrew First Names,* Jonathan David Publishers, 1984.

An excellent resource for English and Hebrew names, their meanings and origins.

Lanton, Sandy, *Daddy's Chair,* Kar-Ben Copies, 1991.

This book deals sensitively with the issue of a parent's death and its effect on a young child. The story takes place during the week of shiva and we see the gradual healing process as the week progresses.

Leneman, Helen, ed., *Bar/Bat Mitzvah Basics: A Practical Family Guide to Coming of Age Together,* Jewish Lights Publishing, 1996.

This book offers valuable information on bar and bat mitzvah preparation, the ceremony, service, and celebration, and on how to maintain spirituality. Authors also include interesting personal reflections on family.

Liss-Levinson, Nechama, Ph.D., *When a Grandparent Dies,* Jewish Lights Publishing, 1995.

Geared for children ages 7-11, this workbook-style book helps children express their feelings as they come to terms with the death of a grandparent.

Meier, Marcie, *A Fitting Bar Mitzvah,* Gefen Publishing House, 1996.

This is another bar mitzvah story, but with a difference. Not once in this book is the party or celebration mentioned! It deals with the suit fitting as well as the practice of donning tefillin and the meanings of these rituals. It is a wonderful change to read a children's story about a bar mitzvah that focuses on the meaning of the event.

Oberman, Sheldon, *The Always Prayer Shawl,* Boyds Mills Press, 1994.

This is a story about a young boy, his grandfather, and their tallith. The book beautifully illustrates the many life changes one encounters as one matures as well as the many things that remain the same.

Orenstein, Rabbi Debra, *Lifecycles: Jewish Women on Life Passages and Personal Milestones,* Jewish Lights Publishing, 1994.

This is a compilation of new rituals that have been created by and for women to recognize and celebrate women's life-cycle events. Rabbi Orenstein has performed a real service to Jewish women by gathering these ceremonies together in one source, particularly those ceremonies for previously unrecognized events.

Pomeranc, Marion Hess, *The Hand-Me-Down Horse,* Albert Whitman & Company, 1996.

This book for young children deals with immigration, family values, and the ideas of tradition and inheritance. It's a great book for family discussion as well as a compact history lesson for young children.

Pomerantz, Barbara, *Who Will Lead Kiddush?,* UAHC Press, 1985.

The story of a young girl and the changes in her life after her parents' divorce. The author handles a tough subject well and weaves in the message that life does go on and that both parents continue to love the children.

Pushker, Gloria Teles, *A Belfer Bar Mitzvah,* Pelican Publishing, 1995.

One of a series of children's books about the Belfer family, this book offers good descriptions of customs and ceremonies. It describes a cousin's bar mitzvah and how the family is incorporated into the celebration.

Riemer, Jack, ed., *Wrestling with the Angel,* Schocken Books, 1995.

This book explains traditional Jewish practice related to death, including the shiva period, the year of mourning, and Jewish views on the afterlife. It contains essays written by popular Jewish writers, who relate how the customs and traditions of mourning affected them personally.

Riemer, Jack, and Nathaniel Stampfer, eds., *So That Your Values Live On: Ethical Wills,* Jewish Lights Publishing, 1991.

This book includes instructions and ideas about writing an ethical will that will express the val-ues you want to pass on through your children, and includes samples of ethical wills written by others.

Salkin, Rabbi Jefrey K., *Putting God on the Guest List,* Jewish Lights Publishing, 1993.

Rabbi Salkin has written a wonderful book that explains the spirituality and meaning in today's b'nai mitzvah. This book describes the origin of the ceremony, explains the Shabbat morning service, and offers suggestions of ways to incorporate non-Jewish family members into the celebration.

Sidi, Smadar Shir, *The Complete Book of Hebrew Baby Names,* HarperCollins, 1989.

A comprehensive book of Hebrew names, that are defined and coded to indicate whether the name is old, popular, or unique.

Syme, Daniel B., and Rifat Sonsino, *What Happens After I Die?,* UAHC Press, 1990.

This book deals with many questions relating to Judaism's view of afterlife, drawing on textual sources, medieval thought, mystical literature, and contemporary writers from each denomination of Judaism.

Techner, David, and Judith Hirt-Manheimer, *A Candle for Grandpa,* UAHC Press, 1993.

A moving story that explains Jewish funeral and burial practices to children, while including explanations for parents to help them better understand and discuss these practices with their children.

Viorst, Judith, *The Tenth Good Thing about Barney,* Aladdin Paperbacks, 1976.

This secular children's book deals with the topic of death through the story of the death of a family pet, and suggests ways to help children cope. It is a solid introduction to the topic of death and a useful aid for parents who find it difficult to broach the subject with their children.

Religious Education

Antonelli, Judith S., *In the Image of God: A Feminist Commentary on the Torah*, Jason Aronson, 1995.

Judith Antonelli manages to combine feminism with traditional Judaism, and this unique combination has earned this book high respect from readers from each Jewish denomination. The book is divided into the different Torah portions and as a result makes an excellent study guide. All of the women who appear in the Torah, as well as those theological issues that involve women, are examined and discussed in a thoughtful manner.

Beiner, Stan J., *Sedra Scenes: Skits for Every Torah Portion*, Alternatives in Religious Education, 1982.

Written in play form, this book provides a skit for each Torah portion, creating a fun way for families to study and discuss the *parashah*. "How did you feel when Joseph said . . .?"

Cohen, Rabbi Norman J., *Self, Struggle & Change*, Jewish Lights Publishing, 1995.

Rabbi Cohen believes that the "starting point of our search for personal meaning is in the Bible itself." His book, both interesting and instructive, is based on the book of Genesis, and examines biblical stories for insight into contemporary life.

Cone, Molly, *Listen to the Trees*, UAHC Press, 1995.

Each chapter of this children's book begins with a photograph and Torah quote. These are followed by a brief description of and commentary on the quote, along with related stories and legends.

Donin, Rabbi Hayim Halevy, *To Pray as a Jew*, Basic Books, 1980.

This wonderful resource, written by a Conservative rabbi, explains the prayer book and synagogue service. Rabbi Donin details the meaning for each prayer, as well as explaining its origin and usage. Additionally, he talks about the different body positions used for different prayers. A great book for anyone interested in Jewish prayer.

Fields, Rabbi Harvey J., *A Torah Commentary for Our Times*, UAHC Press, 1993.

This three-volume commentary includes a summary of the Torah portions as well as interesting interpretations and insights. Questions for study and discussion are included for each portion.

Fox, Everett, *The Five Books of Moses*, Schocken Books, 1995.

This new translation of the Hebrew text is easy to read and understand while maintaining the rhythm of the Hebrew.

Grishaver, Joel Lurie, and Rabbi Stuart Kelman, eds., *Learn Torah with 1994–1995 Torah Annual: A Collection of the Year's Best Torah*, Alef Design Group, 1996.

A wonderful resource for studying the weekly parashot, this is a compilation of a weekly commentary written by contemporary Judaic scholars such as Arthur Green, Marcia Falk, Danny Siegel, Burton Visotzky, Joseph Telushkin, Amy Eilberg, W. Gunther Plaut, Everett Fox, Jo Milgrom, and others. The fax is available on a weekly basis by subscription, although you're better off buying the book, which has a full year's worth of insights in a single volume.

Jaffe, Nina, and Steve Zeitlin, *While Standing on One Foot*, Henry Holt, 1993.

This book is a compilation of puzzle stories and wisdom tales for children, intended to be read as a family and discussed. The stories are set in many different periods of Jewish history. It's fun to debate the possible answers and see if they match the rabbinical opinion.

Kravitz, Rabbi Leonard, and Rabbi Kerry M. Olitzky, *Pirke Avot: A Modern Commentary on Jewish Ethics*, UAHC Press, 1993.

This very readable commentary on *Pirke Avot* makes a classic Jewish text available to all. The English translations and modern commentary will help to reawaken an interest in studying Jewish ethics, and the commentary sections include writings by some of today's more popular Jewish scholars and authors.

Kushner, Lawrence S., and Rabbi Kerry M. Olitzky, *Sparks Beneath the Surface,* Jason Aronson, 1993.

> This spiritual commentary on the Torah is an excellent guide for family study. The pages are set up like the pages of the Talmud. In the center of each page is a phrase or verse from the Torah surrounded by commentary and insights for discussion.

Plaut, Gunther, *Torah: A Modern Commentary/ Hebrew Opening,* UAHC Press, 1981.

> This Torah commentary is particularly useful for study and family discussion. In addition to the text of the Torah and Haftarah in both Hebrew and English, there are well-written commentaries. Each chapter contains information about the historical period discussed as well as an explanation of modern usage.

Rosenblatt, Naomi H., and Joshua Horowitz, *Wrestling with Angels,* Delacorte Press, 1989.

> This book, based on the book of Genesis, uses the biblical stories to teach us about ourselves and our spiritual identity, sexuality, and personal relationships. A very readable book that lends itself to family discussion.

Rosman, Steven M., *Sidrah Stories: A Torah Companion,* UAHC Press, 1989.

> A wonderful collection of short stories to be read weekly and discussed. Each chapter begins with a brief quote from the *parashah* which is followed by a midrashic or talmudic tale.

Rossel, Seymour, *Sefer Ha-Aggadah: The Book of Legends for Young Readers,* UAHC Press, 1996.

> A children's book adapted from the newly translated *Book of Legends* that our sages used to create a world of lessons and values. The illustrations are beautiful and sure to hold a child's interest.

Tucker, Joanne, and Susan Freeman, *Torah in Motion,* Alternatives in Religious Education, 1990.

> This book deals with creating dance midrash as a way to interpret the weekly Torah portion. A unique vehicle for families to enhance their study sessions. Guaranteed to keep you moving!

Observing Shabbat

Feinberg, Miriam P., *Just Enough Room,* United Synagogue of America, 1991.

> This is a lovely story about a family visiting friends for Shabbat dinner, conveying the feelings of this special time together. The concept of Shabbat as a time to welcome all is also illustrated.

Palatnik, Lori, *Friday Night and Beyond: The Shabbat Experience Step-By-Step,* Jason Aronson, 1994.

> Great description of Orthodox daily and Shabbat observance.

Rosenblum, Richard, *The Old Synagogue,* Jewish Publication Society, 1989.

> Although not specifically about Shabbat, this book tells the story of an old synagogue—how it was founded, used, closed down, and eventually reopened. This is a great book for discussion of city life and the migration of American Jewish communities through the years.

Schwartz, Howard, *The Sabbath Lion,* HarperCollins, 1992.

> This wonderful Jewish folk tale from Algeria has marvelous illustrations that are sure to catch the imagination of children, just as the story manages to convey the essence of Shabbat observance and express its importance.

Shapiro, Mark Dov, *Gates of Shabbat,* CCAR Press, 1991.

> This guide for observing Shabbat includes the blessings as well as explanations of the origins of different Shabbat rituals and their meaning.

Swartz, Daniel J., *Bim and Bom: A Shabbat Tale,* Kar-Ben Copies, 1996.

> This wonderful children's book tells the tale of two people who live in an old-fashioned town and spend their week working (she builds houses and he is a baker) and looking forward to Shabbat. The story and pictures are great.

Holidays

Apisdorf, Shimon, *Passover Survival Kit,* Leviathan Press, 1994.

Shimon Apisdorf's easy-to-read writing style and love of Judaism make his books a real treasure for those looking to enhance their holiday celebrations. This book is recommended both for those with significant knowledge and for those who don't know a lot about Passover. The author's enthusiasm is certain to add excitement and meaning to the holiday celebration.

Apisdorf, Shimon, *Rosh Hashanah Yom Kippur Survival Kit,* Leviathan Press, 1992.

This book is ideal for people who dread the high holidays and the long hours at services. It will add meaning to your holidays and bring spirituality to services.

Berrin, Susan, *Celebrating the New Moon,* Jason Aronson, 1996.

This Rosh Chodesh anthology offers an in-depth discussion of the history and evolution of today's Rosh Chodesh celebrations. Not only does it describe present-day celebrations but it also lists important information about the different Hebrew months.

Bohm, Rabbi Lenore, *Holiday Study Guide,* Women of Reform Judaism, 1995.

This book offers a brief description of the Jewish calendar, holidays, and rituals. Each section includes suggestions to make celebrations memorable and questions for discussion. The guide is a valuable resource for study groups, family learning, and individual study.

Drucker, Malka, *The Family Treasury of Jewish Holidays,* Little, Brown and Company, 1994.

This wonderful book is particularly useful for families just starting their Jewish education or for those with young children who are looking for basic holiday information because it includes brief descriptions of the holidays as well as recipes, craft ideas, games, and stories for each holiday.

Gal, Martin, *Eight Great Dreidel Stories,* Alef Design Group, 1994.

This collection of short stories about dreidels (one is even set in Las Vegas!) can be shared with children ages 13 and up, but you might want to read the stories to your children and modify the language.

Greenberg, Irving, *The Jewish Way: Living the Holidays,* Touchstone Books, 1988.

This beautifully written book by an Orthodox rabbi provides useful information about the holidays and how they are celebrated. It describes both the theological origin and spiritual meaning found in particular celebrations. In addition, the background, interconnection, and religious significance of Jewish holidays are explained.

Isaacs, Rabbi Ronald H., and Rabbi Kerry M. Olitzky, *Sacred Celebrations,* KTAV Publishing House, 1994.

Written in a clear and concise manner, this book provides useful information for the home and synagogue celebration of Jewish holidays. Each chapter includes insights from Jewish texts, and descriptions of holiday celebrations, rituals, blessings, and family activities.

Jaffe, Nina, *The Uninvited Guest,* Scholastic Inc., 1993.

A great collection of short stories about each holiday, this book provides brief descriptions of each holiday and supplies folk tales and legends that will enhance any celebration.

Klagsbrun, Francine, *Jewish Days,* Farrar Straus Giroux, 1996.

Subtitled "A Book of Jewish Life and Culture Around the Year," this beautifully illustrated book will spark your curiosity with little-known facts about the Hebrew months as well as legends surrounding the holidays.

Renberg, Dalia Hardof, *The Complete Family Guide to Jewish Holidays,* Adama Books, 1985.

A good one-volume holiday kit for families looking for basic information and ideas for celebrating the holidays. In addition to the basic facts about the holiday, each chapter contains stories, songs, craft ideas, and recipes.

Ross, Lesli Koppelman, *Celebrate! The Complete Jewish Holidays Handbook*, Jason Aronson, 1994.

This comprehensive holiday book describes the origin of individual holidays, and how they have been celebrated throughout history.

Strassfeld, Michael, *The Jewish Holidays: A Guide and Commentary*, HarperCollins, 1985.

In addition to an in-depth discussion of the holidays and the Jewish calendar, this book includes commentaries, ideas for family holiday involvement, and suggestions for new traditions.

Sussman, Susan, *There's No Such Thing as a Chanukah Bush, Sandy Goldstein*, Albert Whitman & Co., 1993.

This children's book describes the "December Dilemma" and how it is handled by Sandy Goldstein and her family. While acknowledging the difficulty in being a minority, the book nicely illustrates the difference between "sharing" a holiday and observing it. With the help of a very special grandfather, Sandy comes to terms with the holiday season and learns to appreciate her own celebrations.

Wolfson, Dr. Ron, *The Art of Jewish Living*, Federation of Jewish Men's Clubs, 1990.

Written by a well-known Jewish family educator, this series includes books about Shabbat, Hanukkah, and Passover. Each starts with a basic definition of the holiday, moves on to a guide for observance, and concludes with suggestions, such as recipes, crafts, and family activities, for enhancing observance.

Values

Amsel, Nachum, *The Jewish Encyclopedia of Moral & Ethical Issues*, Jason Aronson, 1994.

This is a great book about contemporary issues, each of which is addressed from an Orthodox Jewish perspective in two to three pages.

Artson, Bradley Shavit, *It's a Mitzvah*, Behrman House/Rabbinical Assembly, 1995.

Defines and explains core mitzvot and values, tells the sources of the mitzvot, and gives suggestions for how to observe mitzvot.

Bernstein, Ellen, and Dan Fink, *Let the Earth Teach You Torah*, Shomrei Adamah, 1992.

Although written for schools and groups, this book is also an excellent family reference for learning about Judaism and ecology, supplying some wonderful activities and ideas for action.

Feinberg, Miriam, and Rena Rotenberg, *Lively Legends—Jewish Values*, Alternatives in Religious Education, 1993.

Although intended for teachers, this is also a great book for families to use with young children because each section focuses on a different Jewish value and includes a story along with a craft and game ideas. This book also comes in handy for play groups or on rainy days.

Frankel, Ellen, Ph.D., and Sarah Levine, *Tell It Like It Is*, KTAV Publishing House, 1995.

This book discusses issues faced by today's Jewish teens. It follows the life of Sarah as she moves into a new neighborhood and starts a new school. The challenges she faces regarding Shabbat, drugs, kindness to others, and so on are sure to capture the interest of teenagers and their parents.

Gilman, Phoebe, *Something from Nothing*, North Winds Press, 1992.

This is a wonderful children's story about a young boy and his special relationship with his grandfather. The book identifies values essential to Jewish life. The illustrations contain a story within the story that adds to the beauty of the book.

Gittelsohn, Roland Bertram, *How Do I Decide?: A Contemporary Jewish Approach to What's Right and What's Wrong*, Behrman House, 1989.

This book applies traditional texts to modern-day situations and covers a vast array of topics.

Goldin, Barbara Diamond, *A Child's Book of Midrash*, Jason Aronson, 1990.

This is an excellent collection of midrashim that illuminate Jewish moral and ethical values. A treasure for families to read and enjoy together.

Gopin, Rabbi Marc, Rabbi Mark H. Levine, and Rabbi Sid Schwarz, *Jewish Civics: A Tikkun Olam World Repair Manual*, CAJE/WIJLV, 1994.

Published jointly by the Coalition for the Advancement of Jewish Education and the Washington Institute for Jewish Leadership and Values, this book is an excellent resource book for families and educators because it contains some wonderful primary text material on *tikkun olam*.

Gordon, Sol, *When Living Hurts*, UAHC Press, 1995.
This book is one of the few available that deal with helping Jewish teens who are depressed or suicidal. It helps teens develop coping skills for dealing with the issues that are upsetting them.

Hadassah with Shomrei Adamah, *Judaism and Ecology*, Hadassah Department of Education, 1993.
This is a great study guide for Jewish viewpoints on ecology. Textual sources are included and discussed.

Isaacs, Rabbi Ronald H., and Rabbi Kerry M. Olitzky, *Doing Mitzvot*, KTAV Publishing House, 1995.
This is a workbook-style book with great family *tikkun olam* projects geared toward children. There are twelve projects, one for each month, and attached to each is a different mitzvah.

Kadden, Barbara Binder, and Bruce Kadden, *Teaching Mitzvot*, Alternatives in Religious Education, 1988.
Although written for educators, this is an excellent book for families as well. The different mitzvot are explained and there are activity suggestions, concepts, and values for each one.

Kroloff, Rabbi Charles A., *When Elijah Knocks*, Behrman House, 1992.
This book deals with the Jewish responsibility toward the homeless, and includes religious texts as well as practical suggestions.

Levine, Arthur A., *Pearl Moscowitz's Last Stand*, Tambourine Books, 1993.
This children's book introduces us to Pearl Moscowitz, a woman who has lived in the city for a long time and watched many changes take place in her neighborhood. When she finds out

that the last tree on her block is to be torn down she decides that this is one change that she will not just sit and watch.

Olitzky, Rabbi Kerry M., and Rachael T. Sabath, *Striving Towards Virtue*, KTAV Publishing House, 1996.
A contemporary guide for Jewish ethical behavior and moral living that explores subjects such as the appeal of evil, the value of good deeds, and the implications of gossip. Rabbis Olitzky and Sabath recommend actions that we can take to help strengthen and heal ourselves and our world.

Polish, Daniel F., Daniel B. Syme, and Bernard M. Zlotowitz, *Drugs, Sex, and Integrity*, UAHC Press, 1991.
This book deals with many difficult issues faced by today's Jewish teenagers. The authors present traditional and halakhic views, along with modern commentary, and leave decision making to the readers. An excellent resource that will help guide family discussions on these issues.

Rael, Elsa Okon, *What Zeesie Saw on Delancey Street*, Simon & Schuster, 1996.
This book for young readers teaches about mitzvot and immigration. It tells the story of a "package party" given on Delancey Street to raise funds to bring new immigrants to America. Also in the story is the "money room"—a place for those who have money to give to tzedakah, and for those who don't, to receive help. Excellent for family discussions!

Rosenfield, Dina Herman, *The Very Best Place for a Penny*, Merkos L'inyonei Chinuch, 1984.
A cute picture book about a penny that gets lost and all the adventures it has before being put right where it belongs—in the tzedakah box.

Siegel, Danny, *Mitzvahs*, Town House Press, 1992.
Danny Siegel describes many different tzedakah projects in the hope that readers will stop periodically while reading and say, "I can do that—I WILL do that." A good resource for families to read together. It may even inspire your family to decide on a family mitzvah project.

303

Siegel, Danny, *Tell Me A Mitzvah*, Kar-Ben Copies, 1994.

> This children's book briefly describes a dozen projects that are easy to implement in your own community. Children will be able to identify with the ideas and the message of the book.

Slonin, Rivkah, ed., *Total Immersion: A Mikvah Anthology*, Jason Aronson, 1996.

> Consisting of a number of essays on the value of the mikvah, all written from a modern yet traditional point of view, this book is an excellent resource for those who wish to learn more about the relevance of this custom today.

Spitzer, Rabbi Julie Ringold, *When Love Is Not Enough*, Women of Reform Judaism, 1995.

> This book fills a void in literature about domestic violence and how it is dealt with in rabbinic Judaism and contemporary practice. Domestic violence *is* an issue in Jewish homes and should be dealt with by the Jewish community, and this book provides us with a tool for doing just that.

Syme, Deborah Shayne, *Partners*, UAHC Press, 1990.

> A children's story about two young boys who discover the many ways they can become God's partners by reaching out to others. Perfect for children ages 4–8.

Vorspan, Albert, and David Saperstein, *Tough Choices*, UAHC Press, 1992.

> This book, written by two Reform rabbis, covers a wide range of topics relating to Jewish perspectives on social justice, including topics such as civil rights, Israel, anti-Semitism, the evolving concept of the Jewish family, and homosexuality.

Relationships/Sexuality

Balka, Christie, and Andy Rosen, eds., *Twice Blessed*, Beacon Press, 1989.

> This book is a rare find because it deals with the issue of homosexuality and Judaism. It includes a collection of writings by and about homosexual Jewish couples who are maintaining their ties to the Jewish community.

Cowan, Paul, and Rachel Cowan, *Mixed Blessings: Overcoming the Stumbling Blocks in an Interfaith Marriage*, Penguin USA, 1989.

> This book has become a classic source on intermarriage and raising children when there are two different religions in the home. The Cowans, who lectured extensively on intermarriage, were married fifteen years before Rachel converted.

Eilberg-Schwartz, Howard, *People of the Body*, SUNY Press, 1992.

> This book discusses the centrality of the body in Jewish thought and practice and includes consideration of gender issues.

Paasche-Orlow, Rabbi Sara, Rabbi J. B. Rosen-Sacks, and Rabbi David Rosenn, eds., *Kaafikim B'Negev—Welcoming Gays and Lesbians*, distributed by JAGL (Jewish Activists Gay and Lesbian).

> This collection of articles, responsa, and stories is designed to assist Jewish organizations in creating communities that are responsive to and understanding of the views and needs of gay and lesbian Jews.

Dietary Laws

Dresner, Seymour H., Seymour Siegel, and David M. Pollack, *The Jewish Dietary Laws*, Rabbinical Assembly/United Synagogue, 1982.

> This book is divided into two sections. The first section, "Their Meaning for Our Time," discusses how *kashrut* shapes our lives and where it fits into modern Jewish living. The second section, "A Guide to Observance," explains how to observe the dietary laws according to the guidelines of Conservative Judaism.

Grunfeld, Dr. Dayan I., *The Jewish Dietary Laws*, Soncino Press, 1989.

> This two-volume set examines the intricacies of the Jewish dietary laws. Volume One covers forbidden and permitted food, with special reference to meat and meat products. Volume Two discusses plants and vegetables, particularly the produce grown in Israel.

Lebeau, James M., *The Jewish Dietary Laws: Sanctify Life*, United Synagogue of America, 1983.

> Written from a Conservative Jewish viewpoint, this book deals with the spiritual aspects of observing *kashrut*, explaining the basic textual source material for observing the dietary laws as well as how these laws affect Jewish people both personally and spiritually.

Miller, Deborah Uchill, *Fins and Scales*, Kar-Ben Copies, 1991.

> Written in rhyme and containing illustrations that are both ingenious and fun, this delightful children's book explains the rules of *kashrut* in a charming manner.

Schwartz, Richard H., *Judaism and Vegetarianism*, Micah Publications, 1989.

> The author demonstrates that vegetarianism is an important personal and social choice supported by Jewish values.

AUDIO TAPES AND COMPACT DISCS

Instead of listing specific tapes and CDs, we have provided the names of performers whose work we recommend.

Debbie Friedman is a popular Jewish musician who recently performed in a sold-out concert at Carnegie Hall. She sings mostly in English, and her songs deal with Jewish issues, holidays, and prayers. A particularly good tape for children is *Miracles and Wonders*, which contains songs for Purim and Hanukkah, including the feminist favorite, "Vashti's Song."

Craig Taubman (best known to children as the Disney "toon town" singer) has produced a number of great tapes that deal with Jewish identity and the life cycle. A new disc, called *My Jewish Discovery*, is geared toward children and contains upbeat holiday songs. One of the most appealing features of Craig Taubman's music is the beat, which appeals to children of all ages!

Jeff Klepper and Dan Freelander sing together and call themselves Kol B'Seder (Everything is okay). Their music has a folk sound and is pleasant to listen to and sing along with. *Growin'* and *Growin'* 2 are two tapes that are particularly suitable for children: they contain basic blessings and Hebrew phrases, and they teach Jewish values while providing hours of family entertainment. They have also made many tapes for adults: one of our favorites is *Sparks of Torah.*

Safam has been a favorite in our house for years. The songs are mostly in English and deal with Jewish history and issues as diverse as the Marranos, Soviet Russia, Jewish immigration to America, and Israel. The group has been together for twenty years and we are lucky to have them! Treat yourself and your family to Safam for hours of Jewish musical enjoyment!

Doug Cotler is a third-generation cantor and a contemporary favorite on the Jewish music scene. He has only one tape and although it is specifically geared to children, his music appeals to all ages.

David Paskin is a sensitive, original composer/performer whose music charms and inspires Jews across the religious spectrum. Great for children and adults.

Sam Glaser takes a hard rock approach to Jewish music that is sure to appeal to Jewish teens everywhere. Parents, too, will find themselves enjoying this music, particularly because some of the songs deal with historical Jewish events.

Linda Hirschorn and Vocolot have a great sound that combines Jewish prayer and spirituality. Their music shows their pride in Jewish women; the matriarchs and other important biblical women are prominently placed in their music.

Rabbi Joe Black is a popular Jewish children's musician. His music has children tapping their toes and singing along. Some of you might be familiar with his "Aleph Bet Boogie," a favorite in many religious schools.

Cindy Paley has many holiday and children's tapes out. Children really enjoy her work because it is easy to sing along with.

Paul Zim has been singing holiday songs for children for years. His works are classics and easy to sing along with. Your children can learn the words of all the Jewish favorites and some new Jewish songs as well! A great addition to your family holiday collection.

Margie and Ilene have some lovely Shabbat, holiday, and Hebrew children's tapes out. Their voices are pleasant and even the youngest children seem to enjoy the sound of their music. Don't miss their tape of Jewish lullabies, *Where Dreams Are Born!*

Jill Moskowitz is a good choice for those with young children. Her Shabbat song tape is enjoyable and your children will be sure to ask for it over and over again.

Robyn Helzner has a collection of children's songs in Hebrew, Yiddish, and English for Shabbat and for every day. Children and parents love both her lyrics and her music.

Rene Boni's tape *Hands of Time* is loved by children and their parents. In fact, it's the type of music parents play even when their children aren't there! Her tape includes old classics as well as some original songs in Hebrew, Yiddish, and English.

VIDEOS

A Hanukkah Adventure, Tzivos Hashem and Comet International.
This video includes Hanukkah songs, stories, and candle-lighting ceremonies from all over the world.

Hanukkah Tales and Tunes, Video Treasures Inc.
Adults and children sing Hanukkah songs, dance, and tell Hanukkah stories in this video.

Shalom Sesame.
This is the Israel-based version of Sesame Street. Bert, Ernie, Grover, Cookie Monster, and Elmo go to Israel to sing, dance, and discover exciting and interesting places. This great video collection includes favorite Sesame Street personalities and their Israeli counterparts.

Alef-Bet Blast Off.
The puppet characters discover their own Judaism through modern life experiences and through time travel in which they meet the great Jewish heroes and sages.

Shirim K'tanim.
Songs in English and Hebrew with dances, skits, and some animation.

Miracle Days, Esther Deutsch Productions.
A musical adventure based on the Jewish holidays.

A Passover Seder, A Vision Entertainment.
A combination of live action, original illustrations, and animation guides the viewer through highlights of the seder. The video incorporates some of Elie Wiesel's poetic interpretation of this holiday.

Noah's Ark, Lightyear Entertainment.
An animated version of this classic story narrated by James Earl Jones.

Queen Esther, Turner Home Entertainment.
An animated version of the biblical Book of Esther.

Moses, Turner Home Entertainment.
An animated version of the story of Moses and the Israelite exodus from Egypt.

Stories from the Jewish Tradition, Children's Circle, narrated by Theodore Bikel.
Two traditional stories, "In the Month of Kislev" and "Zlatah the Goat," that combine illustrations and live action.

Daniel the Prophet, Jewish Pictures.
The biblical story of Daniel told with puppets.

Chanukah at Bubbe's/Passover at Bubbe's, Doumanian Productions.
A group of idiosyncratic puppet characters prepare to celebrate the holidays along with Bubbe, who relates the holiday story.

The Greatest Adventure Stories from the Bible, 1986, Hanna-Barbera, Turner Home Entertainment.
An animated series in which modern-day teens travel in time and experience biblical events and biblical characters.

Rugrats Passover: Let My Babies Go.
The Rugrats act out the exodus story.

WEB RESOURCES

All addresses are preceded by: http://www.

JCN18.com—Daily news and discussions from Israel and the United States.

Jewishblessings.com—English, Hebrew, and transliterated versions of Jewish prayers that are relevant to Jewish families.

Jewishculture.com—Commentary on and reviews of films, videos, CDs, tapes, plays, websites, radio programs, etc. that are of special interest to Jewish families.

Jewishfamily.com—Award-winning webzine featuring over a dozen departments, weekly columns, and great discussions. Links to Jewish cyberstores.

Jewishgiving.com—Thoughts on social justice and healing the world from the perspective of Jewish families and Jewish thought.

Jewishholidays.com—Suggestions on how to turn a Jewish holiday into a meaningful family experience; analysis of issues that may arise for families as they celebrate the holiday; recipes, craft ideas, "how-to" projects, reviews of holiday-related books, CDs, and tapes.

Jewishhome.com—Practical articles on how to enrich your home with Judaism. Includes crafts for children, gardening to grow vegetables needed for Jewish holidays, food-related articles, discussions of items needed for Jewish life passages or holiday celebrations, and reviews of books about these topics.

Aliza.org—Provocative questions about Judaism and life are posed by an inquisitive four-year-old. Includes a discussion of the questions contributed by on-line readers.

Challah.org—Award-winning recipes for challah submitted by readers of Jewishfamily.com, along with photos and brief biographies of the winners.

Chickensoup.org—Lively articles on a wide range of health concerns of interest to Jewish families, ranging from the heart-healthy benefit of grape juice to the value of the Shabbat nap.

Jewishbooks.org—Reviews and articles about books of interest to Jewish family members of all ages.

Jewishfood.org—Articles on food-related issues of interest to Jewish families. Includes recipes for holidays, Shabbat, and kosher meals, as well as reviews of cookbooks, essays on memorable holiday meals, and suggestions for successful family eating experiences.

Jewishtravel.org—Articles on travel destinations of interest to Jewish families, on group tours with a Jewish slant (such as some led by bicycling rabbis), on how to offer your children a Jewish moral perspective when visiting places of general interest (such as Disneyland), and on Jewish family travel experiences.

Kaddish.org—Articles on the meaning of death for Jews, the relevance of Jewish rituals at this time, how to handle the subject of death with your children, the impact of a death in the family, and reviews of books dealing with the topic.

Mazeltov.org—Articles on bar/bat mitzvah celebrations, such as how to make them meaningful, alternatives to the traditional mode of celebration, suggestions on what to say to your child at this special time, reviews of relevant books, reflections on past bar/bat mitzvahs, and advice on reducing stress and enjoying the experience. Also includes articles with similar content about Jewish weddings.

Mitzvah.org—Articles on good deeds done by Jews and thoughts about how Jewish families can do more to improve the world.

Passover.org—Articles about celebrating Passover, including features on how to engage family members of all ages, crafts for children, how to present Passover in your child's school, growing a Passover garden, relevant book reviews, recipes, reflections on the meaning of Passover, celebrity seders, and more.

Shabbat.org—Substantive articles on how to have a meaningful Shabbat, Shabbat memories, "how-to" articles on Shabbat-related crafts, reviews of books on Shabbat, and recipes for Shabbat.

Shamash.org—The Jewish internet consortium.

Shmooze.org—Where community comes alive. Dozens of provocative and thoughtful readers' questions and responses on a wide range of issues.

ORGANIZATIONS

Social Action

American Israel Public Affairs Committee
440 First St. NW
Washington, DC 20001
(202)639-5200
Web address: www.aipac.org
Lobbying organization that promotes a strong U.S.–Israel relationship.

American Joint Distribution Committee
711 Third Ave.
New York, NY 10017
(212)687-6200
Web address: www.jdc.org.il
The foreign relief arm of the American Jewish Community.

Anti-Defamation League of B'nai B'rith
823 United Nations Plaza
New York, NY 10017
(212)490-2525
Web address: www.adl.org
Combats anti-Semitism and racism and monitors hate groups.

Mazon: A Jewish Response to Hunger
12401 Wilshire Blvd., Suite 303
Los Angeles, CA 90025
(310)442-0020
Web address: www.shamash.org/soc-action/mazon
Raises money by "taxing" Jewish celebrations and distributes it to organizations that combat hunger.

New Israel Fund
1101 15th St. NW
Suite 304
Washington, DC 20005
(202)223-3333
Web address: www.nif.org
Israelis and North Americans working together for social justice, religious pluralism, and democracy in Israel.

North American Conference on Ethiopian Jews
165 East 56th St.
New York, NY 10022
(212)752-6340
Web address: www.cais.com/nacoej
Provides assistance to Ethiopian Jews in Israel and in Ethiopia.

Panim el Panim: High School in Washington
11710 Hunter's Lane
Rockville, MD 20852
(301)770-5070
E-mail address: panim@aol.com
This organization, linking Jewish sources to public policy issues and activism, runs four-day seminars for high school students.

Religious Action Center
2027 Massachusetts Ave. NW
Washington, DC 20036
(202)387-2800
> *Activist and lobbying arm of the Reform movement that promotes progressive social policy on a wide range of national issues.*

Shomrei Adamah
50 West 77th Street
New York, NY 10011
(212)807-6376
> *Promotes Jewish environmentalism.*

Union of Councils for Soviet Jews
1819 H St. NW
Suite 230
Washington, DC 20006
(202)775-9770
> *Fights for the rights and welfare of Jews in the former Soviet Union and of those who have immigrated to the United States.*

Family Services

Association of Jewish Family and Children's Agencies
3086 State Highway 27
Suite 11, P.O. Box 248
Kendall Park, NJ 08824
(800)634-7346
> *Umbrella group of local social service agencies providing assistance and counseling to individuals and families.*

Facing History and Ourselves
16 Hurd Rd.
Brookline, MA 02146
(617)232-1595
> *A national educational and teacher training organization whose mission is to engage students of diverse backgrounds in an examination of racism, prejudice, and anti-Semitism in order to promote the development of a more humane, informed citizenry.*

Hadassah—Training Wheels Program
50 West 58th St.
New York, NY 10019
(212)355-7900
Web address: www.hadassah.org
> *An innovative monthly educational program for parents, grandparents, and their preschoolers.*

Israel Trips
Israel Experience, Inc.
730 Broadway
New York, NY 10003
(212)253-9334
> *Promotes and coordinates teen trips to Israel.*

Jewish Book Council
15 East 26th St.
New York, NY 10010
Web address: www.jewishbooks.org
> *Sponsors Jewish Book Month and Jewish book fairs.*

Jewish Books and Education Coalition for the Advancement of Jewish Education
261 West 35th St., Number 12A
New York, NY 10001
(212)268-4210
> *Premiere association promoting innovation in Jewish education.*

Jewish Family & Life!
1845 Commonwealth Ave.
Brighton, MA 02135
(617)789-4410
Web: www.Jewishfamily.com
> *Publishes webzines, newsletters, and books of interest to Jewish families.*

Stars of David
P. O. Box 1023
Denville, NJ 07834
(201)627-7752
> *Facilitates adoptions by Jewish adults.*

Jewish Community Organizations

American Jewish Committee
165 East 56th St.
New York, NY 10022
(212)751-4000
Web address: www.ajc.org
Produces materials on Jewish identity.

Jewish Community Centers Association
15 East 26th St.
New York, NY 10010
(212)532-4949
Web address: www.jcca.org
Umbrella organization for Jewish Community Centers and many Jewish camps in the United States.

Cultural and Historical Organizations

American Guild of Judaic Art
P.O. Box 1794
Murray Hill Station
New York, NY 10156
(212)481-8181
Promotes Jewish visual arts.

National Foundation for Jewish Culture
Web address: www.nfjc.org
Promotes Jewish culture in the United States.

National Yiddish Book Center
48 Woodbridge St.
South Hadley, MA 01075
(413)535-1303
Collects and disseminates Yiddish books and promotes the revitalization of Yiddish.

Congregational

Aleph: The Alliance for Jewish Renewal
(215)247-9700
Collection of progressive and alternative religious and Jewish political organizations.

Federation of Reconstructionist Congregations and Havurot
Church Rd. and Greenwood Ave.
Wyncote, PA 19095
(215)887-1988
Web address: www.shamash.org/jrf
The umbrella organization for Reconstructionist congregations.

National Havurah Committee
7318 Germantown Ave.
Philadelphia, PA 19119
(215)248-9760
Promotes independent and informal Jewish renewal and prayer communities.

Union of American Hebrew Congregations
838 Fifth Ave.
New York, NY 10021
(212)249-0100
Web address: www.shamash.org/reform
The umbrella organization for Reform congregations.

Union of Orthodox Jewish Congregations
333 Seventh Ave.
New York, NY 10001
(212)563-4000
Web address: www.ou.org
The umbrella organization for Orthodox congregations.

United Synagogue of Conservative Judaism
155 Fifth Ave.
New York, NY 10010
(212)533-7800
Web address: www.uscj.org
The umbrella organization for Conservative congregations.

Glossary

Afikomen: Literally, dessert. The matzah that is hidden at the beginning of the Passover seder. The children later look for it and ransom it back to the adults.

Aleph-bet: The Hebrew alphabet. *Aleph* and *bet* are the first two letters.

Aliyah: Going up. Used to refer to someone who is going up to say the blessing over the Torah reading. Also used in the phrase "making *aliyah*," which means moving from the diaspora to Israel.

Arevut: Responsibility. Refers to our Jewish responsibility for one another.

Bal tashchit: You shall not waste. The prohibition against wastefulness. Used in reference to natural resources.

Bar/bat mitzvah: Son/daughter of commandment. The change of status for a 13 year old (technically 12 for girls). At that age they become adults in terms of their obligations and privileges in the eyes of the Jewish community. It is often celebrated in the context of a religious ceremony followed by a reception.

Basar: Meat.

Beit knesset: House of meeting. Often used in reference to a synagogue.

Beit midrash: House of study.

Benscher: The book of blessings and songs for Shabbat.

Bikkurim: First fruits, such as the first fruits that were brought as offerings to the Temple.

Bimah: The raised platform at the front of the sanctuary upon which rests the ark in which the Torah is kept.

Birkat Ha-Mazon: The grace after meals.

Blintzes: Crepes filled with ricotta cheese. Often served with applesauce and sour cream. Blintzes are a common dish for Shavuot, when it is traditional to eat only dairy and parve foods.

Brakhah (plural: *brakhot*): A blessing.

Bris: The Ashkenazi pronunciation of *brit*, which means "covenant." *Bris* is the colloquial for a *brit milah* (covenant of circumcision) ceremony.

Brit milah: Covenant of circumcision.

B'tzelem Elohim: In the image of God. The Jewish concept that every human being is made by God in the Divine image.

Chalavi: Milk or a milk product. The term is used in speaking about *kashrut*.

Challah: Actually refers to the piece of bread separated from the loaf and thrown in the oven or fire as an offering to God. But it is used today to describe the special braided bread eaten on Shabbat.

Chametz: Literally, vinegar. Category of food that is not kosher for Passover.

Chanukat bayit: A ceremony celebrating the dedication of one's home in which the mezuzahs are put on the doorposts.

Charoset: The mixture that symbolizes the mortar used by the Israelite slaves to stack bricks for the Egyptians. Often made of apples, walnuts, and wine or crushed walnuts and date syrup. Charoset appears on the seder plate.

Chasidic: Pious. A sect of Jews, "orthodox" in practice and mystical, who have a tradition of joy and celebration. Chasidism originated in Eastern Europe but is now found mainly in the United States and Israel.

Cheder: Literally, room. A place of religious study for Jewish children.

Chesed: Compassion. One of the qualities of God that we try to emulate.

Chol ha-moed: The less stringent days of a seven- or eight-day festival.

Cholent: A special stew of beans, potatoes, and sometimes meat, traditionally made on Shabbat.

Chumash: From the same root letters as the word *chamesh,* meaning "five." The five Books of Moses.

Chuppah: Wedding canopy.

Daven: (Yiddish) Pray.

Dayenu: "It would have been enough for us." The title and chorus of a favorite Passover song.

Diaspora: The lands of Jews outside of Israel.

Eco-kashrut: A term coined by Rabbi Zalman Schachter-Shalomi in the 1970s and expanded upon by Rabbi Arthur Waskow. It refers to a way of thinking about *kashrut* that applies Jewish principles and values to the way we consume in general.

Eloheinu: Our God.

Elohim: God.

Eretz Yisrael: The Land of Israel.

Erev Shabbat: The evening of Shabbat (Friday night).

Etrog: A citron. The lemon-like fruit that is used, along with a *lulav,* in Sukkot ritual.

Eyshet chayil: From the Book of Proverbs. The title and first two words of a section of Proverbs traditionally recited by a husband to his wife after Kiddush (the blessing over the wine sanctifying Shabbat) on Friday nights.

Fleishig: (Yiddish) Meat or meat products.

G'milut chasadim (singular: *g'milut chesed*): Acts of lovingkindness.

Grogger: The noisemaker used to drown out Haman's name each time it is uttered during the public reading of the Scroll of Esther during Purim.

Ha-aretz: The land. Refers to the Land of Israel.

Haftarah: A reading from the book of Prophets that is read following the weekly Torah reading. There is a Haftarah for each Torah portion.

Haggadah: Literally, telling. The book used during the Passover seder.

Ha-khnasat orchim: Welcoming guests. Refers to the mitzvah of doing so.

Halakhah: Way. Jewish law.

Hamantashen: (Yiddish) Haman's hat. The triangular cookies eaten during Purim.

Ha-Navi: The prophet. In the Havdalah service, refers to Elijah.

Ha-Nevia: The prophetess. In the Havdalah service, refers to Miriam.

Hanukkah: Dedication. The winter holiday celebrating the success of the Maccabees over the Greeks, and the subsequent reclamation and dedication of the Holy Temple in Jerusalem.

Hanukkiyah: The eight (nine including the *shammas*) candle-holder menorah used for Hanukkah.

Ha-olam: The world.

Ha-Shem: The Name. Refers to God.

Havdalah: Literally, distinction. The Saturday night ceremony marking the separation between Shabbat and the rest of the week.

Havurah: Friendship gathering. A gathering of Jews to worship and study together. Often affiliated with the Reconstructionist movement.

Hazzan/Hazzanit: Cantor.

Hiddur mitzvah: The beautification of a mitzvah. For example, we make beautiful the mitzvah of Shabbat observance by setting a table with our best tablecloth and dishes.

Kabbalah: Jewish mysticism.

Kabbalat Shabbat: The welcoming of Shabbat.

Kaddish: The prayer extolling God that is said by mourners and those observing a *yahrzeit*.

Kadosh: Holy.

Karpas: The parsley that is placed on the seder plate and dipped in salt water during the seder.

Kashrut: Jewish dietary observance.

Kavanah: Intention, focus. Often used in the context of prayer.

Ketubah: Jewish marriage contract.

Kiddush: Sanctification. The name of the blessing sanctifying Shabbat that is recited over wine.

Kippah (plural: *kippot*): Cap. Yarmulke. The skullcap worn by Jews. Traditionally worn only by males, now often worn by females as well.

Klaf: The paper inserted in the mezuzah on which the Shema is written.

K'lal Yisrael: All of the people Israel. A concept that all Jews are of one people.

Kokhavim: Stars.

Kosher: Within the bounds of *kashrut*.

Lag B'Omer: The 33rd day of the counting of the omer: the days between Passover and Shavuot. On this day the omer prohibitions, such as cutting hair, shaving, and weddings, are lifted.

Latkes: Potato pancakes traditionally eaten during Hanukkah.

L'shem shamayim: For the sake of heaven.

Lulav: The willow branch used during Sukkot.

Ma'ariv: Evening. The name of the evening prayers.

Ma'asim tovim: Good deeds.

Ma'ayan: Wellspring. Used as a name for God.

Maggid: Storyteller.

Mah nishtanah?: What is different? The first words and title of the four questions recited at the Passover seder.

Makhberet: Notebook.

Makom: Place. Used as a name for God.

Matanot la'evyonim: Gifts for the poor. Generally refers to those given during Purim.

Matzah: The unleavened bread eaten during the Passover seder and throughout Passover.

Mayim: Water.

Mazal tov: Good luck. Generally used like "Congratulations."

Megillah: Scroll. Often refers to the scroll of Esther read on Purim.

Melekh: King. Used in the traditional blessing formula "King of the universe" to refer to God.

Menorah: Religious candelabra with seven candlestick holders.

Mensch: (Yiddish) Gentleman. Used in reference to males and females, and refers to someone who is particularly kind and generous of spirit.

Menschlich: *Mensch*-like.

Menuchah: Rest. We speak of *Shabbat menuchah,* "Sabbath rest."

Mezuzah: The vessel that holds the handwritten scroll with the Shema and that is affixed to the doorposts of Jewish homes.

Midrash: Jewish interpretive literature. Can refer to one particular rabbinic interpretation or to the whole expansive body of texts.

Mikdash: Holy temple.

Mikdash me'at: Little temple. This term is used to refer to the home.

Mikvah: Ritual bath.

Milchig: Of or containing milk or dairy products.

Minchah: Afternoon. The name of the afternoon prayers.

Mishloach manot: The gift baskets brought to friends and neighbors on Purim.

Mitzvah (plural: mitzvot): A religious obligation.

Mizrach: East. Often refers to a wallhanging that is placed on the eastern wall of western homes to indicate the direction of Jerusalem.

M'kor Ha-Chayim: Source of Life. Used to refer to God.

M'lakhah (plural: m'lakhot): Type of work that may not be done on Shabbat.

Modeh Ani: I am thankful. The name of the morning blessing said upon waking.

Mohel: The one who performs the circumcision and often also the circumcision ceremony.

Motzi: Blessing recited before meals.

Ner: Light.

Netilat yadayim: Ritual washing of the hands, usually accompanied by a blessing.

Nidah: A woman's state of being during her menstrual cycle.

Niggunim: Songs, often without words.

Omer: The time from the second day of Passover until Shavuot, during which we count each day and observe certain prohibitions, such as those against cutting hair and getting married.

Oneg: Joy. Often used to refer to the celebration part of a religious event.

Oseh Shalom: Maker of Peace. A name for God.

Parashat ha'shavua: The weekly Torah portion.

Parve: Kashrut term referring to a food item that is neither a milk nor meat product. Includes kosher fish and eggs.

Passover: The spring holiday remembering and celebrating the exodus of the Jews from Egypt.

Payes: Sidecurls. Worn by some Orthodox men.

Pirkei Avot: Chapters of the Fathers. A section of the Mishnah with collected wise sayings and aphorisms of rabbis spanning hundreds of years around the time of the beginning of the Common Era.

Purim: The raucous holiday celebrating Esther's saving of the Jews from the plans of the evil Haman.

Purimshpiel: The humorous, original performance or group of performances given in celebration of Purim, which often playfully mock the community of which one is a part.

Pushke: (Yiddish) Tzedakah box.

Rachamim: Compassion. An attribute of God.

Rebbe: Eastern European term for one's teacher, or a great rabbi.

Rebbitzen: Term for the wife of a rabbi. (The husband of a rabbi is called *rebbitz*.)

Responsa: Rabbinic responses to contemporary questions and issues.

Rosh Chodesh: Head of the month. The first day of a new month. In the diaspora, the first two days of a new month. Often celebrated by women.

Rosh Hashanah: Head of the year. The Jewish new year.

Ruach: Wind, spirit. Often refers to the spirit in the sense of a spiritually high, joyous mood.

Seder: Literally, order. Refers to the traditional course of events, or service, surrounding the Passover and Tu B'Shevat meals.

Seudah: Meal.

Seudah shlishit: Third meal. Refers to the third meal of Shabbat.

Shabbat: The Sabbath.

Shacharit: Morning, dawn. Name of the morning worship service.

Shaddai: Biblical name for God.

Shalokh manot: Purim gift baskets.

Shalom: Peace. Used as a greeting and word of departure.

Shalom bayit: Peace in the house. The value of harmony in a family.

Shamayim: Heaven.

Shammas: The candle on a hanukkiyah that is used to light the others. It does not count as one of the eight lights for Hanukkah.

Shavua Tov: Good week. The greeting given for a day or so after Shabbat ends.

Shavuot: The feast of weeks. Comes 50 days after Passover begins. Commemorates the receiving of the Torah at Mount Sinai.

Shechitah: Ritual slaughter of kosher animals for meat.

Shehekheyanu: Who has given us life. The word in a blessing thanking God for bringing us to a special moment.

Shekhinah: God's presence. A name for God.

Shema: Hear. The first word and name of the central Jewish prayer and statement of faith.

Shir Ha-Shirim: The Song of Songs. Biblical book found in "Writings" that describes erotic love between two lovers. Traditionally interpreted as an allegory of the love between God and Israel.

Shiva: The seven days of mourning following the funeral of a family member.

Shloshim: The 30 days of mourning following the funeral of a family member.

Sh'mini Atzeret: The final day of Sukkot.

Sh'mirat ha-guf: Protecting the body. The obligation to care well for our bodies.

Shofar: Ram's horn that is blown on Rosh Hashanah and Yom Kippur.

Shtetl: A small Jewish village of Eastern Europe.

Shul: (Yiddish) Synagogue.

Siddur: Prayer book.

Simchah: Joy.

Simchat Torah: Joy of Torah. The celebration, after Sukkot, of the completion of a Torah cycle and the immediate commencement of a new one.

Succah: The hut in which Jews dwell or eat during the festival of Sukkot.

Sukkot: A harvest festival in which we commemorate the Israelite wandering in the desert and recall our fragility and ultimate dependence on God.

Taharat ha-neshek: Purity of the weapon. The idea that a weapon should be used only for good.

Tallith: Prayer shawl.

Talmud: The body of texts that comprise Jewish law.

Tashlikh: Literally, you will send. The custom of casting bread into a natural body of water at Rosh Hashanah to symbolically cast away our sins.

Tefilat Ha-Derekh: Prayer for the road. A prayer said by travelers embarking on a journey.

Tefillin: Phylacteries. Black leather straps for the arm and head each with a small box containing a scroll upon which is written the Shema. Traditionally worn during weekday morning prayer.

Tikkun olam: Repairing the world. A purpose of our covenant with God.

Tisha B'Av: A day of mourning commemorating the destructions of both Temples in Jerusalem, which are said to have happened on this day.

Treife: Nonkosher food, usually used in reference to pork or shellfish.

Tu B'Av: The 15th of the month of Av. A Jewish love holiday.

Tu B'Shevat: The 15th of the month of Shevat. A holiday celebrating nature.

Tzayar: Artist. A rabbinic image of God.

Tzedakah: Righteous giving. The obligation to give 10 percent of one's net income to those in need.

Tzedek: Righteousness.

Tzelem Elohim: Image of God. The Jewish concept that every human being is made by God in the Divine image.

Tzur: Rock. An image of and name for God.

V'shamru: And they shall keep. First word and name of blessing sung before Kiddush on Shabbat morning.

Yahrzeit: The anniversary of someone's death. Commemorated by relatives, who light a *yahrzeit* candle that burns for the 24-hour period.

Yarmulke: (Yiddish) Skullcap worn by Jews, either at all times or during specifically religious occasions.

Yisrael: Israel. Refers to both the country and the Jewish national peoplehood. Also the name given to our patriarch Jacob.

Yizkor: Memorial. The worship service in which we remember relatives who have died.

Yom Ha-Shoah: Holocaust remembrance day.

Yom Kippur: The Day of Atonement. Last and culminating day of the ten days of repentance that begin with Rosh Hashanah.

Yom tov: Good day. The part of a holiday when observance is not very strict.

Yontiff: Yiddish for *yom tov.*

Zeide: (Yiddish) Grandfather.

Zemirot: Shabbat songs.

Index

Credits

Quotes by Kirk Douglas, Sigmund Freud, William Safire, Lauren Bacall, Letty Cottin Pogrebin, Buddy Hackett, Natan Sharansky, Anne Frank, Ruth Bader Ginsburg, Bette Midler, Albert Einstein, Bella Abzug, Arlen Specter, Ruth Westheimer, Goldie Hawn, Marc Chagall, and Sammy Davis, Jr., excerpted from *Great Jewish Quotations*, by Alfred J. Kolatch, copyright © 1996. Reprinted by arrangement with Jonathan David Publishers, Middle Village, NY 11379.

Quotes by Melissa Gilbert, Jane Seymour, Richard Dreyfuss, excerpted from Tim Boxer's *Jewish Celebrity Anecdotes*, by Tim Boxer, copyright © 1996. Reprinted by arrangement with Jonathan David Publishers, Middle Village, NY 11379.

Henry Winkler quotation reprinted with permission from the *Connecticut Jewish Ledger*.

p.27 "Bath time" excerpt from *Our Share of Night, Our Share of Morning*, by Nancy Fuchs. HarperSan Francisco, 1996, p.111.

p.28 *Twinkle, Twinkle, Little Star* adaptation by Rene Boni, printed with permission of the writer.

p.29 Interpretive version of *Ahavat Olam*, by Rabbi Rami M. Shapiro. *Kol Haneshamah: Shabbat Vehagim*, The Reconstructionist Press, copyright 1994. p. 61. Reprinted with permission from the publisher.

p.31 "Creative Bedtime Rituals" by Debra Nussbaum Cohen. Reprinted from *Jewish Family & Life!* with permission of the author.

p.33 "When Mystery Rocked Me to Sleep" by Tovah Lazaroff. Reprinted from *Jewish Family & Life!* with permission of the author.

p.40 Shabbat sidebar reprinted from *Down-to-Earth Judaism* by Arthur Waskow, with permission of the author.

p.43 Story of the Chasidic teacher, as found in *Gates of Shabbat*, Marc Dov Shapiro, Central Conference of American Rabbis, New York, 1991. Reprinted with permission.

p.56 Poem by Aviva Rosman published with permission of the author.

p.61 *Miriam ha'Nevia* by Rabbi Leila Gal Berner, printed with permission of the author.

p.68 Seinfeld quote: Reprinted with permission from the *B'nai B'rith Jewish Monthly*.

p.71 *B'ruchot Ha'ba'ot*: music and lyrics by Debbie Friedman. © 1988 Deborah Lynn Friedman (ASCAP), Sounds Write Productions, Inc.

p.78 "Birthdays, Jewishly" by Lisa Farber Miller and Sandra Widener. Reprinted with permission from *Moment* magazine and the authors.

p.83 Spielberg quote reprinted with permission from the *B'nai B'rith Jewish Monthly*.

p.83 "How to Choose a Hebrew School" by Ethan Feinsilver, reprinted from Jewishfamily.com with permission from the author.

p.89 "Putting the Mitzvah Back in Bar and Bat Mitzvah" by Suzanne Borden, printed with permission of the author.

p.99 "Helping Children Grieve" by Rabbi Rafael Grossman with Anna Olswanger, printed with permission of the authors.

p.105 Response on mourning a pet by Rabbi Shohama Wiener originally appeared in *Moment* magazine. Reprinted with permission of the author.

p.117 "Creating a Library for Your Children" by Miriam Rinn. Reprinted from *Jewish Family & Life!* with permission of the author.

p.125 "A Holy Moment at McDonald's" by Dr. Eugene B. Borowitz. Reprinted from *Renewing the Covenant* with permission of the author.

p.132 Eco-kashrut excerpted from *Down-To-Earth Judaism*, by Arthur Waskow, with permission of the author.

p.147 Seinfeld quote reprinted with permission from the *B'nai B'rith Monthly*.

p.149 "A Daughter and a Shofar," by Mitchell Eisen, printed with permission from the author.

p.153 "Hands-On Judaism" by Julie Hilton Danan. Reprinted from Jewishfamily.com with permission from the author.

p.155 "Sukkah Memories" by Julie Hilton Danan. Reprinted from Jewishfamily.com with permission from the author.

p.156 "A Sukkot Theme Dinner" by Carol Goodman Kaufman. Printed with permission from the author.

p.162 "Close Encounters with Steven Spielberg" by Tom Tugend. Reprinted from *Jewish Family & Life!* with the permission of the author.

p.165 Latke Recipes by Faith R. Corman. Reprinted with the permission of the author.

p. 173 "Seven Silly and Serious Suggestions..." by Julie Hilton Danan. Reprinted from Jewishfamily.com with the permission of the author.

p.184 "Ten Tips to Enliven the Seder" by Ron Wolfson. Reprinted from *Jewish Family & Life!* with the permission of the author.

p.191 "Talking to Your Children about the Holocaust" by Ann Moline. Reprinted from Jewishfamily.com with the permission of the author.

p.211 "Making Time for Togetherness" by Debra B. Darvick. Reprinted from Jewishfamily.com with the permission of the author.

p.216 "Is Halloween...?" by Ted Roberts. Printed by permission of the author.

p.221 "Interfaith Families and the December Dilemma" by Nancy Mades. Printed by permission of the author.

p.224 "'Tis the Season..." by Ann Moline. Reprinted from Jewishfamily.com with the permission of the author.

p.240-244 "The Power of One," "Get Involved!" and "The Role of Parents" by Ann Moline. Reprinted from Jewishfamily.com by permission of the author.

p.245 "How to Raise Moral and Jewish Children" by Helen Mintz Belitsky. Reprinted from *Jewish Family & Life!* with the permission of the author.

p.251 "Talking to Kids about Sex" by Rahel Musleah. Reprinted from Jewishfamily.com with the permission of the author.

p.259 "The Jewish View of Sex." Reprinted from *Heavenly Sex: Sexuality in the Jewish Tradition* by Dr. Ruth K. Westheimer and Jonathan Mark, © 1995, New York University Press.

p.262 "Custodians of Creation" written by Sharon Goldman Edry for Jewishfamily.com. Printed by permission of the author.

p.275 "An Allowance Is Not a Bribe" by Allan Gonsher. Printed with the permission of the author.

p.284 "Interfaith Dating" by Helen Mintz Belitsky. Reprinted from Jewishfamily.com with the permission of the author.

About the Authors

Yosef I. Abramowitz, an award-winning journalist, contributes regularly to more than fifty Jewish newspapers across the United States. A graduate of Boston University and the Columbia Graduate School of Journalism, where he was awarded a Wexner Graduate Fellowship, he is the co-founder and editor-in-chief of the *Jewish Family & Life!* online magazine, and was an editor at *Moment.* He has extensive experience working with young people, including a three-year term as chairperson of the World Union of Jewish Students. He is also president of the Union of Councils for Soviet Jews, and lectures nationally and internationally on a wide variety of Jewish topics. He is the author of *Jews, Zionism, and South Africa* and co-author of *How Americans Feel About Israel.*

Rabbi Susan Silverman, contributing editor and co-founder of *Jewish Family & Life!,* received a B.A. from Boston University and an M.A. from Harvard University, and was ordained by Hebrew Union College-Jewish Institute of Religion in New York City. She served two years as spiritual leader of Congregation Or Chadash, a Reform synagogue in Germantown, Maryland, that prides itself on how actively its members—particularly the children—participate in the life of the congregation. She is the author of the new "Grace after Meals," written in inclusive language, that has been reprinted in *A Feminist Passover Haggadah* by the American Jewish Congress Feminist Center in Los Angeles.

Yosef and Susan are married and the parents of two daughters, Aliza and Hallel. They live in Newton, Massachusetts.

About Jewish Family & Life!

Jewish Family & Life! is the organizational umbrella for a dozen family-friendly Jewish webzines. The publisher of a weekly e-letter (subscribe on www.jewishfamily.com), a bimonthly printed newsletter (1-888-I-LUV-JFL), and other materials, *Jewish Family & Life!* is a non-profit that reaches out to bring the magic of Jewish life into the homes of families where at least one parent is Jewish. *Jewish Family & Life!* is independent of any religious movement or organization, and depends on foundation and individual grants to continue its pioneering work.

Editorial office: 1845 Commonwealth Avenue, Brighton, MA 02135
E-mail: Jewishlife@aol.com
Telephone: 617-789-4410
Web: http://www.jewishfamily.com